jQuery Cookbook

jQuery Cookbook

jQuery Community Experts

O'REILLY®

Beijing · Cambridge · Farnham · Köln · Sebastopol · Taipei · Tokyo

jQuery Cookbook
by jQuery Community Experts

Published by O'Reilly Media, Inc., 1005 Gravenstein Highway North, Sebastopol, CA 95472.

O'Reilly books may be purchased for educational, business, or sales promotional use. Online editions are also available for most titles (*http://my.safaribooksonline.com*). For more information, contact our corporate/institutional sales department: 800-998-9938 or *corporate@oreilly.com*.

Editor: Simon St.Laurent	**Indexer:** Fred Brown
Production Editor: Sarah Schneider	**Cover Designer:** Karen Montgomery
Copyeditor: Kim Wimpsett	**Interior Designer:** David Futato
Proofreader: Andrea Fox	**Illustrator:** Robert Romano
Production Services: Molly Sharp	

Printing History:

November 2009: First Edition.

 This book uses RepKover, a durable and flexible lay-flat binding.

ISBN: 978-0-596-15977-1

[S]

1257542253

Table of Contents

Foreword

When I first started work on building jQuery, back in 2005, I had a simple goal in mind: I wanted to be able to write a web application and have it work in all the major browsers—without further tinkering and bug fixing. It was a couple of months before I had a set of utilities that were stable enough to achieve that goal for my personal use. I thought I was relatively done at this point; little did I know that my work was just beginning.

Since those simple beginnings, jQuery has grown and adapted as new users use the library for their projects. This has proven to be the most challenging part of developing a JavaScript library; while it is quite easy to build a library that'll work for yourself or a specific application, it becomes incredibly challenging to develop a library that'll work in as many environments as possible (old browsers, legacy web pages, and strange markup abound). Surprisingly, even as jQuery has adapted to handle more use cases, most of the original API has stayed intact.

One thing I find particularly interesting is to see how developers use jQuery and make it their own. As someone with a background in computer science, I find it quite surprising that so many designers and nonprogrammers find jQuery to be compelling. Seeing how they interact with the library has given me a better appreciation of simple API design. Additionally, seeing many advanced programmers take jQuery and develop large, complex applications with it has been quite illuminating. The best part of all of this, though, is the ability to learn from everyone who uses the library.

A side benefit of using jQuery is its extensible plugin structure. When I first developed jQuery, I was sure to include some simple ways for developers to extend the API that it provided. This has blossomed into a large and varied community of plugins, encompassing a whole ecosystem of applications, developers, and use cases. Much of jQuery's growth has been fueled by this community—without it, the library wouldn't be where it is today, so I'm glad that there are chapters dedicated to some of the most interesting plugins and what you can do with them. One of the best ways to expand your preconceived notion of what you can do with jQuery is to learn and use code from the jQuery plugin community.

This is largely what makes something like a cookbook so interesting: it takes the cool things that developers have done, and have learned, in their day-to-day coding and distills it to bite-sized chunks for later consumption. Personally, I find a cookbook to be one of the best ways to challenge my preconceived notions of a language or library. I love seeing cases where an API that I thought I knew well is turned around and used in new and interesting ways. I hope this book is able to serve you well, teaching you new and interesting ways to use jQuery.

—John Resig
Creator, Lead Developer, jQuery

Contributors

Chapter Authors

Jonathan Sharp has been passionate about the Internet and web development since 1996. Over the years that have followed, he has worked for startups and for Fortune 500 corporations. Jonathan founded Out West Media, LLC, in greater Omaha, Nebraska, and provides frontend engineering and architecture services with a focus on custom XHTML, CSS, and jQuery development. Jonathan is a jQuery core team member and an author and presenter when not coding. Jonathan is most grateful for his wife, Erin; daughter, Noel; two dogs, and two horses.

Rob Burns develops interactive web applications at A Mountain Top, LLC. For the past 12 years he has been exploring website development using a wide range of tools and technologies. In his spare time, he enjoys natural-language processing and the wealth of opportunity in open source software projects.

Rebecca Murphey is an independent frontend architecture consultant, crafting custom frontend solutions that serve as the glue between server and browser. She also provides training in frontend development, with an emphasis on the jQuery library. She lives with her partner, two dogs, and two cats in Durham, North Carolina.

Ariel Flesler is a web developer and a video game programmer. He's been contributing to jQuery since January 2007 and joined the core team in May 2008. He is 23 years old and was born in Buenos Aires, Argentina. He's studying at the National Technological University (Argentina) and is hoping to become a systems analyst by 2010 and a systems engineer by 2012. He started working as an ASP.NET(C#) programmer and then switched to client-side development of XHTML sites and Ajax applications. He's currently working at QB9 where he develops AS3-based casual games and MMOs.

Cody Lindley is a Christian, husband, son, father, brother, outdoor enthusiast, and professional client-side engineer. Since 1997 he has been passionate about HTML, CSS, JavaScript, Flash, interaction design, interface design, and HCI. He is most well known in the jQuery community for the creation of ThickBox, a modal/dialog solution. In 2008 he officially joined the jQuery team as an evangelist. His current focus has been on client-side optimization techniques as well as speaking and writing about jQuery. His website is *http://www.codylindley.com.*

Remy Sharp is a developer, author, speaker, and blogger. Remy started his professional web development career in 1999 as the sole developer for a finance website and, as such, was exposed to all aspects of running the website during, and long after, the dotcom boom. Today he runs his own development company called Left Logic in Brighton, UK, writing and coding JavaScript, jQuery, HTML 5, CSS, PHP, Perl, and anything else he can get his hands on.

Mike Hostetler is an inventor, entrepreneur, programmer, and proud father. Having worked with web technologies since the mid-1990s, Mike has had extensive experience developing web applications with PHP and JavaScript. Currently, Mike works at the helm of A Mountain Top, LLC, a web technology consulting firm in Denver, Colorado. Heavily involved in open source, Mike is a member of the jQuery core team, leads the QCubed PHP5 Framework project, and participates in the Drupal project. When not in front of a computer, Mike enjoys hiking, fly fishing, snowboarding, and spending time with his family.

Ralph Whitbeck is a graduate of the Rochester Institute of Technology and is currently a senior developer for BrandLogic Corporation (*http://brandlogic.com*) in Rochester, New York. His responsibilities at BrandLogic include interface design, usability testing, and web and application development. Ralph is able to program complex web application systems in ASP.NET, C#, and SQL Server and also uses client-side technologies such as XHTML, CSS, and JavaScript/jQuery in order to implement client-approved designs. Ralph officially joined the jQuery team as an evangelist in October 2009. Ralph enjoys spending time with his wife, Hope, and his three boys, Brandon, Jordan, and Ralphie. You can find out more about Ralph on his personal blog (*http://ralphwhitbeck .com*).

Nathan Smith is a goofy guy who has been building websites since late last century. He enjoys hand-coding HTML, CSS, and JavaScript. He also dabbles in design and information architecture. He has written for online and paper publications such as Adobe Developer Center, Digital Web, and .NET Magazine. He has spoken at venues including Adobe MAX, BibleTech, Drupal Camp, Echo Conference, Ministry 2.0, Refresh Dallas, and Webmaster Jam Session. Nathan works as a UX developer at FellowshipTech.com. He holds a Master of Divinity degree from Asbury Theological Seminary. He started Godbit.com, a community resource aimed at helping churches and ministries make better use of the Web. He also created the 960 Grid System (*http:// www.960.gs*), a framework for sketching, designing, and coding page layouts.

Brian Cherne is a software developer with more than a decade of experience blueprinting and building web-based applications, kiosks, and high-traffic e-commerce websites. He is also the author of the hoverIntent jQuery plugin. When not geeking out with code, Brian can be found ballroom dancing, practicing martial arts, or studying Russian culture and language.

Jörn Zaefferer is a professional software developer from Cologne, Germany. He creates application programming interfaces (APIs), graphical user interfaces (GUIs), software architectures, and databases, for both web and desktop applications. His work focuses on the Java platform, while his client-side scripting revolves around jQuery. He started contributing to jQuery in mid-2006 and has since cocreated and maintained QUnit, jQuery's unit testing framework; released and maintained a half dozen very popular jQuery plugins; and contributed to jQuery books as both author and tech reviewer. He is also a lead developer for jQuery UI.

James Padolsey is an enthusiastic web developer and blogger based in London, UK. He's been crazy about jQuery since he first discovered it; he's written tutorials teaching it, articles and blog posts discussing it, and plenty of plugins for the community. James' plans for the future include a computer science degree from the University of Kent and a career that allows him to continually push boundaries. His website is *http://james .padolsey.com*.

Scott González is a web application developer living in Raleigh, North Carolina, who enjoys building highly dynamic systems and flexible, scalable frameworks. He has been contributing to jQuery since 2007 and is currently the development lead for jQuery UI, jQuery's official user interface library. Scott also writes tutorials about jQuery and jQuery UI on nemikor.com and speaks about jQuery at conferences.

Michael Geary started developing software when editing code meant punching a paper tape on a Teletype machine, and "standards-compliant" meant following ECMA 10 Standard for Data Interchange on Punched Tape. Today Mike is a web and Android developer with a particular interest in writing fast, clean, and simple code, and he enjoys helping other developers on the jQuery mailing lists. Mike's recent projects include a series of 2008 election result and voter information maps for Google; and StrataLogic, a mashup of traditional classroom wall maps and atlases overlaid on Google Earth. His website is *http://mg.to*.

Maggie Wachs, **Scott Jehl**, **Todd Parker**, and **Patty Toland** are Filament Group. Together, they design and develop highly functional user interfaces for consumer- and business-oriented websites, wireless devices, and installed and web-based applications, with a specific focus on delivering intuitive and usable experiences that are also broadly accessible. They are sponsor and design leads of the jQuery UI team, for whom they designed and developed ThemeRoller.com, and they actively contribute to ongoing development of the official jQuery UI library and CSS Framework.

Richard D. Worth is a web UI developer. He is the release manager for jQuery UI and one of its longest-contributing developers. He is author or coauthor of the Dialog, Progressbar, Selectable, and Slider plugins. Richard also enjoys speaking and consulting on jQuery and jQuery UI around the world. Richard is raising a growing family in Northern Virginia (Washington, D.C. suburbs) with his lovely wife, Nancy. They have been blessed to date with three beautiful children: Naomi, Asher, and Isaiah. Richard's website is *http://rdworth.org/*.

Tech Editors

Karl Swedberg, after having taught high school English, edited copy for an advertising agency, and owned a coffee house, began his career as a web developer four years ago. He now works for Fusionary Media in Grand Rapids, Michigan, where he specializes in client-side scripting and interaction design. Karl is a member of the jQuery project team and coauthor of *Learning jQuery 1.3* and *jQuery Reference Guide* (both published by Packt). You can find some of his tips and tutorials at *http://www.learningjquery.com*.

Dave Methvin is the chief technology officer at PCPitstop.com and one of the founding partners of the company. He has been using jQuery since 2006, is active on the jQuery help groups, and has contributed several popular jQuery plugins including Corner and Splitter. Before joining PC Pitstop, Dave served as executive editor at both *PC Tech Journal* and *Windows Magazine*, where he wrote a column on JavaScript. He continues to write for several PC-related websites including InformationWeek. Dave holds bachelor's and master's degrees in computer science from the University of Virginia.

David Serduke is a frontend programmer who is recently spending much of his time server side. After programming for many years, he started using jQuery in late 2007 and shortly after joined the jQuery core team. David is currently creating websites for financial institutions and bringing the benefits of jQuery to ASP.NET enterprise applications. David lives in northern California where he received a bachelor's degree from the University of California at Berkeley in electrical engineering and an MBA from St. Mary's College.

Scott Mark is an enterprise application architect at Medtronic. He works on web-based personalized information portals and transactional applications with an eye toward maintaining high usability in a regulated environment. His key interest areas at the moment are rich Internet applications and multitouch user interface technologies. Scott lives in Minnesota with his lovely wife, two sons, and a black lab. He blogs about technology at *http://scottmark.wordpress.com* and long-distance trail running at *http://runlikemonkey.com*.

Preface

The jQuery library has taken the frontend development world by storm. Its dead-simple syntax makes once-complicated tasks downright trivial—enjoyable, even. Many a developer has been quickly seduced by its elegance and clarity. If you've started using the library, you're already adding rich, interactive experiences to your projects.

Getting started is easy, but as is the case with many of the tools we use to develop websites, it can take months or even years to fully appreciate the breadth and depth of the jQuery library. The library is chock-full of features you might never have known to wish for. Once you know about them, they can dramatically change how you approach the problems you're called upon to solve.

The goal of this cookbook is to expose you, dear reader, to the patterns and practices of some of the leading frontend developers who use jQuery in their everyday projects. Over the course of 18 chapters, they'll guide you through solutions to problems that range from straightforward to complex. Whether you're a jQuery newcomer or a grizzled JavaScript veteran, you're likely to gain new insight into harnessing the full power of jQuery to create compelling, robust, high-performance user interfaces.

Who This Book Is For

Maybe you're a designer who is intrigued by the interactivity that jQuery can provide. Maybe you're a frontend developer who has worked with jQuery before and wants to see how other people accomplish common tasks. Maybe you're a server-side developer who's frequently called upon to write client-side code.

Truth be told, this cookbook will be valuable to anyone who works with jQuery—or who hopes to work with jQuery. If you're just starting out with the library, you may want to consider pairing this book with *Learning jQuery 1.3* from Packt, or *jQuery in Action* from Manning. If you're already using jQuery in your projects, this book will serve to enhance your knowledge of the library's features, hidden gems, and idiosyncrasies.

What You'll Learn

We'll start out by covering the basics and general best practices—including jQuery in your page, making selections, and traversing and manipulation. Even frequent jQuery users are likely to pick up a tip or two. From there, we move on to real-world use cases, walking you through tried-and-true (and tested) solutions to frequent problems involving events, effects, dimensions, forms, and user interface elements (with and without the help of jQuery UI). At the end, we'll take a look at testing your jQuery applications and integrating jQuery into complex sites.

Along the way, you'll learn strategies for leveraging jQuery to solve problems that go far beyond the basics. We'll explore how to make the most of jQuery's event management system, including custom events and custom event data; how to progressively enhance forms; how to position and reposition elements on the page; how to create user interface elements such as tabs, accordions, and modals from scratch; how to craft your code for readability and maintainability; how to optimize your code to ease testing, eliminate bottlenecks, and ensure peak performance; and more.

Because this is a cookbook and not a manual, you're of course welcome to cherry-pick the recipes you read; the individual recipes alone are worth the price of admission. As a whole, though, the book provides a rare glimpse into the problem-solving approaches of some of the best and brightest in the jQuery community. With that in mind, we encourage you to at least skim it from front to back—you never know which line of code will provide the "Aha!" moment you need to take your skills to the next level.

jQuery Style and Conventions

jQuery places a heavy emphasis on *chaining*—calling methods on element selections in sequence, confident in the knowledge that each method will give you back a selection of elements you can continue to work with. This pattern is explained in depth in Chapter 1—if you're new to the library, you'll want to understand this concept, because it is used heavily in subsequent chapters.

jQuery's features are organized into a handful of simple categories: core functionality, selecting, manipulating, traversing, CSS, attributes, events, effects, Ajax, and utilities. Learning these categories, and how methods fit into them, will greatly enhance your understanding of the material in this book.

One of the best practices this book will cover is the concept of storing element selections in a variable, rather than making the same selection repeatedly. When a selection is stored in a variable, it is commonplace for that variable to begin with the $ character, indicating that it is a jQuery object. This can make code easier to read and maintain, but it should be understood that starting the variable name with the $ character is merely a convention; it carries no special meaning, unlike in other languages such as PHP.

In general, the code examples in this book strive for clarity and readability over compactness, so the examples may be more verbose than is strictly necessary. If you see an opportunity for optimization, you should not hesitate to take it. At the same time, you'll do well to strive for clarity and readability in your own code and use minification tools to prepare your code for production use.

Other Options

If you're looking for other jQuery resources, here are some we recommend:

- *Learning jQuery 1.3*, by Jonathan Chaffer, Karl Swedberg, and John Resig (Packt)
- *jQuery in Action*, by Bear Bibeault, Yehuda Katz, and John Resig (Manning)
- *jQuery UI 1.6: The User Interface Library for jQuery*, by Dan Wellman (Packt)

If You Have Problems Making Examples Work

Before you check anything else, ensure that you are loading the jQuery library on the page—you'd be surprised how many times this is the solution to the "It's not working!" problem. If you are using jQuery with another JavaScript library, you may need to use `jQuery.noConflict()` to make it play well with others. If you're loading scripts that require the presence of jQuery, make sure you are loading them after you've loaded the jQuery library.

Much of the code in this book requires the document to be "ready" before JavaScript can interact with it. If you've included code in the head of the document, make sure your code is enclosed in `$(document).ready(function() { ... });` so that it knows to wait until the document is ready for interaction.

Some of the features discussed in this book are available only in jQuery 1.3 and later. If you are upgrading from an older version of jQuery, make sure you've upgraded any plugins you're using as well—outdated plugins can lead to unpredictable behavior.

If you're having difficulty getting an example to work in an existing application, make sure you can get the example working on its own before trying to integrate it with your existing code. If that works, tools such as Firebug for the Firefox browser can be useful in identifying the source of the problem.

If you're including a minified version of jQuery and running into errors that point to the jQuery library itself, you may want to consider switching to the full version of jQuery while you are debugging the issue. You'll have a much easier time locating the line that is causing you trouble, which will often lead you in the direction of a solution.

If you're still stuck, consider posting your question to the jQuery Google group. Many of this book's authors are regular participants in the group, and more often than not, someone in the group will be able to offer useful advice. The `#jquery` IRC channel on Freenode is another valuable resource for troubleshooting issues.

If none of this works, it's possible we made a mistake. We worked hard to test and review all of the code in the book, but errors do creep through. Check the errata (described in the next section) and download the sample code, which will be updated to address any errata we discover.

If You Like (or Don't Like) This Book

If you like—or don't like—this book, by all means, please let people know. Amazon reviews are one popular way to share your happiness (or lack of happiness), or you can leave reviews at the site for the book:

> *http://oreilly.com/catalog/9780596159771/*

There's also a link to errata there. Errata gives readers a way to let us know about typos, errors, and other problems with the book. That errata will be visible on the page immediately, and we'll confirm it after checking it out. O'Reilly can also fix errata in future printings of the book and on Safari, making for a better reader experience pretty quickly. We hope to keep this book updated for future versions of jQuery, and will also incorporate suggestions and complaints into future editions.

Conventions Used in This Book

The following typographical conventions are used in this book:

Italic
> Indicates Internet addresses, such as domain names and URLs, and new items where they are defined.

`Constant width`
> Indicates command lines and options that should be typed verbatim; names and keywords in programs, including method names, variable names, and class names; and HTML element tags, switches, attributes, keys, functions, types, namespaces, modules, properties, parameters, values, objects, events, event handlers, macros, the contents of files, or the output from commands.

`Constant width bold`
> Indicates emphasis in program code lines.

`Constant width italic`
> Indicates text that should be replaced with user-supplied values.

 This icon signifies a tip, suggestion, or general note.

This icon indicates a warning or caution.

Using Code Examples

This book is here to help you get your job done. In general, you may use the code in this book in your programs and documentation. You do not need to contact us for permission unless you're reproducing a significant portion of the code. For example, writing a program that uses several chunks of code from this book does not require permission. Answering a question by citing this book and quoting example code does not require permission. Selling or distributing a CD-ROM of examples from O'Reilly books *does* require permission. Incorporating a significant amount of example code from this book into your product's documentation *does* require permission.

We appreciate, but do not require, attribution. An attribution usually includes the title, author, publisher, and ISBN. For example: "*jQuery Cookbook*, by Cody Lindley. Copyright 2010 Cody Lindley, 978-0-596-15977-1." If you feel your use of code examples falls outside fair use or the permission given above, feel free to contact us at *permissions@oreilly.com*.

Safari® Books Online

 Safari Books Online is an on-demand digital library that lets you easily search over 7,500 technology and creative reference books and videos to find the answers you need quickly.

With a subscription, you can read any page and watch any video from our library online. Read books on your cell phone and mobile devices. Access new titles before they are available for print, and get exclusive access to manuscripts in development and post feedback for the authors. Copy and paste code samples, organize your favorites, download chapters, bookmark key sections, create notes, print out pages, and benefit from tons of other time-saving features.

O'Reilly Media has uploaded this book to the Safari Books Online service. To have full digital access to this book and others on similar topics from O'Reilly and other publishers, sign up for free at *http://my.safaribooksonline.com*.

How to Contact Us

Please address comments and questions concerning this book to the publisher:

O'Reilly Media, Inc.
1005 Gravenstein Highway North
Sebastopol, CA 95472

800-998-9938 (in the United States or Canada)
707-829-0515 (international or local)
707-829-0104 (fax)

To comment or ask technical questions about this book, send email to:

bookquestions@oreilly.com

For more information about our books, conferences, Resource Centers, and the O'Reilly Network, see our website at:

http://oreilly.com

—Rebecca Murphey and Cody Lindley

jQuery Basics

Cody Lindley

1.0 Introduction

Since you've picked up a cookbook about jQuery, the authors of this book for the most part are going to assume that you have a loose idea about what exactly jQuery is and what it does. Frankly, cookbooks in general are typically written for an audience who seeks to enhance a foundation of knowledge that has already been established. Thus, the recipe-solution-discussion format is used to quickly get you solutions to common problems. However, if you are a jQuery newbie, don't throw this book against the wall and curse us just yet. We've dedicated this chapter to you.

If you are in need of a review or are jumping into this cookbook with little or no working knowledge of jQuery, this first chapter alone (the other chapters assume you know the basics) will aid you in learning the jQuery essentials. Now, realistically, if you have absolutely zero knowledge of JavaScript and the DOM, you might want to take a step back and ask yourself whether approaching jQuery *without* a basic understanding of the JavaScript core language and its relationship with the DOM is plausible. It would be my recommendation to study up on the DOM and JavaScript core before approaching jQuery. I highly recommend *JavaScript: The Definitive Guide (http://oreilly.com/ catalog/9780596000486)* by David Flanagan (O'Reilly) as a primer before reading this book. But don't let my humble opinion stop you if you are attempting to learn jQuery before you learn about the DOM and JavaScript. Many have come to a working knowledge of these technologies by way of jQuery. And while not ideal, let's face it, it can still be done.

With that said, let's take a look at a formal definition of jQuery and a brief description of its functionality:

> jQuery is an open source JavaScript library that simplifies the interactions between an HTML document, or more precisely the Document Object Model (aka the DOM), and JavaScript.

In plain words, and for the old-school JavaScript hackers out there, jQuery makes Dynamic HTML (DHTML) dead easy. Specifically, jQuery simplifies HTML document traversing and manipulation, browser event handling, DOM animations, Ajax interactions, and cross-browser JavaScript development.

With a formal explanation of jQuery under our belts, let's next explore why you might choose to use jQuery.

Why jQuery?

It might seem a bit silly to speak about the merits of jQuery within this cookbook, especially since you're reading this cookbook and are likely already aware of the merits.

So, while I might be preaching to the choir here, we're going to take a quick look at why a developer might choose to use jQuery. My point in doing this is to foster your basic knowledge of jQuery by first explaining the "why" before we look at the "how."

In building a case for jQuery, I'm not going to compare jQuery to its competitors in order to elevate jQuery's significance. That's because I just don't believe that there really is a direct competitor. Also, I believe the only library available today that meets the needs of both designer types and programmer types is jQuery. In this context, jQuery is in a class of its own.

Of the notorious JavaScript libraries and frameworks in the wild, I truly believe each has its own niche and value. A broad comparison is silly, but it's nevertheless attempted all the time. Heck, I am even guilty of it myself. However, after much thought on the topic, I truly believe that all JavaScript libraries are good at something. They all have value. What makes one more valuable than the other depends more upon who is using it and how it's being used than what it actually does. Besides, it has been my observation that micro differences across JavaScript libraries are often trivial in consideration of the broader goals of JavaScript development. So, without further philosophical ramblings, here is a list of attributes that builds a case for why you should use jQuery:

- It's open source, and the project is licensed under an MIT and a GNU General Public License (GPL) license. It's free, yo, in multiple ways!
- It's small (18 KB minified) and gzipped (114 KB, uncompressed).
- It's incredibly popular, which is to say it has a large community of users and a healthy amount of contributors who participate as developers and evangelists.
- It normalizes the differences between web browsers so that you don't have to.
- It's intentionally a lightweight footprint with a simple yet clever plugin architecture.
- Its repository of plugins (*http://plugins.jquery.com/*) is vast and has seen steady growth since jQuery's release.

- Its API is fully documented, including inline code examples, which in the world of JavaScript libraries is a luxury. Heck, any documentation at all was a luxury for years.
- It's friendly, which is to say it provides helpful ways to avoid conflicts with other JavaScript libraries.
- Its community support is actually fairly useful, including several mailing lists, IRC channels, and a freakishly insane amount of tutorials, articles, and blog posts from the jQuery community.
- It's openly developed, which means anyone can contribute bug fixes, enhancements, and development help.
- Its development is steady and consistent, which is to say the development team is not afraid of releasing updates.
- Its adoption by large organizations has and will continue to breed longevity and stability (e.g., Microsoft, Dell, Bank of America, Digg, CBS, Netflix).
- It's incorporating specifications from the W3C before the browsers do. As an example, jQuery supports a good majority of the CSS3 selectors.
- It's currently tested and optimized for development on modern browsers (Chrome 1, Chrome Nightly, IE 6, IE 7, IE 8, Opera 9.6, Safari 3.2, WebKit Nightly, Firefox 2, Firefox 3, Firefox Nightly).
- It's downright powerful in the hands of designer types as well as programmers. jQuery does not discriminate.
- Its elegance, methodologies, and philosophy of changing the way JavaScript is written is becoming a standard in and of itself. Consider just how many other solutions have borrowed the selector and chaining patterns.
- Its unexplainable by-product of feel-good programming is contagious and certainly unavoidable; even the critics seem to fall in love with aspects of jQuery.
- Its documentation has many outlets (e.g., API browser, dashboard apps, cheat sheets) including an offline API browser (AIR application).
- It's purposely bent to facilitate unobtrusive JavaScript practices.
- It has remained a JavaScript library (as opposed to a framework) at heart while at the same time providing a sister project for user interface widgets and application development (jQuery UI).
- Its learning curve is approachable because it builds upon concepts that most developers and designers already understand (e.g., CSS and HTML).

It is my opinion that the combination of the aforementioned jQuery points, and not any single attribute on its own, sets it apart from all other solutions. The total jQuery package is simply unmatched as a JavaScript tool.

The jQuery Philosophy

The jQuery philosophy is "Write less, do more." This philosophy can be further broken down into three concepts:

- Finding some elements (via CSS selectors) and doing something with them (via jQuery methods)
- Chaining multiple jQuery methods on a set of elements
- Using the jQuery wrapper and implicit iteration

Understanding these three concepts in detail is foundational when it comes time to write your own jQuery code or augment the recipes found in this book. Let's examine each of these concepts in detail.

Find some elements and do something with them

Or more specifically stated, locate a set of elements in the DOM, and then do something with that set of elements. For example, let's examine a scenario where you want to hide a <div> from the user, load some new text content into the hidden <div>, change an attribute of the selected <div>, and then finally make the hidden <div> visible again.

This last sentence translated into jQuery code would look something like this:

```
<!DOCTYPE html PUBLIC "-//W3C//DTD XHTML 1.0 Transitional//EN"
"http://www.w3.org/TR/xhtml1/DTD/xhtml1-transitional.dtd">
<html>
<head>
<script type="text/JavaScript"
src="http://ajax.googleapis.com/ajax/libs/jquery/1.3.2/jquery.min.js"></script>
</head>
<body>
<div>old content</div>
<script>

//hide all divs on the page
jQuery('div').hide();

//update the text contained inside of all divs
jQuery('div').text('new content');

//add a class attribute with a value of updatedContent to all divs
jQuery('div').addClass("updatedContent");

//show all divs on the page
jQuery('div').show();

</script>
</body>
</html>
```

Let's step through these four jQuery statements:

- Hide the `<div>` element on the page so it's hidden from the user's view.
- Replace the text inside the hidden `<div>` with some new text (`new content`).
- Update the `<div>` element with a new attribute (`class`) and value (`updatedContent`).
- Show the `<div>` element on the page so it's visible again to the viewing user.

If the jQuery code at this point is mystical syntax to you, that's OK. We'll dive into the basics with the first recipe in this chapter. Again, what you need to take away from this code example is the jQuery concept of "find some elements and do something with them." In our code example, we found all the `<div>` elements in the HTML page using the jQuery function (`jQuery()`), and then using jQuery methods we did something with them (e.g., `hide()`, `text()`, `addClass()`, `show()`).

Chaining

jQuery is constructed in a manner that will allow jQuery methods to be chained. For example, why not find an element once and then chain operations onto that element? Our former code example demonstrating the "Find some elements and do something with them" concept could be rewritten to a single JavaScript statement using chaining.

This code, using chaining, can be changed from this:

```
//hide all divs on the page
jQuery('div').hide();

//update the text contained inside of the div
jQuery('div').text('new content');

//add a class attribute with a value of updatedContent to all divs
jQuery('div').addClass("updatedContent");

//show all divs on the page
jQuery('div').show();
```

to this:

```
jQuery('div').hide().text('new content').addClass("updatedContent").show();
```

or, with indenting and line breaks, to this:

```
jQuery('div')
    .hide()
    .text('new content')
    .addClass("updatedContent")
    .show();
```

Plainly speaking, chaining simply allows you to apply an endless chain of jQuery methods on the elements that are currently selected (currently wrapped with jQuery functionality) using the jQuery function. Behind the scenes, the elements previously selected before a jQuery method was applied are always returned so that the chain can continue. As you will see in future recipes, plugins are also constructed in this manner (returning wrapped elements) so that using a plugin does not break the chain.

If it's not immediately obvious, and based on the code in question, chaining also cuts down on processing overhead by selecting a set of DOM elements only once, to then be operated on numerous times by jQuery methods by way of chaining. Avoiding unnecessary DOM traversing is a critical part of page performance enhancements. Whenever possible, reuse or cache a set of selected DOM elements.

The jQuery wrapper set

A good majority of the time, if jQuery is involved, you're going to be getting what is known as a *wrapper*. In other words, you'll be selecting DOM elements from an HTML page that will be wrapped with jQuery functionality. Personally, I often refer to this as a "wrapper set" or "wrapped set" because it's a set of elements wrapped with jQuery functionality. Sometimes this wrapper set will contain one DOM element; other times it will contain several. There are even cases where the wrapper set will contain no elements. In these situations, the methods/properties that jQuery provides will fail silently if methods are called on an empty wrapper set, which can be handy in avoiding unneeded if statements.

Now, based on the code we used to demonstrate the "Find some elements and do something with them" concept, what do you think would happen if we added multiple <div> elements to the web page? In the following updated code example, I have added three additional <div> elements to the HTML page, for a total of four <div> elements:

```
<!DOCTYPE html PUBLIC "-//W3C//DTD XHTML 1.0 Transitional//EN"
"http://www.w3.org/TR/xhtml1/DTD/xhtml1-transitional.dtd">
<html>
<head>
<script type="text/JavaScript" src="http://ajax.googleapis.com/ajax/libs/
jquery/1.3.0/jquery.min.js"></script> </head>
<body>
<div>old content</div>
<div>old content</div>
<div>old content</div>
<div>old content</div>
<script>
//hide all divs on the page
jQuery('div').hide().text('new content').addClass("updatedContent").show();

</script>
</body>
</html>
```

You may not have explicitly written any programmatic loops here, but guess what? jQuery is going to scan the page and place all <div> elements in the wrapper set so that the jQuery methods I am using here are performed (aka implicit iteration) on each DOM element in the set. For example, the .hide() method actually applies to each element in the set. So if you look at our code again, you will see that each method that we use will be applied to each <div> element on the page. It's as if you had written a loop here to invoke each jQuery method on each DOM element. The updated code example will result in each `<div>` in the page being hidden, filled with updated text, given a new class value, and then made visible again.

Wrapping your head around (pun intended) the wrapper set and its default looping system (aka implicit iteration) is critical for building advanced concepts around looping. Just keep in mind that a simple loop is occurring here before you actually do any additional looping (e.g., `jQuery('div').each(function(){}`). Or another way to look at this is each element in the wrapper will typically be changed by the jQuery method(s) that are called.

Something to keep in mind here is there are scenarios that you will learn about in the coming chapters where only the first element, and not all the elements in the wrapper set, is affected by the jQuery method (e.g., `attr()`).

How the jQuery API Is Organized

There is no question that when I first started out with jQuery, my main reason for selecting it as my JavaScript library was simply that it had been properly documented (and the gazillion plugins!). Later, I realized another factor that cemented my love affair with jQuery was the fact that the API was organized into logical categories. Just by looking at how the API was organized, I could narrow down the functionality I needed.

Before you really get started with jQuery, I suggest visiting the documentation online (*http://docs.jquery.com/Main_Page*) and simply digesting how the API is organized. By understanding how the API is organized, you'll more quickly navigate the documentation to the exact information you need, which is actually a significant advantage given that there are really a lot of different ways to code a jQuery solution. It's so robust that it's easy to get hung up on implementation because of the number of solutions for a single problem. I've replicated here for you how the API is organized. I suggest memorizing the API outline, or at the very least the top-level categories.

- jQuery Core
  - The jQuery Function
  - jQuery Object Accessors
  - Data
  - Plugins
  - Interoperability
- Selectors
  - Basics
  - Hierarchy
  - Basic Filters
  - Content Filters
  - Visibility Filters

- —Attribute Filters
- —Child Filters
- —Forms
- —Form Filters
- Attributes
  - —Attr
  - —Class
  - —HTML
  - —Text
  - —Value
- Traversing
  - —Filtering
  - —Finding
  - —Chaining
- Manipulation
  - —Changing Contents
  - —Inserting Inside
  - —Inserting Outside
  - —Inserting Around
  - —Replacing
  - —Removing
  - —Copying
- CSS
  - —CSS
  - —Positioning
  - —Height and Widths
- Events
  - —Page Load
  - —Event Handling
  - —Live Events
  - —Interaction Helpers
  - —Event Helpers
- Effects
  - —Basics
  - —Sliding

- —Fading
- —Custom
- —Settings
- Ajax
- —AJAX Requests
- —AJAX Events
- —Misc.
- Utilities
- —Browser and Feature Detection
- —Array and Object Operations
- —Test Operations
- —String Operations
- —Urls

Before we jump into a sequence of basic jQuery recipes, I would like to mention that the recipes found in this chapter build on each other. That is, there is a logical formation of knowledge as you progress from the first recipe to the last. It's my suggestion, for your first reading of these recipes, that you read them in order from 1.1 to 1.17.

1.1 Including the jQuery Library Code in an HTML Page

Problem

You want to use the jQuery JavaScript library on a web page.

Solution

There are currently two ideal solutions for embedding the jQuery library in a web page:

- Use the Google-hosted content delivery network (CDN) to include a version of jQuery (used in this chapter).
- Download your own version of jQuery from jQuery.com and host it on your own server or local filesystem.

Discussion

Including the jQuery JavaScript library isn't any different from including any other external JavaScript file. You simply use the HTML `<script>` element and provide the element a value (URL or directory path) for its `src=""` attribute, and the external file you are linking to will be included in the web page. For example, the following is a template that includes the jQuery library that you can use to start any jQuery project:

```
<!DOCTYPE html PUBLIC "-//W3C//DTD XHTML 1.0 Transitional//EN"
"http://www.w3.org/TR/xhtml1/DTD/xhtml1-transitional.dtd">
<html>
<head>
<meta http-equiv="Content-Type" content="text/html; charset=UTF-8" />
<script type="text/JavaScript"
src="http://ajax.googleapis.com/ajax/libs/jquery/1.3.2/jquery.min.js"></script>
</head>
<body>
<script type="text/JavaScript">
    alert('jQuery ' + jQuery.fn.jquery);
</script>
</body>
</html>
```

Notice that I am using—and highly recommend using for public web pages—the Google-hosted minified version of jQuery. However, debugging JavaScript errors in minified code is not ideal. During code development, or on the production site, it actually might be better to use the nonminified version from Google for the purpose of debugging potential JavaScript errors. For more information about using the Google-hosted version of jQuery, you can visit the Ajax libraries API site on the Web at *http://code.google.com/apis/ajaxlibs/*.

It's of course also possible, and mostly likely old hat, to host a copy of the jQuery code yourself. In most circumstances, however, this would be silly to do because Google has been kind enough to host it for you. By using a Google-hosted version of jQuery, you benefit from a stable, reliable, high-speed, and globally available copy of jQuery. As well, you reap the benefit of decreased latency, increased parallelism, and better caching. This of course could be accomplished without using Google's solution, but it would most likely cost you a dime or two.

Now, for whatever reason, you might not want to use the Google-hosted version of jQuery. You might want a customized version of jQuery, or your usage might not require/have access to an Internet connection. Or, you simply might believe that Google is "The Man" and wish not to submit to usage because you are a control freak and conspiracy fanatic. So, for those who do not need, or simply who do not want, to use a Google-hosted copy of the jQuery code, jQuery can be downloaded from jQuery.com (*http://docs.jquery.com/Downloading_jQuery*) and hosted locally on your own server or local filesystem. Based on the template I've provided in this recipe, you would simply replace the src attribute value with a URL or directory path to the location of the jQuery JavaScript file you've downloaded.

1.2 Executing jQuery/JavaScript Coded After the DOM Has Loaded but Before Complete Page Load

Problem

Modern JavaScript applications using unobtrusive JavaScript methodologies typically execute JavaScript code only after the DOM has been completely loaded. And the reality of the situation is that any DOM traversing and manipulation will require that the DOM is loaded before it can be operated on. What's needed is a way to determine when the client, most often a web browser, has completely loaded the DOM but has possibly not yet completely loaded all assets such as images and SWF files. If we were to use the `window.onload` event in this situation, the entire document including all assets would need to be completely loaded before the `onload` event fired. That's just too time-consuming for most web surfers. What's needed is an event that will tell us when the DOM alone is ready to be traversed and manipulated.

Solution

jQuery provides the `ready()` method, which is a custom event handler that is typically bound to the DOM's document object. The `ready()` method is passed a single parameter, a function, that contains the JavaScript code that should be executed once the DOM is ready to be traversed and manipulated. The following is a simple example of this event opening an `alert()` window once the DOM is ready but before the page is completely loaded:

```
<!DOCTYPE html PUBLIC "-//W3C//DTD XHTML 1.0 Transitional//EN"
"http://www.w3.org/TR/xhtml1/DTD/xhtml1-transitional.dtd">
<html>
<head>
<meta http-equiv="Content-Type" content="text/html; charset=UTF-8" />
<script type="text/JavaScript"
src="http://ajax.googleapis.com/ajax/libs/jquery/1.3.2/jquery.min.js"></script>
<script type="text/JavaScript">
    jQuery(document).ready(function(){//DOM not loaded, must use ready event
        alert(jQuery('p').text());
    });
</script>
</head>
<body>
<p>The DOM is ready!</p>
</body>
</html>
```

Discussion

The `ready()` event handler method is jQuery's replacement for using the JavaScript core `window.onload` event. It can be used as many times as you like. When using this custom event, it's advisable that it be included in your web pages after the inclusion of stylesheet declarations and includes. Doing this will ensure that all element properties are correctly defined before any jQuery code or JavaScript code will be executed by the `ready()` event.

Additionally, the jQuery function itself provides a shortcut for using the jQuery custom ready event. Using this shortcut, the following `alert()` example can be rewritten like so:

```
<!DOCTYPE html PUBLIC "-//W3C//DTD XHTML 1.0 Transitional//EN"
"http://www.w3.org/TR/xhtml1/DTD/xhtml1-transitional.dtd">
<html>
<head>
<meta http-equiv="Content-Type" content="text/html; charset=UTF-8" />
<script type="text/JavaScript"
src="http://ajax.googleapis.com/ajax/libs/jquery/1.3.2/jquery.min.js"></script>
<script type="text/JavaScript">
    jQuery(function(){ //DOM not loaded, must use ready event
        alert(jQuery('p').text());
    });
</script>
</head>
<body>
<p>The DOM is ready!</p>
</body>
</html>
```

The use of this custom jQuery event is necessary only if JavaScript has to be embedded in the document flow at the top of the page and encapsulated in the <head> element. I simply avoid the usage of the `ready()` event by placing all JavaScript includes and inline code before the closing <body> element. I do this for two reasons.

First, modern optimization techniques have declared that pages load faster when the JavaScript is loaded by the browser at the end of a page parse. In other words, if you put JavaScript code at the bottom of a web page, then the browser will load everything in front of it before it loads the JavaScript. This is a good thing because most browsers will typically stop processing other loading initiatives until the JavaScript engine has compiled the JavaScript contained in a web page. It's sort of a bottleneck in a sense that you have JavaScript at the top of a web page document. I realize that for some situations it's easier to place JavaScript in the <head> element. But honestly, I've never seen a situation where this is absolutely required. Any obstacle that I've encountered during my development by placing JavaScript at the bottom of the page has been easily overcome and well worth the optimization gains.

Second, if speedy web pages are our goal, why wrap more functionality around a situation that can be elevated by simply moving the code to the bottom of the page? When given the choice between more code or less code, I choose less code. Not using the `ready()` event results in using less code, especially since less code always runs faster than more code.

With some rationale out of the way, here is an example of our `alert()` code that does not use the `ready()` event:

```
<!DOCTYPE html PUBLIC "-//W3C//DTD XHTML 1.0 Transitional//EN"
"http://www.w3.org/TR/xhtml1/DTD/xhtml1-transitional.dtd">
<html>
<head>
<meta http-equiv="Content-Type" content="text/html; charset=UTF-8" />
</head>
<body>
<p>The DOM is ready!</p>
<script type="text/JavaScript"
src="http://ajax.googleapis.com/ajax/libs/jquery/1.3.2/jquery.min.js"></script>
<script type="text/JavaScript">
    alert(jQuery('p').text());//go for it the DOM is loaded
</script>
</body>
</html>
```

Notice that I have placed all of my JavaScript before the closing </body> element. Any additional markup should be placed above the JavaScript in the HTML document.

1.3 Selecting DOM Elements Using Selectors and the jQuery Function

Problem

You need to select a single DOM element and/or a set of DOM elements in order to operate on the element(s) using jQuery methods.

Solution

jQuery provides two options when you need to select element(s) from the DOM. Both options require the use of the jQuery function (jQuery() or alias $()). The first option, which uses CSS selectors and custom selectors, is by far the most used and most eloquent solution. By passing the jQuery function a string containing a selector expression, the function will traverse the DOM and locate the DOM nodes defined by the expression. As an example, the following code will select all the <a> elements in the HTML document:

```
<!DOCTYPE html PUBLIC "-//W3C//DTD XHTML 1.0 Transitional//EN"
"http://www.w3.org/TR/xhtml1/DTD/xhtml1-transitional.dtd">
<html>
<head>
<meta http-equiv="Content-Type" content="text/html; charset=UTF-8" />
</head>
<body>
<a href='#'>link</a>
<a href='#'>link</a>
<a href='#'>link</a>
<a href='#'>link</a>
<a href='#'>link</a>
<a href='#'>link</a>
```

```
<script type="text/JavaScript"
src="http://ajax.googleapis.com/ajax/libs/jquery/1.3.2/jquery.min.js"></script>
<script type="text/JavaScript">
    //alerts there are 6 elements
    alert('Page contains ' + jQuery('a').length +  ' <a> elements!');
</script>
</body>
</html>
```

If you were to run this HTML page in a web browser, you would see that the code executes a browser `alert()` that informs us that the page contains six `<a>` elements. I passed this value to the `alert()` method by first selecting all the `<a>` elements and then using the `length` property to return the number of elements in the jQuery wrapper set.

You should be aware that the first parameter of the jQuery function, as we are using it here, will also accept multiple expressions. To do this, simply separate multiple selectors with a comma inside the same string that is passed as the first parameter to the jQuery function. Here is an example of what that might look like:

```
jQuery('selector1, selector2, selector3').length;
```

Our second option for selecting DOM elements and the less common option is to pass the jQuery function an actual JavaScript reference to DOM element(s). As an example, the following code will select all the `<a>` elements in the HTML document. Notice that I'm passing the jQuery function an array of `<a>` elements collected using the `getElementsByTagName` DOM method. This example produces the same exact results as our previous code example:

```
<!DOCTYPE html PUBLIC "-//W3C//DTD XHTML 1.0 Transitional//EN"
"http://www.w3.org/TR/xhtml1/DTD/xhtml1-transitional.dtd">
<html>
<head>
<meta http-equiv="Content-Type" content="text/html; charset=UTF-8" />
</head>
<body bgcolor="yellow"> <!-- yes the attribute is depreciated, I know, roll
with it -->
<a href='#'>link</a>
<a href='#'>link</a>
<a href='#'>link</a>
<a href='#'>link</a>
<a href='#'>link</a>
<a href='#'>link</a>
<script type="text/JavaScript"
src="http://ajax.googleapis.com/ajax/libs/jquery/1.3.2/jquery.min.js"></script>
<script type="text/JavaScript">
    //alerts there are 6 elements
    alert('Page contains ' + jQuery(document.getElementsByTagName('a')).length +
' <a> Elements, And has a '
    + jQuery(document.body).attr('bgcolor') + ' background');
</script>
</body>
</html>
```

Discussion

The heavy lifting that jQuery is known for is partially based on the selector engine, Sizzle (*http://sizzlejs.com/*), that selects DOM element(s) from an HTML document. While you have the option, and it's a nice option when you need it, passing the jQuery function DOM references is not what put jQuery on everyone's radar. It's the vast and powerful options available with selectors that make jQuery so unique.

Throughout the rest of the book, you will find powerful and robust selectors. When you see one, make sure you fully understand its function. This knowledge will serve you well with future coding endeavors using jQuery.

1.4 Selecting DOM Elements Within a Specified Context

Problem

You need a reference to a single DOM element or a set of DOM elements in the context of another DOM element or document in order to operate on the element(s) using jQuery methods.

Solution

The jQuery function when passed a CSS expression will also accept a second parameter that tells the jQuery function to which context it should search for the DOM elements based on the expression. The second parameter in this case can be a DOM reference, jQuery wrapper, or document. In the following code, there are 12 `<input>` elements. Notice how I use a specific context, based on the `<form>` element, to select only particular `<input>` elements:

```
<!DOCTYPE html PUBLIC "-//W3C//DTD XHTML 1.0 Transitional//EN"
"http://www.w3.org/TR/xhtml1/DTD/xhtml1-transitional.dtd">
<html>
<head>
<meta http-equiv="Content-Type" content="text/html; charset=UTF-8" />
</head>
<body>

<form>
<input name="" type="checkbox" />
<input name="" type="radio" />
<input name="" type="text" />
<input name="" type="button" />
</form>

<form>
<input name="" type="checkbox" />
<input name="" type="radio" />
<input name="" type="text" />
<input name="" type="button" />
```

```
    </form>

    <input name="" type="checkbox" />
    <input name="" type="radio" />
    <input name="" type="text" />
    <input name="" type="button" />

    <script type="text/JavaScript"
    src="http://ajax.googleapis.com/ajax/libs/jquery/1.3.2/jquery.min.js"></script>
    <script type="text/JavaScript">

        //searches within all form elements, using a wrapper for context, alerts "8 inputs"
        alert('selected ' + jQuery('input',$('form')).length + ' inputs');

        //search with the first form element, using DOM reference as the context, alerts
        //"4 inputs"
        alert('selected' + jQuery('input',document.forms[0]).length + ' inputs');

        //search within the body element for all input elements using an expression,
        //alerts "12 inputs"
        alert('selected' + jQuery('input','body').length + ' inputs');

    </script>
    </body>
    </html>
```

Discussion

It's also possible, as mentioned in the solution of this recipe, to select documents as the context for searching. For example, it's possible to search within the context of an XML document that is sent back from doing an XHR request (Ajax). You can find more details about this usage in Chapter 16.

1.5 Filtering a Wrapper Set of DOM Elements

Problem

You have a set of selected DOM elements in a jQuery wrapper set but want to remove DOM elements from the set that do not match a new specified expression(s) in order to create a new set of elements to operate on.

Solution

The jQuery filter method, used on a jQuery wrapper set of DOM elements, can exclude elements that *do not* match a specified expression(s). In short, the filter() method allows you to filter the current set of elements. This is an important distinction from the jQuery find method, which will reduce a wrapped set of DOM elements by finding (via a new selector expression) new elements, including child elements of the current wrapped set.

To understand the filter method, let's examine the following code:

```
<!DOCTYPE html PUBLIC "-//W3C//DTD XHTML 1.0 Transitional//EN"
"http://www.w3.org/TR/xhtml1/DTD/xhtml1-transitional.dtd">
<html>
<head>
<meta http-equiv="Content-Type" content="text/html; charset=UTF-8" />
</head>
<body>
<a href="#" class="external">link</a>
<a href="#" class="external">link</a>
<a href="#"></a>
<a href="#" class="external">link</a>
<a href="#" class="external">link</a>
<a href="#"></a></li>
<a href="#">link</a>
<a href="#">link</a>
<a href="#">link</a>
<a href="#">link</a>
<script type="text/JavaScript"
src="http://ajax.googleapis.com/ajax/libs/jquery/1.3.2/jquery.min.js"></script>
<script type="text/JavaScript">

    //alerts 4 left in the set
        alert(jQuery('a').filter('.external').length + ' external links');
</script>
</body>
</html>
```

The HTML page in the code example just shown contains a web page with 10 <a> elements. Those links that are external links are given a class name of external. Using the jQuery function, we select all <a> elements on the page. Then, using the filter method, all those elements that do not have a class attribute value of external are removed from the original set. Once the initial set of DOM elements are altered using the filter() method, I invoke the length property, which will tell me how many elements are now in my new set after the filter has been applied.

Discussion

It's also possible to send the filter() method a function that can be used to filter the wrapped set. Our previous code example, which passes the filter() method a string expression, can be changed to use a function instead:

```
alert(
   jQuery('a')
      .filter(function(index){ return $(this).hasClass('external');})
      .length + ' external links'
);
```

Notice that I am now passing the filter() method an anonymous function. This function is called with a context equal to the current element. That means when I use $(this) within the function, I am actually referring to each DOM element in the wrapper set. Within the function, I am checking each <a> element in the wrapper set to see whether the element has a class value (`hasClass()`) of `external`. If it does, Boolean true, then keep the element in the set, and if it doesn't (false), then remove the element from the set. Another way to look at this is if the function returns false, then the element is removed. If the function returns any other data value besides false, then the element will remain in the wrapper set.

You may have noticed that I have passed the function a parameter named `index` that I am not using. This parameter, if needed, can be used to refer numerically to the index of the element in the jQuery wrapper set.

1.6 Finding Descendant Elements Within the Currently Selected Wrapper Set

Problem

You have a set of selected DOM elements (or a single element) and want to find descendant (children) elements within the context of the currently selected elements.

Solution

Use the `.find()` method to create a new wrapper set of elements based on the context of the current set and their descendants. For example, say that you have a web page that contains several paragraphs. Encapsulated inside of these paragraphs are words that are emphasized (italic). If you'd like to select only `<em>` elements contained within `<p>` elements, you could do so like this:

```
<!DOCTYPE html PUBLIC "-//W3C//DTD XHTML 1.0 Transitional//EN"
"http://www.w3.org/TR/xhtml1/DTD/xhtml1-transitional.dtd">
<html>
<head>
<meta http-equiv="Content-Type" content="text/html; charset=UTF-8" />
</head>
<body>
<p>Ut ad videntur facilisis <em>elit</em> cum. Nibh insitam erat facit
<em>saepius</em> magna.  Nam ex liber iriure et imperdiet. Et mirum eros
iis te habent. </p>
<p>Claram claritatem eu amet dignissim magna. Dignissim quam elit facer eros
illum. Et qui ex esse <em>tincidunt</em> anteposuerit. Nulla nam odio ii
vulputate feugait.</p>
<p>In quis <em>laoreet</em> te legunt euismod. Claritatem <em>consuetudium</em>
wisi sit velit facilisi.</p>
<script type="text/JavaScript"
src="http://ajax.googleapis.com/ajax/libs/jquery/1.3.2/jquery.min.js"></script>
<script type="text/JavaScript">
 //alerts total italic words found inside of <p> elements
        alert('The three paragraphs in all contain ' +
        jQuery('p').find('em').length + '
italic words');
</script>
```

```
</body>
</html>
```

Keep in mind that we could have also written this code by passing a contextual reference as a second parameter to the jQuery function:

```
alert('The three paragraphs in all contain ' + jQuery('em',$('p')).length +
' italic words');
```

Additionally, it's worth mentioning that the last two code examples are demonstrative in purpose. It is likely more logical, if not pragmatic, to use a CSS selector expression to select all the descendant italic elements contained within the ancestor `<p>` elements.

```
alert('The three paragraphs in all contain ' + jQuery('p em').length +
' italic words');
```

Discussion

The jQuery `.find()` method can be used to create a new set of elements based on context of the current set of DOM elements and their children elements. People often confuse the use of the `.filter()` method and `.find()` method. The easiest way to remember the difference is to keep in mind that `.find()` will operate/select the children of the current set while `.filter()` will only operate on the current set of elements. In other words, if you want to change the current wrapper set by using it as a context to further select the children of the elements selected, use `.find()`. If you only want to filter the current wrapped set and get a new subset of the current DOM elements in the set only, use `.filter()`. To boil this down even more, `find()` returns children elements, while `filter()` only filters what is in the current wrapper set.

1.7 Returning to the Prior Selection Before a Destructive Change

Problem

A destructive jQuery method (e.g., `filter()` or `find()`) that was used on a set of elements needs to be removed so that the set prior to the use of the destructive method is returned to its previous state and can then be operated as if the destructive method had never been invoked.

Solution

jQuery provides the `end()` method so that you can return to the previous set of DOM elements that were selected before using a destructive method. To understand the `end()` method, let's examine the following HTML.

```
<!DOCTYPE html PUBLIC "-//W3C//DTD XHTML 1.0 Transitional//EN"
"http://www.w3.org/TR/xhtml1/DTD/xhtml1-transitional.dtd">
<html>
```

```
<head>
<meta http-equiv="Content-Type" content="text/html; charset=UTF-8" />
</head>
<body>
<p>text</p>
<p class="middle">Middle <span>text</span></p>
<p>text</p>
<script type="text/JavaScript"
src="http://ajax.googleapis.com/ajax/libs/jquery/1.3.2/jquery.min.js"></script>
<script type="text/JavaScript">
    alert(jQuery('p').filter('.middle').length); //alerts 1
    alert(jQuery('p').filter('.middle').end().length); //alerts 3
    alert(jQuery('p').filter('.middle').find('span')
.end().end().length); //alerts 3
</script>
</body>
</html>
```

The first `alert()` statement in the code contains a jQuery statement that will search the document for all `<p>` elements and then apply `filter()` to the selected `<p>` elements in the set selecting only the one(s) with a class of `middle`. The `length` property then reports how many elements are left in the set:

```
alert(jQuery('p').filter('.middle').length); //alerts 1
```

The next `alert()` statement makes use of the `end()` method. Here we are doing everything we did in the prior statement except that we are undoing the `filter()` method and returning to the set of elements contained in the wrapper set before the `filter()` method was applied:

```
alert(jQuery('p').filter('.middle').end().length); //alerts 3
```

The last `alert()` statement demonstrates how the `end()` method is used twice to remove both the `filter()` and `find()` destructive changes, returning the wrapper set to its original composition:

```
alert(jQuery('p').filter('.middle').find('span').end().end().length); //alerts 3
```

Discussion

If the `end()` method is used and there were no prior destructive operations performed, an empty set is returned. A destructive operation is any operation that changes the set of matched jQuery elements, which means any traversing or manipulation method that returns a jQuery object, including `add()`, `andSelf()`, `children()`, `closes()`, `filter()`, `find()`, `map()`, `next()`, `nextAll()`, `not()`, `parent()`, `parents()`, `prev()`, `prevAll()`, `siblings()`, `slice()`, `clone()`, `appendTo()`, `prependTo()`, `insertBefore()`, `insertAfter()`, and `replaceAll()`.

1.8 Including the Previous Selection with the Current Selection

Problem

You have just manipulated a set of elements in order to acquire a new set of elements. However, you want to operate on the prior set as well as the current set.

Solution

You can combine a prior selection of DOM elements with the current selection by using the andSelf() method. For example, in the following code, we are first selecting all <div> elements on the page. Next we manipulate this set of elements by finding all <p> elements contained within the <div> elements. Now, in order to operate on both the <div> and the <p> elements found within the <div>, we could include the <div> into the current set by using andSelf(). Had I omitted the andSelf(), the border color would have only been applied to the <p> elements:

```
<!DOCTYPE html PUBLIC "-//W3C//DTD XHTML 1.0 Transitional//EN"
"http://www.w3.org/TR/xhtml1/DTD/xhtml1-transitional.dtd">
<html>
<head>
<meta http-equiv="Content-Type" content="text/html; charset=UTF-8" />
</head>
<body>
<div>
<p>Paragraph</p>
<p>Paragraph</p>
</div>
<script type="text/JavaScript" src="http://ajax.googleapis.com/
ajax/libs/jquery/1.3.2/jquery.min.js"></script>
<script type="text/JavaScript">
    jQuery('div').find('p').andSelf().css('border','1px solid #993300');
</script>
</body>
</html>
```

Discussion

Keep in mind that when you use the andSelf() method, it will only add into the current set being operated on and the prior set, but not all prior sets.

1.9 Traversing the DOM Based on Your Current Context to Acquire a New Set of DOM Elements

Problem

You have selected a set of DOM elements, and based on the position of the selections within the DOM tree structure, you want to traverse the DOM to acquire a new set of elements to operate on.

Solution

jQuery provides a set of methods for traversing the DOM based on the context of the currently selected DOM element(s).

For example, let's examine the following HTML snippet:

```
<div>
<ul>
<li><a href="#">link</a></li>
<li><a href="#">link</a></li>
<li><a href="#">link</a></li>
<li><a href="#">link</a></li>
</ul>
</div>
```

Now, let's select the second `<li>` element using the `:eq()` index custom selector:

```
//selects the second element in the set of <li>'s by index, index starts at 0
jQuery('li:eq(1)');
```

We now have a context, a starting point within the HTML structure. Our starting point is the second `<li>` element. From here we can go anywhere—well, almost anywhere. Let's see where we can go using a couple of the methods jQuery provides for traversing the DOM. Read the comments in the code for clarification:

```
jQuery('li:eq(1)').next() //selects the third <li>

jQuery('li:eq(1)').prev() //selects the first <li>

jQuery('li:eq(1)').parent() //selects the <ul>

jQuery('li:eq(1)').parent().children() //selects all <li>s

jQuery('li:eq(1)').nextAll() //selects all the <li>s after the second <li>

jQuery('li:eq(1)').prevAll() //selects all the <li>s before the second <li>
```

Keep in mind that these traversing methods produce a new wrapper set, and to return to the previous wrapper set, you can use `end()`.

Discussion

The traversing methods shown thus far have demonstrated simple traverses. There are two additional concepts that are important to know about traversing.

The first concept and likely most obvious is that traversing methods can be chained. Let's examine again the following jQuery statement from earlier:

```
jQuery('li:eq(1)').parent().children() //selects all <li>'s
```

Notice that I have traversed from the second <li> element to the parent <ul> element and then again traversed from the parent element to selecting all the children elements of the <ul> element. The jQuery wrapper set will now contain all the <li> elements contained within the <ul>. Of course, this is a contrived example for the purpose of demonstrating traversing methods. Had we really wanted a wrapper set of just <li> elements, it would have been much simpler to select all the <li> elements from the get-go (e.g., jQuery('li')).

The second concept that you need to keep in mind when dealing with the traversing methods is that many of the methods will accept an optional parameter that can be used to filter the selections. Let's take our chained example again and look at how we could change it so that only the last <li> element was selected. Keep in mind that this is a contrived example for the purpose of demonstrating how a traversing method can be passed an expression used for selecting a very specific element:

```
jQuery('li:eq(1)').parent().children(':last') //selects the last <li>
```

jQuery provides additional traversing methods that were not shown here. For a complete list and documentation, have a look at *http://docs.jquery.com/Traversing*. You will find these additional traversing methods used throughout this book.

1.10 Creating, Operating on, and Inserting DOM Elements

Problem

You want to create new DOM elements (or a single element) that are immediately selected, operated on, and then injected into the DOM.

Solution

If you haven't figured it out yet, the jQuery function is multifaceted in that this one function performs differently depending upon the makeup of the parameter(s) you send it. If you provide the function with a text string of raw HTML, it will create these elements for you on the fly. For example, the following statement will create an <a> element wrapped inside of a <p> element with a text node encapsulated inside of the <p> and <a> elements:

```
jQuery('<p><a>jQuery</a></p>');
```

Now, with an element created, you can use jQuery methods to further operate on the elements you just created. It's as if you had selected the <p> element from the get-go in an existing HTML document. For example, we could operate on the <a> by using the .find() method to select the <a> element and then set one of its attributes. In the case of the following code, we are setting the href attribute with a value of http://www.jquery.com:

```
jQuery('<p><a>jQuery</a></p>').find('a').attr('href','http://www.jquery.com');
```

This is great, right? Well, it's about to get better because all we have done so far is create elements on the fly and manipulate those elements in code. We have yet to actually change the currently loaded DOM, so to speak. To do this, we'll have to use the manipulation methods provided by jQuery. The following is our code in the context of an HTML document. Here we are creating elements, operating on those elements, and then inserting those elements into the DOM using the appendTo() manipulation method:

```
<!DOCTYPE html PUBLIC "-//W3C//DTD XHTML 1.0 Transitional//EN"
"http://www.w3.org/TR/xhtml1/DTD/xhtml1-transitional.dtd">
<html>
<head>
<meta http-equiv="Content-Type" content="text/html; charset=UTF-8" />
</head>
<body>
<script type="text/JavaScript"
src="http://ajax.googleapis.com/ajax/libs/jquery/1.3.2/jquery.min.js"></script>
<script type="text/JavaScript">
jQuery('<p><a>jQuery</a></p>').find('a').attr('href','http://www.jquery.com')
  .end().appendTo('body');
</script>
</body>
</html>
```

Notice how I am using the end() method here to undo the find() method so that when I call the appendTo() method, it appends what was originally contained in the initial wrapper set.

Discussion

In this recipe we've passed the jQuery function a string of raw HTML that is taken and used to create DOM elements on the fly. It's also possible to simply pass the jQuery function a DOM object created by the DOM method createElement():

```
jQuery(document.createElement('p')).appendTo('body'); //adds an empty p element
to the page
```

Of course, this could be rather laborious depending upon the specifics of the usage when a string of HTML containing multiple elements will work just fine.

It's also worth mentioning here that we've only scratched the surface of the manipulation methods by using the appendTo() method. In addition to the appendTo() method, there are also the following manipulation methods:

- `append()`
- `prepend()`
- `prependTo()`
- `after()`
- `before()`
- `insertAfter()`
- `insertBefore()`
- `wrap()`
- `wrapAll()`
- `wrapInner()`

1.11 Removing DOM Elements

Problem

You want to remove elements from the DOM.

Solution

The `remove()` method can be used to remove a selected set of elements and their children elements from the DOM. Examine the following code:

```
<!DOCTYPE html PUBLIC "-//W3C//DTD XHTML 1.0 Transitional//EN"
"http://www.w3.org/TR/xhtml1/DTD/xhtml1-transitional.dtd">
<html>
<head>
<meta http-equiv="Content-Type" content="text/html; charset=UTF-8" />
</head>
<body>
<h3>Anchors</h3>
<a href='#'>Anchor Element</a>
<a href='#'>Anchor Element</a>
<a href='#'>Anchor Element</a>
<script type="text/JavaScript"
src="http://ajax.googleapis.com/ajax/libs/jquery/1.3.2/jquery.min.js"></script>
<script type="text/JavaScript">
  jQuery('a').remove();
</script>
</body>
</html>
```

When the preceding code is loaded into a browser, the anchor elements will remain in the page until the JavaScript is executed. Once the `remove()` method is used to remove all anchor elements from the DOM, the page will visually contain only an `<h3>` element.

It's also possible to pass the method an expression to filter the set of elements to be removed. For example, our code could change to remove only anchors with a specific class:

```
<!DOCTYPE html PUBLIC "-//W3C//DTD XHTML 1.0 Transitional//EN"
"http://www.w3.org/TR/xhtml1/DTD/xhtml1-transitional.dtd">
<html>
<head>
<meta http-equiv="Content-Type" content="text/html; charset=UTF-8" />
</head>
<body>
<h3>Anchors</h3>
<a href='#' class='remove'>Anchor Element</a>
<a href='#'>Anchor Element</a>
<a href='#' class="remove">Anchor Element</a>
<script type="text/JavaScript"
src="http://ajax.googleapis.com/ajax/libs/jquery/1.3.2/jquery.min.js"></script>
<script type="text/JavaScript">
  jQuery('a').remove('.remove');
</script>
</body>
</html>
```

Discussion

When using the jQuery `remove()` method, you need to keep two things in mind:

- While the elements selected are removed from the DOM using `remove()`, they have not been removed from the jQuery wrapper set. That means in theory you could continue operating on them and even add them back into the DOM if desired.

- This method will not only remove the elements from the DOM, but it will also remove all event handlers and internally cached data that the elements removed might have contained.

1.12 Replacing DOM Elements

Problem

You need to replace DOM nodes currently in the DOM with new DOM nodes.

Solution

Using the `replaceWith()` method, we can select a set of DOM elements for replacement. In the following code example, we use the `replaceWith()` method to replace all `<li>` elements with a `class` attribute of `remove` with a new DOM structure:

```
<!DOCTYPE html PUBLIC "-//W3C//DTD XHTML 1.0 Transitional//EN"
"http://www.w3.org/TR/xhtml1/DTD/xhtml1-transitional.dtd">
<html>
<head>
```

```
<meta http-equiv="Content-Type" content="text/html; charset=UTF-8" />
</head>
<body>
<ul>
<li class='remove'>name</li>
<li>name</li>
<li class='remove'>name</li>
<li class='remove'>name</li>
<li>name</li>
<li class='remove'>name</li>
<li>name</li>
<li class='remove'>name</li>
</ul>
<script type="text/JavaScript"
src="http://ajax.googleapis.com/ajax/libs/jquery/1.3.2/jquery.min.js"></script>
<script type="text/JavaScript">
  jQuery('li.remove').replaceWith('<li>removed</li>');
</script>
</body>
</html>
```

The new DOM structure added to the DOM is a string parameter passed into the `replaceWith()` method. In our example, all the `<li>` elements, including children elements, are replaced with the new structure, `<li>removed</li>`.

Discussion

jQuery provides an inverse to this method called `replaceAll()` that does the same task with the parameters reversed. For example, we could rewrite the jQuery code found in our recipe code like so:

```
jQuery('<li>removed</li>').replaceAll('li.remove');
```

Here we are passing the jQuery function the HTML string and then using the `replaceAll()` method to select the DOM node and its children that we want to be removed and replaced.

1.13 Cloning DOM Elements

Problem

You need to clone/copy a portion of the DOM.

Solution

jQuery provides the `clone()` method for copying DOM elements. Its usage is straightforward. Simply select the DOM elements using the jQuery function, and then call the `clone()` method on the selected set of element(s). The result is a copy of the DOM structure being returned for chaining instead of the originally selected DOM elements. In the following code, I am cloning the `<ul>` element and then appending this copy back

into the DOM using the inserting method appendTo(). Essentially, I am adding another
<ul> structure to the page exactly like the one that is already there:

```
<!DOCTYPE html PUBLIC "-//W3C//DTD XHTML 1.0 Transitional//EN"
"http://www.w3.org/TR/xhtml1/DTD/xhtml1-transitional.dtd">
<html>
<head>
<meta http-equiv="Content-Type" content="text/html; charset=UTF-8" />
</head>
<body>
<ul>
<li>list</li>
<li>list</li>
<li>list</li>
<li>list</li>
</ul>
<script type="text/JavaScript"
src="http://ajax.googleapis.com/ajax/libs/jquery/1.3.2/jquery.min.js"></script>
<script type="text/JavaScript">
 jQuery('ul').clone().appendTo('body');
</script>
</body>
</html>
```

Discussion

The cloning method is actually very handy for moving DOM snippets around inside of
the DOM. It's especially useful when you want to not only copy and move the DOM
elements but also the events attached to the cloned DOM elements. Closely examine
the HTML and jQuery here:

```
<!DOCTYPE html PUBLIC "-//W3C//DTD XHTML 1.0 Transitional//EN"
"http://www.w3.org/TR/xhtml1/DTD/xhtml1-transitional.dtd">
<html>
<head>
<meta http-equiv="Content-Type" content="text/html; charset=UTF-8" />
</head>
<body>
<ul id="a">
<li>list</li>
<li>list</li>
<li>list</li>
<li>list</li>
</ul>
<ul id="b"></ul>
<script type="text/JavaScript"
src="http://ajax.googleapis.com/ajax/libs/jquery/1.3.2/jquery.min.js"></script>
<script type="text/JavaScript">
 jQuery('ul#a li')
    .click(function(){alert('List Item Clicked')})
    .parent()
        .clone(true)
            .find('li')
            .appendTo('#b')
        .end()
```

```
        .end()
        .remove();
</script>
</body>
</html>
```

If you were to run this code in a browser, it would clone the `<li>` elements on the page that have a click event attached to them, insert these newly cloned elements (including events) into the empty `<ul>`, and then remove the `<ul>` element that we cloned.

This might stretch a new jQuery developer's mind, so let's examine this jQuery statement by stepping through this code in order to explain the chained methods:

1. `jQuery('ul#a li')` = Select `<ul>` element with an `id` attribute of `a` and then select all the `<li>` elements inside of the `<ul>`.
2. `.click(function(){alert('List Item Clicked')})` = Add a click event to each `<li>`.
3. `.parent()` = Traverse the DOM, by changing my selected set to the `<ul>` element.
4. `.clone(true)` = Clone the `<ul>` element and all its children, including any events attached to the elements that are being cloned. This is done by passing the `clone()` method a Boolean value of `true`.
5. `.find('li')` = Now, within the cloned elements, change the set of elements to only the `<li>` elements contained within the cloned `<ul>` element.
6. `.appendTo('#b')` = Take these selected cloned `<li>` elements and place them inside of the `<ul>` element that has an `id` attribute value of `b`.
7. `.end()` = Return to the previous selected set of elements, which was the cloned `<ul>` element.
8. `.end()` = Return to the previous selected set of elements, which was the original `<ul>` element we cloned.
9. `.remove()` = Remove the original `<ul>` element.

If it's not obvious, understanding how to manipulate the selected set of elements or revert to the previous selected set is crucial for complex jQuery statements.

1.14 Getting, Setting, and Removing DOM Element Attributes

Problem

You have selected a DOM element using the jQuery function and need to get or set the value of the DOM element's attribute.

Solution

jQuery provides the `attr()` method for getting and setting attribute values. In the following code, we are going to be setting and then getting the value of an `<a>` element's `href` attribute:

```
<!DOCTYPE html PUBLIC "-//W3C//DTD XHTML 1.0 Transitional//EN"
"http://www.w3.org/TR/xhtml1/DTD/xhtml1-transitional.dtd">
<html>
<head>
<meta http-equiv="Content-Type" content="text/html; charset=UTF-8" />
</head>
<body>
<a>jquery.com</a>
<script type="text/JavaScript"
src="http://ajax.googleapis.com/ajax/libs/jquery/1.3.2/jquery.min.js">
</script>
<script type="text/JavaScript">
// alerts the jQuery home page URL
alert(
    jQuery('a').attr('href','http://www.jquery.com').attr('href')
);
</script>
</body>
</html>
```

As you can see in the code example, we are selecting the only <a> element in the HTML document, setting its href attribute, and then getting its value with the same attr() method by passing the method the attribute name alone. Had there been multiple <a> elements in the document, the attr() method would access the first matched element. The code when loaded into a browser will alert() the value that we set for the href attribute.

Now, since most elements have more than one attribute available, it's also possible to set multiple attribute values using a single attr() method. For example, we could also set the title attribute in the previous example by passing the attr() method an object instead of two string parameters:

```
jQuery('a').attr({'href':'http://www.jquery.com','title':'jquery.com'}).attr('href')
```

With the ability to add attributes to elements also comes the ability to remove attributes and their values. The removeAttr() method can be used to remove attributes from HTML elements. To use this method, simply pass it a string value of the attribute you'd like to remove (e.g., jQuery('a')removeAttr('title')).

Discussion

In addition to the attr() method, jQuery provides a very specific set of methods for working with the HTML element class attribute. Since the class attribute can contain several values (e.g., class="class1 class2 class3"), these unique attribute methods are used to manage these values.

These jQuery methods are as follows:

addClass()
Updates the class attribute value with a new class/value including any classes that were already set

hasClass()
> Checks the value of the **class** attribute for a specific class

removeClass()
> Removes a unique class from the **class** attribute while keeping any values already set

toggleClass()
> Adds the specified class if it is not present; removes the specified class if it is present

1.15 Getting and Setting HTML Content

Problem

You need to get or set a chunk of HTML content in the current web page.

Solution

jQuery provides the html() method for getting and setting chunks (or DOM structures) of HTML elements. In the following code, we use this method to set and then get the HTML value of the <p> element found in the HTML document:

```
<!DOCTYPE html PUBLIC "-//W3C//DTD XHTML 1.0 Transitional//EN"
"http://www.w3.org/TR/xhtml1/DTD/xhtml1-transitional.dtd">
<html>
<head>
<meta http-equiv="Content-Type" content="text/html; charset=UTF-8" />
</head>
<body>
<p></p>
<script type="text/JavaScript"
src="http://ajax.googleapis.com/ajax/libs/jquery/1.3.2/jquery.min.js">
</script>
<script type="text/JavaScript">
jQuery('p').html('<strong>Hello World</strong>, I am a <em>&lt;p&gt;</em> element.');
alert(jQuery('p').html());
</script>
</body>
</html>
```

Running this code in a browser will result in a browser alerting the HTML content contained within the <p> element, which we set using the html() method and then retrieved using the html() method.

Discussion

This method uses the DOM **innerHTML** property to get and set chunks of HTML. You should also be aware that html() is not available on XML documents (although it will work for XHTML documents).

1.16 Getting and Setting Text Content

Problem

You need to get or set the text that is contained inside of an HTML element(s).

Solution

jQuery provides the text() method for getting and setting the text content of elements. In the following code, we use this method to set and then get the text value of the <p> element found in the HTML document:

```
<!DOCTYPE html PUBLIC "-//W3C//DTD XHTML 1.0 Transitional//EN"
"http://www.w3.org/TR/xhtml1/DTD/xhtml1-transitional.dtd">
<html>
<head>
<meta http-equiv="Content-Type" content="text/html; charset=UTF-8" />
</head>
<body>
<p></p>
<script type="text/JavaScript"
src="http://ajax.googleapis.com/ajax/libs/jquery/1.3.2/jquery.min.js">
</script>
<script type="text/JavaScript">
    jQuery('p').text('Hello World, I am a <p> element.');
    alert(jQuery('p').text());
</script>
</body>
</html>
```

Running this code in a browser will result in a browser alerting the content of the <p> element, which we set using the text() method and then retrieved using the text() method.

Discussion

It's important to remember that the text() method is not unlike html() except that the text() method will escape HTML (replace < and > with their HTML entities). This means that if you place tags inside of the text string passed to the text() method, it will convert these tags to their HTML entities (< and >).

1.17 Using the $ Alias Without Creating Global Conflicts

Problem

You want to use the shortcut $ alias instead of typing the global namespace name (jQuery) without fear of global conflicts.

Solution

The solution here is to create an anonymous self-invoking function that we pass the jQuery object to and then use the $ character as a parameter pointer to the jQuery object.

For example, all jQuery code could be encapsulated inside the following self-invoking function:

```
(function($){ //function to create private scope with $ parameter
    //private scope and using $ without worry of conflict
})(jQuery); //invoke nameless function and pass it the jQuery object
```

Discussion

Essentially, what is going on here is that we have passed the global reference to jQuery to a function that creates a private scope. Had we not done this and chosen to use the shorthand $ alias in the global scope, we would be taking a risk by assuming that no other scripts included in the HTML document (or scripts included in the future) use the $ character. Why risk it when you can just create your own private scope?

Another advantage to doing this is that code included inside of the anonymous self-invoking function will run in its own private scope. You can rest assured that anything that is placed inside the function will likely never cause a conflict with other JavaScript code written in the global scope. So, again, why risk programmatic collisions? Just create your own private scope.

Selecting Elements with jQuery

James Padolsey

2.0 Introduction

At the very core of jQuery is its selector engine, allowing you to select elements within any document based on names, attributes, states, and more. Because of CSS's popularity, it made sense to adopt its selector syntax to make it simple to select elements in jQuery. As well as supporting most of the selectors specified in the CSS 1–3 specifications, jQuery adds quite a few *custom selectors* that can be used to select elements based on special states and characteristics. Additionally, you can create your own custom selectors! This chapter discusses some of the more common problems encountered while selecting elements with jQuery.

Before the first recipe, let's discuss a few basic principles.

The easiest way to target a specific element or a set of elements within a document is by using a CSS selector within the jQuery wrapper function, like so:

```
jQuery('#content p a');
    // Select all anchor elements within all paragraph elements within #content
```

Now that we've selected the elements we're after, we can run any of jQuery's methods on that collection. For example, adding a class of `selected` to all links is as simple as:

```
jQuery('#content p a').addClass('selected');
```

jQuery offers many DOM traversal methods to aid in the element selection process, such as `next()`, `prev()`, and `parent()`. These and other methods accept a selector expression as their only parameter, which filters the returned results accordingly. So, you can use CSS selectors in a number of places, not just within `jQuery(...)`.

When constructing selectors, there's one general rule for optimization: be only as specific as you need to be. It's important to remember that the more complicated a selector is, the more time it will take jQuery to process the string. jQuery uses native DOM methods to retrieve the elements you're after. The fact that you can use selectors is only a product of a nicely polished abstraction; there's nothing wrong with this, but it is very important to understand the ramifications of what you're writing. Here is a typical example of an unnecessarily complicated selector:

```
jQuery('body div#wrapper div#content');
```

A higher degree of specificity does not necessarily mean it's faster. The previous selector can be rewritten to this:

```
jQuery('#content');
```

This has the same effect but manages to shave off the overhead of the previous version. Also note that sometimes you can further optimize by specifying a context for your selectors; this will be discussed later in the chapter (see Recipe 2.11).

2.1 Selecting Child Elements Only

Problem

You need to select one or more direct children of a particular element.

Solution

Use the *direct descendant* combinator (>). This combinator expects two selector expressions, one on either side. For example, if you want to select all anchor elements that reside directly beneath list items, you could use this selector: li > a. This would select all anchors that are children of a list item; in other words, all anchors that exist directly beneath list items. Here's an example:

```
<a href="/category">Category</a>
<ul id="nav">
    <li><a href="#anchor1">Anchor 1</a></li>
    <li><a href="#anchor2">Anchor 2</a></li>
    <li><span><a href="#anchor3">Anchor 3</a></span></li>
</ul>
```

Now, to select only the anchors within each list item, you would call jQuery like so:

```
jQuery('#nav li > a');
// This selects two elements, as expected
```

The third anchor within the #nav list is not selected because it's not a child of a list item; it's a child of a <span> element.

Discussion

It's important to distinguish between a child and a descendant. A *descendant* is any element existing within another element, whereas a *child* is a direct descendant; the analogy of children and parents helps massively since the DOM's hierarchy is largely similar to that.

It's worth noting that combinators like > can be used without an expression on the left side if a context is already specified:

```
jQuery('> p', '#content');
    // Fundamentally the same as jQuery('#content > p')
```

Selecting children in a more programmatic environment should be done using jQuery's `children()` method, to which you can pass a selector to filter the returned elements. This would select all direct children of the #content element:

```
jQuery('#content').children();
```

The preceding code is essentially the same as `jQuery('#content > *')` with one important difference; it's faster. Instead of parsing your selector, jQuery knows what you want immediately. The fact that it's faster is not a useful differential, though. Plus, in some situations, the speed difference is marginal verging on irrelevant, depending on the browser and what you're trying to select. Using the `children()` method is especially useful when you're dealing with jQuery objects stored under variables. For example:

```
var anchors = jQuery('a');

// Getting all direct children of all anchor elements
// can be achieved in three ways:

// #1
anchors.children();

// #2
jQuery('> *', anchors);

// #3
anchors.find('> *');
```

In fact, there are even more ways of achieving it! In this situation, the first method is the fastest. As stated earlier, you can pass a selector expression to the `children()` method to filter the results:

```
jQuery('#content').children('p');
```

Only paragraph elements that are direct children of #content will be returned.

2.2 Selecting Specific Siblings

Problem

You need to select only a specific set of siblings of a particular element.

Solution

If you're looking to select the adjacent sibling of a particular element, then you can use the *adjacent sibling* combinator (+). Similar to the child (>) combinator, the sibling combinator expects a selector expression on each side. The righthand expression is the subject of the selector, and the lefthand expression is the sibling you want to match. Here's some example HTML markup:

```
<div id="content">
    <h1>Main title</h1>
    <h2>Section title</h2>
    <p>Some content...</p>
    <h2>Section title</h2>
    <p>More content...</p>
</div>
```

If you want to select only <h2> elements that immediately follow <h1> elements, you can use the following selector:

```
jQuery('h1 + h2');
// Selects ALL H2 elements that are adjacent siblings of H1 elements
```

In this example, only one <h2> element will be selected (the first one). The second one is not selected because, while it is a sibling, it is not an *adjacent* sibling of the <h1> element.

If, on the other hand, you want to select and filter all siblings of an element, adjacent or not, then you can use jQuery's `siblings()` method to target them, and you can pass an optional selector expression to filter the selection:

```
jQuery('h1').siblings('h2,h3,p');
// Selects all H2, H3, and P elements that are siblings of H1 elements.
```

Sometimes you'll want to target siblings dependent on their position relative to other elements; for example, here's some typical HTML markup:

```
<ul>
    <li>First item</li>
    <li class="selected">Second item</li>
    <li>Third item</li>
    <li>Fourth item</li>
    <li>Fifth item</li>
</ul>
```

To select all list items beyond the second (after `li.selected`), you could use the following method:

```
jQuery('li.selected').nextAll('li');
```

The `nextAll()` method, just like `siblings()`, accepts a selector expression to filter the selection before it's returned. If you don't pass a selector, then `nextAll()` will return all siblings of the subject element that exist after the subject element, although not before it.

With the preceding example, you could also use another CSS combinator to select all list items beyond the second. The *general sibling* combinator (~) was added in CSS3, so you probably haven't been able to use it in your actual style sheets yet, but fortunately you can use it in jQuery without worrying about support, or lack thereof. It works in exactly the same fashion as the adjacent sibling combinator (+) except that it selects *all* siblings that follow, not just the adjacent one. Using the previously specified markup, you would select all list items after `li.selected` with the following selector:

```
jQuery('li.selected ~ li');
```

Discussion

The adjacent sibling combinator can be conceptually tricky to use because it doesn't follow the top-down hierarchical approach of most other selector expressions. Still, it's worth knowing about and is certainly a useful way of selecting what you want with minimal hassle.

The same functionality might be achieved without a selector, in the following way:

```
jQuery('h1').next('h2');
```

The `next()` method can make a nice alternative to the selector syntax, especially in a programmatic setting when you're dealing with jQuery objects as variables, for example:

```
var topHeaders = jQuery('h1');
topHeaders.next('h2').css('margin','0');
```

2.3 Selecting Elements by Index Order

Problem

You need to select elements based on their order among other elements.

Solution

Depending on what you want to do, you have the following filters at your disposal. These may look like CSS pseudoclasses, but in jQuery they're called *filters*:

`:first`
    Matches the first selected element

`:last`
    Matches the last selected element

`:even`
    Matches even elements (zero-indexed)

`:odd`
    Matches odd elements (zero-indexed)

`:eq(n)`
    Matches a single element by its index (*n*)

`:lt(n)`
    Matches all elements with an index below *n*

:gt(*n*)

    Matches all elements with an index above *n*

Assuming the following HTML markup:

```
<ol>
    <li>First item</li>
    <li>Second item</li>
    <li>Third item</li>
    <li>Fourth item</li>
</ol>
```

the first item in the list could be selected in a number of different ways:

```
jQuery('ol li:first');
jQuery('ol li:eq(0)');
jQuery('ol li:lt(1)');
```

Notice that both the `eq()` and `lt()` filters accept a number; since it's zero-indexed, the first item is 0, the second is 1, etc.

A common requirement is to have alternating styles on table rows; this can be achieved with the `:even` and `:odd` filters:

```
<table>
    <tr><td>0</td><td>even</td></tr>
    <tr><td>1</td><td>odd</td></tr>
    <tr><td>2</td><td>even</td></tr>
    <tr><td>3</td><td>odd</td></tr>
    <tr><td>4</td><td>even</td></tr>
</table>
```

You can apply a different class dependent on the index of each table row:

```
jQuery('tr:even').addClass('even');
```

You'd have to specify the corresponding class (**even**) in your CSS style sheet:

```
table tr.even {
    background: #CCC;
}
```

This code would produce the effect shown in Figure 2-1.

0	even
1	odd
2	even
3	odd
4	even

Figure 2-1. Table with even rows darkened

Discussion

As mentioned, an element's index is zero-based, so if an element is the first one, then its index is zero. Apart from that fact, using the preceding filters is very simple. Another thing to note is that these filters require a collection to match against; the index can be determined only if an initial collection is specified. So, this selector wouldn't work:

```
jQuery(':even');
```

 Actually, this selector does work, but only because jQuery does some corrective postprocessing of your selector behind the scenes. If no initial collection is specified, then jQuery will assume you meant all elements within the document. So, the selector would actually work, since it's effectively identical to this: `jQuery('*:even')`.

An initial collection is required on the lefthand side of the filter, i.e., something to apply the filter to. The collection can be within an already instantiated jQuery object, as shown here:

```
jQuery('ul li').filter(':first');
```

The filter method is being run on an already instantiated jQuery object (containing the list items).

2.4 Selecting Elements That Are Currently Animating

Problem

You need to select elements based on whether they're animating.

Solution

jQuery offers a convenient filter for this very purpose. The `:animated` filter will match only elements that are currently animating:

```
jQuery('div:animated');
```

This selector would select all `<div>` elements currently animating. Effectively, jQuery is selecting all elements that have a nonempty animation queue.

Discussion

This filter is especially useful when you need to apply a blanket function to all elements that are not currently animated. For example, to begin animating all `<div>` elements that are not already animating, it's as simple as this:

```
jQuery('div:not(div:animated)').animate({height:100});
```

Sometimes you might want to check whether an element is animating. This can be done with jQuery's useful `is()` method:

```
var myElem = jQuery('#elem');
if( myElem.is(':animated') ) {
    // Do something.
}
```

2.5 Selecting Elements Based on What They Contain

Problem

You need to select an element based on what it contains.

Solution

There are normally only two things you would want to query in this respect: the text contents and the element contents (other elements). For the former, you can use the `:contains()` filter:

```
<!-- HTML -->
<span>Hello Bob!</span>

// Select all SPANs with 'Bob' in:
jQuery('span:contains("Bob")');
```

Note that it's case sensitive, so this selector wouldn't match anything if we searched for *bob* (with a lowercase *b*). Also, quotes are not required in all situations, but it's a good practice just in case you encounter a situation where they are required (e.g., when you want to use parentheses).

To test for nested elements, you can use the `:has()` filter. You can pass any valid selector to this filter:

```
jQuery('div:has(p a)');
```

This selector would match all `<div>` elements that encapsulate `<a>` elements (anchors) within `<p>` elements (paragraphs).

Discussion

The `:contains()` filter might not fit your requirements. You may need more control over what text to allow and what to disallow. If you need that control, I suggest using a regular expression and testing against the text of the element, like so:

```
jQuery('p').filter(function(){
    return /(^|\s)(apple|orange|lemon)(\s|$)/.test(jQuery(this).text());
});
```

This would select all paragraphs containing the word *apple*, *orange*, or *lemon*. To read more about jQuery's `filter()` method, have a look at Recipe 2.10.

2.6 Selecting Elements by What They Don't Match

Problem

You need to select a number of elements that don't match a specific selector.

Solution

For this, jQuery gives us the :not filter, which you can use in the following way:

```
jQuery('div:not(#content)'); // Select all DIV elements except #content
```

This filter will remove any elements from the current collection that are matched by the passed selector. The selector can be as complex as you like; it doesn't have to be a simple expression, e.g.:

```
jQuery('a:not(div.important a, a.nav)');
// Selects anchors that do not reside within 'div.important' or have the class 'nav'
```

 Passing complex selectors to the :not filter is possible only in jQuery version 1.3 and beyond. In versions previous to that, only simple selector expressions were acceptable.

Discussion

In addition to the mentioned :not filter, jQuery also supplies a method with very similar functionality. This method accepts both selectors and DOM collections/nodes. Here's an example:

```
var $anchors = jQuery('a');
$anchors.click(function(){
    $anchors.not(this).addClass('not-clicked');
});
```

According to this code, when an anchor is clicked, all anchors apart from that one will have the class not-clicked added. The this keyword refers to the clicked element.

The not() method also accepts selectors:

```
$('#nav a').not('a.active');
```

This code selects all anchors residing within #nav that do not have a class of active.

2.7 Selecting Elements Based on Their Visibility

Problem

You need to select an element based on whether it's visible.

Solution

You can use either the `:hidden` or `:visible` filter as necessary:

```
jQuery('div:hidden');
```

Here are some other examples of usage:

```
if (jQuery('#elem').is(':hidden')) {
    // Do something conditionally
}
jQuery('p:visible').hide(); // Hiding only elements that are currently visible
```

Discussion

 Since jQuery 1.3.2, these filters have dramatically changed. Before 1.3.2 both filters would respond like you would expect for the CSS `visibility` property, but that is no longer taken into account. Instead, jQuery tests for the height and width of the element in question (relative to its `offsetParent`). If either of these dimensions is zero, then the element is considered hidden; otherwise, it's considered visible.

If you need more control, you can always use jQuery's `filter()` method, which allows you to test the element in any way you want. For example, you may want to select all elements that are set to `display:none` but not those that are set to `visibility:hidden`. Using the `:hidden` filter won't work because it matches elements with either of those characteristics (< v1.3.2) or doesn't take either property into consideration at all (>= v1.3.2):

```
jQuery('*').filter(function(){
    return jQuery(this).css('display') === 'none'
            && jQuery(this).css('visibility') !== 'hidden';
});
```

The preceding code should leave you with a collection of elements that are set to `display:none` but not `visibility:hidden`. Note that, usually, such a selection won't be necessary—the `:hidden` filter is perfectly suitable in most situations.

2.8 Selecting Elements Based on Attributes

Problem

You need to select elements based on attributes and those attributes' values.

Solution

Use an attribute selector to match specific attributes and corresponding values:

```
jQuery('a[href="http://google.com"]');
```

The preceding selector would select all anchor elements with an `href` attribute equal to the value specified (`http://google.com`).

There are a number of ways you can make use of the attribute selector:

[attr]
> Matches elements that have the specified attribute

[attr=val]
> Matches elements that have the specified attribute with a certain value

[attr!=val]
> Matches elements that don't have the specified attribute or value

[attr^=val]
> Matches elements with the specified attribute and that start with a certain value

[attr$=val]
> Matches elements that have the specified attribute and that end with a certain value

[attr~=val]
> Matches elements that contain the specified value with spaces, on either side (i.e., `car` matches `car` but not `cart`)

 Prior to jQuery 1.2 you had to use XPath syntax (i.e., putting an @ sign before an attribute name). This is now deprecated.

You can also combine multiple attribute selectors:

```
// Select all elements with a TITLE and HREF:
jQuery('*[title][href]');
```

Discussion

As always, for special requirements it may be more suitable to use the `filter()` method to more specifically outline what you're looking for:

```
jQuery('a').filter(function(){
    return (new RegExp('http:\/\/(?!' + location.hostname + ')')).test(this.href);
});
```

In this filter, a regular expression is being used to test the `href` attribute of each anchor. It selects all external links within any page.

The attribute selector is especially useful for selecting elements based on slightly varying attributes. For example, if we had the following HTML:

```
<div id="content-sec-1">...</div>
<div id="content-sec-2">...</div>
<div id="content-sec-3">...</div>
<div id="content-sec-4">...</div>
```

we could use the following selector to match all of the `<div>` elements:

```
jQuery('div[id^="content-sec-"]');
```

2.9 Selecting Form Elements by Type

Problem

You need to select form elements based on their types (`hidden`, `text`, `checkbox`, etc.).

Solution

jQuery gives us a bunch of useful filters for this very purpose, as shown in Table 2-1.

Table 2-1. jQuery form filters

jQuery selector syntax	Selects what?
:text	`<input type="text" />`
:password	`<input type="password" />`
:radio	`<input type="radio" />`
:checkbox	`<input type="checkbox" />`
:submit	`<input type="submit" />`
:image	`<input type="image" />`
:reset	`<input type="reset" />`
:button	`<input type="button" />`
:file	`<input type="file" />`
:hidden	`<input type="hidden" />`

So, as an example, if you needed to select all text inputs, you would simply do this:

```
jQuery(':text');
```

There is also an `:input` filter that selects all `input`, `textarea`, `button`, and `select` elements.

Discussion

Note that the `:hidden` filter, as discussed earlier, does not test for the type `hidden`; it works by checking the computed height of the element. This works with input elements of the type `hidden` because they, like other hidden elements, have an `offsetHeight` of zero.

As with all selectors, you can mix and match as desired:

```
jQuery(':input:not(:hidden)');
    // Selects all input elements except those that are hidden.
```

These filters can also be used with regular CSS syntax. For example, selecting all text input elements plus all `<textarea>` elements can be done in the following way:

```
jQuery(':text, textarea');
```

2.10 Selecting an Element with Specific Characteristics

Problem

You need to select an element based not only on its relationship to other elements or simple attribute values but also on varying characteristics such as programmatic states not expressible as selector expressions.

Solution

If you're looking for an element with very specific characteristics, selector expressions may not be the best tool. Using jQuery's DOM filtering method (`filter()`), you can select elements based on anything expressible within a function.

The filter method in jQuery allows you to pass either a string (i.e., a selector expression) or a function. If you pass a function, then its return value will define whether certain elements are selected. The function you pass is run against every element in the current selection; every time the function returns false, the corresponding element is removed from the collection, and every time you return true, the corresponding element is not affected (i.e., it remains in the collection):

```
jQuery('*').filter(function(){
    return !!jQuery(this).css('backgroundImage');
});
```

The preceding code selects all elements with a background image.

The initial collection is of all elements (*); then the `filter()` method is called with a function. This function will return true when a `backgroundImage` is specified for the element in question. The `!!` that you see is a quick way of converting any type in JavaScript to its Boolean expression. Things that evaluate to false include an empty string, the number zero, the value `undefined`, the null type, and, of course, the false Boolean itself. If any of these things are returned from querying the `backgroundImage`, the function will return false, thus removing any elements without background images from the collection. Most of what I just said is not unique to jQuery; it's just JavaScript fundamentals.

In fact, the `!!` is not necessary because jQuery evaluates the return value into a Boolean itself, but keeping it there is still a good idea; anyone looking at your code can be absolutely sure of what you intended (it aids readability).

Within the function you pass to `filter()`, you can refer to the current element via the `this` keyword. To make it into a jQuery object (so you can access and perform jQuery methods), simply wrap it in the jQuery function:

```
this; // Regular element object
jQuery(this); // jQuery object
```

Here are some other filtering examples to spark your imagination:

```
// Select all DIV elements with a width between 100px and 200px:
jQuery('div').filter(function(){
    var width = jQuery(this).width();
    return width > 100 && width < 200;
});

// Select all images with a common image extension:
jQuery('img').filter(function(){
    return /\.(jpe?g|png|bmp|gif)(\?.+)?$/.test(this.src);
});

// Select all elements that have either 10 or 20 children:
jQuery('*').filter(function(){
    var children = jQuery(this).children().length;
    return children === 10 || children === 20;
});
```

Discussion

There will always be several different ways to do something; this is no less true when selecting elements with jQuery. The key differential is usually going to be speed; some ways are fast, others are slow. When you use a complicated selector, you should be thinking about how much processing jQuery has to do in the background. A longer and more complex selector will take longer to return results. jQuery's native methods can sometimes be much faster than using a single selector, plus there's the added benefit of readability. Compare these two techniques:

```
jQuery('div a:not([href^=http://]), p a:not([href^=http://])');
```

```
jQuery('div, p').find('a').not('[href^=http://]');
```

The second technique is shorter and much more readable than the first. Testing in Firefox (v3) and Safari (v4) reveals that it's also faster than the first technique.

2.11 Using the Context Parameter

Problem

You've heard of the context parameter but have yet to encounter a situation where it's useful.

Solution

As well as passing a selector expression to `jQuery()` or `$()`, you can pass a second argument that specifies the context. The context is where jQuery will search for the elements matched by your selector expression.

The context parameter is probably one of the most underused of jQuery's features. The way to use it is incredibly simple: pass a selector expression, a jQuery object, a DOM collection, or a DOM node to the context argument, and jQuery will search only for elements within that context.

Here's an example: you want to select all input fields within a form before it's submitted:

```
jQuery('form').bind('submit', function(){
    var allInputs = jQuery('input', this);
    // Now you would do something with 'allInputs'
});
```

Notice that `this` was passed as the second argument; within the handler just shown, `this` refers to the form element. Since it's set as the context, jQuery will only return `input` elements within that form. If we didn't include that second argument, then all of the document's `input` elements would be selected—not what we want.

As mentioned, you can also pass a regular selector as the context:

```
jQuery('p', '#content');
```

The preceding code returns exactly the same collection as the following selector:

```
jQuery('#content p');
```

Specifying a context can aid in readability and speed. It's a useful feature to know about!

Discussion

The default context used by jQuery is `document`, i.e., the topmost item in the DOM hierarchy. Only specify a context if it's different from this default. Using a context can be expressed in the following way:

```
jQuery( context ).find( selector );
```

In fact, this is exactly what jQuery does behind the scenes.

Considering this, if you already have a reference to the context, then you should pass that instead of a selector—there's no point in making jQuery go through the selection process again.

2.12 Creating a Custom Filter Selector

Problem

You need a reusable filter to target specific elements based on their characteristics. You want something that is succinct and can be included within your selector expressions.

Solution

You can extend jQuery's selector expressions under the `jQuery.expr[':']` object; this is an alias for `Sizzle.selectors.filters`. Each new filter expression is defined as a property of this object, like so:

```
jQuery.expr[':'].newFilter = function(elem, index, match){
    return true; // Return true/false like you would on the filter() method
};
```

The function will be run on all elements in the current collection and needs to return true (to keep the element in the collection) or false (to remove the element from the collection). Three bits of information are passed to this function: the element in question, the index of this element among the entire collection, and a match array returned from a regular expression match that contains important information for the more complex expressions.

For example, you might want to target all elements that have a certain property. This filter matches all elements that are displayed inline:

```
jQuery.expr[':'].inline = function(elem) {
    return jQuery(elem).css('display') === 'inline';
};
```

Now that we have created a custom selector, we can use it in any selector expression:

```
// E.g. #1
jQuery('div a:inline').css('color', 'red');
// E.g. #2
jQuery('span').filter(':not(:inline)').css('color', 'blue')
```

jQuery's custom selectors (`:radio`, `:hidden`, etc.) are created in this way.

Discussion

As mentioned, the third parameter passed to your filter function is an array returned from a regular expression match that jQuery performs on the selector string. This match is especially useful if you want to create a filter expression that accepts *parameters*. Let's say that we want to create a selector that queries for data held by jQuery:

```
jQuery('span').data('something', 123);

// We want to be able to do this:
jQuery('*:data(something,123)');
```

The purpose of the selector would be to select all elements that have had data attached to them via jQuery's `data()` method—it specifically targets elements with a datakey of `something`, equal to the number 123.

The proposed filter (`:data`) could be created as follows:

```
jQuery.expr[':'].data = function(elem, index, m) {

    // Remove ":data(" and the trailing ")" from
    // the match, as these parts aren't needed:
    m[0] = m[0].replace(/:data\(|\)$/g, '');

    var regex = new RegExp('([\'"]?)((?:\\\\\\1|.)+?)\\1(,|$)', 'g'),
        // Retrieve data key:
        key = regex.exec( m[0] )[2],
        // Retrieve data value to test against:
        val = regex.exec( m[0] );

    if (val) {
        val = val[2];
    }

    // If a value was passed then we test for it, otherwise
    // we test that the value evaluates to true:
    return val ? jQuery(elem).data(key) == val : !!jQuery(elem).data(key);

};
```

The reason for such a complex regular expression is that we want to make it as flexible as possible. The new selector can be used in a number of different ways:

```
// As we originally mused (above):
jQuery('div:data("something",123)');

// Check if 'something' is a "truthy" value
jQuery('div:data(something)');

// With or without (inner) quotes:
jQuery('div:data(something, "something else")');
```

Now we have a totally new way of querying data held by jQuery on an element.

If you ever want to add more than one new selector at the same time, it's best to use jQuery's `extend()` method:

```
jQuery.extend(jQuery.expr[':'], {
    newFilter1 : function(elem, index, match){
        // Return true or false.
    },
    newFilter2 : function(elem, index, match){
        // Return true or false.
    },
    newFilter3 : function(elem, index, match){
        // Return true or false.
    }
});
```

Beyond the Basics

Ralph Whitbeck

3.0 Introduction

jQuery is a very lightweight library that is capable of helping you do the simple selections of DOM elements on your page. You saw these simple uses in Chapter 1. In this chapter, we'll explore how jQuery can be used to manipulate, traverse, and extend jQuery to infinite possibilities. As lightweight as jQuery is, it was built to be robust and expandable.

3.1 Looping Through a Set of Selected Results

Problem

You need to create a list from your selected set of DOM elements, but performing any action on the selected set is done on the set as a whole. To be able to create a list with each individual element, you'll need to perform a separate action on each element of the selected set.

Solution

Let's say you wanted to make a list of every link within a certain DOM element (perhaps it's a site with a lot of user-provided content, and you wanted to quickly glance at the submitted links being provided by users). We would first create our jQuery selection, `$("div#post a[href]")`, which will select all links with an `href` attribute within the `<div>` with the `id` of `post`. Then we want to loop through each matched element and append it to an array. See the following code example:

```
var urls = [];
 $("div#post a[href]").each(function(i) {
    urls[i] = $(this).attr('href');
});
```

```
    alert(urls.join(","));
```

We were able to make an array because we iterated through each element in the jQuery object by using the `$().each();` method. We are able to access the individual elements and execute jQuery methods against those elements because we wrapped the `this` variable in a jQuery wrapper, `$()`, thus making it a jQuery object.

Discussion

jQuery provides a core method that you can use to loop through your set of selected DOM elements. `$().each()` is jQuery's `for` loop, which will loop through and provide a separate function scope for each element in the set. `$().each();` will iterate exclusively through jQuery objects.

 `$().each();` is not the same as the jQuery utility method `jQuery.each(object, callback);`. The `jQuery.each` method is a more generalized iterator method that will iterate through both objects and arrays. See jQuery's online documentation for more information on `jQuery.each()` at *http://docs.jquery.com/Utilities/jQuery.each*.

In each iteration, we are getting the `href` attribute of the current element from the main selection. We are able to get the current DOM element by using the `this` keyword. We then wrap it in the jQuery object, `$(this)`, so that we can perform jQuery methods/actions against it—in our case, pulling the `href` attribute from the DOM element. The last action is to assign the `href` attribute to a global array, `urls`.

Just so we can see what we have, the array URL is joined together with a `,` and displayed to the user in an alert box. We could also have added the list to an unordered list DOM element for display to the user. More practically, we might want to format the list of URLs into JSON format and send it to the server for processing into a database.

Let's look at another example using `$().each();`. This example is probably the most obvious use of `$().each();`. Let's say we have an unordered list of names, and we want each name to stand out. One way to accomplish this is to set an alternate background color for every other list item:

```
<!DOCTYPE html
    PUBLIC "-//W3C//DTD XHTML 1.0 Transitional//EN"
    "http://www.w3.org/TR/xhtml1/DTD/xhtml1-transitional.dtd">
<html xmlns="http://www.w3.org/1999/xhtml">
<head>
    <meta http-equiv="Content-Type" content="text/html;charset=UTF-8" />
    <title>Chapter 3 - Recipe 1 - Looping through a set of selected results</title>
    <style type="text/css">
        .even { background-color: #ffffff; }
        .odd  { background-color: #cccccc; }
    </style>
    <script src="http://ajax.googleapis.com/ajax/libs/jquery/1.3.2/jquery.min.js"
type="text/javascript"></script>
```

```
<script type="text/javascript">
    (function($){
        $(document).ready(function() {
            $("ul > li").each(function(i) {
                if (i % 2 == 1)
                {
                    $(this).addClass("odd");
                }
                else
                {
                    $(this).addClass("even");
                }
            });
        });
    })(jQuery);
</script>
</head>
<body>
    <h2>Family Members</h2>
    <ul>
        <li>Ralph</li>
        <li>Hope</li>
        <li>Brandon</li>
        <li>Jordan</li>
        <li>Ralphie</li>
    </ul>
</body>
</html>
```

Figure 3-1 shows the code output.

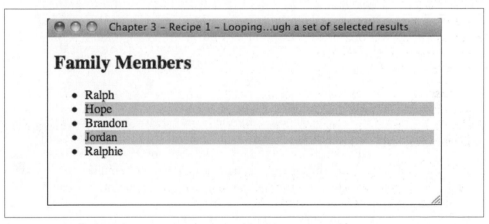

Figure 3-1. Code output

As we iterate through each <li> element, we are testing whether the current index, which is passed in as a single argument to the function when executed, modded by 2 is equal to 1. Based on that condition, we either set one CSS class (.odd) or another CSS class (.even).

Even though this may be the most obvious way to use $().each(), it isn't the most efficient way to handle making alternating background colors. We could have accomplished this with one line:

```
$("ul > li:odd").addClass("odd");
```

All we needed to do was set all the <li> elements to the class .even in the CSS so that we could override the odd <li> elements with the .odd class with jQuery.

The basic function of $.each(); is to take the matched set and iterate through each element via reference of the index, perform some action, and iterate to the next element in the matched set until there are no more elements left.

3.2 Reducing the Selection Set to a Specified Item

Problem

A jQuery selector is broad and selects all elements on the page based on your query. The need may rise when you need to select a single item, based on its position, but there isn't an easy way to select that item without editing the code.

Solution

After you make your selection with jQuery, you can chain the .eq() method and pass in the index of the selection you want to work with.

The selection index is zero-based, so the first item in the selection would be $().eq(0); where 0 represents the first item in the selection. $().eq(4); represents the fifth item.

Let's use the end of the season standings for the National Hockey League (NHL) conferences as an example of how we can show which teams made the playoffs and which didn't. What we need to do is list all the teams in each conference in the order they finished the season in. Since the top eight teams in each conference make it to the playoff round, we just need to figure out the eighth entry in each list and draw a line:

```
<!DOCTYPE html
    PUBLIC "-//W3C//DTD XHTML 1.0 Transitional//EN"
    "http://www.w3.org/TR/xhtml1/DTD/xhtml1-transitional.dtd">
<html xmlns="http://www.w3.org/1999/xhtml">
<head>
    <meta http-equiv="Content-Type" content="text/html;charset=UTF-8" />
    <title>Chapter 3 - Recipe 2 - Reducing the selection set to specified item</title>
    <script type="text/javascript"
src="http://ajax.googleapis.com/ajax/libs/jquery/1.3.2/jquery.min.js"></script>
```

```
<script type="text/javascript">
    (function($){
        $(document).ready(function(){
            $("ol#east > li").eq(7).css("border-bottom", "1px solid #000000");
            $("ol#west > li").eq(7).css("border-bottom", "1px solid #000000");
        });
    })(jQuery);
</script>
</head>
<body>
    <h2>Eastern Conference</h2>
    <ol id="east">
        <li>Boston Bruins</li>
        <li>Washington Capitals</li>
        <li>New Jersey Devils</li>
        <li>Pittsburgh Penguins</li>
        <li>Philadelphia Flyers</li>
        <li>Carolina Hurricanes</li>
        <li>New York Rangers</li>
        <li>Montreal Canadians</li>
        <li>Florida Panthers</li>
        <li>Buffalo Sabres</li>
        <li>Ottawa Senators</li>
        <li>Toronto Maple Leafs</li>
        <li>Atlanta Thrashers</li>
        <li>Tampa Bay Lightning</li>
        <li>New York Islanders</li>
    </ol>

    <h2>Western Conference</h2>
    <ol id="west">
        <li>San Jose Sharks</li>
        <li>Detroit Red Wings</li>
        <li>Vancouver Canucks</li>
        <li>Chicago Blackhawks</li>
        <li>Calgary Flames</li>
        <li>St. Louis Blues</li>
        <li>Columbus Blue Jackets</li>
        <li>Anaheim Ducks</li>
        <li>Minnesota Wild</li>
        <li>Nashville Predators</li>
        <li>Edmonton Oilers</li>
        <li>Dallas Stars</li>
        <li>Phoenix Coyotes</li>
        <li>Los Angeles Kings</li>
        <li>Colorado Avalanche</li>
    </ol>
</body>
</html>
```

Figure 3-2 shows the code output.

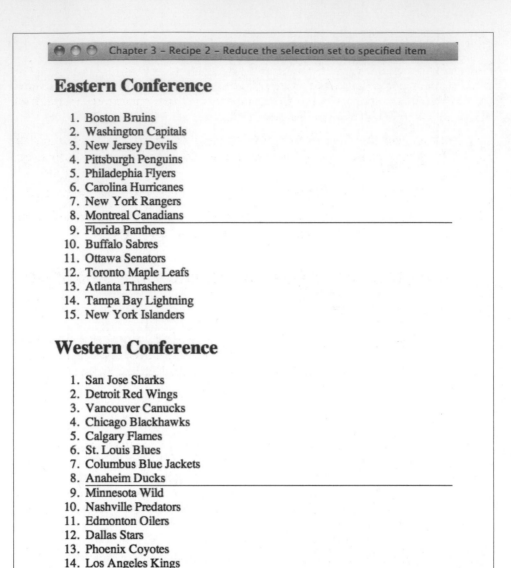

Eastern Conference

1. Boston Bruins
2. Washington Capitals
3. New Jersey Devils
4. Pittsburgh Penguins
5. Philadephia Flyers
6. Carolina Hurricanes
7. New York Rangers
8. Montreal Canadians
9. Florida Panthers
10. Buffalo Sabres
11. Ottawa Senators
12. Toronto Maple Leafs
13. Atlanta Thrashers
14. Tampa Bay Lightning
15. New York Islanders

Western Conference

1. San Jose Sharks
2. Detroit Red Wings
3. Vancouver Canucks
4. Chicago Blackhawks
5. Calgary Flames
6. St. Louis Blues
7. Columbus Blue Jackets
8. Anaheim Ducks
9. Minnesota Wild
10. Nashville Predators
11. Edmonton Oilers
12. Dallas Stars
13. Phoenix Coyotes
14. Los Angeles Kings
15. Colorado Avalanche

Figure 3-2. Code output

As you can see, we just use an ordered list to list the teams in the order they placed, then we use jQuery to add a bottom border to the eighth item in each list. We need to add an ID to each ordered list so that we can specify each list in a separate query. If we were to do `$("li").eq(7);`, it would select only from the first list because the query would have counted all the `<li>` elements on the page together.

Discussion

The `.eq()` method is used to take a selection set and reduce it to a single item from that set. The argument is the index that you want to reduce your selection to. The index starts at 0 and goes to length –1. If the argument is an invalid index, the method will return an empty set of elements instead of null.

The `.eq()` method is similar to using the `$(":eq()")`; right in your selection, but the `.eq()` method allows you to chain to the selection and fine-tune further. For example:

```
$("li").css("background-color","#CCCCCC").eq(0).css("background-color","#ff0000");
```

This will change the background color of all `<li>` elements and then select the first one and give it a different color to signify that it is perhaps a header item.

3.3 Convert a Selected jQuery Object into a Raw DOM Object

Problem

Selecting elements on a page with jQuery returns a set as a jQuery object and not as a raw DOM object. Because it's a jQuery object, you can only run jQuery methods against the selected set. To be able to run DOM methods and properties against the selected set, the set needs to be converted to a raw DOM object.

Solution

jQuery provides a core method `get()`, which will convert all matched jQuery objects back into an array of DOM objects. Additionally, you can pass an index value in as an argument of `get()`, which will return the element at the index of the matched set as a DOM object, `$.get(1);`. Now, even though you can get at a single element's DOM object via `$.get(index)`, it is there for historical reasons; the "best practices" way is to use the `[]` notation, `$("div")[1];`.

 We are discussing the core `.get()` method, which transforms a jQuery object to a DOM array. We are not discussing the Ajax get method, which will load a remote page using an HTTP GET request.

Because `get()` returns an array, you can traverse the array to get at each DOM element. Once it's a DOM element, you can then call traditional DOM properties and methods against it. Let's explore a simple example of pulling the `innerHTML` of an element:

```
<!DOCTYPE html
    PUBLIC "-//W3C//DTD XHTML 1.0 Transitional//EN"
    "http://www.w3.org/TR/xhtml1/DTD/xhtml1-transitional.dtd">
<html xmlns="http://www.w3.org/1999/xhtml">
<head>
```

```
    <meta http-equiv="Content-Type" content="text/html;charset=UTF-8" />
    <title>Chapter 3 - Recipe 3 - Converting a selected jQuery object into a
raw DOM object</title>
    <script type="text/javascript"
src="http://ajax.googleapis.com/ajax/libs/jquery/1.3.2/jquery.min.js"></script>
    <script type="text/javascript">
        (function($){
            $(document).ready(function(){
                var inner = $("div")[0].innerHTML;
                alert(inner);
            });
        })(jQuery);
    </script>
</head>
<body>
    <div>
        <p>
            jQuery, the write less, do more JavaScript library.  Saving the day
for web developers since 2006.
        </p>
    </div>
</body>
</html>
```

Figure 3-3 shows the output.

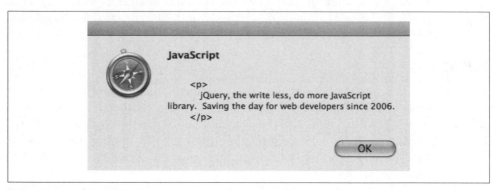

Figure 3-3. Code output

We start by selecting all the `<div>` elements on the page and calling `[0]`. We pass in the index of the selection we want to work with; since there is only one `<div>` on the page, we can pass in index `0`. Finally, we call a property, in this case `innerHTML`, to retrieve the raw DOM element.

Discussion

The core `get()` method can be very useful, as there are some non-JavaScript methods that we can utilize for our advantage. Let's say we have a list and we need to show that list in reverse order. Since `get()` returns an array, we can use native array methods to reverse sort the list and then redisplay the list:

```html
<!DOCTYPE html
    PUBLIC "-//W3C//DTD XHTML 1.0 Transitional//EN"
    "http://www.w3.org/TR/xhtml1/DTD/xhtml1-transitional.dtd">
<html xmlns="http://www.w3.org/1999/xhtml">
<head>
    <meta http-equiv="Content-Type" content="text/html;charset=UTF-8" />
    <title>Chapter 3 - Recipe 3 - Converting a selected jQuery object into a raw DOM
object</title>
    <script type="text/javascript"
src="http://ajax.googleapis.com/ajax/libs/jquery/1.3.2/jquery.min.js"></script>
    <script type="text/javascript">
    <!--
        (function($){
            $(document).ready(function(){
                var lis = $("ol li").get().reverse();
                $("ol").empty();
                $.each(lis, function(i){
                    $("ol").append("<li>" + lis[i].innerHTML + "</li>");
                });
            });
        })(jQuery);
    //-->
    </script>
</head>
<body>
    <h2>New York Yankees - Batting Line-up</h2>
    <ol>
        <li>Jeter</li>
        <li>Damon</li>
        <li>Teixeira</li>
        <li>Posada</li>
        <li>Swisher</li>
        <li>Cano</li>
        <li>Cabrera</li>
        <li>Molina</li>
        <li>Ransom</li>
    </ol>
</body>
</html>
```

Figure 3-4 shows the output.

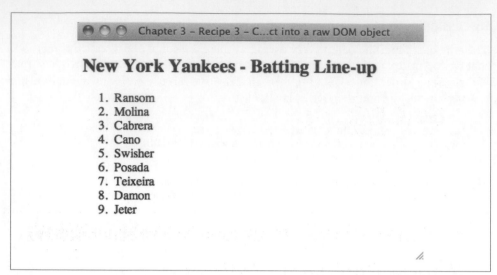

Figure 3-4. Code output

3.4 Getting the Index of an Item in a Selection

Problem

When binding an event for a wide range of selected elements on a page, you need to know exactly which item was clicked from the selected set to "personalize" the action of the bound event.

Solution

When we click an item, we can use the core method `index()` to search through a selection to see what index the item is at:

```
<!DOCTYPE html
    PUBLIC "-//W3C//DTD XHTML 1.0 Transitional//EN"
    "http://www.w3.org/TR/xhtml1/DTD/xhtml1-transitional.dtd">
<html xmlns="http://www.w3.org/1999/xhtml">
<head>
    <meta http-equiv="Content-Type" content="text/html;charset=UTF-8" />
    <title>Chapter 3 - Recipe 4 - Getting the index of an item in a selection</title>
    <script type="text/javascript"
src="http://ajax.googleapis.com/ajax/libs/jquery/1.3.2/jquery.min.js"></script>
    <script type="text/javascript">
    <!--
        (function($){
            $(document).ready(function(){
                $("div").click(function() {
                    alert("You clicked on div with an index of " +
$("div").index(this));
```

```
                });
            });
        })(jQuery);
    //-->
    </script>
</head>
<body>
    <div>click me</div>
    <div class="test">test</div>
    <div>click me</div>
</body>
</html>
```

Figure 3-5 shows the output.

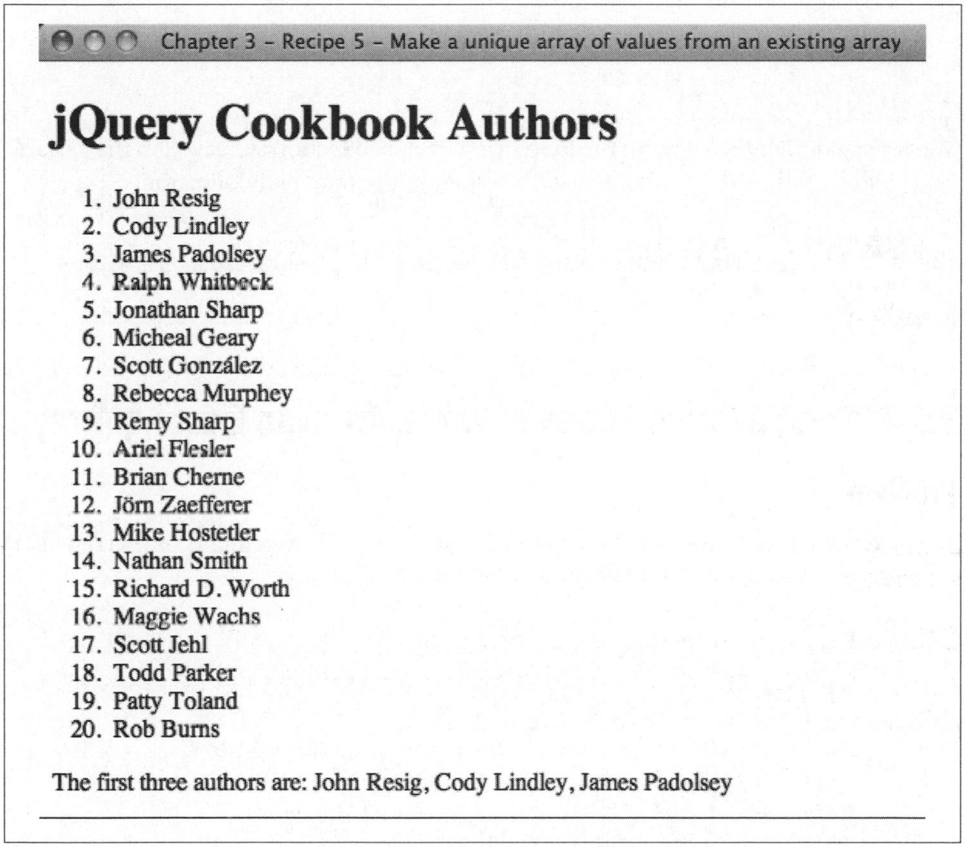

Figure 3-5. Code output

We start by binding all `<div>` elements to a click event. Then when a `<div>` is clicked, we can figure out which `<div>` was clicked by searching for the item in the same selection: `$("div").index(this);`, where `this` is the `<div>` that was clicked.

Discussion

The core method `index()` allows you to get the index of the DOM element you are looking for from a jQuery set. As of jQuery 1.2.6, you can also pass in the index of a jQuery collection to search for. The method will return the index of the first occurrence it finds:

```
var test = $("div.test");

$("div").each(function(i){
    if ($(this).index(test) >= 0)
    {
        //do something
    }
    else
    {
        //do something else
    }
});
```

We'll see whether the `<div>` in the loop matches the collection we saved in the variable `test`, and if so, it will perform a custom action on the matched collection.

 If the index method cannot find the subject that was passed in, it will return –1.

3.5 Making a Unique Array of Values from an Existing Array

Problem

You have an ordered list on your page. You select all the `<li>` elements of that list using jQuery; now you need to transform that list into another list.

Solution

Let's say we have a list of people in an ordered list. We would like to display the first three people from that ordered list as a sentence:

```
<!DOCTYPE html
    PUBLIC "-//W3C//DTD XHTML 1.0 Transitional//EN"
    "http://www.w3.org/TR/xhtml1/DTD/xhtml1-transitional.dtd">
<html xmlns="http://www.w3.org/1999/xhtml">
<head>
    <meta http-equiv="Content-Type" content="text/html;charset=UTF-8" />
    <title>Chapter 3 - Recipe 5 - Making a unique array of values from an existing
array</title>
    <script type="text/javascript"
src="http://ajax.googleapis.com/ajax/libs/jquery/1.3.2/jquery.min.js"></script>
    <script type="text/javascript">
```

```
<!--
    (function($){
        $(document).ready(function(){
            var arr = $.map($("LI"), function(item, index){
                while (index < 3)
                {
                    return $(item).html();
                }
                return null;
            });

            $(document.body).append("<span>The first three authors are: " +
arr.join(", ") + "</span>");
        });
    })(jQuery);
    //-->
    </script>
</head>
<body>
    <h1>jQuery Cookbook Authors</h1>
    <ol>
        <li>John Resig</li>
        <li>Cody Lindley</li>
        <li>James Padolsey</li>
        <li>Ralph Whitbeck</li>
        <li>Jonathan Sharp</li>
        <li>Michael Geary</li>
        <li>Scott González</li>
        <li>Rebecca Murphey</li>
        <li>Remy Sharp</li>
        <li>Ariel Flesler</li>
        <li>Brian Cherne</li>
        <li>Jörn Zaefferer</li>
        <li>Mike Hostetler</li>
        <li>Nathan Smith</li>
        <li>Richard D. Worth</li>
        <li>Maggie Wachs</li>
        <li>Scott Jehl</li>
        <li>Todd Parker</li>
        <li>Patty Toland</li>
        <li>Rob Burns</li>
    </ol>
</body>
</html>
```

Figure 3-6 shows the output.

We start by making an array of the <li> elements from the ordered list. We will select all <li> elements on the page by using a jQuery selector and pass that in as an argument of the jQuery utility method $.map(), which will take an existing array and "map" it into another array. The second argument is the function that will iterate through the array, perform translations, and return a new value to be stored into a new array.

jQuery Cookbook Authors

1. John Resig
2. Cody Lindley
3. Ralph Whitbeck
4. Jonathan Sharp
5. Michael Geary
6. Scott González
7. Rebecca Murphy
8. Remy Sharp
9. Ariel Flesler
10. Brian Cherne
11. Jörn Zaefferer
12. Mike Hostetler
13. Nathan Smith
14. Richard Worth
15. James Padolsey

The first three authors are: John Resig, Cody Lindley, Ralph Whitbeck

Figure 3-6. Code output

In the preceding example, we iterate through the array we made, return only the `html()` values of the first three list elements, and map these values into a new array. We then take that array and use the join method to make a single string out of the array and inject it into the end of the document.

Discussion

In the solution, we are using the jQuery utility method `$.map()`, which will transform an existing array into another array of items. `$.map()` takes two arguments, an array and a callback function:

```
$.map([1,2,3], function(n,i) { return n+i;});

//Output: [1,3,5]
```

`$.map()` will iterate through each item of the original array and pass in the item to be translated and the index of the current location within the array. The method is expecting a value to be returned. The returned value will be inserted into the new array.

> If the null value is returned, no value will be saved into the new array.
> Returning null basically removes the item from the new array.

3.6 Performing an Action on a Subset of the Selected Set

Problem

You need to perform an action on a set of tags, but there is no way to isolate these tags from all the other tags on the page in a jQuery selection set.

Solution

We can use the slice() method to filter the selection set to a subset. We pass it a starting index value and an ending index value, then we can chain our action at the end:

```
<!DOCTYPE html
    PUBLIC "-//W3C//DTD XHTML 1.0 Transitional//EN"
    "http://www.w3.org/TR/xhtml1/DTD/xhtml1-transitional.dtd">
<html xmlns="http://www.w3.org/1999/xhtml">
<head>
    <meta http-equiv="Content-Type" content="text/html;charset=UTF-8" />
    <title>Chapter 3 - Recipe 6 - Performing an action on a subset of the selected
set</title>
    <script type="text/javascript"
src="http://ajax.googleapis.com/ajax/libs/jquery/1.3.2/jquery.min.js"></script>
    <script type="text/javascript">
    <!--
        (function($){
            $(document).ready(function(){

    $("p").slice(1,3).wrap("<i></i>");
        });
    })(jQuery);
    //-->
    </script>
</head>
<body>
    <p>
        Lorem ipsum dolor sit amet, consectetur adipiscing elit. Proin eget nibh ut
tortor egestas pharetra. Nullam a hendrerit urna. Aenean augue arcu, vestibulum eget
faucibus nec, auctor vel velit. Fusce eget velit non nunc auctor rutrum id et ante.
Donec nec malesuada arcu. Suspendisse eu nibh nulla, congue aliquet metus. Integer
porta dignissim magna, eu facilisis magna luctus ac. Aliquam convallis condimentum
purus, at lacinia nisi semper volutpat. Nulla non risus justo. In ac elit vitae elit
posuere adipiscing.
    </p>
    <p>
        Aliquam gravida metus sit amet orci facilisis eu ultricies risus iaculis. Nunc
tempus tristique magna, molestie adipiscing nibh bibendum vel. Donec sed nisi luctus
sapien scelerisque pretium id eu augue. Mauris ipsum arcu, feugiat non tempor
tincidunt, tincidunt sit amet turpis. Vestibulum scelerisque rutrum luctus. Curabitur
eu ornare nisl. Cras in sem ut eros consequat fringilla nec vitae felis. Nulla
facilisi. Mauris suscipit feugiat odio, a condimentum felis luctus in. Nulla interdum
dictum risus, accumsan dignissim tortor ultricies in. Duis justo mauris, posuere vel
convallis ut, auctor non libero. Ut a diam magna, ut egestas dolor. Nulla convallis,
orci in sodales blandit, lorem augue feugiat nulla, vitae dapibus mi ligula quis
```

```
ligula. Aenean mattis pulvinar est quis bibendum.
    </p>
    <p>
        Donec posuere pulvinar ligula, nec sagittis lacus pharetra ac. Cras nec
tortor mi. Pellentesque et magna vel erat consequat commodo a id nunc. Donec velit
elit, vulputate nec tristique vitae, scelerisque ac sem. Proin blandit quam ut magna
ultrices porttitor. Fusce rhoncus faucibus tincidunt. Cras ac erat lacus, dictum
elementum urna. Nulla facilisi. Praesent ac neque nulla, in rutrum ipsum. Aenean
imperdiet, turpis sit amet porttitor hendrerit, ante dui eleifend purus, eu fermentum
dolor enim et elit.
    </p>
    <p>
        Suspendisse facilisis molestie hendrerit. Aenean congue congue sapien, ac
luctus nulla rutrum vel. Fusce vitae dui urna. Fusce iaculis mattis justo sit amet
varius. Duis velit massa, varius in congue ut, tristique sit amet lorem. Curabitur
porta, mauris non pretium ultrices, justo elit tristique enim, et elementum tellus
enim sit amet felis. Sed sollicitudin rutrum libero sit amet malesuada. Duis vitae
gravida purus. Proin in nunc at ligula bibendum pharetra sit amet sit amet felis.
Integer ut justo at massa ullamcorper sagittis. Mauris blandit tortor lacus,
convallis iaculis libero. Etiam non pellentesque dolor. Fusce ac facilisis ipsum.
Suspendisse eget ornare ligula. Aliquam erat volutpat. Aliquam in porttitor purus.
    </p>
    <p>
        Suspendisse facilisis euismod purus in dictum. Vivamus ac neque ut sapien
fermentum placerat. Sed malesuada pellentesque tempor. Aenean cursus, metus a
lacinia scelerisque, nulla mi malesuada nisi, eget laoreet massa risus eu felis.
Vivamus imperdiet rutrum convallis. Proin porta, nunc a interdum facilisis, nunc dui
aliquet sapien, non consectetur ipsum nisi et felis. Nullam quis ligula nisi, sed
scelerisque arcu. Nam lorem arcu, mollis ac sodales eget, aliquet ac eros. Duis
hendrerit mi vitae odio convallis eget lobortis nibh sodales. Nunc ut nunc vitae
nibh scelerisque tempor at malesuada sapien. Nullam elementum rutrum odio nec aliquet.
    </p>
</body>
</html>
```

Figure 3-7 shows the output.

The preceding example selects the subset starting at index 1 and ending before index 3 and wraps an italics tag around the subselection.

Discussion

The jQuery method `slice()` takes a couple of options; the first is the starting index position, and the second argument, which is optional, is the ending index position. So, say you wanted all `<P>` tags except the first one; you could do `$("p").slice(1)`, and it would start the selection at the second item and select the rest that is in the jQuery selection.

`slice()` also takes a negative number. If a negative number is given, it'll count in from the selection's end. So, `$("p").slice(-1);` will select the last item in the selection. Additionally, `$("p").slice(1, -2);` will start the selection at the second item and select to the second-to-last item.

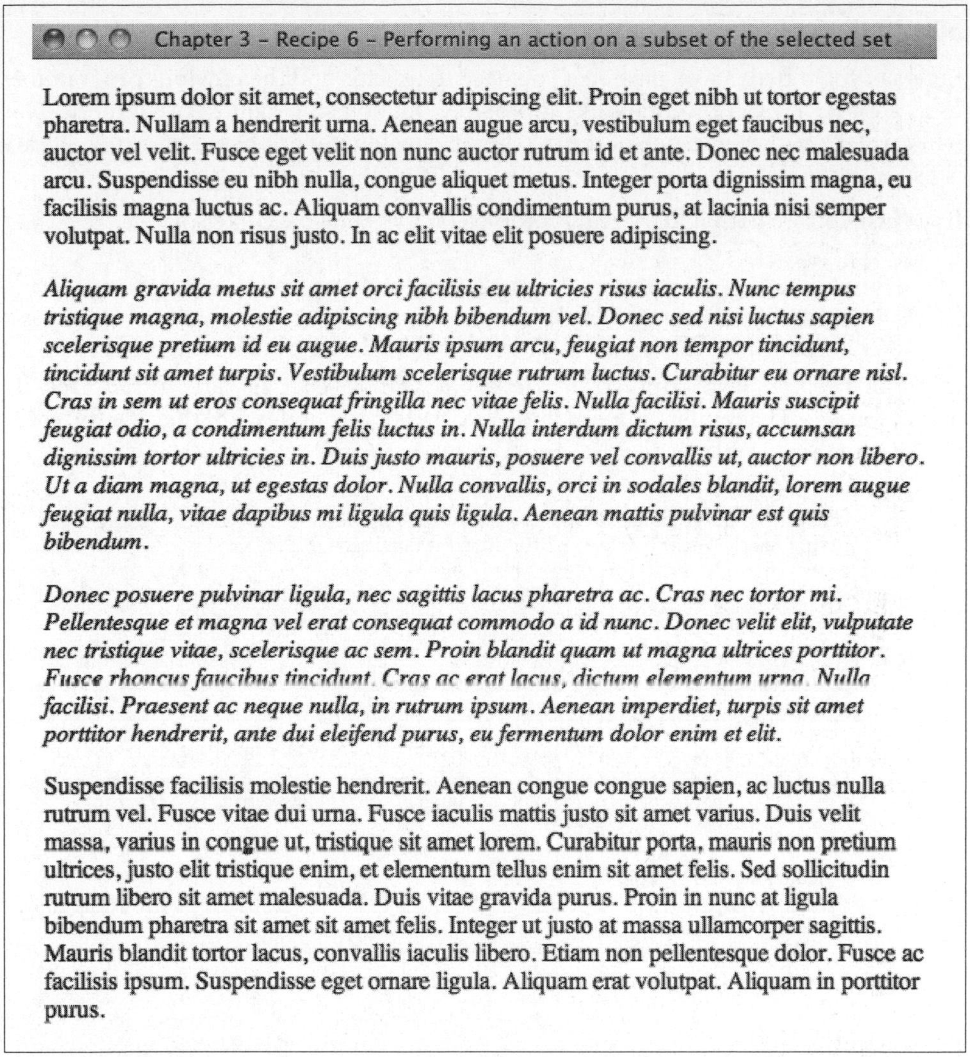
Chapter 3 - Recipe 6 - Performing an action on a subset of the selected set
Lorem ipsum dolor sit amet, consectetur adipiscing elit. Proin eget nibh ut tortor egestas pharetra. Nullam a hendrerit urna. Aenean augue arcu, vestibulum eget faucibus nec, auctor vel velit. Fusce eget velit non nunc auctor rutrum id et ante. Donec nec malesuada arcu. Suspendisse eu nibh nulla, congue aliquet metus. Integer porta dignissim magna, eu facilisis magna luctus ac. Aliquam convallis condimentum purus, at lacinia nisi semper volutpat. Nulla non risus justo. In ac elit vitae elit posuere adipiscing.
Aliquam gravida metus sit amet orci facilisis eu ultricies risus iaculis. Nunc tempus tristique magna, molestie adipiscing nibh bibendum vel. Donec sed nisi luctus sapien scelerisque pretium id eu augue. Mauris ipsum arcu, feugiat non tempor tincidunt, tincidunt sit amet turpis. Vestibulum scelerisque rutrum luctus. Curabitur eu ornare nisl. Cras in sem ut eros consequat fringilla nec vitae felis. Nulla facilisi. Mauris suscipit feugiat odio, a condimentum felis luctus in. Nulla interdum dictum risus, accumsan dignissim tortor ultricies in. Duis justo mauris, posuere vel convallis ut, auctor non libero. Ut a diam magna, ut egestas dolor. Nulla convallis, orci in sodales blandit, lorem augue feugiat nulla, vitae dapibus mi ligula quis ligula. Aenean mattis pulvinar est quis bibendum.
Donec posuere pulvinar ligula, nec sagittis lacus pharetra ac. Cras nec tortor mi. Pellentesque et magna vel erat consequat commodo a id nunc. Donec velit elit, vulputate nec tristique vitae, scelerisque ac sem. Proin blandit quam ut magna ultrices porttitor. Fusce rhoncus faucibus tincidunt. Cras ac erat lacus, dictum elementum urna. Nulla facilisi. Praesent ac neque nulla, in rutrum ipsum. Aenean imperdiet, turpis sit amet porttitor hendrerit, ante dui eleifend purus, eu fermentum dolor enim et elit.
Suspendisse facilisis molestie hendrerit. Aenean congue congue sapien, ac luctus nulla rutrum vel. Fusce vitae dui urna. Fusce iaculis mattis justo sit amet varius. Duis velit massa, varius in congue ut, tristique sit amet lorem. Curabitur porta, mauris non pretium ultrices, justo elit tristique enim, et elementum tellus enim sit amet felis. Sed sollicitudin rutrum libero sit amet malesuada. Duis vitae gravida purus. Proin in nunc at ligula bibendum pharetra sit amet sit amet felis. Integer ut justo at massa ullamcorper sagittis. Mauris blandit tortor lacus, convallis iaculis libero. Etiam non pellentesque dolor. Fusce ac facilisis ipsum. Suspendisse eget ornare ligula. Aliquam erat volutpat. Aliquam in porttitor purus.

Figure 3-7. Code output

3.7 Configuring jQuery Not to Conflict with Other Libraries

Problem

If jQuery is loaded on the same page as another JavaScript library, both libraries may have implemented the `$` variable, which results in only one of those methods working correctly.

Solution

Let's say you inherit a web page that you need to update, and the previous programmer used another JavaScript library like Prototype, but you still want to use jQuery. This will cause a conflict, and one of the two libraries will not work based on which library is listed last in the page head.

If we just declare both jQuery and Prototype on the same page like so:

```
<script type="text/javascript"
src="http://ajax.googleapis.com/ajax/libs/prototype/1.6.0.3/prototype.js"></script>
<script type="text/javascript"
src="http://ajax.googleapis.com/ajax/libs/jquery/1.3.2/jquery.min.js"></script>
```

this will cause a JavaScript error: *element.dispatchEvent is not a function in prototype.js*. Thankfully, jQuery provides a workaround with the jQuery.noConflict() method:

```
<!DOCTYPE html
    PUBLIC "-//W3C//DTD XHTML 1.0 Transitional//EN"
    "http://www.w3.org/TR/xhtml1/DTD/xhtml1-transitional.dtd">
<html xmlns="http://www.w3.org/1999/xhtml">
<head>
    <meta http-equiv="Content-Type" content="text/html;charset=UTF-8" />
    <title>Chapter 3 - Recipe 7 - Configuring jQuery to free up a conflict with
another library</title>

    <script type="text/javascript"
src="http://ajax.googleapis.com/ajax/libs/prototype/1.6.0.3/prototype.js"></script>
    <script type="text/javascript"
src="http://ajax.googleapis.com/ajax/libs/jquery/1.3.2/jquery.min.js"></script>
    <script type="text/javascript">
    <!--
        jQuery.noConflict();

        // Use jQuery via jQuery(...)
        jQuery(document).ready(function(){
          jQuery("div#jQuery").css("font-weight","bold");
        });

        // Use Prototype with $(...), etc.
        document.observe("dom:loaded", function() {
            $('prototype').setStyle({
                fontSize: '10px'
            });
        });
    //-->
    </script>

</head>
<body>
    <div id="jQuery">Hello, I am a jQuery div</div>
    <div id="prototype">Hello, I am a Prototype div</div>
</body>
</html>
```

Figure 3-8 shows the output.

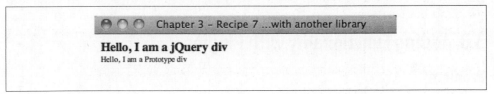

Figure 3-8. Code output

When you call `jQuery.noConflict()`, it gives control of the $ variable back to whomever implemented it first. Once you free up the $ variable, you only will be able to access jQuery with the `jQuery` variable. For example, when you used to use `$("div p")`, you would now use `jQuery("div p")`.

Discussion

The jQuery library and virtually all of its plugins are constrained by the jQuery name-space. You shouldn't get a conflict with the jQuery variable and any other library (i.e., Prototype, YUI, etc.). jQuery does however use $ as a shortcut for the jQuery object. This shortcut definition is what conflicts with other libraries that also use the $ variable. As we've seen in the solution, we can free jQuery of the $ shortcut and revert to using the jQuery object.

There is another option. If you want to make sure jQuery won't conflict with another library but still have the benefit of a short name, you can call `jQuery.noConflict()` and assign it to a variable:

```
var j = jQuery.noConflict();

j(document).ready(function(){
  j("div#jQuery").css("font-weight","bold");
});
```

You can define your own short name by choosing the variable name you assign, `jQuery.noConflict()`.

Finally, another option is to encapsulate your jQuery code inside a closure:

```
jQuery.noConflict();

(function($){
    $("div#jQuery").css("font-weight","bold");
})(jQuery);
```

By using a closure, you temporarily make the $ variable available to the jQuery object while being run inside the function. Once the function ends, the $ variable will revert to the library that had initial control.

If you use this technique, you will not be able to use other libraries' methods within the encapsulated function that expect the $.

3.8 Adding Functionality with Plugins

Problem

The jQuery library is a small, slick, powerful JavaScript library, but it doesn't come preloaded with every piece of functionality that you may need.

Solution

jQuery was built with extensibility in mind. If the core jQuery library can't do what you want, chances are a jQuery plugin author has written a plugin that will handle your need, probably in as little as one line of code.

To include a plugin on your page, all you need to do is download the plugin *.js* file, include the jQuery library on the page, then immediately after, include your plugin on the page. Then, in either another *.js* file or in a script block on the page, you'll typically need to call the plugin and provide any options that may be required.

Here is an example using the jQuery cycle plugin (*http://jquery-cookbook.com/go/plugin -cycle*) developed by Mike Alsup:

```
<!DOCTYPE html
    PUBLIC "-//W3C//DTD XHTML 1.0 Transitional//EN"
    "http://www.w3.org/TR/xhtml1/DTD/xhtml1-transitional.dtd">
<html xmlns="http://www.w3.org/1999/xhtml">
<head>
    <meta http-equiv="Content-Type" content="text/html;charset=UTF-8" />
    <title>Chapter 3 - Recipe 8 - Adding Functionality with Plugins</title>
    <style type="text/css">
        .pics {
            height:  232px;
            width:   232px;
            padding: 0;
            margin:  0;
        }

        .pics img {
            padding: 15px;
            border:  1px solid #ccc;
            background-color: #eee;
            width:   200px;
            height: 200px;
            top:  0;
            left: 0
        }
    </style>
    <script type="text/javascript"
```

```
    src="http://ajax.googleapis.com/ajax/libs/jquery/1.3.2/jquery.min.js"></script>
      <!--Now include your plugin declarations after you've declared jQuery on the page-->
      <script type="text/javascript" src="scripts/2.8/jquery.cycle.all.min.js?
v2.60"></script>
      <script type="text/javascript">
      <!--
         (function($){
            $(document).ready(function(){
               $('.pics').cycle('fade');
            });
         })(jQuery);
      //-->
      </script>

   </head>
   <body>
      <div class="pics">
         <img src="images/2.8/beach1.jpg" width="200" height="200" alt="Beach 1" />
         <img src="images/2.8/beach2.jpg" width="200" height="200" alt="Beach 2" />
         <img src="images/2.8/beach3.jpg" width="200" height="200" alt="Beach 3" />
      </div>
   </body>
</html>
```

Figure 3-9 shows the output.

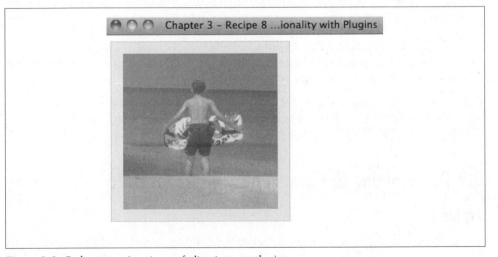

Figure 3-9. Code output (one image fading into another)

With one line of code, we are able to make a slideshow effect that will show one image
at a time and then fade to the next image automatically. The cycle plugin is also extensible because it was written so developers can provide different options to have
different transition effects and layouts.

Discussion

jQuery has one of the largest communities of developers of any of the JavaScript libraries. This large community contributes to a large base of plugins and tutorials that are available on the Web. jQuery hosts a repository of plugins that have been written and submitted to *http://plugins.jquery.com* by the authors. There are currently more than 1,600 plugins listed in the repository, and you can find plugins in many different categories. Plugin authors are invited to submit their plugins and to give a description, a link to the plugin, and a link to the plugin's documentation. The repository makes it easy for developers to search for the specific functionality they want.

Chances are that, as a developer, you will eventually find a plugin that meets your requirements. But on the off chance that a plugin doesn't exist, creating a plugin yourself is fairly straightforward. Here are some points to remember:

- Name your file *jquery.[name of plugin].js*, as in *jquery.debug.js*.
- All new methods are attached to the `jQuery.fn` object; all functions to the jQuery object.
- Inside methods, `this` is a reference to the current jQuery object.
- Any methods or functions you attach must have a semicolon (`;`) at the end—otherwise, the code will break when compressed.
- Your method must return the jQuery object, unless explicitly noted otherwise.
- You should use `this.each` to iterate over the current set of matched elements—it produces clean and compatible code that way.
- Always use `jQuery` instead of `$` inside your plugin code—that allows users to change the alias for jQuery in a single place.

For more information and examples on creating plugins, you can go to the Authoring page on the jQuery documentation site (*http://docs.jquery.com/Plugins/Authoring*), or you can skip ahead to Chapter 12 where Mike Hostetler will go into more detail.

3.9 Determining the Exact Query That Was Used

Problem

While writing a plugin or a method that extends jQuery, you need to know exactly what the selection and the context used when calling the method so that the method can be recalled.

Solution

We can use the core properties `.selector` and `.context` in conjunction with each other so we can re-create the original query that was passed through. We need to use both in conjunction because not all queries to our function or plugin will be within the default document context:

```
<!DOCTYPE html
    PUBLIC "-//W3C//DTD XHTML 1.0 Transitional//EN"
    "http://www.w3.org/TR/xhtml1/DTD/xhtml1-transitional.dtd">
<html xmlns="http://www.w3.org/1999/xhtml">
<head>
    <meta http-equiv="Content-Type" content="text/html;charset=UTF-8" />
    <title>Chapter 3 - Recipe 9 - Determining the exact query that was used</title>
    <script type="text/javascript"
src="http://ajax.googleapis.com/ajax/libs/jquery/1.3.2/jquery.min.js"></script>
    <script type="text/javascript">
    <!--
        (function($){
            $.fn.ShowQuery = function(i) {
                alert("$(\""+ $(this).selector + "\", " + $(this).context +")");
                if (i < 3)
                {
                    $($(this).selector, $(this).context).ShowQuery(i+1);
                }
            };
            $("div").ShowQuery(1);
        })(jQuery);
    //-->
    </script>
</head>
<body>
    <div>
        This is a div.
    </div>
</body>
</html>
```

Figure 3-10 shows the output.

Figure 3-10. Code output (alert box)

Discussion

In the preceding example, we define a method that can be called from a jQuery selection, ShowQuery. Within that method, we alert the query as it was passed in and then recursively recall ShowQuery again with the same jQuery selector. The if statement is there so that we don't get into a recursive loop.

The core properties .selector and .context were introduced in jQuery 1.3, which was released in January 2009. These methods are geared more toward plugin developers who may need to perform an action against the original query passed in. A potential use case of using these methods is to rerun the selection query or to check to see whether an element is in the selection.

.selector returns as a string the actual selector that was used to match the given elements. .selector will return the whole selector if, say, the selection is broken up where there is a selector and then the matched set is narrowed with the use of the find() method:

```
$("div").find("a").selector;

//returns: "div a"
```

.context will return the DOM node originally passed in to jQuery(). If no context was set in the selector, the context will default to the document.

jQuery Utilities

Jonathan Sharp

4.0 Introduction

Often, when thinking and talking about jQuery, the main concepts that come to mind are DOM and style manipulation and behavior (events). Yet there are also a number of "core" features and utility functions tucked away for the developer's benefit. This chapter is focused on exposing, disclosing, and explaining these not-so-common utility methods of jQuery.

4.1 Detecting Features with jQuery.support

Problem

You need to attach a special `click` handler to all anchor tags that have just a hash for the current page, and you don't want to risk it breaking because of browser support issues.

Solution

```
(function($) {
    $(document).ready(function() {
    $('a')
        .filter(function() {
            var href = $(this).attr('href');
            // Normalize the URL
            if ( !jQuery.support.hrefNormalized ) {
                var loc = window.location;
                href = href.replace( loc.protocol + '//' + loc.host + loc.pathname,
'');
            }
            // This anchor tag is of the form <a href="#hash">
            return ( href.substr(0, 1) == '#' );
        })
```

```
        .click(function() {
            // Special click handler code
        });
    });
})(jQuery);
```

Discussion

The `jQuery.support` object was added in version 1.3 and contains Boolean flags to help write code using browser feature detection. In our example, Internet Explorer (IE) has a different behavior in how it handles the `href` attribute. IE will return the full URL instead of the exact `href` attribute. Using the `hrefNormalized` attribute, we have future-proofed our solution in the event that a later version of IE changes this behavior. Otherwise, we would have needed a conditional that contained specific browser versions. While it may be tempting, it is best to avoid this approach because it requires future maintenance as new versions of browsers are released. Another reason to avoid targeting specific browsers is that it is possible for clients to intentionally or unintentionally report an incorrect user agent string. In addition to the `hrefNormalized` attribute, a number of additional attributes exist:

`boxModel`
> True if the browser renders according to the W3C CSS box model specification

`cssFloat`
> True if `style.cssFloat` is used to get the current CSS float value

`hrefNormalized`
> True if the browser leaves intact the results from `getAttribute('href')`

`htmlSerialize`
> True if the browser properly serializes link elements with the `innerHTML` attribute

`leadingWhitespace`
> True if the browser preserves leading whitespace when `innerHTML` is used

`noCloneEvent`
> True if the browser does not clone event handlers when elements are cloned

`objectAll`
> True if `getElementsByTagName('*')` on an element returns all descendant elements

`opacity`
> True if the browser can interpret the CSS opacity style

`scriptEval`
> True if using `appendChild` for a `<script>` tag will execute the script

`style`
> True if `getAttribute('style')` is able to return the inline style specified by an element

`tbody`
> True if the browser allows `<table>` elements without a `<tbody>` element

---

4.2 Iterating Over Arrays and Objects with jQuery.each

Problem

You need to iterate or loop over each element in an array or attribute of an object.

Solution

```
(function($) {
    $(document).ready(function() {
        var months = [  'January', 'February', 'March', 'April', 'May',
                        'June', 'July', 'August', 'September', 'October',
                        'November', 'December'];
        $.each(months, function(index, value) {
            $('#months').append('<li>' + value + '</li>');
        });

        var days = {    Sunday: 0, Monday: 1, Tuesday: 2, Wednesday: 3,
                        Thursday: 4, Friday: 5, Saturday: 6 };
        $.each(days, function(key, value) {
            $('#days').append('<li>' + key + ' (' + value + ')</li>');
        });
    });
})(jQuery);
```

Discussion

In this recipe, we iterate over both an array and an object using `$.each()`, which provides an elegant interface to the common task of iteration. The first argument to the `$.each()` method is the array or object to iterate over, with the second argument being the callback method that is executed for each element. (Note that this is slightly different from the jQuery collection method `$('div').each()`, whose first argument is the callback function.)

When the callback function defined by the developer is executed, the `this` variable is set to the value of the element currently being iterated. Thus, the previous recipe could be rewritten as follows:

```
(function($) {
    $(document).ready(function() {
        var months = [  'January', 'February', 'March', 'April', 'May',
                        'June', 'July', 'August', 'September', 'October',
                        'November', 'December'];
        $.each(months, function() {
            $('#months').append('<li>' + this + '</li>');
        });

        var days = {    Sunday: 0, Monday: 1, Tuesday: 2, Wednesday: 3,
                        Thursday: 4, Friday: 5, Saturday: 6 };
        $.each(days, function(key) {
            $('#days').append('<li>' + key + ' (' + this + ')</li>');
        });
```

```
        });
    })(jQuery);
```

4.3 Filtering Arrays with jQuery.grep

Problem

You need to filter and remove elements in an array.

Solution

```
(function($) {
    $(document).ready(function() {
        var months = [  'January', 'February', 'March', 'April', 'May',
                        'June', 'July', 'August', 'September', 'October',
                        'November', 'December'];
        months = $.grep(months, function(value, i) {
            return ( value.indexOf('J') == 0 );
        });
        $('#months').html( '<li>' + months.join('</li><li>') + '</li>' );
    });
})(jQuery);
```

Discussion

This recipe uses the $.grep() method to filter the months array so that it only includes
entries that begin with the capital letter J. The $.grep method returns the filtered array.
The callback method defined by the developer takes two arguments and is expected to
return a Boolean value of true to keep an element or false to have it removed. The first
argument specified is the value of the array element (in this case, the month), and the
second argument passed in is the incremental value of the number of times the
$.grep() method has looped. So, for example, if you want to remove every other month,
you could test whether (i % 2) == 0, which returns the remainder of i / 2. (The % is
the modulus operator, which returns the remainder of a division operation. So, when
i = 4, i divided by 2 has a remainder of 0.)

```
(function($) {
    $(document).ready(function() {
        var months = [  'January', 'February', 'March', 'April', 'May',
                        'June', 'July', 'August', 'September', 'October',
                        'November', 'December'];
        months = $.grep(months, function(value, i) {
            return ( i % 2 ) == 0;
        });
        $('#months').html( '<li>' + months.join('</li><li>') + '</li>' );
    });
})(jQuery);
```

4.4 Iterating and Modifying Array Entries with jQuery.map

Problem

You need to loop over each element in an array and modify its value.

Solution

```
(function($) {
    $(document).ready(function() {
        var months = [  'January', 'February', 'March', 'April', 'May',
                        'June', 'July', 'August', 'September', 'October',
                        'November', 'December'];
        months = $.map(months, function(value, i) {
            return value.substr(0, 3);
        });
        $('#months').html( '<li>' + months.join('</li><li>') + '</li>' );
    });
})(jQuery);
```

Discussion

In this recipe, `$.map()` is iterating over the `months` array and returns the abbreviation (first three characters). The `$.map()` method takes an array and a callback method as arguments and iterates over each array element executing the callback as defined by the developer. The array entry will be updated with the return value of the callback.

4.5 Combining Two Arrays with jQuery.merge

Problem

You have two arrays that you need to combine or concatenate.

Solution

```
(function($) {
    $(document).ready(function() {
        var horseBreeds = ['Quarter Horse', 'Thoroughbred', 'Arabian'];
        var draftBreeds = ['Belgian', 'Percheron'];

        var breeds = $.merge( horseBreeds, draftBreeds );
        $('#horses').html( '<li>' + breeds.join('</li><li>') + '</li>' );
    });
})(jQuery);
```

Discussion

In this example, we have two arrays that contain a list of horse breeds. The arrays are combined in the order of first + second. So, the final **breeds** array will look like this:

```
['Quarter Horse', 'Thoroughbred', 'Arabian', 'Belgian', 'Percheron']
```

4.6 Filtering Out Duplicate Array Entries with jQuery.unique

Problem

You have two jQuery DOM collections that need to have duplicate elements removed:

```
(function($) {
    $(document).ready(function() {
        var animals = $('li.animals').get();
        var horses = $('li.horses').get();
        $('#animals')
            .append( $(animals).clone() )
            .append( $(horses).clone() );
    });
})(jQuery);
```

Solution

```
(function($) {
    $(document).ready(function() {
        var animals = $('li.animals').get();
        var horses = $('li.horses').get();
        var tmp = $.merge( animals, horses );
        tmp = $.unique( tmp );
        $('#animals').append( $(tmp).clone() );
    });
})(jQuery);
```

Discussion

jQuery's `$.unique()` function will remove duplicate DOM elements from an array or collection. In the previous recipe, we combine the `animals` and `horses` arrays using `$.merge()`. jQuery makes use of `$.unique()` throughout most of its core and internal functions such as `.find()` and `.add()`. Thus, the most common use case for this method is when operating on an array of elements not constructed with jQuery.

4.7 Testing Callback Functions with jQuery.isFunction

Problem

You have written a plugin and need to test whether one of the settings is a valid callback function.

Solution

```
(function($) {
    $.fn.myPlugin = function(settings) {
        return this.each(function() {
            settings = $.extend({ onShow: null }, settings);
            $(this).show();
            if ( $.isFunction( settings.onShow ) ) {
                settings.onShow.call(this);
            }
        });
    };
    $(document).ready(function() {
        $('div').myPlugin({
            onShow: function() {
                alert('My callback!');
            }
        });
    });
})(jQuery);
```

Discussion

While the JavaScript language provides the `typeof` operator, inconsistent results and edge cases across web browsers need to be taken into account. jQuery provides the `.isFunction()` method to ease the developer's job. Worth pointing out is that since version 1.3, this method works for user-defined functions and returns inconsistent results with built-in language functions such as this:

```
jQuery.isFunction( document.getElementById );
```

which returns false in versions of Internet Explorer.

4.8 Removing Whitespace from Strings or Form Values with jQuery.trim

Problem

You have an input form and need to remove the whitespace that a user may have entered at either the beginning or end of a string.

Solution

```
<input type="text" name="first_name" class="cleanup" />
<input type="text" name="last_name" class="cleanup" />

(function($) {
    $(document).ready(function() {
        $('input.cleanup').blur(function() {
            var value = $.trim( $(this).val() );
            $(this).val( value );
```

```
        });
    });
})(jQuery);
```

Discussion

Upon the user blurring a field, the value as entered by the user—`$(this).val()`—is retrieved and passed through the `$.trim()` method that strips all whitespace characters (space, tab, and newline characters) from the beginning and end of the string. The trimmed string is then set as the value of the input field again.

4.9 Attaching Objects and Data to DOM with jQuery.data

Problem

Given the following DOM code:

```
var node = document.getElementById('myId');
node.onclick = function() {
    // Click handler
};
node.myObject = {
    label: document.getElementById('myLabel')
};
```

you have metadata associated with a DOM element for easy reference. Because of flawed garbage collection implementations of some web browsers, the preceding code can cause memory leaks.

Solution

Properties added to an object or DOM node at runtime (called *expandos*) exhibit a number of issues because of flawed garbage collection implementations in some web browsers. jQuery provides developers with an intuitive and elegant method called `.data()` that aids developers in avoiding memory leak issues altogether:

```
$('#myId').data('myObject', {
    label: $('#myLabel')[0]
});

var myObject = $('#myId').data('myObject');
myObject.label;
```

Discussion

In this recipe, we use the `.data()` method, which manages access to our data and provides a clean separation of data and markup.

One of the other benefits of using the `data()` method is that it implicitly triggers get Data and `setData` events on the target element. So, given the following HTML:

```
<div id="time" class="updateTime"></div>
```

we can separate our concerns (model and view) by attaching a handler for the setData event, which receives three arguments (the event object, data key, and data value):

```
// Listen for new data
$(document).bind('setData', function(evt, key, value) {
    if ( key == 'clock' ) {
        $('.updateTime').html( value );
    }
});
```

The `setData` event is then triggered every time we call `.data()` on the document element:

```
// Update the 'time' data on any element with the class 'updateTime'
setInterval(function() {
    $(document).data('clock', (new Date()).toString() );
}, 1000);
```

So, in the previous recipe, every 1 second (1,000 milliseconds) we update the `clock` data property on the `document` object, which triggers the `setData` event bound to the document, which in turn updates our display of the current time.

4.10 Extending Objects with jQuery.extend

Problem

You have developed a plugin and need to provide default options allowing end users to overwrite them.

Solution

```
(function($) {
    $.fn.myPlugin = function(options) {
        options = $.extend({
            message: 'Hello world',
            css: {
                color: 'red'
            }
        }, options);
        return this.each(function() {
            $(this).css(options.css).html(options.message);
        });
    };
})(jQuery);
```

Discussion

In this recipe, we use the `$.extend()` method provided by jQuery. `$.extend()` will return a reference to the first object passed in with the latter objects overwriting any properties they define. The following code demonstrates how this works in practice:

```
var obj = { hello: 'world' };
obj = $.extend(obj, { hello: 'big world' }, { foo: 'bar' });

alert( obj.hello ); // Alerts 'big world'
alert( obj.foo ); // Alerts 'bar';
```

This allows for `myPlugin()` in our recipe to accept an `options` object that will overwrite our default settings. The following code shows how an end user would overwrite the default CSS `color` setting:

```
$('div').myPlugin({ css: { color: 'blue' } });
```

One special case of the `$.extend()` method is that when given a single object, it will extend the base jQuery object. Thus, we could define our plugin as follows to extend the jQuery core:

```
$.fn.extend({
    myPlugin: function() {
        options = $.extend({
            message: 'Hello world',
            css: {
                color: 'red'
            }
        }, options);
        return this.each(function() {
            $(this).css(options.css).html(options.message);
        });
    }
});
```

`$.extend()` also provides a facility for a deep (or recursive) copy. This is accomplished by passing in Boolean `true` as the first parameter. Here is an example of how a deep copy would work:

```
var obj1 = { foo: { bar: '123', baz: '456' }, hello: 'world' };
var obj2 = { foo: { car: '789' } };

var obj3 = $.extend( obj1, obj2 );
```

Without passing in `true`, `obj3` would be as follows:

```
{ foo: { car: '789' }, hello: 'world' }
```

If we specify a deep copy, `obj3` would be as follows after recursively copying all properties:

```
var obj3 = $.extend( true, obj1, obj2 );
// obj3
{ foo: { bar: '123', baz: '456', car: '789' }, hello: 'world' }
```

Faster, Simpler, More Fun

Michael Geary and Scott González

5.0 Introduction

Nearly every day, someone asks on the jQuery Google Group how they can make their code simpler or faster, or how to debug a piece of code that isn't working.

This chapter will help you simplify your jQuery code, making it easier to read and more fun to work on. And we'll share some tips for finding and fixing those bugs.

We'll also help you make your code run faster, and equally important, find out which parts of your code you need to speed up. So your site's visitors will have more fun using the snappy pages on your site.

That's what we call a win-win situation. Happy coding!

5.1 That's Not jQuery, It's JavaScript!

Problem

You're a web designer who is new to jQuery, and you're having trouble with the syntax of an `if/else` statement. You know it must be a simple problem, and before asking on the jQuery mailing list, you do your homework: you search the jQuery documentation and find nothing. Web searches for terms like *jquery if else statement* aren't proving helpful either.

You also need to split an email address into two parts, separating it at the @ sign. You've heard that there is a function to split strings, but there doesn't seem to be any information in the jQuery documentation about this either.

Is jQuery really that poorly documented?

Solution

The `if/else` statement and the `.split()` method for strings are part of JavaScript, not part of jQuery.

So, these web searches will turn up more useful results:

> *javascript if else statement*
> *javascript split string*

Discussion

JavaScript experts, please don't bite the newbies.

Newbies, don't feel bad if you've scratched your head over something like this.

If you're an old pro at JavaScript, you may laugh at these questions. But they come up fairly often on the jQuery mailing list, and understandably so. jQuery is designed to make simple JavaScript coding so easy that someone who's never programmed before can pick up the basics and add useful effects to a page, without having to learn a "real" programming language.

But jQuery *is* JavaScript. jQuery itself is 100% pure JavaScript code, and every line of jQuery you write is also a line of JavaScript.

You can indeed get many simple tasks done with jQuery without really understanding its relationship to JavaScript, but the more you learn about the underlying language, the more productive—and less frustrating—your jQuery experience will be.

5.2 What's Wrong with $(this)?

Problem

You have an event handler that adds a class to a DOM element, waits one second using `setTimeout()`, and then removes that class:

```
$(document).ready( function() {
    $('.clicky').click( function() {
        $(this).addClass('clicked');
        setTimeout( function() {
            $(this).removeClass('clicked');
        }, 1000 );
    });
});
```

The class gets added when you click, but it never gets removed. You have confirmed that the code inside `setTimeout()` is being called, but it doesn't seem to do anything. You've used `.removeClass()` before, and that code looks correct. You are using `$(this)` the same way in both places, but it doesn't seem to work inside the `setTimeout()` call.

Solution

Save this in a variable before calling setTimeout():

```
$(document).ready( function() {
    $('.clicky').click( function() {
        var element = this;
        $(element).addClass('clicked');
        setTimeout( function() {
            $(element).removeClass('clicked');
        }, 1000 );
    });
});
```

Even better, since you're calling $() in both places, follow the advice in Recipe 5.3 and copy $(this) to a variable instead of this:

```
$(document).ready( function() {
    $('.clicky').click( function() {
        var $element = $(this);
        $element.addClass('clicked');
        setTimeout( function() {
            $element.removeClass('clicked');
        }, 1000 );
    });
});
```

Discussion

What *is* $(this) anyway, and why doesn't it always work? It's easier to understand if you separate it into its two parts, $() and this.

$() looks mysterious, but it really isn't: it's just a function call. $ is a reference to the jQuery function, so $() is simply a shorter way to write jQuery(). It's just an ordinary JavaScript function call that happens to return an object.

> If you're using another JavaScript library that redefines $, that's a different matter—but then you wouldn't use $() in your jQuery code; you'd use jQuery() or a custom alias.

this is one of the more confusing features in JavaScript, because it's used for so many different things. In object-oriented JavaScript programming, this is used in an object's methods to refer to that object, just like self in Python or Ruby:

```
function Foo( value ) {
    this.value = value;
}

Foo.prototype.alert = function() {
    alert( this.value );
};
```

```
var foo = new Foo( 'bar' );
foo.alert();  // 'bar'
```

In the code for a traditional *onevent* attribute, this refers to the element receiving the event—but only in the attribute itself, not in a function called from the attribute:

```
<a href="#" id="test" onclick="clicked(this);">Test</a>

function clicked( it ) {
    alert( it.id );            // 'test'
    alert( this.id );          // undefined
    alert( this === window );  // true (what?)
}
```

As you can see from the third alert(), this is actually the window object inside the function. For historical reasons, window is the "default" meaning of this when a function is called directly (i.e., not called as a method of an object).

In a jQuery event handler, this is the DOM element handling the event, so $(this) is a jQuery wrapper for that DOM element. That's why $(this).addClass() works as expected in our "Problem" code.

But the code then calls setTimeout(), and setTimeout() works like a direct function call: this is the window object. So when the code calls $(this).removeClass(), it's actually trying to remove the class from the window object!

Why does copying this or $(this) into a local variable fix this? (Pun intended.) JavaScript creates a *closure* for the parameters and local variables of a function.

Closures may seem mysterious at first, but they really boil down to three simple rules:

* You can nest JavaScript functions one inside another, with multiple levels of nesting.
* A function can read and write not only its own parameters and local variables but also those of any functions it's nested in.
* The previous rule *always* works, even if the outer function has already returned and the inner function is called later (e.g., an event handler or setTimeout() callback).

These rules apply equally to all functions, both named and anonymous. However, this is not a function parameter or local variable—it's a special JavaScript keyword—so these rules do not apply. By copying the value of this into a local variable, we take advantage of the closure to make that value available in any nested functions.

5.3 Removing Redundant Repetition

Problem

You need to hide, show, or otherwise manipulate some DOM elements when the page loads, and you also need to take the same actions later in response to a couple of different events:

```javascript
$(document).ready( function() {

    // Set visibility at startup
    $('#state').toggle( $('#country').val() == 'US' );
    $('#province').toggle( $('#country').val() == 'CA' );

    // Update visibility when country selector changes via mouse
    $('#country').change( function() {
        $('#state').toggle( $(this).val() == 'US' );
        $('#province').toggle( $(this).val() == 'CA' );
    });

    // Also update when country selector changes via keyboard
    $('#country').keyup( function() {
        $('#state').toggle( $(this).val() == 'US' );
        $('#province').toggle( $(this).val() == 'CA' );
    });

});
```

The code is working, but you want to simplify it so there's not so much duplicate code.

 Why handle both the change and keyup events? Many websites handle only the change event on a select list. This works fine if you make a selection with the mouse, but if you click the select list and then use the up and down arrow keys to select among the options, nothing happens: keystrokes in a select list do not fire the change event. If you also handle the keyup event, the select list will respond to the arrow keys, providing a better experience for keyboard users.

Solution 1

Move the duplicate code into a function, and call the function both at load time and in response to the event. Use jQuery's `.bind()` method to wire up both event handlers at the same time. And save data used more than once in variables:

```javascript
$(document).ready( function() {

    var $country = $('#country');

    function setVisibility() {
        var value = $country.val();
        $('#state').toggle( value == 'US' );
```

```
        $('#province').toggle( value == 'CA' );
    }

    setVisibility();
    $country.bind( 'change keyup', setVisibility );
});
```

Solution 2

Use jQuery's event triggering to fire the event immediately after attaching it, along with the `.bind()` trick and local variables from solution 1:

```
$(document).ready( function() {

    $('#country')
        .bind( 'change keyup', function() {
            var value = $(this).val();
            $('#state').toggle( value == 'US' );
            $('#province').toggle( value == 'CA' );
        })
        .trigger('change');

});
```

Discussion

It's standard programming practice in just about any language to take duplicate code and move it into a separate function that can be called from multiple places. Solution 1 follows this approach: instead of repeating the code to set the visibility, it appears once in the `setVisibility()` function. The code then calls that function directly at startup and indirectly when the `change` event is fired.

Solution 2 also uses a common function for both of these cases. But instead of giving the function a name so it can be called directly at startup, the code merely sets the function as the event handler for the `change` event and then uses the `trigger()` method to trigger that same event—thus calling the function indirectly.

These approaches are more or less interchangeable; it's largely a matter of taste which you prefer.

5.4 Formatting Your jQuery Chains

Problem

You have a lengthy jQuery chain that includes methods like `.children()` and `.end()` to operate on several related groups of elements. It's getting hard to tell which operations apply to which elements:

```
$('#box').addClass('contentBox').children(':header')
    .addClass('contentTitle').click(function() {
        $(this).siblings('.contentBody').toggle();
```

```
}).end().children(':not(.contentTitle)')
.addClass('contentBody').end()
.append('<div class="contentFooter"></div>')
.children('.contentFooter').text('generated content');
```

Solution

Put each method call in the chain on its own line, and put the . operators at the beginning of each line. Then, indent each part of the chain to indicate where you are switching to different sets of elements.

Increase the indentation when you use methods like .children() or .siblings() to select different elements, and decrease the indentation when you call .end() to return to the previous jQuery selection.

If you're new to jQuery, you'll probably want to read the recipes about basic chaining and .end() in Chapter 1:

```
$('#box')
    .addClass('contentBox')
    .children(':header')
        .addClass('contentTitle')
        .click(function() {
            $(this).siblings('.contentBody').toggle();
        })
    .end()
    .children(':not(.contentTitle)')
        .addClass('contentBody')
    .end()
    .append('<div class="contentFooter"></div>')
    .children('.contentFooter')
        .text('generated content');
```

Discussion

By breaking each call out onto its own line, it becomes very easy to scan the code and see what is happening. Using indentation to indicate when you're modifying the set of elements makes it easy to keep track of when destructive operations are occurring and being undone via .end().

This style of indentation results in every call for any given set of elements always being lined up, even if they're not consecutive. For example, it's clear that the wrapper <div> has an element prepended and appended to it, even though there are operations on other elements in between.

Putting the . operators at the beginning of the lines instead of the end is just a finishing touch: it gives a better visual reminder that these are method calls and not ordinary function calls.

Did jQuery invent chaining? No. jQuery does make very good use of method chaining, but it's something that has been around since the earliest days of JavaScript.

For example, here is a familiar use of chaining with a string object:

```
function htmlEscape( text ) {
    return text
        .replace( '&', '&amp;' )
        .replace( '<', '&lt;' )
        .replace( '>', '&gt;' );
}
```

5.5 Borrowing Code from Other Libraries

Problem

You found a useful function in another JavaScript library and want to use the same technique in your jQuery code. In this case, it's the `.radioClass()` method from the Ext Core library (*http://jquery-cookbook.com/go/ext-core*), which adds a class to the matching element(s) and *removes* the same class from all siblings of the matching element(s).

The name `.radioClass()` comes from the behavior of radio buttons in both web applications and desktop apps, where clicking one button selects it and deselects the other buttons in the same radio button group.

The name *radio button* for those input elements comes from the station buttons in old car radios—the mechanical ones where pushing in one button caused all of the other buttons to pop out.

Given this HTML:

```
<div>
    <div id="one" class="hilite">One</div>
    <div id="two">Two</div>
    <div id="three">Three</div>
    <div id="four">Four</div>
</div>
```

you'd like to run code like this:

```
// Add the 'hilite' class to div#three, and
// remove the class from all of its siblings
// (e.g. div#one)

$('#three').radioClass('hilite');
```

You may even want to allow a "multiple-select" radio class:

```
// Add the 'hilite' class to div#two and
// div#four, and remove the class from the
```

```
// other siblings (div#one and div#three)

$('#two,#four').radioClass('hilite');
```

Solution

Write a simple plugin to add the .radioClass() method to jQuery:

```
// Remove the specified class from every sibling of the selected
// element(s), then add that class to the selected element(s).
// Doing it in that order allows multiple siblings to be selected.
//
// Thanks to Ext Core for the idea.

jQuery.fn.radioClass = function( cls ) {
    return this.siblings().removeClass(cls).end().addClass(cls);
};
```

This is a short enough function that it's not too hard to follow as a one-liner, but indenting the code as described in Recipe 5.4 makes it completely clear how it works:

```
jQuery.fn.radioClass = function( cls ) {
    return this                 // Start chain, will return its result
        .siblings()             // Select all siblings of selected elements
            .removeClass(cls)   // Remove class from those siblings
        .end()                  // Go back to original selection
        .addClass(cls);         // Add class to selected elements
};
```

Discussion

The composer Igor Stravinsky is reported to have said, "Good composers borrow; great composers steal." He apparently stole the quote from T.S. Eliot, who wrote, "Immature poets imitate; mature poets steal."

Good ideas come from many places, and other JavaScript libraries are chock-full of good code and ideas. If there is code in another open source library that you can use or that you can translate to work with jQuery, you're free to do that—if you respect the other author's copyright and license.

 For information on open source and free software, see the following sites:

- *http://www.opensource.org/*
- *http://www.fsf.org/*

You may not even need the actual code in a case like this one, where the implementation is very simple and just the *idea* of having a "radio class" method is the missing link. While not required, it's a good courtesy to give credit to the source of the idea.

Whether the idea comes from elsewhere or is something you thought of yourself, in a surprising number of cases you can write a useful jQuery plugin in one or a few lines of code.

What Is jQuery.fn, and Why Do jQuery Plugins Use It?

jQuery.fn is a reference to the same object as jQuery.prototype. When you add a function to the jQuery.fn object, you're really adding it to jQuery.prototype.

When you create a jQuery object with jQuery() or $(), you're actually calling new jQuery(). (The jQuery code automatically does the new for you.) As with any other JavaScript constructor, jQuery.prototype provides methods and default properties for the objects returned by each new jQuery() call. So, what you're really doing when you write a jQuery.fn plugin is traditional object-oriented JavaScript programming, adding a method to an object using the constructor's prototype.

Then why does jQuery.fn exist at all? Why not just use jQuery.prototype like any other object-oriented JavaScript code? It's not just to save a few characters.

The very first version of jQuery (long before 1.0) didn't use JavaScript's prototype feature to provide the methods for a jQuery object. It *copied* references to every property and method in jQuery.fn (then called $.fn) into the jQuery object by looping through the object.

Since this could be hundreds of methods and it happened every time you called $(), it could be rather slow. So, the code was changed to use a JavaScript prototype to eliminate all the copying. To avoid breaking plugins that already used $.fn, it was made an alias of $.prototype:

```
$.fn = $.prototype;
```

So that's why jQuery.fn exists today—because plugins used $.fn in early 2006!

5.6 Writing a Custom Iterator

Problem

You've selected multiple elements into a jQuery object, and you need to iterate through those elements with a pause between each iteration, for example, to reveal elements one by one:

```
<span class="reveal">Ready? </span>
<span class="reveal">On your mark! </span>
<span class="reveal">Get set! </span>
<span class="reveal">Go!</span>
```

You tried using each(), but of course that revealed the elements all at once:

```
$('.reveal').each( function() {
    $(this).show();
});
```

```
// That was no better than this simpler version:
$('.reveal').show();
```

Solution

Write a custom iterator that uses setTimeout() to delay the callbacks over time:

```
// Iterate over an array (typically a jQuery object, but can
// be any array) and call a callback function for each
// element, with a time delay between each of the callbacks.
// The callback receives the same arguments as an ordinary
// jQuery.each() callback.
jQuery.slowEach = function( array, interval, callback ) {
    if( ! array.length ) return;
    var i = 0;
    next();

    function next() {
        if( callback.call( array[i], i, array[i] ) !== false )
            if( ++i < array.length )
                setTimeout( next, interval );
    }

    return array;
};
// Iterate over "this" (a jQuery object) and call a callback
// function for each element, with a time delay between each
// of the callbacks.
// The callback receives the same arguments as an ordinary
// jQuery(...).each() callback.
jQuery.fn.slowEach = function( interval, callback ) {
    return jQuery.slowEach( this, interval, callback );
};
```

Then simply change your .each() code to use .slowEach() and add the timeout value:

```
// Show an element every half second
$('.reveal').slowEach( 500, function() {
    $(this).show();
});
```

Discussion

jQuery's .each() method is not rocket science. In fact, if we strip the jQuery 1.3.2 implementation down to the code actually used in the most typical use (iterating over a jQuery object), it's a fairly straightforward loop:

```
jQuery.each = function( object, callback ) {
    var value, i = 0, length = object.length;
    for(
        value = object[0];
        i < length && callback.call( value, i, value ) !== false;
        value = object[++i]
    ) {}
```

```
        return object;
    };
```

That could also be coded in a more familiar way:

```
jQuery.each = function( object, callback ) {
    for(
        var i = 0, length = object.length;
        i < length;
        ++i
    ) {
        var value = object[i];
        if( callback.call( value, i, value ) === false )
            break;
    }

    return object;
};
```

We can write similar functions to iterate over arrays or jQuery objects in other useful ways. A simpler example than `.slowEach()` is a method to iterate over a jQuery object in reverse:

```
// Iterate over an array or jQuery object in reverse order
jQuery.reverseEach = function( object, callback ) {
    for( var value, i = object.length;   --i >= 0; ) {
        var value = object[i];
        console.log( i, value );
        if( callback.call( value, i, value ) === false )
            break;
    }
};
// Iterate over "this" (a jQuery object) in reverse order
jQuery.fn.reverseEach = function( callback ) {
    jQuery.reverseEach( this, callback );
    return this;
};
```

This doesn't attempt to handle all of the cases that `.each()` handles, just the ordinary case for typical jQuery code.

Interestingly enough, a custom iterator may not use a loop at all. `.reverseEach()` and the standard `.each()` both use fairly conventional loops, but there's no explicit Java-Script loop in `.slowEach()`. Why is that, and how does it iterate through the elements without a loop?

JavaScript in a web browser does not have a `sleep()` function as found in many languages. There's no way to pause script execution like this:

```
doSomething();
sleep( 1000 );
doSomethingLater();
```

Instead, as with any asynchronous activity in JavaScript, the `setTimeout()` function takes a callback that is called when the time interval elapses. The `.slowEach()` method increments the "loop" variable i in the `setTimeout()` callback, using a closure to preserve the value of that variable between "iterations." (See Recipe 5.2 for a discussion of closures.)

Like .each(), .slowEach() operates directly on the jQuery object or array you give it, so any changes you make to that array before it finishes iterating will affect the iteration. Unlike .each(), .slowEach() is asynchronous (the calls to the callback function happen *after* .slowEach() returns), so if you change the jQuery object or its elements after .slowEach() returns but before all the callbacks are done, that can also affect the iteration.

5.7 Toggling an Attribute

Problem

You need a way to toggle all of the checkmarks in a group of checkboxes. Each checkbox should be toggled independently of the others.

Solution

Write a .toggleCheck() plugin that works like the .toggle() and .toggleClass() methods in the jQuery core to allow you to set, clear, or toggle a checkbox or group of checkboxes:

```
// Check or uncheck every checkbox element selected in this jQuery object
// Toggle the checked state of each one if check is omitted.

jQuery.fn.toggleCheck = function( check ) {
    return this.toggleAttr( 'checked', true, false, check );
};
```

Then you can enable a group of buttons:

```
$('.toggleme').toggleCheck( true );
```

or disable them:

```
$('.toggleme').toggleCheck( false );
```

or toggle them all, each one independent of the rest:

```
$('.toggleme').toggleCheck();
```

This .toggleCheck() method is built on top of a more general-purpose .toggleAttr() method that works for any attribute:

```
// For each element selected in this jQuery object,
// set the attribute 'name' to either 'onValue' or 'offValue'
// depending on the value of 'on. If 'on' is omitted,
// toggle the attribute of each element independently
// between 'onValue' and 'offValue'.
// If the selected value (either 'onValue' or 'offValue') is
```

```
    // null or undefined, remove the attribute.
    jQuery.fn.toggleAttr = function( name, onValue, offValue, on ) {

        function set( $element, on ) {
            var value = on ? onValue : offValue;
            return value == null ?
                $element.removeAttr( name ) :
                $element.attr( name, value );
        }
        return on !== undefined ?
            set( this, on ) :
            this.each( function( i, element ) {
                var $element = $(element);
                set( $element, $element.attr(name) !== onValue );
            });
    };
```

Why go to the trouble of building something so general-purpose? Now we can write similar togglers for other attributes with almost no effort. Suppose you need to do the same thing as .toggleCheck(), but now you're enabling and disabling input controls. You can write a .toggleEnable() in one line of code:

```
// Enable or disable every input element selected in this jQuery object.
// Toggle the enable state of each one if enable is omitted.

jQuery.fn.toggleEnable = function( enable ) {
    return this.toggleAttr( 'disabled', false, true, enable );
};
```

Note how the onValue and offValue parameters let us swap the true and false attribute values, making it easy to talk about "enabling" the element instead of the less intuitive "disabling" that the disabled attribute provides normally.

As another example, suppose we need to toggle a foo attribute where its "on" state is the string value bar, and its "off" state is to remove the attribute. That's another one-liner:

```
// Add or remove an attribute foo="bar".
// Toggle the presence of the attribute if add is omitted.

jQuery.fn.toggleFoo = function( add ) {
    return this.toggleAttr( 'foo', 'bar', null, add );
};
```

Discussion

It's always good to beware of feeping creaturism (aka creeping featurism). If all we really needed were to toggle checkboxes, we could code the whole thing like this:

```
jQuery.fn.toggleCheck = function( on ) {
    return on !== undefined ?
        this.attr( 'checked', on ) :
        this.each( function( i, element ) {
            var $element = $(element);
            $element.attr( 'checked', ! $element.attr('checked') );
```

```
        });
    };
```

That is a bit simpler than our `.toggleAttr()` method, but it's only useful for the `checked` attribute and nothing else. What would we do if we later needed that `.toggleEnable()` method? Duplicate the whole thing and change a few names?

The extra work in `.toggleAttr()` buys us a lot of flexibility: we now can write a whole family of attribute togglers as straightforward one-liners.

 Check the documentation for the version of jQuery you're using before writing new utility methods like this. It's always possible that similar methods could be added to future versions of jQuery, saving you the trouble of writing your own.

5.8 Finding the Bottlenecks

Problem

Your site is too slow to load or too slow to respond to clicks and other user interaction, and you don't know why. What part of the code is taking so much time?

Solution

Use a profiler, either one of the many available ones or a simple one you can code yourself.

Discussion

A profiler is a way to find the parts of your code that take the most time. You probably already have at least one good JavaScript profiler at your fingertips. Firebug has one, and others are built into IE 8 and Safari 4. These are all function profilers: you start profiling, interact with your page, and stop profiling, and then you get a report showing how much time was spent in each function. That may be enough right there to tell you which code you need to speed up.

There are also some profilers specific to jQuery that you can find with a web search for *jquery profiler*. These let you profile selector performance and look more deeply at jQuery function performance.

For really detailed profiling, where you need to analyze individual sections of code smaller than the function level, you can write a simple profiler in just a few lines of code. You may have coded this ad hoc classic:

```
var t1 = +new Date;
// ... do stuff ...
var t2 = +new Date;
alert( ( t2 - t1 ) + ' milliseconds' );
```

The +new Date in this code is just a simpler way of coding the more familiar new Date().getTime(): it returns the current time in milliseconds.

Why does it work? Well, the new Date part is the same: it gives you a Date object representing the current time. (The () are optional, as there are no arguments.) The + operator converts that object to a number. The way JavaScript converts an object to a number is by calling the object's .valueOf() method. And the .valueOf() method for a Date object happens to be the same thing as .getTime(), giving the time in milliseconds.

We can make something more general-purpose and easier to use with only 15 lines of code:

```
(function() {

    var log = [], first, last;

    time = function( message, since ) {
        var now = +new Date;
        var seconds = ( now - ( since || last ) ) / 1000;
        log.push( seconds.toFixed(3) + ': ' + message + '<br />' );
        return last = +new Date;
    };

    time.done = function( selector ) {
        time( 'total', first );
        $(selector).html( log.join('') );
    };

    first = last = +new Date;
})();
```

Now we have a time() function that we can call as often as we want to log the elapsed time since the last time() call (or, optionally, since a specific prior time). When we're ready to report the results, we call time.done(). Here's an example:

```
// do stuff
time( 'first' );
// do more stuff
time( 'second' );
// and more
time( 'third' );
time.done( '#log' );
```

That JavaScript code requires this HTML code to be added to your page:

```
<div id="log">
</div>
```

After the code runs, that `<div>` would get filled with a list like this:

0.102 first
1.044 second
0.089 third
1.235 total

We can see that the largest amount of time is being spent between the `time('first')` and `time('second')` calls.

 Beware of Firebug! If you have Firebug enabled on the page you are timing, it can throw off the results considerably. JavaScript's `eval()` function, which jQuery 1.3.2 and earlier use to evaluate downloaded JSON data, is affected to an extreme degree: an array of 10,000 names and addresses in the format from Recipe 5.11 takes 0.2 seconds in Firefox normally, but *55 seconds* with Firebug's Script panel enabled. Later versions of jQuery use `Function()` for this, which isn't affected by Firebug.

If Firebug affects your page as badly as that and if you can't find a workaround, you may want to detect Firebug and display a warning:

```
<div id="firebugWarning" style="display:none;">
    Your warning here
</div>

$(document).ready( function() {
    if( window.console && console.firebug )
        $('#firebugWarning').show();
});
```

For many optimization exercises, this code may be sufficient. But what if the code we need to test is inside a loop?

```
for( var i = 0; i < 10; ++i ) {
    // do stuff
    time( 'first' );
    // do more stuff
    time( 'second' );
    // and more
    time( 'third' );
}
time.done( '#log' );
```

Now our little profiler will list those first, second, and third entries 10 times each! That's not too hard to fix—we just need to accumulate the time spent for each specific message label when it's called multiple times:

```
(function() {

    var log = [], index = {}, first, last;

    // Accumulate seconds for the specified message.
    // Each message string has its own total seconds.
    function add( message, seconds ) {
        var i = index[message];
        if( i == null ) {
            i = log.length;
            index[message] = i;
            log[i] = { message:message, seconds:0 };
        }
        log[i].seconds += seconds;
    }

    time = function( message, since ) {
        var now = +new Date;
        add( message, ( now - ( since || last ) ) / 1000 );
        return last = +new Date;
    }

    time.done = function( sel ) {
        time( 'total', first );
        $(sel).html(
            $.map( log, function( item ) {
                return(
                    item.seconds.toFixed(3) +
                    ': ' +
                    item.message + '<br />'
                );
            }).join('')
        );
    };

    first = last = +new Date;
})();
```

With this change, we'll get useful results from that loop:

```
0.973 first
9.719 second
0.804 third
11.496 total
```

When Timing Test Results Vary

When you run timing tests on a web page, you won't get the same result every time. In fact, the timing results will probably vary quite a bit if you reload a page or rerun a test multiple times.

What should you do to get the "real" number? Average the results?

Probably not. Here's a chart of the fillTable() timing from Recipe 5.11 for 50 consecutive runs, taken about 10 seconds apart:

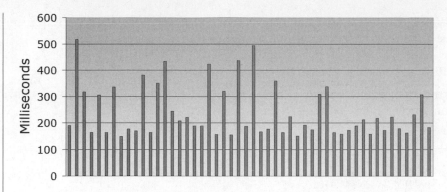

There's a distinct pattern here: a large majority of runs in the 150–200 millisecond range, with a small number of scattered runs taking longer. It seems likely that something around 175 milliseconds is the real timing, and the runs taking much longer were affected by other processes on the machine.

It's also possible that some of the longer runs are caused by garbage collection in the browser. It would be hard to distinguish that from time taken by other processes, so the most practical thing is probably just to disregard these outliers.

5.9 Caching Your JQuery Objects

Problem

You're logging the various properties of the event object for a mousemove event, and the code lags behind because it uses $('.classname') selectors to find and update table cells with the event data.

Your page contains this HTML code for the log:

```
<table id="log">
    <tr><td>Client X:</td><td class="clientX"></td></tr>
    <tr><td>Client Y:</td><td class="clientY"></td></tr>
    <tr><td>Page X:</td><td class="pageX"></td></tr>
    <tr><td>Page Y:</td><td class="pageY"></td></tr>
    <tr><td>Screen X:</td><td class="screenX"></td></tr>
    <tr><td>Screen Y:</td><td class="screenY"></td></tr>
</table>
```

and this JavaScript code:

```
$('html').mousemove( function( event ) {
    $('.clientX').html( event.clientX );
    $('.clientY').html( event.clientY );
    $('.pageX').html( event.pageX );
    $('.pageY').html( event.pageY );
    $('.screenX').html( event.screenX );
    $('.screenY').html( event.screenY );
});
```

The page also contains a large number (thousands!) of other DOM elements. In a simpler test page, the code performs fine, but in this complex page it is too slow.

Solution

Cache the jQuery objects returned by the $(...) calls, so the DOM queries only have to be run once:

```
var
    $clientX = $('.clientX'),
    $clientY = $('.clientY'),
    $pageX = $('.pageX'),
    $pageY = $('.pageY'),
    $screenX = $('.screenX'),
    $screenY = $('.screenY');
$('html').mousemove( function( event ) {
    $clientX.html( event.clientX );
    $clientY.html( event.clientY );
    $pageX.html( event.pageX );
    $pageY.html( event.pageY );
    $screenX.html( event.screenX );
    $screenY.html( event.screenY );
});
```

You may also be able to speed up those selectors considerably; see the next recipe for ways to do that. But simply calling them once each instead of over and over again may be enough of an improvement right there.

Discussion

One of the classic ways to optimize code is to "hoist" repeated calculations out of a loop so you have to do them only once. Any values that don't change inside the loop should be calculated one time, before the loop starts. If those are expensive calculations, the loop will then be much faster.

This works just as well when the "loop" is a series of frequently fired events such as mousemove and the "calculation" is a jQuery selector. Hoisting the selector out of the event handler makes the event handler respond faster.

Of course, if you're calling multiple selectors inside a loop, that will also benefit from moving them outside the loop in the same manner.

Why do $clientX and the other variable names begin with the $ character?

$ doesn't have any special meaning in JavaScript—it's treated just like a letter of the alphabet. It's simply a popular convention in jQuery code to use the $ prefix as a reminder that the variable contains a reference to a jQuery object and not, say, a DOM element, because a variable name of $foobar has a visual resemblance to the jQuery operation $('#foobar').

This is especially helpful when you need to use both a jQuery object and its underlying DOM element, e.g.:

```
var $foo = $('#foo'), foo = $foo[0];
// Now you can use the jQuery object:
$foo.show();
// or the DOM element:
var id = foo.id;
```

5.10 Writing Faster Selectors

Problem

Your code contains a large number of $('.classname') selectors. You're caching them as described in the previous recipe, but the selectors are still affecting your page load time. You need to make them faster.

Solution

First, make sure you are using a recent version of jQuery (1.3.2 or later) for faster selector performance in most browsers, especially with class selectors.

If you have control over the HTML page content, change the page to use id attributes and '#xyz' selectors instead of class attributes and '.xyz' selectors:

```
<div class="foo"></div>
<div id="bar"></div>

$('.foo')  // Slower
$('#bar')  // Faster
```

If you must use class name selectors, see whether there is a parent element that you can find with a faster ID selector, and then drill down from there to the child elements. For example, using the HTML from the previous recipe:

```
<table id="log">
    <tr><td>Client X:</td><td id="clientX"></td></tr>
    ...
</table>
```

you could use this:

```
$('.clientX')         // Slower
$('td.clientX')       // May be faster
$('#log .clientX')    // May be much faster
$('#log td.clientX')  // Possibly faster in some browsers
```

 Beware of selector speed test pages that don't reflect the actual page content you are using. In a very simple page, a simple $('.clientX') selector may test out faster than a fancier selector like $('#log td.clientX')—even in browsers and jQuery versions where you might expect the class selector to be slow.

That's just because the more complicated selector takes more time to set up, and in a simple page that setup time may dominate performance.

The test page for this recipe deliberately contains a very large number of elements to provoke selector performance problems that only show up in large pages.

Neither one, of course, shows exactly what any selector's performance will be in *your* page. The only way to be sure which selector is fastest in a particular page is to test each in that page.

Discussion

It's easy to forget that an innocent-looking call like $('.clientX') may take considerable time. Depending on the browser and version of jQuery, that selector may have to make a list of every DOM element in your page and loop through it looking for the specified class.

jQuery versions prior to 1.3 use this slow method in *every* browser. jQuery 1.3 introduced the Sizzle selector engine, which takes advantage of faster DOM APIs in newer browsers such as getElementsByClassName() and querySelectorAll().

However, for most websites you'll probably need to support IE 7 for some time to come, and class selectors are slow in IE 7 when you have a complex page.

If you can use it, selecting by ID as in $('#myid') is generally very fast in all browsers, because it simply uses a single call to the getElementById() API.

It also helps to narrow down the number of elements that need to be searched, either by specifying a parent element, by making the class selector more specific with a tag name, or by combining those and other tricks.

5.11 Loading Tables Faster

Problem

You're loading a JSON data object with 1,000 names and addresses and using jQuery to create a table with this data. It takes 5–10 seconds to create the table in IE 7—and that's not even counting the download time.

Your JSON data is in this format:

```
{
    "names": [
        {
            "first": "Azzie",
            "last": "Zalenski",
            "street": "9554 Niemann Crest",
            "city": "Quinteros Divide",
            "state": "VA",
            "zip": "48786"
        },
        // and repeat for 1000 names
    ]
}
```

Your JavaScript code is as follows:

```
// Return a sanitized version of text with & < > escaped for HTML
function esc( text ) {
    return text
        .replace( '&', '&amp;' )
        .replace( '<', '&lt;' )
        .replace( '>', '&gt;' );
}
$(document).ready( function() {

    function fillTable( names ) {
        $.each( names, function() {
            $('<tr>')
                .append( $('<td>').addClass('name').html(
                    esc(this.first) + ' ' + esc(this.last)
                ) )
                .append( $('<td>').addClass('address').html(
                    esc(this.street) + '<br />' +
                    esc(this.city) + ', ' +
                    esc(this.state) + ' ' + esc(this.zip)
                ) )
                .appendTo('#nameTable');
        });
    }

    $.getJSON( 'names/names-1000.json', function( json ) {
        fillTable( json.names );
    });
});
```

And you have this HTML code in your document:

```
<table id="nameTable">
</table>
```

It works fine, resulting in the browser display shown in Figure 5-1.

Arica Hence	5473 Brallier Crossing Bejar Centers, MA 37967
Vicente Hofmann	4070 Cree Pike Gosier Cove, LA 67602
Renna Pastorius	4666 Moorer Tunnel Marmo Centers, PO 53702
Exie Duca	7139 Langenfeld Court Albrecht, RE 24425
Sean Pickerel	9956 Urquidez Rest Iveson Islands, EN 05425
Justa Ocasio	3463 Lair Terrace Stanislawski, SE 80277
Sommer Lafortune	9101 Palmateer Road

Figure 5-1. Browser output for name table

It's just much too slow.

Solution

Combine several optimizations:

- Insert a single `<table>` or `<tbody>` instead of multiple `<tr>` elements
- Use `.innerHTML` or `.html()` instead of DOM manipulation
- Build an array with `a[++i]` and `.join()` it instead of string concatenation
- Use a bare-metal `for` loop instead of `$.each`
- Reduce name lookups

The result is this new version of the code (using the same `esc()` function as before):

```
$(document).ready( function() {

    function fillTable( names ) {
        // Reduce name lookups with local function name
        var e = esc;
        //
        var html = [], h = -1;
        html[++h] = '<table id="nameTable">';
        html[++h] = '<tbody>';
        for( var name, i = -1;   name = names[++i]; ) {
            html[++h] = '<tr><td class="name">';
            html[++h] =     e(name.first);
```

```
            html[++h] =      ' ';
            html[++h] =      e(name.last);
            html[++h] = '</td><td class="address">';
            html[++h] =      e(name.street);
            html[++h] =      '<br />';
            html[++h] =      e(name.city);
            html[++h] =      ', ';
            html[++h] =      e(name.state);
            html[++h] =      ' ';
            html[++h] =      e(name.zip);
            html[++h] = '</td></tr>';
        }
        html[++h] = '</tbody>';
        html[++h] = '</table>';

        $('#container')[0].innerHTML = html.join('');
    }

    $.getJSON( 'names/names-1000.json', function( json ) {
        fillTable( json.names );
    });
});
```

The new code requires the HTML code in your document to be changed to the
following:

```
<div id="container">
</div>
```

On one test system in IE 7, the new code runs in 0.2 seconds compared with 7 seconds
for the original code. That's 35 times faster!

Granted, the code is not as clean and elegant as the original, but your site's visitors will
never know or care about that. What they will notice is how much faster your page
loads.

Discussion

Sometimes you'll get lucky and find that one specific optimization is all it takes to fix
a performance problem. Sometimes, as in this recipe, you'll need several tricks to get
the speed you want.

The biggest speed boost in this code comes from inserting a single `<table>` element with
all its children in a single DOM operation, instead of inserting a lengthy series of
`<tr>` elements one by one. In order to do this, you need to generate the entire table as
HTML. That means you need to paste together a large number of strings to build the
HTML, which can be very fast or very slow depending on how you do it. And with
1,000 items to loop though, it's worth finding the fastest way to write the loop itself.

You may wonder, "Is this still jQuery code? It looks like plain old JavaScript!" The
answer is yes, and yes. It's quite all right to mix and match jQuery code with other
JavaScript code. You can use simpler jQuery ways of coding in most of your site, and

when you discover the slow parts, you can either find faster jQuery techniques or use plain old JavaScript as needed for performance.

5.12 Coding Bare-Metal Loops

Problem

You're calling `$.each(array,fn)` or `$(selector).each(fn)` to iterate over thousands of items in your code, and you suspect that all those function calls may be adding to your load time:

```
$.each( array, function() {
    // do stuff with this
});
```

or:

```
$('.lotsOfElements').each( function() {
    // do stuff with this or $(this)
});
```

Solution

Use a `for` loop instead of `.each()`. To iterate over an array, it's hard to beat this loop:

```
for( var item, i = -1; item = array[++i] ) {
    // do stuff with item
}
```

But there is a catch: this loop works only if your array has no "false" elements, that is, elements whose value is undefined, null, false, 0, or "". Even with that restriction, this loop is useful in many common cases, such as iterating over a jQuery object. Just be sure to cache the object in a variable:

```
var $items = $('.lotsOfElements');
for( var item, i = -1; item = $item[++i] ) {
    // do stuff with item (a DOM node)
}
```

It's also common to have JSON data that contains an array of objects as in our example from Recipe 5.11:

```
{
    "names": [
        {
            // ...
            "zip": "48786"
        },
        // and repeat for 1000 names
    ]
}
```

If you know that none of the objects making up the elements of the `names` array will ever be null, it's safe to use the fast loop.

For a more general-purpose loop that works with any array, there is always the classic loop that you'll see in many places:

```
for( var i = 0; i < array.length; i++ ) {
    var item = array[i];
    // do stuff with item
}
```

But you can improve that loop in three ways:

- Cache the array length.
- Use `++i`, which is faster than `i++` in some browsers.
- Combine the test and increment of the loop variable to remove one name lookup.

The result is as follows:

```
for( var i = -1, n = array.length; ++i < n; ) {
    var item = array[i];
    // do stuff with item
}
```

Would it be even faster to use a `while` loop or a `do...while` loop? Probably not. You could rewrite the previous loop as follows:

```
var i = -1, n = array.length;
while( ++i < n ) {
    var item = array[i];
    // do stuff with item
}
```

or:

```
var i = 0, n = array.length;
if( i < n ) do {
    var item = array[i];
    // do stuff with item
}
while( ++i < n );
```

But neither one is any faster than the more readable `for` loop.

To iterate over an object (not an array), you can use a `for..in` loop:

```
for( var key in object ) {
    var item = object[key];
    // do stuff with item
}
```

A Warning About for..in Loops

Never use a `for..in` loop to iterate over a jQuery object or an array of any type. If the array has any custom properties or methods, those will be iterated along with the numeric array elements. For example, this code enumerates a single DOM element, the document body (with i = 0):

```
$('body').each( function( i ) { console.log( i ); });
```

This code may look like it would do the same thing, but it enumerates all of the jQuery methods such as `show` and `css` along with the [0] element:

```
for( var i in $('body') ) console.log( i ); // BAD
```

Instead, use one of the array loops listed previously.

Even the "safe" use of a `for..in` loop to iterate over an object can get in trouble if any code on your page has modified `Object.prototype` to extend all objects with additional methods or properties. The loop will enumerate those methods or properties along with the ones you want.

Extending `Object.prototype` is strongly discouraged because it breaks so much code. In fact, at least through jQuery 1.3.2, it breaks jQuery itself by causing `each()` to enumerate those added methods or properties. If your code has to work in such an environment, you need to take extra precautions on all your loops, such as testing the `hasOwnProperty()` method of each object property. Unfortunately, these extra tests slow the code down, so you have to choose between speed and robustness.

Discussion

`$(selector).each(fn)` is the customary way to create a jQuery object and iterate over it, but it's not the only way. The jQuery object is an "array-like" object with `.length` and [0], [1], ..., [length-1] properties. Therefore, you can use any of the looping techniques you would use with any other array. And because the jQuery object never contains "false" elements, you can use the fastest `for` loop listed at the beginning of the solution.

If you use the `time()` function from Recipe 5.2 or another profiler to measure loop performance, be sure to test your actual code, not a simplified test case that just runs the loop without the full loop body. The simplified test would miss one potential benefit of the `for` loop: fewer name lookups resulting from less function nesting. See Recipe 5.13 for the details.

5.13 Reducing Name Lookups

Problem

Your code has an inner loop, down inside several levels of nested functions, that runs hundreds or thousands of times. The inner loop calls several global functions, and it references some variables defined in the outer functions or globally.

Each of these references is triggering several name lookups because of the nested functions. It's slowing down your code, but profilers don't show what the problem is, and it isn't obvious from looking at the code that there's a problem!

Solution

Investigate every name that appears in your innermost loop, and figure out how many name lookups it requires. Reduce the number of name lookups by caching object references locally or using fewer nested functions.

Discussion

Closures are a wonderful thing. They make it trivial to capture state information and pass it along to asynchronous functions such as event handlers or timer callbacks. If JavaScript didn't have closures, then every asynchronous callback would need to have a way to pass that state around. Instead, you can simply use a nested function.

The dynamic nature of JavaScript is also a wonderful thing. You can add properties and methods to any object, any time, and the JavaScript runtime will happily chase down those references when you need them.

Put these together, and you can get a lot of name lookups.

 The most modern JavaScript interpreters have improved greatly in this area. But if you want your code to run fast in the most popular browsers—such as any version of IE— you still need to worry about the number of name lookups.

Consider this code:

```
// A typical function wrapper to get a local scope
(function() {
    // Find the largest absolute value in an array of numbers
    function maxMagnitude( array ) {
        var largest = -Infinity;
        $.each( array, function() {
            largest = Math.max( largest, Math.abs(this) );
        });
    return largest;
    }
```

```
    // Other code here calls maxMagnitude on a large array
})();
```

Remember that JavaScript looks up a name first in the local scope (function), and if the name isn't found there, it works its way up through the parent nested functions and finally the global scope. Not only does the JavaScript runtime have to look up each name every time you use it, it also has to repeat those lookups when the names are actually defined in parent functions or in the global scope.

So, if this block of code is in the global scope, the each() callback does the following name lookups in every iteration:

1. largest in local scope [fail]
2. largest in MaxMagnitude() [success]
3. Math in local scope [fail]
4.   Math in MaxMagnitude() [fail]
5.   Math in anonymous wrapper function [fail]
6.   Math in global scope [success]
7.   abs in Math object [success]
8. Math in local scope [fail]
9. Math in MaxMagnitude() [fail]
10.   Math in anonymous wrapper function [fail]
11.   Math in global scope [success]
12.   max in Math object [success]
13. largest in local scope [fail]
14. largest in MaxMagnitude() [success]

Now rewrite the code as follows:

```
// A typical wrapper to get a local scope
(function() {
    // Find the largest absolute value in an array of numbers
    function maxMagnitude( array ) {
        var abs = Math.abs, max = Math.max;
        var largest = -Infinity;
        for( var i = -1, n = array.length; ++i < n; ) {
            largest = max( largest, abs(array[i]) );
        }
        return largest;
    }
    // Other code here calls maxMagnitude on a large array
})();
```

This not only eliminates the callback function call in every iteration, it also reduces the number of name lookups per iteration by 10 or more. The loop body in this version does these name lookups:

1. largest in local scope [success]
2. abs in local scope [success]
3. max in local scope [success]
4. largest in local scope [success]

That's more than a 70 percent improvement over the first version.

If this code is nested even deeper inside another function, the difference is even greater, since each nested function adds one more lookup for each of the Math object lookups.

 In this discussion we're omitting the this and array[i] lookups, as well as the lookups in the for loop itself. Those are roughly comparable between the two versions.

In Recipe 5.11, a single name lookup optimization accounts for a 100 ms improvement. That's not a huge difference, but a tenth of a second off your page load time for a one-line code change is good value.

The original code calls esc() six times in each loop iteration, for a total of 6,000 calls in the thousand-name test case. These calls are inside three nested functions, and esc() is a global function, so it takes four name lookups simply to resolve the function name for each call. That's 24,000 name lookups!

The improved code reduces the function nesting by one, so that cuts it down to 18,000 name lookups (two nested functions and the global scope at 6,000 each), but then it uses one last trick in the innermost function:

```
function fillTable( names ) {
    var e = esc;
    // and now call e() in the inner loop instead of esc()
}
```

Now, the 6,000 calls to e() are each resolved in a single name lookup. That's a reduction of 12,000 name lookups. No wonder it knocks a tenth of a second off the load time.

5.14 Updating the DOM Faster with .innerHTML

Problem

You're creating a large block of HTML code and using $('#mydiv').html(myhtml); to insert it into the DOM. You've profiled the code and found that the .html() method is taking longer than expected.

Solution

Use $('#mydiv')[0].innerHTML = myhtml; for faster DOM updates—if you don't require any of the special processing that .html() provides.

Discussion

The .html() method uses the .innerHTML property to actually insert the HTML content into the DOM, but it does quite a bit of preprocessing first. In most cases this won't matter, but in performance-critical code you can save some time by setting the `.innerHTML` property directly.

It's actually jQuery's internal `.clean()` method that does this processing. If you read the source code for `.clean()`, you'll see that it goes to quite a bit of work to clean up the HTML input.

 The easiest way to find most methods in the jQuery source code is to search for the method name with a `:` after it; e.g., to find the `.clean()` method, search for `clean:` in the *uncompressed* jQuery source.

The code in Recipe 5.11 runs afoul of some of this cleanup. That recipe's HTML code contains a large number of `<br />` tags. There's a regular expression in `.clean()` that finds all self-closing tags (tags that end with `/>` and therefore do not require a closing tag) and checks that these tags are indeed in the limited set of HTML tags that can be self-closed. If not, then it converts the HTML to an open–close tag.

For example, if you code `$('#test').html('<div />');`, then this invalid HTML is automatically converted to `$('#test').html('<div></div>');`. This makes coding easier, but if you have a very long HTML string that contains many self-closing tags, `.clean()` has to check them all—even if all those tags are valid like the `<br />` tags in the other recipe.

The `.html()` method replaces any existing content, and it takes care to avoid memory leaks by removing all event handlers that you've attached through jQuery to any of the elements being replaced. If there are any event handlers in the content being replaced, you should stick with `.html()`, or if you just need this event handler cleanup but don't need the other HTML cleanup, you could possibly use `$('#test').empty() [0].innerHTML = myhtml;` to get the event cleanup only.

The bottom line: if you know for sure that your code doesn't require the event cleanup or HTML cleanup that jQuery normally provides, then with caution you can use `.innerHTML` directly. Otherwise, stick with `.html()` for safety.

5.15 Debugging? Break Those Chains

Problem

A chain of jQuery methods is failing somewhere along the way. The HTML code is as follows:

```
<div class="foo">
    before
        <span class="baz" style="display:none;">
            test
        </span>
```

```
    after
</div>
```

and the JavaScript code (part of a button click event handler) is as follows:

```
$('.foo').css({ fontsize: '18px' }).find('.bar').show();
```

But when you run the code, the font size isn't set, and the hidden element isn't shown.

You have Firebug or another JavaScript debugger, but it's hard to trace through the code. How can you tell where in the chain it is failing?

Solution

Break up the chain into individual statements, and store each jQuery object in a variable:

```
// $('.foo').css({ fontsize: '18px' }).find('.bar').show();
var $foo = $('.foo');
$foo.css({ fontsize: '18px' });
var $bar = $foo.find('.bar');
$bar.show();
```

Now you have several debugging options. One is to use the Step Over command in the debugger to single step over each statement and observe your variables and the state of the page after each step.

In this code, you'd want to check $foo and $bar after their values are assigned. What is the value of the .length property of each? That tells you how many DOM elements were selected. Does each object contain the DOM elements you expect? Check the [0], [1], [2], etc., properties to see the DOM elements.

Assuming that $foo contains the correct DOM elements, what happens after the .css() method is called? With Firebug's CSS Inspector, you'll find that the CSS font-size property is unchanged after the method call. Wait a minute! It's font-size, not fontsize? There's the problem. Checking the docs, you find that the correct way to write this is either of these:

```
$foo.css({ fontSize: '18px' });
```

```
$foo.css({ 'font-size': '18px' });
```

That's one problem down, but what about the other one? After $bar is assigned, if we look at its .length property, we'll see that it is zero. This tells us that we didn't succeed in selecting any elements. A look at the HTML and JavaScript code will then reveal that we simply misspelled the class name.

Now we can incorporate these two fixes back in the original chain:

```
$('.foo').css({ fontSize: '18px' }).find('.baz').show();
```

Another alternative is to use Firebug's logging statements:

```
// $('.foo').css({ fontsize: '18px' }).find('.bar').show();
var $foo = $('.foo');
```

```
console.log( $foo );
$foo.css({ fontsize: '18px' });
console.log( $foo.css('fontsize') );
var $bar = $foo.find('.bar');
console.log( $bar );
$bar.show();
```

These `console.log()` calls will reveal that `$bar` doesn't have any elements selected, although we've fallen into a trap on the call that attempts to log the font size: we misspelled `fontSize` in the `console.log()` call as well!

This is where combining multiple debugging techniques helps: log those variables, use Firebug's inspectors, read and reread your source code, and have someone else look at the problem too.

Discussion

jQuery's chaining helps make it easy to write concise code, but it can get in the way when debugging, because it is hard to step through the individual steps of the chain and see their results. Breaking up the chain into individual statements, even on a temporary basis while debugging, makes this task easier.

5.16 Is It a jQuery Bug?

Problem

You're calling some jQuery code to show a hidden element and set its HTML content after a time delay using `setTimeout()`:

```
function delayLog( text ) {
    setTimeout( "$('#log').show().html(text)", 1000 );
}
// ... and somewhere else in the code ...
delayLog( 'Hello' );
```

The `.show()` call works, but the `.html(text)` call fails. The Firebug console reports that the `text` variable is undefined. The same jQuery code works when you don't call it from `setTimeout()`. Is there a problem using jQuery with `setTimeout()`?

Solution

One way to find out whether jQuery is the source of a problem is to replace your jQuery code with other JavaScript code that doesn't use jQuery. In this example, we can replace the jQuery code with a simple `alert()`:

```
function delayLog( text ) {
    setTimeout( "alert(text)", 1000 );
}
```

When we try this version of the code, the same problem occurs: there is no alert, and Firebug again reports that `text` is undefined.

This doesn't identify the problem, but it narrows it down a lot. It clearly isn't jQuery (unless the mere presence of the jQuery library is interfering with your page, but you can rule that out by running the code in a simple test page that doesn't include jQuery). So, it must be something wrong with this code itself, most likely to do with the way we're using `setTimeout()`.

Indeed, the problem here is that when a string argument is passed to `setTimeout()`, it is executed in the *global scope*, i.e., as if the code were located outside of any function. The easiest way to fix it is to use a local function for the callback instead of a text string:

```
function delayLog( text ) {
    setTimeout( function() {
        alert(text);
    }, 1000 );
}
```

Unlike code in a string, a nested function has full access to the outer function's variables and parameters. So, this code will alert the text as expected.

And finally, here is a corrected version of the original jQuery code:

```
function delayLog( text ) {
    setTimeout( function() {
        $('#log').show().html(text);
    }, 1000 );
}
```

Discussion

When debugging, if you aren't sure what is causing a problem, finding out where the problem *isn't* can help you track it down. The purpose of this recipe isn't to help you troubleshoot `setTimeout()` problems—after all, this is a jQuery book, not a general JavaScript book—but to help you focus your debugging efforts by quickly ruling out (or confirming!) jQuery as the source of the problem.

5.17 Tracing into jQuery

Problem 1

You're using the Step Into feature in Firebug or another JavaScript debugger to try to step through the jQuery code to see what it actually does when you make a jQuery call. But when you step into the jQuery code, it's all mashed into one long, unreadable line of code and you can't step through it:

```
(function(){var l=this,g,y=l.jQuery,p=l.$,o=l.jQuery=l.$=function(E,F)...
```

Solution 1

You're using the *minified* version of jQuery. Instead, load the *uncompressed* version of jQuery into your page for testing.

If you are loading the code from the Google Ajax Libraries API with a `<script>` tag, change it like this:

```
<!-- Comment out the minified jQuery -->
<!--
<script type="text/javascript"
  src="http://ajax.googleapis.com/ajax/libs/jquery/1.3.2/jquery.min.js
"></script>
-->
<!-- Use the uncompressed version for testing -->
<script type="text/javascript"
  src="http://ajax.googleapis.com/ajax/libs/jquery/1.3.2/jquery.js"></script>
```

If you're using Google's JavaScript loader, change it like this:

```
// Comment out the minified jQuery
// google.load( 'jquery', '1.3.2' );
// Use the uncompressed version for testing
google.load( 'jquery', '1.3.2', { uncompressed:true });
```

Now you will be able to step into and through the jQuery code.

Problem 2

Having fixed that problem, you want to learn how jQuery's `.html()` and `.show()` methods work. So, you are trying to trace into this code in the debugger:

```
$('#test').html( 'test' ).show();
```

But when you use the Step Into command, the debugger goes into the jQuery constructor instead of either of the methods that you're interested in.

Solution 2

The previous line of code contains *three* function calls: a call to the jQuery (`$`) constructor followed by calls to the `.html()` and `.show()` methods. The Step Into command steps into the first of those calls, the constructor.

At that point you can immediately do a Step Out followed by another Step In. This steps you out of the jQuery constructor (thus putting you back in the *middle* of the original line of code) and then into the `.html()` method.

To get to the `.show()` method, use another pair of Step Out and Step In commands. Each time you do this, you'll work your way one step further through the jQuery chain.

If this gets tedious, break the chain as described in Recipe 5.15, and add `debugger;` statements wherever you want to stop. If you want to trace into the `.show()` method, you can change the code to the following:

```
var $test = $('#test');
$test.html( 'test' );
debugger;
$test.show();
```

Now when the code stops on the debugger; statement, you can just use Step In (twice, first to step to the $test.show(); statement and then to step *into* that function call).

You could use Step Over to step from the debugger; statement to the next line, since after all you're not yet stepping "into" anything, but it's easier to click Step In (or hit the F11 key in Windows) twice, and it works just as well. Or, instead of the debugger; statement, you can set a breakpoint on the $test.show() line itself, and then a single Step In will go into the code for the .show() method.

Discussion

The minified version of jQuery is great for production use but not so good for development. It collapses all of the code into one or two lines, making it nearly impossible to step through the code in a debugger. Also, the common use of chained methods makes it more difficult to step into jQuery methods. Using the tips in this recipe, you can easily trace through the jQuery code in the debugger, whether to chase down a bug or to learn how the code works.

Do not let your test-driven friends talk you out of using a debugger! Even if you find most of your bugs through unit testing and other means, one of the best ways to learn about a piece of code is to step through it in the debugger and study its variables and properties as you go.

After all, as you read code, you have to step through it in your head and form a mental model of what its variables contain. Why not let the computer step through the code and *show* you what's in those variables?

5.18 Making Fewer Server Requests

Problem

You're including jQuery and a number of plugins in your page. The sheer number of server requests is slowing down your page load time:

```
<script type="text/javascript" src="jquery.js"></script>
<script type="text/javascript" src="superfish.js"></script>
<script type="text/javascript" src="cycle.js"></script>
<script type="text/javascript" src="history.js"></script>
<script type="text/javascript" src="hoverintent.js"></script>
<script type="text/javascript" src="jcarousel.js"></script>
```

```
<script type="text/javascript" src="thickbox.js"></script>
<script type="text/javascript" src="validate.js"></script>
```

After the page loads, you are downloading some JSON data using $.getJSON(), thus adding yet another server request:

```
$(document).ready( function() {
    $.getJSON( 'myjson.php?q=test', function( json ) {
        $('#demo').html( json.foo );
    });
});
```

myjson.php is a script on your server that returns JSON data like this:

```
{
    "foo": "bar"
}
```

Solution

Load jQuery from Google's Ajax library, and combine all your plugins into a single file:

```
<script type="text/javascript"

  src="http://ajax.googleapis.com/ajax/libs/jquery/1.3.2/jquery.min.js"></script>

<script type="text/javascript" src="plugins.js">
</script>
```

Or, combine *all* of the JavaScript code you use most frequently (jQuery, plugins, and your own code) into a single file:

```
<script type="text/javascript" src="allmyscripts.js"></script>
```

Either way, it also helps to *minify* the .js files (remove comments and extra whitespace) to reduce their size. And make sure your server is using gzip compression on the files it downloads.

For the JSON data, since this page is generated by your own server application, you can "burn" the JSON data directly into the HTML page as it's generated, using a <script> tag:

```
<script type="text/javascript">
    var myJson = {
        "foo": "bar"
    };
</script>
```

The highlighted portion of that script tag is identical to the JSON data downloaded by myjson.php in the original code. In most server languages it should be easy to include the content in this way.

Now the jQuery code to use the JSON data is simply:

```
$(document).ready( function() {
    $('#demo').html( myJson.foo );
});
```

This eliminates one more server request.

Discussion

One of the keys to fast page loading is to simply minimize the number of HTTP requests. Making requests to different servers can also help. Browsers will make only a small number of simultaneous downloads from any single domain (or subdomain), but if you download some of your files from a different domain, the browser may download them in parallel as well.

 Pointing different `<script>` tags to different domains may allow them to be downloaded in parallel, but it doesn't affect the order of *execution*. `<script>` tags are executed in the order they appear in the HTML source.

You can combine JavaScript files by hand by simply copying and pasting them into one big file. This is inconvenient for development but does speed up downloading.

There are a number of file combiner/minifiers available for various server languages.

Ruby on Rails:

- Bundle-fu (*http://jquery-cookbook.com/go/bundle-fu*)
- AssetPackager (*http://jquery-cookbook.com/go/asset-packager*)
- The packager built into Rails 2.0

PHP:

- Minify (*http://jquery-cookbook.com/go/minify*)

Python:

- JSCompile (*http://jquery-cookbook.com/go/js-compile*)

Java:

- YUI Compressor (*http://jquery-cookbook.com/go/yui-compressor*)

In addition to JavaScript code, check your CSS for multiple `.css` files. Some of the tools listed can merge your `.css` files into a single download, just as they do for `.js` files.

 At one time, "packing" JavaScript was all the rage. This not only removes comments and whitespace but also rewrites all of the JavaScript code so that it's not even JavaScript code anymore. Packing requires an unpacking step at runtime—every time the page loads, even if the JavaScript code is already cached. Because of this, packing has fallen out of favor, and "minifying" the code (removing comments and whitespace) is recommended instead, combined with gzip compression. Much of the benefit of packing comes from removing duplicate strings, and gzip does that for you anyway.

5.19 Writing Unobtrusive JavaScript

Problem

You have a page with inline event handler attributes creating a hover effect for a menu.

Your content (HTML), presentation (CSS), and behavior (JavaScript) are all mixed up, making it hard to maintain each on their own and resulting in duplicate JavaScript and style settings:

```
<!DOCTYPE html PUBLIC "-//W3C//DTD XHTML 1.0 Transitional//EN"
    "http://www.w3.org/TR/xhtml1/DTD/xhtml1-transitional.dtd">
<html xmlns="http://www.w3.org/1999/xhtml" xml:lang="en" lang="en">
<head>
    <meta http-equiv="Content-Type" content="text/html; charset=utf-8" />
    <meta http-equiv="Content-Language" content="en-us" />
    <title>Menu Demo</title>

    <style type="text/css">
        .menu {
            background-color: #ccc;
            list-style: none;
            margin: 0;
            padding: 0;
            width: 10em;
        }
        .menu li {
            margin: 0;
            padding: 5px;
        }
        .menu a {
            color: #333;
        }
    </style>
</head>
<body>
<ul class="menu">
    <li onmouseover="this.style.backgroundColor='#999';"
        onmouseout="this.style.backgroundColor='transparent';">
        <a href="download.html">Download</a>
    </li>
    <li onmouseover="this.style.backgroundColor='#999';"
        onmouseout="this.style.backgroundColor='transparent';">
        <a href="documentation.html">Documentation</a>
    </li>
    <li onmouseover="this.style.backgroundColor='#999';"
        onmouseout="this.style.backgroundColor='transparent';">
        <a href="tutorials.html">Tutorials</a>
    </li>
</ul>
</body>
</html>
```

Solution

Replace inline JavaScript with jQuery event handlers, and add/remove classes instead of manipulating the backgroundColor style directly:

```html
<!DOCTYPE html PUBLIC "-//W3C//DTD XHTML 1.0 Transitional//EN"
    "http://www.w3.org/TR/xhtml1/DTD/xhtml1-transitional.dtd">
<html xmlns="http://www.w3.org/1999/xhtml" xml:lang="en" lang="en">
<head>
    <meta http-equiv="Content-Type" content="text/html; charset=utf-8" />
    <meta http-equiv="Content-Language" content="en-us" />
    <title>Menu Demo</title>

    <style type="text/css">
        .menu {
            background-color: #ccc;
            list-style: none;
            margin: 0;
            padding: 0;
            width: 10em;
        }
        .menu li {
            margin: 0;
            padding: 5px;
        }
        .menu a {
            color: #333;
        }
        .menuHover {
            background-color: #999;
        }
    </style>

    <script type="text/javascript"
src="http://ajax.googleapis.com/ajax/libs/jquery/1.3.2/jquery.js">
    </script>

    <script type="text/javascript">

        $(document).ready( function() {
            $('li').hover(
                function() {
                    $(this).addClass('menuHover');
                },
                function() {
                    $(this).removeClass('menuHover');
                });
        });

    </script>
</head>
<body>

<ul class="menu">
    <li><a href="download.html">Download</a></li>
```

```
        <li><a href="documentation.html">Documentation</a></li>
        <li><a href="tutorials.html">Tutorials</a></li>
    </ul>
    </body>
    </html>
```

We've removed the inline event handlers and replaced them with jQuery event handlers, separating the content and behavior. Now if we want to add more menu items, we don't have to copy and paste the same batch of event handlers; instead, the event handler will automatically be added.

We have also moved the style rules for the hover effect into a CSS class, separating the behavior and presentation. If we want to change the styling for the hover effect later, we can just update the stylesheet instead of having to modify the markup.

Discussion

While an "all in one" HTML file with on*event* attributes works fine in a small, simple page, it doesn't scale up very well. As your pages get more complex, separating presentation and behavior makes the code easier to maintain.

We didn't do it in this simple example, but if you have multiple pages using the same JavaScript or CSS code, move that code to a common .js or .css file. That way it will be downloaded into the browser cache once, instead of being re-sent on every page load. As a result, once one of your pages has been visited, the rest will load faster.

5.20 Using jQuery for Progressive Enhancement

Problem

You want to build a site that allows simple task management with a great user experience using animations and Ajax, but you also want to support users who have JavaScript disabled.

Solution

You can build the site to work without all the flashiness and then unobtrusively add the JavaScript functionality:

```
<!DOCTYPE html PUBLIC "-//W3C//DTD XHTML 1.0 Transitional//EN"
    "http://www.w3.org/TR/xhtml1/DTD/xhtml1-transitional.dtd">
<html xmlns="http://www.w3.org/1999/xhtml" xml:lang="en" lang="en">
<head>
    <meta http-equiv="Content-Type" content="text/html; charset=utf-8" />
    <meta http-equiv="Content-Language" content="en-us" />
    <title>Task List</title>

    <script type="text/javascript"
src="http://ajax.googleapis.com/ajax/libs/jquery/1.3.2/jquery.js">
    </script>
```

```
        <script type="text/javascript">

            $(document).ready( function() {
                var url = $('form').attr('action');
                $(':checkbox').click(function() {
                    $.post(url, this.name + '=1');
                    $(this).parent().slideUp(function() {
                        $(this).remove();
                    });
                });
                $(':submit').hide();
            });

        </script>
    </head>
    <body>
    <form method="post" action="tasklist.html">
        <ul>
            <li>
                <input type="checkbox" name="task1" id="task1" />
                <label for="task1">Learn jQuery</label>
            </li>
            <li>
                <input type="checkbox" name="task2" id="task2" />
                <label for="task2">Learn Progressive Enhancement</label>
            </li>
            <li>
                <input type="checkbox" name="task3" id="task3" />
                <label for="task3">Build Great Websites</label>
            </li>
        </ul>
        <input type="submit" value="Mark Complete" />
    </form>
    </body>
    </html>
```

The input form in this page doesn't require JavaScript. The user checks off the tasks he has completed and submits the form, and then it would be up to the server to load a new page with the completed tasks removed from the list.

Now, we can progressively enhance the page using jQuery: we bind an event handler to the checkboxes that mimics a standard form submit, by getting the submit URL for the form and generating POST data showing that the checkbox was checked. Then we animate the removal of the task to provide feedback to the user. We also hide the submit button because marking tasks complete has become an instantaneous process.

Discussion

Although few people browse without JavaScript these days, it's still a good practice when possible to build your pages so they work fine without JavaScript and then use jQuery and JavaScript to enhance them.

Beware that you don't make the user experience *worse* with JavaScript enhancements. The non-JavaScript version of this page may not give immediate feedback when you check off a task, but it does give you a way to change your mind easily if you make a mistake: either uncheck it before submitting or just don't submit the form at all.

If you "submit" each checkbox immediately when it's clicked, be sure you provide a way for your visitor to undo that action. If the task item disappears from the page, people will be afraid to click for fear of clicking the wrong item. You could either leave the item in the page but move it to a "completed" section or add an explicit Undo option.

5.21 Making Your Pages Accessible

Problem

You're building a web application with complex widgets and lots of Ajax functionality, but you want to accommodate visitors with disabilities.

Solution

Add keyboard accessibility and Accessible Rich Internet Applications (ARIA) semantics to your widgets. In the following code, the changes to support these features are indicated in **bold**:

```
<!DOCTYPE html PUBLIC "-//W3C//DTD XHTML 1.0 Transitional//EN"
    "http://www.w3.org/TR/xhtml1/DTD/xhtml1-transitional.dtd">
<html xmlns="http://www.w3.org/1999/xhtml" xml:lang="en" lang="en">
<head>
    <meta http-equiv="Content-Type" content="text/html; charset=utf-8" />
    <meta http-equiv="Content-Language" content="en-us" />
    <title>Dialog Demo</title>

    <style type="text/css">
        table {
            border-collapse: collapse;
            width: 500px;
        }
        th, td {
            border: 1px solid #000;
            padding: 2px 5px;
        }
        .dialog {
            position: absolute;
            background-color: #fff;
            border: 1px solid #000;
            width: 400px;
            padding: 10px;
        }
        .dialog h1 {
            margin: 0 0 10px;
        }
```

```
        .dialog .close {
            position: absolute;
            top: 10px;
            right: 10px;
        }
    </style>

    <script type="text/javascript"
src="http://ajax.googleapis.com/ajax/libs/jquery/1.3.2/jquery.js">
    </script>

    <script type="text/javascript">

        $(document).ready( function() {
            function close() {
                dialog.hide();
                $('#add-user').focus();
            }

            var title = $('<h1>Add User</h1>')
                    .attr('id', 'add-user-title'),

                closeButton = $('<button>close</button>')
                    .addClass('close')
                    .click(close)
                    .appendTo(title),

                content = $('<div/>')
                    .load('add.html'),

                dialog = $('<div/>')
                    .attr({
                        role: 'dialog',
                        'aria-labelledby': 'add-user-title'
                    })
                    .addClass('dialog')
                    .keypress(function(event) {
                        if (event.keyCode == 27) {
                            close();
                        }
                    })
                    .append(title)
                    .append(content)
                    .hide()
                    .appendTo('body');

            $('#add-user').click(function() {
                var height = dialog.height(),
                    width = dialog.width();

                dialog
                    .css({
                        top: ($(window).height() - height) / 2
                            + $(document).scrollTop(),
                        left: ($(window).width() - width) / 2
```

```
                                    + $(document).scrollLeft()
                    })
                    .show();

                dialog.find('#username').focus();

                return false;
            });
        });

    </script>
</head>
<body>
<h1>Users</h1>
<a id="add-user" href="add.html">add a user</a>
<table>
<thead>
    <tr>
        <th>User</th>
        <th>First Name</th>
        <th>Last Name</th>
    </tr>
</thead>
<tbody>
    <tr>
        <td>jsmith</td>
        <td>John</td>
        <td>Smith</td>
    </tr>
    <tr>
        <td>mrobertson</td>
        <td>Mike</td>
        <td>Robertson</td>
    </tr>
    <tr>
        <td>arodriguez</td>
        <td>Angela</td>
        <td>Rodriguez</td>
    </tr>
    <tr>
        <td>lsamseil</td>
        <td>Lee</td>
        <td>Samseil</td>
    </tr>
    <tr>
        <td>lweick</td>
        <td>Lauren</td>
        <td>Weick</td>
    </tr>
</tbody>
</table>
</body>
</html>
```

We've added several useful features with just a small amount of additional code:

- We added ARIA semantics (`role` and `aria-labelledby`) so that assistive technology devices such as screen readers know that our `<div>` is a dialog and not just additional content on the page.
- We placed the keyboard focus in the dialog's first input field when it opens. This is helpful for all your visitors, sighted and nonsighted alike.
- We moved the keyboard focus back to the Add Users link when the dialog closes.
- We allowed the dialog to be canceled with the Escape key.

Discussion

ARIA is a work in progress, so browser and screen reader support for it is still limited. But by adding it now, you'll be better prepared for those visitors who can use it. And improved keyboard access benefits all your visitors.

For more information about ARIA, see the following:

- WAI-ARIA Overview (*http://jquery-cookbook.com/go/aria-overview*)
- DHTML Style Guide (*http://jquery-cookbook.com/go/dhtml-styleguide*)

Don't be thrown off by the old-school DHTML name; the DHTML Style Guide is an up-to-date keyboard accessibility reference for all the latest widgets.

CHAPTER 6

Dimensions

Rebecca Murphey

6.0 Introduction

Dimensions are a core part of adding advanced behaviors to a website. Once you know how to manipulate the dimensions of elements and their position on the page, you will have a new level of control over your user interface, providing desktop-like behaviors and interactions in your application.

6.1 Finding the Dimensions of the Window and Document

Problem

You want to get the width and height of the window and document in pixels.

Solution

jQuery's width and height methods provide easy access to the basic dimensions of the window or document:

```
jQuery(document).ready(function() {
    alert('Window height: ' + jQuery(window).height()); // returns the height of
the viewport
    alert('Window width: ' + jQuery(window).width()); // returns the width of the
viewport

    alert('Document height: ' + jQuery(document).height()); // returns the height
of the document
    alert('Document width: ' + jQuery(document).width()); // returns the width of
the document
});
```

Discussion

It's important to understand that the width and height of the document can (and likely will) be different from the width and height of the window. The dimensions of the window refer to the size of the viewport—that portion of the browser that is available for displaying a document. The dimensions of the document refer to the size of the document itself. In most cases, the document height will be taller than the window's height. The document's width will always be at least the window's width but may be greater than the window's width. In Figure 6-1, `jQuery('body').width() < jQuery(document).width()`, and `jQuery(document).width() == jQuery(window).width()`. If the body were wider than the window, the document width would increase accordingly.

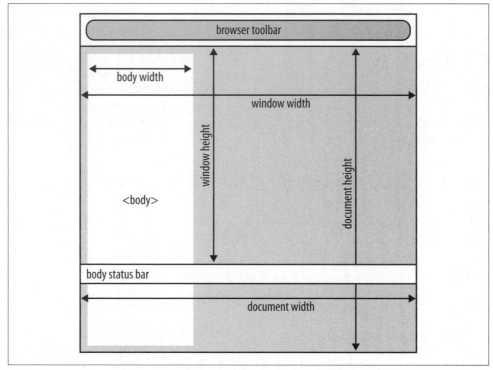

Figure 6-1. The document size and the window size are often different

The `width` and `height` methods can also accept arguments if you want to set the dimensions of an element. The argument can be provided as an integer—in which case it will be interpreted as a pixel measurement—or as a string, in which case it is interpreted as a CSS-like measurement (i.e., `$('#foo').width('300px')`).

6.2 Finding the Dimensions of an Element

Problem

You want to determine the space occupied by an element.

Solution

The `width` and `height` methods can be applied to any element, and they are useful for determining the computed width or height of an element. However, they fall short if you need to determine the actual real estate that an element is occupying on the screen. In addition to `width` and `height`, jQuery provides the following methods for determining more specific dimensions of an element:

`innerWidth`
> Returns the width *excluding* the border and *including* the padding

`innerHeight`
> Returns the height *excluding* the border and *including* the padding

`outerWidth`
> Returns the width including *both* the border *and* the padding

`outerHeight`
> Returns the height *including* the border and *including* the padding

For a visual reference, see Figure 6-2.

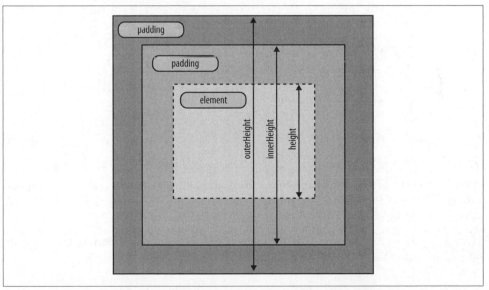

Figure 6-2. Illustration of an element's height, innerHeight, and outerHeight

Given the following HTML:

```
<div id="results"></div>
<div id="myDiv">Some text.</div>
```

and the following CSS:

```
#myDiv {
    width:100px;
    height:30px;
    padding:10px;
    border:1px;
}
```

you could expect the following:

```
jQuery(document).ready(function() {
    var $myDiv = jQuery('#myDiv');
    var $results = jQuery('#results');

    jQuery('<p>Computed width: ' + $myDiv.width() + '</p>')
        .appendTo($results); // 100
    jQuery('<p>Computed height: ' + $myDiv.height() + '</p>')
        .appendTo($results); // 30
    jQuery('<p>Inner width: ' + $myDiv.innerWidth() + '</p>')
        .appendTo($results); // 120
    jQuery('<p>Inner height: ' + $myDiv.innerHeight() + '</p>')
        .appendTo($results); // 50
    jQuery('<p>Outer width: ' + $myDiv.outerWidth() + '</p>')
        .appendTo($results); // 122
    jQuery('<p>Outer height: ' + $myDiv.outerHeight() + '</p>')
        .appendTo($results); // 52

    jQuery('<p>Document outer height: ' + jQuery(document).outerHeight() + '</p>')
        .appendTo($results); // NaN
    jQuery('<p>Document inner height: ' + jQuery(document).innerHeight() + '</p>')
        .appendTo($results); // NaN
    jQuery('<p>Window outer height: ' + jQuery(window).outerHeight() + '</p>')
        .appendTo($results); // NaN
    jQuery('<p>Window inner height: ' + jQuery(window).innerHeight() + '</p>')
        .appendTo($results); // NaN
});
```

Discussion

The innerWidth/innerHeight and outerWidth/outerHeight methods are useful tools for determining the actual dimension that you're after—the basic width and height methods are of limited use when you are trying to measure the actual real estate that an element with border and padding occupies on the screen.

Note that using innerWidth, innerHeight, outerWidth, or outerHeight methods on jQuery(document) or jQuery(window) objects will return NaN.

6.3 Finding the Offset of an Element

Problem

You want to determine the location of an element in the document.

Solution

jQuery offers three methods that are useful in determining an element's position:

offset
:   Returns an object containing the position of the top-left corner of the element relative to the document's top-left corner

position
:   Returns an object containing the position of the top-left corner of the element relative to the top-left corner of the first positioned parent of the element (the offsetParent)

offsetParent
:   Returns a jQuery object containing the offsetParent of the element

The offset method is useful for determining the location of an element on the page—for example, if you want to scroll the window to an element. The position method is useful for repositioning elements and for finding the position of an element in a scrolling container. Both tasks will be discussed in subsequent sections; this section seeks to serve as an overview to the positioning methods.

Given the following HTML where the <body> element has 0-pixel margin and 10-pixel padding:

```
<body id="the_offset_parent">
    <h1>Finding the Offset of an Element</h1>
    <div id="foo">
        <div id="bar">Some text inside #bar, which is inside #foo</div>
    </div>

    <div id="results"></div>
</body>
```

you can use the following code to determine the position, offset, and offset parent of the two DIVs:

```
jQuery(document).ready(function() {
    var $foo = jQuery('#foo');
    var $bar = jQuery('#bar');

    var $results = jQuery('#results');
    var fooPosition = $foo.position();
    var barPosition = $bar.position();
    var fooOffset = $foo.offset();
    var barOffset = $bar.offset();
```

```
        var $fooOffsetParent = $foo.offsetParent();
        var $barOffsetParent = $bar.offsetParent();

        $results
            .append('<p>#foo position.top: ' + fooPosition.top + '</p>') // 10
            .append('<p>#foo position.left: ' + fooPosition.left + '</p>') // 10
            .append('<p>#bar position.top: ' + barPosition.top + '</p>') // 10
            .append('<p>#bar position.left: ' + barPosition.left + '</p>') // 10

            .append('<p>#foo offset.top: ' + fooOffset.top + '</p>') // 10
            .append('<p>#foo offset.left: ' + fooOffset.left + '</p>') // 10
            .append('<p>#bar offset.top: ' + barOffset.top + '</p>') // 10
            .append('<p>#bar offset.left: ' + barOffset.left + '</p>') // 10

            .append('<p>ID of #foo offsetParent: '
                + $fooOffsetParent.attr('id')) // the_offset_parent
            .append('<p>ID of #bar offsetParent: '
                + $barOffsetParent.attr('id')); // the_offset_parent
});
```

In this case, both elements have the same position, and both have the same offsetParent (the document's <body> element).

However, if #foo is positioned using CSS:

```
<body id="the_offset_parent">
    <div id="foo" style="position:absolute; top:10px; left:10px;">
        <div id="bar">Some text inside #bar, which is inside the
absolutely-positioned #foo</div>
    </div>

    <div id="results" style="position:absolute; top:60px; left:10px;"></div>
</body>
```

then the results change. The #foo DIV hasn't actually moved and its offsetParent hasn't changed, so its position and offset stay the same; the #bar DIV hasn't moved either, but since its offsetParent has changed, its position has changed—remember, an element's position is relative to its offset parent.

```
jQuery(document).ready(function() {
    var $foo = jQuery('#foo');
    var $bar = jQuery('#bar');

    var $results = jQuery('#results');
    var fooPosition = $foo.position();
    var barPosition = $bar.position();
    var fooOffset = $foo.offset();
    var barOffset = $bar.offset();

    var $fooOffsetParent = $foo.offsetParent();
    var $barOffsetParent = $bar.offsetParent();

    $results
        .append('<p>#foo position.top: ' + fooPosition.top + '</p>') // 10
        .append('<p>#foo position.left: ' + fooPosition.left + '</p>') // 10
```

```
    .append('<p>#bar position.top: ' + barPosition.top + '</p>') // 0
    .append('<p>#bar position.left: ' + barPosition.left + '</p>') // 0

    .append('<p>#foo offset.top: ' + fooOffset.top + '</p>') // 10
    .append('<p>#foo offset.left: ' + fooOffset.left + '</p>') // 10
    .append('<p>#bar offset.top: ' + barOffset.top + '</p>') // 10
    .append('<p>#bar offset.left: ' + barOffset.left + '</p>') // 10

    .append('<p>ID of #foo offsetParent: '
        + $fooOffsetParent.attr('id')) // the_offset_parent
    .append('<p>ID of #bar offsetParent: '
        + $barOffsetParent.attr('id')); // foo
});
```

Discussion

The important thing to remember is this: the offset method will always give you an element's position relative to the document. The return value of the position method *may* be the element's position relative to the document, depending on whether the element has an offsetParent. If the element has an offsetParent—that is, a parent element that has positioning applied to it—then the position method will provide information about the position of the element relative to the offsetParent, *not* to the document.

 jQuery's offsetParent method provides a replacement for the standard JavaScript offsetParent DOM node property. In certain cases—such as when an element has a fixed position—some browsers will return null when asked for the offsetParent property of the element.

6.4 Scrolling an Element into View

Problem

You want to scroll the document or an element to bring another element into view.

Solution: Scrolling the Whole Window

If you need to scroll the whole window, you'll use the offset method to determine the location of the destination element relative to the document and then use the scrollTop method to scroll the document to bring the element into view.

For example, let's say you want to scroll to the #foo element when the user clicks the #bar element:

```
jQuery('#bar').click(function() {
    var fooOffset = jQuery('#foo').offset(),
        destination = fooOffset.top;
    jQuery(document).scrollTop(destination);
});
```

Solution: Scrolling Inside an Element

If your destination element is inside a scrolling container, you'll use the `position` method to determine the location of the destination element relative to the container, add it to the current scroll position of the container, and then use the `scrollTop` method to scroll the container to bring the element into view. Note that the scrolling container must be positioned—using `position: relative`, `position: absolute`, or `position: fixed`—in order for this to work.

For example, consider the following markup, styled so that #foo is not large enough to show both paragraphs at once.

```
<head>
    <style>
    #foo {
    width:300px;
    padding:10px;
    height:20px;
    border:1px solid black;
    overflow:auto;
    position:relative;
    }
    </style>
</head>
<body>
    <input type="button" id="bar" value="Click to scroll to last paragraph" />
    <input type="button" id="bam" value="Click to scroll to last paragraph with
animation" />
    <div id="foo">
    <p>This is the first paragraph. Lorem ipsum dolor sit amet, consectetur
adipisicing elit, sed do eiusmod tempor incididunt ut labore et dolore magna
aliqua. Ut enim ad minim veniam, quis nostrud exercitation ullamco laboris nisi
ut aliquip ex ea commodo consequat. Duis aute irure dolor in reprehenderit in
voluptate velit esse cillum dolore eu fugiat nulla pariatur. Excepteur sint
occaecat cupidatat non proident, sunt in culpa qui officia deserunt mollit anim
id est laborum.</p>
    <p>This is the second paragraph. Lorem ipsum dolor sit amet, consectetur
adipisicing elit, sed do eiusmod tempor incididunt ut labore et dolore magna
aliqua. Ut enim ad minim veniam, quis nostrud exercitation ullamco laboris nisi
ut aliquip ex ea commodo consequat. Duis aute irure dolor in reprehenderit in
voluptate velit esse cillum dolore eu fugiat nulla pariatur. Excepteur sint
occaecat cupidatat non proident, sunt in culpa qui officia deserunt mollit anim
id est laborum.</p>
    <!-- several more paragraphs -->
    </div>
</body>
```

Scrolling #foo to show the last paragraph is simple:

```
var $foo = jQuery('#foo');
$('#bar').click(function() {
    var lastParagraphPosition = jQuery('#foo p:last').position();
    var scrollPosition = $foo.scrollTop() + lastParagraphPosition.top;
    $foo.scrollTop(scrollPosition);
});
```

In both of these examples, the scrolling happens instantaneously—efficient, but not necessarily attractive. The animate method will animate an element's **scrollTop** property, so animating the transition is trivial. Here's how we would do it for the scrolling container:

```
var $foo = jQuery('#foo');
$('#bam').click(function() {
    var lastParagraphPosition = jQuery('#foo p:last').position();
    var scrollPosition = $foo.scrollTop() + lastParagraphPosition.top;
    jQuery('#foo').animate({scrollTop: scrollPosition}, 300);
});
```

 jQuery also includes a **scrollLeft** method, with behavior analogous to scrollTop.

6.5 Determining Whether an Element Is Within the Viewport

Problem

You want to determine whether an element is visible within the viewport; further, you want to determine the percentage of the element that is visible and scroll to it if it is less than 50 percent visible.

Solution

This makes use of several of the methods discussed in earlier sections of this chapter.

There are several steps to this process:

1. Determine the size of the viewport.
2. Determine the scroll position of the document.
3. Figure out the minimum and maximum values for the top and left positions of the element if the element is visible.
4. Test the position of the element against those values.

```
jQuery(document).ready(function() {
    var viewportWidth = jQuery(window).width(),
        viewportHeight = jQuery(window).height(),

        documentScrollTop = jQuery(document).scrollTop(),
        documentScrollLeft = jQuery(document).scrollLeft(),

        minTop = documentScrollTop,
        maxTop = documentScrollTop + viewportHeight,
        minLeft = documentScrollLeft,
        maxLeft = documentScrollLeft + viewportWidth,
```

```
        $myElement = jQuery('#myElement'),
        elementOffset = $myElement.offset();
    if (
        (elementOffset.top > minTop && elementOffset.top < maxTop) &&
        (elementOffset.left > minLeft &&elementOffset.left < maxLeft)
    ) {
        alert('element is visible');
    } else {
        alert('element is not visible');
    }
});
```

With this solution, we know whether the top of the element is visible in the viewport; a better solution would test whether the entire element was contained in the viewport:

```
jQuery(document).ready(function() {
    var viewportWidth = jQuery(window).width(),
        viewportHeight = jQuery(window).height(),
        documentScrollTop = jQuery(document).scrollTop(),
        documentScrollLeft = jQuery(document).scrollLeft(),

        $myElement = jQuery('#myElement'),

        elementOffset = $myElement.offset(),
        elementHeight = $myElement.height(),
        elementWidth = $myElement.width(),

        minTop = documentScrollTop,
        maxTop = documentScrollTop + viewportHeight,
        minLeft = documentScrollLeft,
        maxLeft = documentScrollLeft + viewportWidth;

    if (
        (elementOffset.top > minTop && elementOffset.top + elementHeight < maxTop) &&
        (elementOffset.left > minLeft && elementOffset.left + elementWidth < maxLeft)
    ) {
        alert('entire element is visible');
    } else {
        alert('entire element is not visible');
    }
});
```

Alternatively, we could look at how much of the element is visible—if it is less than a certain amount, then we can scroll to the element:

```
jQuery(document).ready(function() {

var viewportWidth = jQuery(window).width(),
    viewportHeight = jQuery(window).height(),

    documentScrollTop = jQuery(document).scrollTop(),
    documentScrollLeft = jQuery(document).scrollLeft(),

    $myElement = jQuery('#myElement'),

    verticalVisible, horizontalVisible,
```

```
        elementOffset = $myElement.offset(),
        elementHeight = $myElement.height(),
        elementWidth = $myElement.width(),

        minTop = documentScrollTop,
        maxTop = documentScrollTop + viewportHeight,
        minLeft = documentScrollLeft,
        maxLeft = documentScrollLeft + viewportWidth;

    function scrollToPosition(position) {
        jQuery('html,body').animate({
            scrollTop : position.top,
            scrollLeft : position.left
        }, 300);
    }

    if (
        ((elementOffset.top > minTop && elementOffset.top < maxTop) ||
        (elementOffset.top + elementHeight > minTop && elementOffset.top +
    elementHeight < maxTop))
    &&
        ((elementOffset.left > minLeft && elementOffset.left < maxLeft) ||
        (elementOffset.left + elementWidth > minLeft && elementOffset.left +
    elementWidth < maxLeft))
    ) {
        alert('some portion of the element is visible');

        if (elementOffset.top >= minTop && elementOffset.top + elementHeight
    <= maxTop) {
            verticalVisible = elementHeight;
        } else if (elementOffset.top < minTop) {
            verticalVisible = elementHeight - (minTop - elementOffset.top);
        } else {
            verticalVisible = maxTop - elementOffset.top;
        }

        if (elementOffset.left >= minLeft && elementOffset.left + elementWidth
    <= maxLeft) {
            horizontalVisible = elementWidth;
        } else if (elementOffset.left < minLeft) {
            horizontalVisible = elementWidth - (minLeft - elementOffset.left);
        } else {
            horizontalVisible = maxLeft - elementOffset.left;
        }

        var percentVerticalVisible = (verticalVisible / elementHeight) * 100;
        var percentHorizontalVisible = (horizontalVisible / elementWidth) * 100;

        if (percentVerticalVisible < 50 || percentHorizontalVisible < 50) {
            alert('less than 50% of element visible; scrolling');
            scrollToPosition(elementOffset);
        } else {
            alert('enough of the element is visible that there is no need to scroll');
        }
```

```
    } else {
        // element is not visible; scroll to it
        alert('element is not visible; scrolling');
        scrollToPosition(elementOffset);
    }

});
```

 The scrollTo plugin (*http://jquery-cookbook.com/go/plugin-scrollto*) by
Ariel Flesler provides excellent shorthand access to many of these methods by allowing you to simply write `$.scrollTo('#myElement')`; it takes
care of determining the position of the destination element.

6.6 Centering an Element Within the Viewport

Problem

You want to scroll the window to center an element within the viewport.

Solution

Get the viewport's dimensions; determine the width, height, and offset of the element;
and use a little math to center the element in the viewport:

```
jQuery(document).ready(function() {
    jQuery('#bar').click(function() {
        var viewportWidth = jQuery(window).width(),
            viewportHeight = jQuery(window).height(),

            $foo = jQuery('#foo'),
            elWidth = $foo.width(),
            elHeight = $foo.height(),
            elOffset = $foo.offset();

        jQuery(window)
            .scrollTop(elOffset.top + (elHeight/2) - (viewportHeight/2))
            .scrollLeft(elOffset.left + (elWidth/2) - (viewportWidth/2));
    });
});
```

In the final lines, we add the top offset of the element to half the element's height in
order to determine the vertical center of the element. Then we subtract half the viewport's height to determine the position to which we want the window to scroll. Finally,
we do an analogous calculation to center the viewport horizontally.

6.7 Absolutely Positioning an Element at Its Current Position

Problem

You want to turn a static or relatively positioned element into being absolutely positioned.

Solution

To accomplish this, we simply get the position of the element and then use it to set the element's CSS properties accordingly:

```
var $myElement = jQuery('#foo p').eq(0),
        elPosition = $myElement.position();

    $myElement.css({
        position : 'absolute',
        top : elPosition.top,
        left : elPosition.left
    });
```

We can also easily reposition an element relative to its current position:

```
var $myElement = jQuery('#foo p').eq(1),
        elPosition = $myElement.position();

    $myElement.css({
        position : 'absolute',
        top : elPosition.top + 20,
        left : elPosition.left + 20
    });
```

6.8 Positioning an Element Relative to Another Element

Problem

You want to position a new element relative to an existing element.

Solution

Get the width, height, and offset of the existing element, and use the values to position the new element accordingly.

Given the following HTML:

```
<style>
#foo {
    width: 300px;
    height: 100px;
    border: 1px solid red;
    padding: 5px;
}
```

```
#tooltip {
    border: 1px solid black;
    padding: 5px;
    background-color: #fff;
}
</style>

<div id="foo">An existing element</div>
```

the following code would add an element as a sibling to the existing element but positioned "inside" the element, 10 pixels from the top and 10 pixels from the left of the existing element's top-left corner, and with a width 20 pixels less than that of the existing element:

```
jQuery(document).ready(function() {
    var $foo = jQuery('#foo'),
        fooPosition = $foo.position(),
        $tooltip = $('<div id="tooltip">A new element</div>').insertAfter($foo);

    $tooltip.css({
        position : 'absolute',
        top : fooPosition.top + 10,
        left : fooPosition.left + 10,
        width : $foo.width() - 20
    });
});
```

If you wanted to add the new element somewhere else in the page—that is, if you didn't want it to be a sibling of the existing element—you could adjust your code to look at the offset of the original element rather than the position:

```
jQuery(document).ready(function() {
    var $foo = jQuery('#foo'),
        fooOffset = $foo.offset(),
        $tooltip = $('<div id="tooltip">A new element</div>').appendTo('body');

    $tooltip.css({
        position : 'absolute',
        top : fooOffset.top + 10,
        left : fooOffset.left + ($foo.width() / 2),
        width : $foo.width() - 20
    });
});
```

6.9 Switching Stylesheets Based on Browser Width

Problem

You want to change the document's CSS based on the width of the browser.

Solutions

There are a few solutions to this problem. One changes the `class` attribute of the body element, another changes the `href` attribute of the stylesheet you want to change, and the third includes all size-related stylesheets on the page but enables only one of them at a time.

In each case, we'll create a function that checks the width of the browser and bind that function to the document's `ready` event and to the window's `resize` event. The `checkWidth` function will then call the `setSize` function, which we'll define based on the approach we're taking:

```
var checkWidth = function() {
    var browserWidth = $(window).width();
    if (browserWidth < 960) {
        setSize('small');
    } else {
        setSize('large');
    }
};

jQuery(document).ready(function() {
    checkWidth();
    $(window).resize(checkWidth);
});
```

The definition of the `setSize` function depends on how you want to switch styles.

Solution 1: Changing the Class on the Body Element

```
var setSize = function(size) {
    var $body = jQuery('body');
    jQuery('body').removeClass('large small').addClass(size);
};
```

Solution 2: Changing the href Attribute of the Stylesheet That's Responsible for Size-Related Styling

Let's assume you have the following size-related stylesheet in your document:

```
<link rel="stylesheet" type="text/css" id="css_size" href="size-small.css" />
```

In this case, you would define the `setSize` function as follows:

```
var setSize = function(size) {
    var $css = jQuery('#css_size');
    $css.attr('href', 'size-' + size + '.css');
};
```

Note that in this case, the new CSS file is requested from the server, which is likely to cause a brief delay in the style change occurring. For this reason, this is perhaps the least-preferable method.

Solution 3: Include All Size-Related Stylesheets in the Page, but Enable Only One at a Time

```
<link rel="stylesheet" type="text/css" class="css_size small" href="size-small.css" />
<link rel="alternate stylesheet" type="text/css" class="css_size large"
    href="size-large.css" disabled=true/>
```

In this case, you would define the setSize function as follows:

```
var setSize = function(size) {

    jQuery('link.css_size').each(function() {
        var $this = $(this);
        if ($this.hasClass(size)) {
            $this
                .removeAttr('disabled')
                .attr('rel', 'stylesheet');
        } else {
            $this
                .attr('disabled', true)
                .attr('rel', 'alternate stylesheet');
        }
    });
};
```

In this approach, all stylesheets are loaded at page load, and nothing new is fetched when switching from one stylesheet to another. This eliminates the delay caused by solution 2 but it also results in potentially unnecessary HTTP requests if your user is unlikely to need the alternate stylesheets.

Discussion

There is no definitive answer to which of the three style-switching methods is the best. When choosing a method, you'll want to consider how likely your users are to need a different stylesheet, how big your size-related stylesheets are, and how you prefer to manage your size-related styles. In many cases, the method from the first solution will be both sufficient and preferable.

Effects

Remy Sharp

7.0 Introduction

Out of the box, jQuery comes with a number of preset effects and the robust low-level animation method for creating your own custom effects.

The preset effects include the following:

- Hiding and showing elements in a toggle fashion
- Scaling and simultaneously fading elements in and out of view
- Sliding up and down and toggling
- Fading in and out and to a specific opacity

All of the preset effects support speeds and callback functions to trigger upon completion.

In addition to these predefined effects, there are also a number of utilities that can help you take more control over your animations:

- `:animated` selector to assess whether an element is in the process of being animated
- The ability to turn off and on all effects across the board
- The ability to add to the animation queue with your own bespoke functions
- Function to change the entire queue of animations

 It's worth noting that the canned animation methods, `hide` (with a duration) and `slideUp`, reduce the margin and padding on the element as they approach zero height. This may affect how you want to mark up the page and CSS for your effect. Also note that jQuery doesn't *officially* support effects in documents using QuirksMode.

Animate Method

Using the `animate` method gives you complete control over the animation to roll your own bespoke effect. Using the `animate` method, you can do the following:

- Control CSS properties (limited to numerical properties only)
- Control `scrollTop` and `scrollLeft` DOM properties (if the element has overflow)
- Use any CSS unit of measure, e.g., pixels, ems, inches, or percentages for the end point values
- Specify the end point of the effect as a fixed value or a relative value from the element's current state
- Use `toggle` as a value to flip between states, e.g., `opacity: toggle`
- Specify an easing method to run the animation over
- Set callbacks at all points of the animation: on each step of the animation and when it finishes
- Specify whether the animation should queue or run immediately allowing for simultaneous animations

When specifying properties to animate, they must be written using camel case, e.g. `marginLeft` rather than `margin-left`. If you don't do it this way, nothing will animate!

Animation Speeds

The `speed` parameter can be specified using either milliseconds or a few predefined strings:

- `slow` has a value of 600 milliseconds.
- `fast` has a value of 200 milliseconds.

If a speed isn't explicitly passed in to the animation functions, the animation will run at a default speed of 400 milliseconds.

If you explicitly pass in a speed of zero, then the animation will run like the `.css()` function, but as of jQuery 1.3, the method call will run *synchronously* rather than *asynchronously* like all other animations would do.

Effects Template

Unless otherwise stated in the recipe, we will use the following template for all the examples, applying a different jQuery snippet for each solution:

```
<!DOCTYPE html PUBLIC "-//W3C//DTD XHTML 1.0 Transitional//EN"
  "http://www.w3.org/TR/xhtml1/DTD/xhtml1-transitional.dtd">
<html>
<head>
  <title>Chapter 6</title>
  <link rel="stylesheet" href="chapter6.css" type="text/css" />
  <script src="jquery-latest.js" type="text/javascript"></script>
</head>
<body id="single">
  <input type="button" id="animate" value="animate" />
  <div class="box">
  <p>Lorem ipsum dolor sit amet, consectetur adipisicing elit, sed do
    eiusmod tempor incididunt ut labore et dolore magna aliqua.</p>
  </div>
</body>
</html>
```

All the individual examples are available online at *http://jquery-cookbook.com/exam ples/06/*, including a complete amalgamated version of the recipes.

7.1 Sliding and Fading Elements in and out of View

Problem

We want to reveal or toggle a block of content into view. This can be triggered by the user clicking some element or can be fired by some other event.

Rather than just showing and hiding, which could be jarring visually, we want to create a gradual effect to reveal the content into view.

For these solutions, I've assumed we want to allow the user to toggle the effect.

Solution

For reference, if we were *just* to show the element, our code would be as follows:

```
$(document).ready(function () {
  $('#animate').click(function () {
    $('.box').show();
  });
);
```

If we were to *toggle* the box but just toggle from visible and hidden, we would use the following instead of .show():

```
$('.box').toggle();
```

However, our solution wants to be a little more visually engaging than just toggling the display property. So, let's look at using the slide and fade methods:

Slide

```
$(document).ready(function () {
  $('#animate').click(function () {
    $('.box').slideToggle('slow');
  });
});
```

Fade

Because there's no opacity toggle function, either we can use a combination of fadeIn and fadeOut:

```
$(document).ready(function () {
  $('#animate').click(function () {
    var $box = $('.box');
    if ($box.is(':visible')) {
      $box.fadeOut('slow');
    } else {
      $box.fadeIn('slow');
    }
  });
});
```

or we can create our own fade toggle animation, using the fadeTo method:

```
$(document).ready(function () {
  $('#animate').click(function () {
    $('.box').fadeTo('slow', 'toggle');
  });
});
```

However, I'm of the opinion that it reads better for future maintenance if we use the animate method:

```
$(document).ready(function () {
  $('#animate').click(function () {
    $('.box').animate({ opacity : 'toggle' }, 'slow');
  });
});
```

Both

If we want to toggle the height and opacity together, we can reuse the previous solution and add the height to toggle at the same time. This would cause the box to fade out *and* slide up at the same time:

```
$(document).ready(function () {
  $('#animate').click(function () {
    $('.box').animate({
      opacity : 'toggle',
      height: 'toggle'
    }, 'slow');
  });
});
```

Discussion

As we can see from the previous solutions, the slide and fade methods are the next step up from the straight show (and hide) and toggle methods. The slide methods come in the following flavors:

- `slideUp`
- `slideDown`
- `slideToggle`

The fade methods don't have an explicit toggle feature, but it can be achieved. Fading has the following methods:

- `fadeIn`
- `fadeOut`
- `fadeTo`

With the exception of `fadeTo`, all these methods take `speed` as the first parameter and a *callback function* as the second—both of which are optional. The callback function is executed once the animation is complete, and the context is set to the element the animation ran against; i.e., the `this` variable is the current element.

The reason I would choose to use `animate` over `fadeTo` to toggle opacity is that the `fadeTo` parameters read the wrong way around. If a new developer were coming to the code, using the animate function almost reads as plain English, therefore making it easier to skim and understand what is happening in the code.

It's worth also adding that if you use the `show` (or `hide`) method using a speed, it will animate the height, width, opacity, margin, and padding all in one animation, as shown in Figure 7-1.

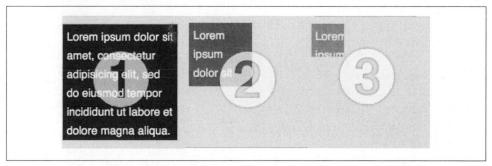

Figure 7-1. Passing a speed in to the show method animates height, width, padding, margin, and opacity

7.2 Making Elements Visible by Sliding Them Up

Problem

You want to slide the content block into view, but the UI design dictates that the content must slide *upward* when being revealed. The slideUp method would hide the element, reducing the height from the top position.

To slide upward, we need to use CSS to position the element and then consider the content that we are revealing.

Solution

HTML

We need to absolutely position the element we are animating to get it to *stick* to the bottom position so it can animate upward when revealing.

To achieve this, we need to wrap the animating element in another <div> (or the element that suits your design) and give it a position: relative style. (This may also be position: absolute. We just need a defined position to trigger the position: absolute on #revealUp to position relatively to; however, since we want the document to flow *normally*, we've used position: relative.)

```
<div class="box">
  <div id="revealUp">
    <p>Lorem ipsum dolor sit amet, consectetur adipisicing elit, sed do
    eiusmod tempor incididunt ut labore et dolore magna aliqua.</p>
  </div>
</div>
```

CSS

Now we need to give the box element a relative position so that we can absolutely position #revealUp relative to it:

```
.box {
  position: relative;
}

#revealUp {
  position: absolute;
  overflow: hidden;
  display: none;
  bottom: 0;
  background-color: #c00;
  height: 0;
}
```

jQuery

We can toggle the `#revealUp` based on the element's height. We're going to longer lengths to animate the height upward (by checking the current height) rather than just using `slideToggle()`—but we'll look at why in the discussion:

```
$(document).ready(function () {
  $('#animate').click(function () {
    var $box = $('#revealUp');

    if ($box.height() > 0) {
      $box.animate({ height : 0 });
    } else {
      $box.animate({ height : '100%' });
    }
  });
});
```

Discussion

This solution requires that we check the height of the box to then determine how we proceed.

Notice how we don't use `slideToggle`, which behind the scenes is very similar, if not the same as, using `.animate({ height: 'toggle' })`.

The reason we're not using the toggle is that for the toggle to work correctly, it needs to capture the *real* height from somewhere. As the element starts with a height of zero, jQuery has no way to work out what the full height is. If we used `slideToggle`, the `#revealUp` element appears briefly as a 1-pixel slither and then disappears again. This is because there's no real height to animate to.

Instead, we determine whether the height is great than zero and then animate the height accordingly. Since the element is nested within another element with `position: relative`, we can give it a height of 100 percent, and it will grow to fill the space.

 In the recipe, I have used `overflow: hidden`. However, if the font size is increased by the user, my example hides some of the content. In your real solutions, make sure you test that the content is still available when the font size is increased, and consider either ensuring that the revealing box is large enough for the content or using `overflow: auto` on the `#revealUp` element.

7.3 Creating a Horizontal Accordion

Problem

The jQuery UI library supports vertical accordions out of the box, and in fact there are a few simple code snippets that can be used to create a rudimentary accordion effect.

However, making the accordion run horizontally requires specific CSS and a slightly different take on the jQuery code.

For this solution we won't be using the template, because the markup is different for the horizontal accordion.

Solution

HTML

```html
<div id="accordionWrapper">
  <h3 class="red"><a href="#red">Red</a></h3>
  <div id="red" class="box"><p>Lorem ipsum dolor sit amet, consectetur
adipisicing.</p></div>

  <h3 class="green"><a href="#green">Green</a></h3>
  <div id="green" class="box"><p>Lorem ipsum dolor sit amet, consectetur
adipisicing.</p></div>

  <h3 class="blue"><a href="#blue">Blue</a></h3>
  <div id="blue" class="box"><p>Lorem ipsum dolor sit amet, consectetur
adipisicing.</p></div>
</div>
```

CSS

```css
#accordionWrapper {
  margin: 10px;
}

#accordionWrapper h3 a {
  text-indent: -9999px;
  height: 150px;
  width: 50px;
  float: left;
}

#accordionWrapper .red {
  background: #c00 url(images/red.png) no-repeat;
}

#accordionWrapper .green {
  background: #0c0 url(images/green.png) no-repeat;
}

#accordionWrapper .blue {
  background: #00c url(images/blue.png) no-repeat;
}

#accordionWrapper div.box {
  float: left;
  height: 150px;
  width: 150px;
  border: 0;
```

```
    margin: 0;

    /* to cancel the image from .red, etc */
    background-image: none;
}
```

jQuery

```
$.fn.horizontalAccordion = function (speed) {
  return this.each(function () {
    var $accordionHeaders = $(this).find('h3'),
      $open = $accordionHeaders.next().filter(':first'),
      width = $open.outerWidth();

    // initialize the display
    $accordionHeaders.next().filter(':not(:first)').css({ display : 'none', width : 0
});

    $accordionHeaders.click(function () {
      if ($open.prev().get(0) == this) {
        return;
      }
      $open.animate({ width: 0 }, { duration : speed });
      $open = $(this).next().animate({ width : width }, { duration : speed });
    });
  });
};

$(document).ready(function () {
  $('#accordionWrapper').horizontalAccordion(200);
});
```

Discussion

The HTML and CSS lay the accordion out so that the elements within it are all floated to the left. If you used this on a web page, you would probably expect to have to add a clearing element directly after the accordion to allow the following content to flow properly.

By floating the elements to the left, our accordion is set up with the h3 > a as the title to the content panel.

If CSS and JavaScript are disabled, then the content flows correctly and is readable by, for instance, Google's search engine.

If CSS is turned on but JavaScript isn't, the default view is to see all the content panels.

Using jQuery, we initialize the display by hiding all the panels except the first, and we hook click handlers to the headers to slide the content in and out of view.

The horizontal accordion has been written as a jQuery plugin, in particular to show that we don't need to hard-code any variables within the accordion effect. We only pass the duration speed variable in to the plugin, which determines the duration of the effect. We could easily upgrade this plugin to also take an easing or callback.

It's important to note that throughout this code, all the click handling and navigation of the DOM happens around the `<h3>` element, *not* the `<a>` element. This still works, keeping the code relatively simple (instead of having to navigate up and down from the `<a>` element to get the parent `<h3>` then the adjacent `<div>` element), but more importantly, offers keyboard accessibility because the `<a>` elements can be tabbed on to and triggered via the keyboard. We don't have to bind the click handler to the `<a>` element, because when the `<a>` element has the click event triggered (via clicking or the keyboard), it *bubbles* up through the DOM and is caught by our click handler on the `<h3>` element.

The plugin first collects the necessary parts of the accordion: the header, which will be clickable; the first visible panel, and the width of the panels (note that this version of the plugin works only for equal sized panels):

```
var $accordionHeaders = $(this).find('h3'),
```

`this` is the current accordion wrapper element, typically a `<div>`.

From the accordion wrapper, our code collects all the `<h3>` elements. Note that we will make use of `next()` and `prev()` to change our DOM collection from the `<h3>` to the next nodes in the DOM tree, in particular the accordion content panels:

```
$open = $accordionHeaders.next().filter(':first'),
```

`$open` is a temporary variable that will point to the current visible panel. We can't use `.is(':visible')` because we're actually reducing the width and the panel still has a CSS property of `display: block`. So, we will keep track of the current panel through this `$open` variable:

```
width = $open.outerWidth();
```

Finally in the initialization, we capture the width of the open panel so that we can animate the width of the panels correctly.

Two tasks are left:

- Initialize the view of panels, showing only the first panel
- Bind the click handles to show and hide the panels

To initialize the view, we must hide all the panels except the first. We must also set the width to zero to allow for the animate function to increase the width, rather than making it *pop* out when it is shown.

To achieve this, we use an inverse filter from the `$open` variable, in particular `:not(:first)`:

```
$accordionHeaders.next().filter(':not(:first)').css({ display : 'none', width : 0 });
```

Once we have our selection of panels that are *not the first*, we change the CSS properties to initialize them.

Finally, we attach the click handler.

Remembering that the `$accordionHeaders` variable contains the `h3` elements, the first thing we do is say this: if the `<h3>` clicked is the same as the currently open panel, then don't do anything.

Since the `$open` variable is the panel, we use `.prev()` to navigate to the previous `<h3>` element and test whether it matches the current context of the clicked element.

If the clicked element is not the current open panel, we animate the `$open` panel width to zero, and the current clicked panel to the captured width.

Notice the very last line of the click handler:

```
$open = $(this).next().animate({ width : width }, { duration : speed });
```

Because jQuery usually returns jQuery (except when getting a value) and we're animating the panel that will now be open, we can capture this at the same time in the `$open` variable, thus overwriting it with the latest panel.

7.4 Simultaneously Sliding and Fading Elements

When some part of the web page is hidden and is shown to the user only on a specific action, sometimes a simple show/hide isn't enough. We want to create more pleasing effects for our visitors.

Depending on the layout of the page, an instant show/hide effect may not make it entirely clear to the visitor what content was revealed. This is another advantage of sliding an element into view because it gives a visual cue to the visitor where the page layout is changing.

We could use jQuery's built-in show method with a duration because this *almost* does the job, but not quite because it also animates the width of the element, as shown earlier in Figure 7-1. As you also noted earlier, the show method will animate any padding and margin around the element, so to solve the problem we will use the animate function to create a custom effect.

Solution

Use the animation function to *toggle* both the height and the opacity at the same time:

```
$(document).ready(function () {
  $('#animate').click(function () {
    $('.box').animate({ opacity: 'toggle', height: 'toggle' });
    return false;
  });
});
```

Discussion

Using the `animate` method allows us to specify exactly which CSS properties we want to animate for the effect.

We are also using `toggle` as the end point value. This way, the `animate` method takes the current height in the initial state and toggles it to either zero or 100 percent of the initial state.

In our example, the initial state of the box is visible. If we want it to slide and fade *into* view, then we only need to set the display property to `none` in the stylesheet.

Warning: there is no need to set the height to zero in the style; in fact, doing so will mean the animate won't expand to the correct height because it will toggle back and forth between zero height (from the CSS) and zero height and display none (the final point of `slideUp`).

7.5 Applying Sequential Effects

Problem

You want an effect to occur on one set of elements after another effect occurs on a different set of elements. This is simple to solve if you just have one other effect to execute, but if you want to apply the effect one-by-one to *any* number of elements, the code *could* become difficult to maintain.

Solution

This solution uses the standard template outlined at the beginning of this chapter, except that we have multiple copies of the `div.box` element on the page. This solution is designed as such that we can be dealing with any number of `div.box` elements, from just one single element to many, because the automatic sequence solution can handle them all.

Manual callback

The basic approach to applying sequential effects would be to use the callback. This would also be used if the next effect is different from the first:

```
$(document).ready(function () {
  var $boxes = $('.box').hide();

  $('#animate').click(function () {
    $boxes.eq(0).fadeIn('slow', function () {
      $boxes.eq(1).slideDown('slow');
    });
  });
});
```

Automatic sequence

This alternative method, based on Dave Methvin's solution, will repeat in sequence the effect on any number of elements:

```
$(document).ready(function () {
  var $boxes = $('.box').hide(),
    div = 0;

  $('#animate').click(function () {
    $($boxes[div++] || []).fadeIn('slow', arguments.callee);
  });
});
```

Discussion

The simple solution uses the callback feature to then step in to the next animation in the sequence. The selector we use targets the first `div.box`; however, this doesn't scale because it is expecting there to be two and only two animated elements. Any less and the code breaks. Any more, and some elements will be missed.

If we have many more, or even an unknown number of elements we need to animate in sequence, then Dave Methvin's solution is perfect.

There are two tricks to the code. The first is the failover to an empty array:

```
$($boxes[div++] || [])
```

This code increments the index counter, and if the element doesn't exist, it passes an empty array to jQuery.

When the jQuery result set is empty, running an animation doesn't do anything. Since the result is empty, jQuery *doesn't* pass any DOM elements to the chained call, and therefore any callbacks given to the chained method *won't* be called either.

For example, if we ran the following code, the alert box would never appear—which is a key ingredient to making this recipe work:

```
$('made-up-element').show(function () {
  alert('will never appear');
});
```

The second trick to this recipe is the callback argument:

```
arguments.callee
```

`arguments` is a keyword in JavaScript referring to a local variable that all functions have access to. The `arguments` object is similar to any array but does not have any of the array methods (such as `slice`) or properties except `length`.

`arguments` also contains a reference to the currently executing function in the `arguments.callee` property. This is useful for recursive function calls, which is exactly how we are using the property in this solution.

This solution says to keep incrementing through the `$boxes` jQuery collection and, on completion of the animation, recursively execute the function. This continues until the `<div>` index goes beyond the length of the `$boxes` jQuery collection (`$boxes.length`), at which point an empty array is used as the jQuery collection, and thus the callback is not executed, causing the code to finish running.

7.6 Determining Whether Elements Are Currently Being Animated

Problem

When an animation is in progress, we may want to prevent the user from triggering the animation to run again until the initial animation has finished.

An example of this may be if the user clicks a button to trigger some animation. This could be to reveal some piece of information. For our particular contrived example, when the user clicks the button, we will shake the box back and forth.

If the user keeps clicking the button, we won't want to keep queuing animations, so we need to test whether the animation is already running and, if it is, ignore the request to animate.

Solution

For this solution, I want to include some debugging information, so I've included a `<div>` element with the ID of `debug`, and we'll append log messages to this to help us see what's happening.

We will use the `:animated` custom jQuery selector to test whether the animation is running:

```
$(document).ready(function () {
  var speed = 100;

  $('#animate').click(function () {
    $('.box')
      .filter(':not(:animated)')
      .animate({ marginLeft: -10 }, speed, function () {
        $('#debug').append('<p>Starting animation.<p>');
      })
      .animate({ marginLeft: 10 }, speed)
      .animate({ marginLeft: -10}, speed)
      .animate({ marginLeft: 10 }, speed)
      .animate({ marginLeft: -10}, speed)
      .animate({ marginLeft: 10 }, speed)
```

```
        .animate({ marginLeft: 0}, speed, function () {
          $('#debug').append('<p>Finished animation.</p>');
        }); // end of our long chain
    });
  });
```

Discussion

In this contrived example, we use multiple calls to the `animate` method to make the box shake back and forth (though if this were required in reality, it might be better to use a bouncing easing instead!).

This animation is triggered when the user clicks the animate button.

I have included two callback functions to show when the animation starts and finishes. Note that even though there are several lines, because of the way chaining works, this is in fact one single line of JavaScript starting from `$('.box')` and ending on `}); // end of our long chain`.

The following line of jQuery filters out any `div.box` element that is currently being animated from our collection and only running the subsequent animations on the remaining elements:

```
    .filter(':not(:animated)')
```

Since we have a single `div.box` element in our example, the animation will run only if the element isn't animating already.

7.7 Stopping and Resetting Animations

Problem

If an animation is running, we may be required to stop it in midflow. A common problem is seen when using a mouseover and a mouseout to trigger an animation to show and hide a particular block of content.

If the mouse is run in and out of the trigger area, the animation continuously triggers; for example, the content block would keep sliding up and down until it completed the number of times it was triggered.

One approach could be to use the `:animated` selector to filter out the element for animation. However, you may want to fade an element back out of view when the user moves the mouse away from the trigger rather than letting it complete. This can be solved with the `stop()` method.

Solution

We have added a CSS style to the `div.box` element to set the opacity to zero.

Instead of having the user *click* the button to trigger the effect, we're running the animation when the mouse *hovers* over the button. This is just to show that without the `stop()` calls, the animation would run out of control:

```
$(document).ready(function () {
  $('#animate').hover(function () {
    $('.box').stop().fadeTo(200, 1);
  }, function () {
    $('.box').stop().fadeTo(200, 0);
  });
});
```

Discussion

Typically this problem would be solved using a combination of `fadeIn()` and `fadeOut()`. However, if this were used, firstly without `stop()`, then the effect keeps repeating each time the mouse hovers over the button.

To prevent this, we insert the `stop()` command before queuing on the next animation. The big advantage of this is that it stops the animation midflow. This means if the opacity of the element is at 0.5 (or 50 in IE), it will proceed with the next animation with the starting point of 0.5.

Since we are now stopping in the middle of the opacity animation, it also means we can't properly use `fadeIn()` and `fadeOut()`. We have to explicitly state where we want to fade to. So, now we are using `fadeTo()`, passing in the duration and then the target opacity.

Now when the user moves their mouse back and forth over the button, the animation doesn't repeat but fades in and out in a single smooth transition.

7.8 Using Custom Easing Methods for Effects

Problem

jQuery comes with only two built-in easing functions: `swing` and `linear`. The default is `swing`. If we want to make our animations a little more interesting, then we might want to use a different easing function—this could give us a bounce animation, or elastic, or perhaps just an animation that slows down as it's coming to its end.

We can manually add easing functions, but we can also include a predefined collection using the `jquery.easing` plugin, which can be downloaded from *http://jquery-cookbook .com/go/easing/*.

Solution

By first including `jquery.easing.1.3.js` after we include the jQuery library, we can now make use of any one of the 31 new easing functions:

```
$(document).ready(function () {
  $('#animate').click(function () {
    $('.box').animate({ scrollTop: '+=100' },
      { duration: 400, easing: 'easeOutElastic' });
  });
});
```

Discussion

By including the easing library, we can specify a large range of values in the `easing` property in the `options` parameter. The `animate` method also supports passing `easing` as the third parameter, so the preceding solution could be written as follows:

```
$('.box').animate({ scrollTop: '+=100' }, 400, 'easeOutElastic');
```

To create your own custom easing function, you can extend the `easing` object using this:

```
jQuery.extend(jQuery.easing, {
  customEasing: function(x, t, b, c, d) {
    return c*(t/=d)*t + b;
  },
});
```

The preceding example is the equation for the `easeInQuad` easing. All easing functions take five parameters:

fraction
> The current position of the animation, as measured in time between 0 (the beginning of the animation) and 1 (the end of the animation)

elapsed
> The number of milliseconds that have passed since the beginning of the animation (seldom used)

attrStart
> The beginning value of the CSS attribute that is being animated

attrDelta
> The difference between the start and end values of the CSS attribute that is being animated

duration
> The total number of milliseconds that will pass during the animation (seldom used)

7.9 Disabling All Effects

Problem

Your user or web application may require that all animations are disabled, but the effect of revealing information or scrolling (or whichever animation type) may still be required.

This may be a personal preference, the user may be using a low-resolution device, or it may be because the user finds the animations problematic in their browsing.

jQuery has a way to disable all animations from one access point but still supports the `animate` method and its final value.

Solution

```
$.fx.off = true;

$(document).ready(function () {
  $('#animate').click(function () {
    $('.box').animate({ width: '+=100', height: '+=100' });
  });
});
```

Discussion

By setting `fx` to `off` using the following line, all animation calls have the same effect as calling `css()` directly:

```
$.fx.off = true;
```

This can be set at any point and it will disable the animations, which means it can be offered as a user preference. To enable animations again, you simply set the flag to `false`:

```
$.fx.off = false;
```

7.10 Using jQuery UI for Advanced Effects

Problem

If you want to create more complicated effects, it is certainly possible using the `animate` method. This might be for a web application that needs to animate a whole range of CSS properties on an element, or perhaps there is a special way a dialog box must disappear when closed—say, for instance, explode away on the screen (see Figure 7-2).

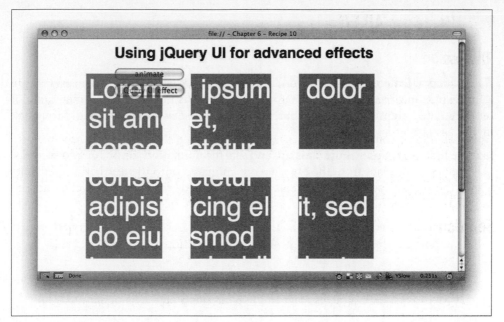

Figure 7-2. The explode effect running against the div.box element

Solution

Download the jQuery UI library from *http://jquery-cookbook.com/go/jqueryui-down load*. The library can now be included after jQuery is included and the new effects plugin is available.

For this solution, I have added an extra button to show two effects and added a new class to our CSS.

CSS

```
.big {
  font-size: 400%;
  width: 500px;
  height: 500px;
  line-height: 100%;
}
```

jQuery

```
$(document).ready(function () {
  $('#animate').click(function () {
    $('.box').toggleClass('big', 2000);
  });

  $('#effect').click(function () {
    $('.box').effect('explode', null, 2000);
```

```
    });
});
```

Discussion

The jQuery UI effects library also modifies the way addClass, removeClass, and toggle Class work; in particular, you can supply a duration as the second parameter, and it will animate a transition from the current state to the new class, working through all new class properties.

So, the first example adds the class big and sets the animation to run for two seconds. All the CSS properties from the big class are animated onto the div.box element. Because the toggleClass method has also been modified by jQuery UI, we are able to toggle back and forth to the original state.

Second, we are using the effect() method, which is bespoke to the jQuery UI library. This method offers a collection of show and hide functions.

 The effect() method requires the option object passed in as the second variable; this can be null or it can be an empty object, but it must be provided to be able to pass in the duration.

Using the string explode, the div.box will split into nine pieces and fade off the page as shown earlier in Figure 7-2.

 At the time of this writing, one or two effect types have slight side effects in Safari 4. They do work in all other A-grade browsers as outlined by Yahoo! at *http://developer.yahoo.com/yui/articles/gbs/*.

To see all the different available effects, you can visit *http://jquery-cookbook.com/go/ jqueryui-effects* and play with all the interactive demos.

Events

Ariel Flesler

8.0 Introduction

Events are the main method of communication between a user and a website or web application. Most of our JavaScript/jQuery coding will be run in response to a variety of user and browser events.

By *user events*, I mean basically keyboard and mouse interaction like `click`, `mousedown`, `keypress`, etc. *Browser events* are mainly DOM events like `document.ready`, `window.onload`, and many other events related to DOM elements.

When coding Ajax applications, we also have custom jQuery *Ajax events* that are dispatched during the process of an Ajax request, that is, `ajaxSend`, `ajaxComplete`, `ajaxError`, and some more.

jQuery's API is very consistent, especially when it comes to events. Attaching a handler to any kind of event is done using the same code structure:

```
jQuery( listener).bind( 'eventName', handlerFunction);
```

This syntax also applies to a fourth category that I haven't mentioned yet. jQuery's event system can be used for *event-driven programming** in which you can create your own *custom events* that can be bound and triggered as regular ones.

jQuery also provides a shortcut method for most common browser and Ajax events. A model call using a shortcut would look like this:

```
jQuery( listener).eventName( handlerFunction);
```

When using `bind()`, `eventName` will be a string wrapped in either single or double quotes. When using the shortcut, you simply put the event's name as the jQuery method's name.

* *http://en.wikipedia.org/wiki/Event-driven_programming*

Here's an example of binding a click handler, with and without the shortcut:

```
// Using bind()
jQuery('div').bind('click',function(e){...});
// Using the shortcut
jQuery('div').click(function(e){...});
```

During this chapter, I'll use the shortcuts when available, just because they're shorter and easier to read, in my opinion. Both work equally, and there's no advantage to using the shortcut other than clarity and brevity; it's simply a matter of taste.

I'll assume that you already read Chapter 1, where the document.ready event is explained in detail (Recipe 1.2). If you have any doubt about its use, do consult that recipe.

I also want to clarify that when I use the term *plugin*, for most cases I mean "plugins, widgets, or simply blocks of code." Most jQuery users tend to organize their code into plugin-like structures, usually adding names to jQuery's namespace.

Finally, jQuery's event module was highly modified in 1.3. I will always mention when something needs to be done differently, according to what jQuery version would be used.

8.1 Attaching a Handler to Many Events

Problem

In many common situations, one needs to bind the same handler function to more than one event (on the same element, that is). You could always do something like this:

```
jQuery('div').click(function(e){
          alert('event');
       })
       .keydown(function(e){
          alert('event');
       });
```

That is not such a problem if the function is short, but for longer blocks of code, repeating them over and over won't be that trivial and is definitely not the best approach.

Solution

There's more than a single solution to this simple but recurrent problem.

One way to solve it without repeating yourself too much would be as follows:

```
function handler(e){
    alert('event');
}

jQuery('div').click(handler)
         .keydown(handler);
```

Defining a function once and then referring to it multiple times is not a bad approach, but there's an even simpler one provided by jQuery.

`bind()` accepts a list of events separated by spaces. That means you can solve the previous problem like this:

```
jQuery('div').bind'click keydown', function(e){
    alert('event');
});
```

Discussion

You can also apply this behavior to `unbind()` and `one()`.

To unbind a certain function, you need to have a reference to it, so even if you are using the multievent feature, you still need to keep a reference to the handler. If you don't pass the function to `unbind()`, then any other event handler bound to that event will be removed as well:

```
function handler(e){
    alert('event');
}

jQuery('div').bind('click keydown', handler);

// ...

jQuery('div').unbind('click keydown', handler);
```

8.2 Reusing a Handler Function with Different Data

Problem

You've come into a situation where you have many bindings, and the handler functions look pretty similar. It doesn't matter whether these bindings are applied to different element/event combinations. The thing is, you don't want to repeat yourself over and over (who does?).

Here's an example:

```
jQuery('#button1').click(function(e){
    jQuery('div.panel').hide();
    jQuery('#panel1').show();
    jQuery('#desc').text('You clicked the red button');
});

jQuery('#button2').click(function(e){
    jQuery('div.panel').hide();
    jQuery('#panel2').show();
    jQuery('#desc').text('You clicked the blue button');
});
```

```
jQuery('#button3').click(function(e){
    jQuery('div.panel').hide();
    jQuery('#panel3').show();
    jQuery('#desc').text('You clicked the green button');
});
```

As you can see, the only differences noticed on each handler are the color and the panel to show. The amount of code would grow as you add more buttons or each time the handler functions get larger.

Solution

bind() accepts an optional data argument to be bound together with each specific handler function. The data values will be accessible from within this function by accessing *event*.data[†] where *event* is the event object argument provided by jQuery.

Note that this value can be anything…an array, a string, a number, or an object literal.

It's a common approach to pass an object literal, even if you are just passing one value, to make the code more readable. This way, the name you give this single attribute within the object will make your code a little more self-explanatory.

Discussion

event.data is used to provide precomputed values to a function, which means the values you will be passing to bind() need to be already available at binding time. To handle more "dynamic" values, there's another way that we'll learn about in Recipe 8.5.

The solution to the previous problem could look something like this:

```
function buttonClicked(e){
    jQuery('div.panel').hide();
    jQuery('#panel'+e.data.panel).show();
    jQuery('#desc').text('You clicked the '+e.data.color+' button');
}

jQuery('#button1').bind('click',{panel:1, color:'red'}, buttonClicked);
jQuery('#button2').bind('click',{panel:2, color:'blue'}, buttonClicked);
jQuery('#button3').bind('click',{panel:3, color:'green'}, buttonClicked);
```

Of course, you could make this even shorter by using a loop. This approach is called a *macro* by some coders, and it's a very common approach for jQuery code.

These *macros* will surely reduce the code length and can sometimes improve code readability. Some other times, they'll just make your code completely unreadable, so use them with caution.

Here's how you could do it:

```
jQuery.each(['red','blue','green'], function(num, color){
    num++; // it's 0-index based
```

[†] *http://docs.jquery.com/Events/jQuery.Event#event.data*

```
    jQuery('#button'+num).bind('click',function(e){
        jQuery('div.panel').hide();
        jQuery('#panel'+num).show();
        jQuery('#desc').text('You clicked the '+color+' button');
    });
})
```

As you can see, I haven't used the data argument because we don't really need it. The code is now somewhat shorter, but not that much, and it's not more readable.

The conclusion is that both approaches can be used on this kind of situation. Depending on the problem, one could be better (shorter, more readable, easier to maintain) than the other.

8.3 Removing a Whole Set of Event Handlers

Problem

So, you've made a plugin-like block of code that binds many event handlers to certain DOM elements.

Later, you want to clean them all up in order to dispose the plugin completely.

This could get a little lengthy if you added many handlers. Maybe you don't even have access to the bound handlers because they belong to another local scope.

You can't unbind every handler for a certain event (or any existing event), because you could be deleting other handlers that you didn't take into account.

Solution

Use a unique namespace for each plugin you make. Any handler bound within this plugin must be added with this namespace.

Later, when cleaning up, you just need to "unbind the whole namespace," and all the related event handlers will go away with one single line of code.

Discussion

How to bind with a namespace?

To add a namespace to an event type, you simply add a **.** followed by the namespace name.

Since jQuery 1.3, you can add more than one (namespace) per event.

This is how you would bind the `click` and `mousedown` functions with a namespace:

```
jQuery.fn.myPlugin = function(){
    return this
        .bind('click.myPlugin', function(){
```

```
            // [code]
        })
        .bind('mousedown.myPlugin', function(){
            // [code]
        });
    };
```

How to clean up my plugin?

To dispose the bindings above, you would do:

```
jQuery.fn.disposeMyPlugin = function(){
    return this.unbind('.myPlugin');
};
```

8.4 Triggering Specific Event Handlers

Problem

You need to trigger an event on a certain element (or many). This element belongs to one or more plugins so it may have event handlers bound to this event.

The problem is that this event is a common one, like click or mousedown. Simply triggering the event could run other event handlers that you didn't expect.

Solution

On the same principle as the previous recipe, namespaces can be used for triggering as well. When binding, you need to make sure you add a unique namespace to each set of handlers.

This can also be used for the opposite situation; if you need to trigger any event except those with a namespace, you can use the ! operator. An example of this will be shown in the discussion.

Discussion

How to trigger handlers with a certain namespace?

Now, say you want to programmatically trigger the click event bound by the plugin myPlugin. You could simply trigger the click event, but that would be a bad approach, because any other handler bound to the same event would get fired as well.

This is how to do this properly:

```
jQuery.fn.runMyPlugin = function(){
    return this.trigger('click.myPlugin');
};
```

How to trigger handlers that do *not* have a namespace?

On the contrary, maybe you need to trigger a click (or any other event), but the target element belongs to one or more plugins. Triggering an event could run undesired event handlers, and that would cause problems that will be pretty hard to debug.

So, assuming all the plugins did use a namespace, this is how to trigger a click safely:

```
jQuery('div.panels').trigger('click!');
```

8.5 Passing Dynamic Data to Event Handlers

Problem

You want to pass certain values to an event handler, but they're not known at "binding time," and they would change with each call to the handler.

Solution

There are two ways of solving this problem:

- Passing extra arguments to `trigger()`
- Passing a custom event object to `trigger()`

Both approaches work, and neither is clearly better than the other. The second approach was a little awkward to use before jQuery 1.3. Since this version, it has become pretty straightforward and less problematic. I'll explain each option in detail in the "Discussion" section.

Passing data to the handler, instead of making the function grab it from somewhere (global variables, jQuery namespace, etc.), makes the code easier to maintain because you keep handler functions simple and agnostic from the environment.

This also allows you to reuse the same handler for many situations.

Discussion

Passing extra arguments

`trigger()` can receive one or more values that will be passed on to the triggered handlers.

These values can be of any type and any amount. When you have more than one, you need to wrap them with an array:

```
jQuery('form').trigger('submit', ['John','Doe', 28, {gender:'M'}]);
```

The bound function for the preceding case would be something like this:

```
jQuery('form').bind('submit', function(e, name, surname, age, extra){
    // Do something with these arguments
});
```

This approach is simple and easy to read. The problem is, it looks pretty bad when you need to receive many arguments; I personally wouldn't go beyond four to five.

It's also kind of misleading if the reader is used to the common `function(e){ }` kind of function.

You start to wonder, where do these other arguments come from ?

Some more examples. Used within a programmatic event:

```
jQuery('#slideshow').bind('add-image', function(e, src){
    var $img = jQuery('<img />').attr('src', src);
    jQuery(this).append($img);
});
jQuery('#slideshow').trigger('add-image', 'img/dogs4.jpg');
```

Used within a real event:

```
jQuery('#button').bind('click', function(e, submit){
    if( submit )
        // Do something
    else
        // Do something else
});
jQuery('#button').trigger('click', true);
```

Passing a custom event object

If you choose to pass a custom event object instead, each value you pass has to be accessed as an attribute on the event object received by the handler.

This means that, no matter how many data you're passing, the handler will always have only a single argument, the event object.

This is already an advantage over the first approach, because it makes the function declaration less verbose.

As mentioned, this approach is much nicer to use since jQuery 1.3. Here's how you'd code the first example with a custom object:

```
jQuery('form').bind('submit', function(e){
    // Do something with e.name, e.surname, etc.
});
jQuery('form').trigger({
    type:'submit',
    name:'John',
    surname:'Doe',
    age: 28,
    gender:'M'
});
```

Passing an object literal is actually a shortcut to creating an instance of jQuery.Event.‡ This is the alternative way:

```
var e = jQuery.Event('submit'); // the new operator can be omitted
e.name = 'John';
e.surname = 'Doe';
e.age = 28;
e.gender = 'M';
jQuery('form').trigger(e);
```

You can, of course, use jQuery.extend instead of setting one attribute at a time.

You do need to create an event object yourself if you plan on retrieving data from this object after the call to trigger(). That's, by the way, a cool technique to pass information from the handler to the caller (we'll get into this in the next chapter).

What's the difference with event.data?

Using event.data is useful for static values that are accessible at the time when the function was bound. When the data you need to pass must be evaluated later (or each time), event.data won't do for you.

8.6 Accessing an Element ASAP (Before document.ready)

Problem

You need to gain access to a certain DOM element as soon as possible.

Using document.ready isn't fast enough; you really want to control this element before the page finishes rendering.

Issues like this are especially noticeable on large pages, where the document.ready event takes longer to be reached.

Solution

This is a very common and generic problem that can be solved in many different ways.

There's one approach that works for all of them, but it requires polling the DOM so it adds overhead to the page-rendering process (definitely undesirable!).

These are some of the usual problems where one could rely on polling:

- Hide an element right away, before it is rendered (or another style operation)
- Bind event handlers to an element ASAP so that it quickly becomes functional
- Any other situation

We'll discuss what's the better approach for each situation in the "Discussion" section.

---

‡ http://docs.jquery.com/Events/jQuery.Event

Discussion

Hide an element right away (or another style operation)

So, your problem is directly related to styling, you want to apply a conditional styling to an element, and this condition needs to be evaluated by JavaScript.

The right way to go about this is adding a specific CSS class to an element that is quickly accessible, like the <html> element, and then style the element accordingly.

Do something like this:

```
<!DOCTYPE html>
<html>
<head>
 <style type="text/css">
    html.no-message #message{ display:none; }
 </style>
 <script src="assets/jquery-latest.js"></script>
 <script type="text/javascript">
    // Bad
    jQuery(document).ready(function($){
       $('#message').hide();
    });
    // Correct
    jQuery('html').addClass('no-message');
    // or...
    document.documentElement.className = 'no-message';
 </script>
</head>
<body>
    <p id="message">I should not be visible</p>
    <!--
      Many more html elements
    -->
</body>
</html>
```

Bind event handlers to an element ASAP

Very often we have this large page with interactive elements, like buttons and links.

You don't want those elements to just hang in there, without any functionality attached while the page loads.

Luckily, there's a great concept called *event delegation* that can save the day. Event delegation is easy to implement with one of several jQuery plugins, and since jQuery 1.3, a plugin is no longer needed, because it has been added to the core jQuery file.

You can now bind event handlers to elements that still don't exist by using the method live().§ That way, you don't need to worry about waiting for the element to be ready in order to bind the events.

To read more about event delegation, check Recipe 8.10.

Any other situation

Your problem isn't about styling or about events. Then you, my friend, fall into the worst group.

But don't panic! There's a better solution than polling if you're concerned about performance. I'll explain it at last.

Polling. Polling can be implemented with a simple interval (`setInterval`) that checks for an element, and once found, a certain function is run, and the interval needs to be cleared.

There are two plugins that can aid you with this. One is `LiveQuery`,‖ which has an option to register a function to be run for each newly found element that matches a selector. This approach is pretty slow but supports the whole set of selectors.

There's another plugin called `ElementReady`# that will also handle this situation properly.

It lets you register pairs of `id`/`function`, and it will poll the DOM. Once an `id` is found, the `function` will be called, and the `id` is removed from the queue.

This plugin implements, probably, the fastest approach to detect elements, that is, using `document.getElementById`. This plugin is pretty fast but only supports `ids`.

Customly positioned scripts. The whole document-ready concept means "after the html is parsed." This means the browser reached the body's closing tag, `</body>`.

In other words, instead of using `document.ready`, you could simply put your scripts right before `</body>`.

You can apply the same principle to other parts of the DOM: you can add a `<script>` right after the element you want to access, and you can know, for certain, that it will be already accessible from it.

Here's an example:

```
<!DOCTYPE html>
<html>
<head>
 <script src="assets/jquery-latest.js"></script>
```

§ *http://docs.jquery.com/Events/live*

‖ *http://plugins.jquery.com/project/LiveQuery*

http://plugins.jquery.com/project/ElementReady

```
    </head>
    <body>
        <p>The time is <span id="time"> </span></p>
        <script type="text/javascript">
        jQuery('#time').text( new Date().toString() );
        </script>
        <!-- Many more html elements -->
    </body>
</html>
```

As you can see, no polling was needed in this case. This is a feasible solution if you don't need to use it a lot or you'll be adding tons of scripts to the page.

8.7 Stopping the Handler Execution Loop

Problem

You have several handlers bound to the same element/event combination.

You want to, from within a handler, prevent the rest from being called, something like what event.stopPropagation()* does. The problem is that event.stopPropagation() only works for elements that are below the current element in the DOM hierarchy.

Solution

Since jQuery 1.3, event objects passed to handlers have a new method called stopImmediatePropagation().† This method will do just that, and no subsequent event handler will be notified of the current event. It will also stop the event's propagation, just like stopPropagation() does.

This method has been taken from ECMAScript's DOM level 3 events specification.‡

If you want to consult the event object, to know whether this method has been called, you can do so by calling event.isImmediatePropagationStopped(),§ which will return either true or false.

Discussion

Examples

Simple form validation. stopImmediatePropagation() can cancel the actual submit binding(s) if a certain situation is met:

---

* *http://docs.jquery.com/Events/jQuery.Event#event.stopPropagation.28.29*

† *http://docs.jquery.com/Events/jQuery.Event#event.stopImmediatePropagation.28.29*

‡ *http://www.w3.org/TR/DOM-Level-3-Events/*

§ *http://docs.jquery.com/Events/jQuery.Event#event.isImmediatePropagationStopped.28.29*

```
jQuery('form')
    .submit(function(e){
        e.preventDefault(); // Don't submit for real
        if( jQuery('#field').val() == '' )
            e.stopImmediatePropagation();
    })
    .submit(function(e){
        // Only executed if the function above
        // didn't call e.stopImmediatePropagation
    });
```

Killing all events. It can also be useful for disabling elements or blocking containers temporarily:

```
(function($){

function checkEnabled(e){
    if( jQuery(this).is('.disabled') ){
        e.stopImmediatePropagation(); // Stop all handlers
        e.preventDefault();
    }
};

jQuery.fn.buttonize = function(){
    return this.css('cursor','pointer')
            .bind('click mousedown mouseup',checkEnabled};
};

})(jQuery);
```

Disadvantages of this approach

While this new feature could be a lifesaver in some situations, you must be aware that basing your logic on this behavior isn't all that safe. When you rely on this feature, you assume that the handlers will be executed in the order you expect and that no other handlers will get in the way.

While events bound with jQuery are executed in the same order they're added, it's not something the API strongly supports, meaning it could fail in some browsers or some special situations. It's also possible that bindings from different plugins could collide because one could call `stopImmediatePropagation()` and the other wouldn't get executed. This could cause unexpected problems that could take a long time to debug.

The conclusion is, don't be afraid to use `stopImmediatePropagation()` if it really suits your problem, but do use it with caution and double-check all the event handlers involved.

You should rather think twice before using it in these situations:

* The listener is a "popular" DOM element that is also used by other plugins.
* The event is a common one like `click` or `ready`. There's a greater chance of collisions.

On the other hand, it should be pretty safe to use it in these situations:

- The listener is a DOM element that is dynamically created and used merely by one plugin.
- The event is a custom event like `change-color` or `addUser`.
- You intentionally want to stop any bound handler (like in the second example).

8.8 Getting the Correct Element When Using event.target

Problem

Your code is relying on the `event.target`[ll] property of an event object, most likely in combination with event delegation, where one single event handler is bound to a container and it manages a variable number of descendant elements.

In some cases, you don't seem to be getting the expected behavior. `event.target` is sometimes pointing to an element that is inside the one you expected.

Solution

The `event.target` property refers to the element that got the event, that is, the specific element.

This means that if, for example, you have an image inside a link and you click the link, the `event.target` will be the image, not the link.

So, how should you work around this? If you're not working with event delegation, then using `this` (scope of the function) or `event.currentTarget` (since jQuery 1.3) should do. It will always point to the element that has the event handler bound.

If you're indeed using event delegation, then you'll need to find the parent element you were expecting.

Since jQuery 1.3, you can use `closest()`.[#] As specified in its documentation, it will return the closest element, beginning with the current element and going up through the parents, that matches a certain selector.

If you're using an older version of jQuery, you can simulate `closest()` with something like this:

```
jQuery.fn.closest = function( selector ){
    return this.map(function(){
        var $parent = jQuery(this).parents();
        return jQuery(this).add($parents).filter( selector )[0];
    });
}
```

---

ll *http://docs.jquery.com/Events/jQuery.Event#event.target*

\# *http://docs.jquery.com/Traversing/closest*

This could be improved a little for performance, but this simple version should do for general purposes.

Here's a small example of a very common situation using `closest()`:

```
jQuery('table').click(function(e){
    var $tr = jQuery(e.target).closest('tr');
    // Do something with the table row
});
```

Discussion

`event.target` is one of the event object's properties normalized by jQuery's event system (`event.srcElement` on IE).

So, how come an event is triggered on this target element and your event handler is called even when bound to an ancestor ? The answer is Event bubbling.[*]

Most standard DOM events do bubble.[†] This means that, after the event was triggered on the target, it will go up to its parent node and trigger the same event (with all its handlers).

This process will continue until either it reaches the `document` or `event.stopPropagation()` is called within an event handler.

Thanks to event bubbling, you don't need to always bind event handlers to specific elements; instead, you can bind to a common container once and handle them all from there. This is the principle of event delegation.

8.9 Avoid Multiple hover() Animations in Parallel

Problem

We all have fallen for this at least once. You set up something like this:

```
jQuery('#something').hover(
    function(){
        // add some cool animation for jQuery(this)
    },
    function(){
        // Revert the cool animation to its initial state
    }
);
```

For example, you could be enlarging an element each time the mouse rolls over it and then shrinking it to its initial size once the mouse rolls out.

All goes well until you quickly move the mouse over and out of the element and...what?!

---

[*] *http://www.quirksmode.org/js/events_order.html*

[†] *http://en.wikipedia.org/wiki/DOM_events#Common.2FW3C_events*

The jQuery('#something') element suddenly gets resized back and forth many times until it finally stops.

Solution

The solution is indeed simple, too simple, but the problem is so recurrent that I really consider this solution a useful one.

What you need to do in order to avoid this nasty effect is simply kill all existing animations on the element before you create a new one.

To do so, you have to use jQuery's stop() method. It will (as the name says) stop the current animation and, optionally, remove the following ones as well.

Discussion

Example

I'll show you an example of animating the opacity CSS property, but it works the same for any other property:

```
jQuery('#something').hover(
    function(){
        jQuery(this).stop().animate({opacity:1}, 1000);
    },
    function(){
        jQuery(this).stop().animate({opacity:0.8}, 1000);
    }
);
```

This also works for custom jQuery animations, like slideUp(), slideDown(), fadeIn(), etc.

This is the former example using the fade methods:

```
jQuery('#something').hover(
    function(){
        jQuery(this).stop().fadeTo( 1, 1000 );
    },
    function(){
        jQuery(this).stop().fadeTo( 0.8, 1000 );
    }
);
```

Not there yet

There's still another related problem that could arise in a situation like this:

```
jQuery('#something').hover(
    function(){
        jQuery(this).stop()
            .fadeTo( 1, 1000 )
            .animate( {height:500}, 1000 );
    },
```

```
    function(){
        jQuery(this).stop()
            .fadeTo( 0.8, 1000 )
            .animate( {height:200}, 1000 );
    }
);
```

If you try this code and move the mouse quickly, the element will get animated crazily again, but only its height (not the opacity) will animate.

The reason is simple; jQuery animations get queued by default. This means that if you add several animations, they'll get executed in sequence.

stop() by default only stops (and removes) the current animation. In our last example, only the opacity animation will be removed each time, leaving the height animation in the queue, ready to run.

To work around this, you have to either call stop() one more time or pass true as the first argument. This will make stop() clean all the queued animations as well. Our hover code should look like this:

```
jQuery('#something').hover(
    function(){
        jQuery(this).stop(true)
            .fadeTo( 1, 1000 )
            .animate( {height:500}, 1000 );
    },
    function(){
        jQuery(this).stop(true)
            .fadeTo( 0.8, 1000 )
            .animate( {height:200}, 1000 );
    }
);
```

8.10 Making Event Handlers Work for Newly Added Elements

Problem

You've bound one or more event handlers, and they suddenly stop working.

It happens after new elements are added dynamically by an Ajax request or simple jQuery operations (append(), wrap(), etc.).

This problem is incredibly common, and we've all fallen for this at least once.

I'll explain the theory behind it in the "Discussion" section. If you feel you need to understand this well before heading to the solutions, check "Why do event handlers get lost ?" on page 188 first.

Solution

There are two possible solutions for this recurring problem, each with its own pros and cons:

Rebinding
> This approach requires you to call bind() again and again, every time new elements are added.
>
> It's pretty easy to implement and doesn't require any plugin or new method.
>
> You can simply have all the bindings in a function and call it again after each update.

Event delegation
> It relies on event bubbling.‡ This is fast and light but requires a little understanding and can be (just) a little tricky at times.
>
> Since jQuery 1.3, there's built-in support for event delegation. Using it is as simple as using the new live() method instead of bind().

Discussion

Why do event handlers get lost ?

JavaScript, as opposed to CSS, isn't a declarative language. You don't describe behaviors, and they get "automagically" applied.

JavaScript, like most other programming languages, is imperative. The developer specifies a sequence of actions to perform, and they get applied as the line of code is reached.

When you add a piece of code like this:

```
function handler(){
    alert('got clicked');
}
jQuery('.clickable').bind('click', handler);
```

this is what you're "doing":

1. Look for all elements with a CSS class "clickable" and save it to the collection.
2. Bind the "handler" function to the click event of each element in the collection.

If JavaScript/jQuery were interpreted declaratively, the previous code would mean the following:

1. Each time an element with CSS class clickable is clicked, run the function handler.

However, because JavaScript/jQuery is interpreted imperatively, the only elements that will get bound are those that match the selector at the time it is run. If you add new

---

‡ *http://www.quirksmode.org/js/events_order.html*

elements with a `clickable` class or you remove the class from an element, the behaviors won't be added or removed for those elements.

A little introduction to event delegation

Event delegation consists of binding once, at the start, and passively listening for events to be triggered. It relies on the fact that many events in the browser bubble up.

As an example, after you click a `<div>`, its parent node receives the click event as well, and then it passes to the parent's parent and so on, until it reaches the `document` element.

Pros and cons of each approach

Rebinding. Rebinding is simple: you just re-add the event handlers. It leads to new problems, such as adding event handlers to elements that were already bound. Some add CSS classes to work around this problem (marking those bound with a certain class).

All this requires CPU cycles every time the elements are updated and requires more and more event handlers to be created.

One way to work around both problems mentioned is to use named functions as event handlers. If you always use the same function, then you've solved the duplication problem, and the overhead is smaller.

Still, rebinding can lead to higher and higher amounts of RAM taken as time passes by.

Event delegation. Event delegation just requires an initial binding and there's no need to deal with rebinding at all. This is quite a relief for the developer and makes the code shorter and clearer. The RAM problem mentioned before doesn't apply to event delegation. The content of the page might change, but the active event handlers are always the same.

Event delegation has a catch, though. In order for it to work, the code that handles it (`live()`, a plugin or your own code) must take the element that got the event (`event.target`) and go through its ancestors to see which ones have event handlers to trigger along with some more processing. This means that, while event delegation requires less binding, it requires more processing each time an event is triggered.

Also, event delegation cannot be used with events that don't bubble, such as `focus` and `blur`. For these events, there's a workaround that works cross-browser, using the `focusin` and `focusout` events in some browsers.

Conclusion

Event delegation seems like a nicer approach, but it requires extra processing.

My advice on this matter is to use live bindings just when you really need them. These are two common situations:

Dynamic elements
> You have a list of DOM elements that changes dynamically.

Large lists
> Event delegation can work faster when you bind one live binding instead of, say, 100 from the regular ones. This is faster at the start and takes less memory.

If there's no reason to use `live()`, then just go for `bind()`. If you then need to make it live, switching should be just a matter of seconds.

Advanced Events

Ariel Flesler

9.0 Introduction

These recipes will deal with edge case problems, advanced optimizations, and certain techniques to make your code cooler. These recipes are mostly for advanced developers who want to take their jQuery code one step further.

As in Chapter 8, I'll refer to code as *plugins*, but that doesn't mean it needs to be an actual plugin. If you don't structure your code as jQuery plugins, then keep my naming convention in mind.

9.1 Getting jQuery to Work When Loaded Dynamically

Problem

You are including jQuery dynamically into the page, by either adding a `<script>` element to the DOM or doing it some other way like Ajax.

Once jQuery is loaded, you expect everything to start working, but for some reason, no script starts.

Solution

You need to include an additional script to be executed after jQuery is loaded. This script will simply call `jQuery.ready()`. After you do this, everything will start working as expected.

Discussion

What is jQuery.ready()?

The jQuery.ready() function is called by jQuery's core when the document is detected as ready. Once called, all the document.ready handlers are triggered automatically.

 You don't need to worry about whether this function might have been called already (for example, by the original detection), triggering all the document.ready handlers again.

jQuery.ready() includes a check for duplicated executions internally. Further calls will be ignored.

Why was this happening?

The document.ready detection is mostly based on events. Depending on the browser, a certain event is bound, and it's supposed to be triggered once the document is ready.

In addition, the window.onload event is bound for all browsers as a fallback measure in case the other options fail.

What was happening to you is that jQuery was finally loaded into the page only after the window.onload event; therefore, all the event handlers remained bound, and none got triggered.

By calling jQuery.ready(), you're "announcing" the document.ready event manually, triggering all the handlers and getting things back to normal.

9.2 Speeding Up Global Event Triggering

Problem

Global event triggering implicates calling all the event handlers bound for a certain event, on all available elements.

It is performed by calling jQuery.trigger() without passing any DOM element as context. It is nearly the same as calling trigger() on all the elements that have one or more bindings to the corresponding event, something like this:

```
jQuery('#a1,#a2,div.b5').trigger('someEvent');
```

Triggering globally is obviously simpler because you don't need to know all the elements that need to be triggered.

It's quite useful for certain situations but can also be a slow process at times. Although it's been optimized since jQuery 1.3, it still requires going through all the elements registered to jQuery's event system. This can cause short (or not so short) hangs every time an event is triggered like this.

Solution

One possible solution is to have one or more global objects that will act as event listeners. These elements can be DOM elements or not. All global events will be bound and triggered on one of these elements.

Instead of doing something like this:

```
jQuery('#text1').bind('change-page', function(e, title){
    jQuery(this).text( 'Page is ' + title );
});
jQuery('#text2').bind('change-page', function(e, title){
    jQuery(this).text( 'At ' + title + ' Page' );
});
jQuery.trigger('change-page', 'Inbox');
```

you'd do something like this:

```
jQuery.page = jQuery({}); // Just an empty object
jQuery.page.bind('change', function(e, title){
    jQuery('#text1').text( 'Page is ' + title );
});
jQuery.page.bind('change', function(e, title){
    jQuery('#text2').text( 'At ' + title + ' Page' );
});
jQuery.page.trigger('change', 'Inbox');
```

The syntax seems pretty much the same, but each call to `trigger` won't be iterating jQuery's data registry (aka `jQuery.cache`).

Even if you decide to use a DOM element, the principle is the same. DOM elements can be more appropriate at times. If, for example, you're creating a table-related plugin, then it'd make sense to use each `<table>` element as an event listener.

The problem with DOM elements in many browsers is that they're the main source of memory leaks. Memory leaks occur when there are certain amounts of RAM memory that cannot be freed by the JavaScript engine as the user leaves a page.

You should be much more careful about how you save data into the objects when you use DOM elements. That's why jQuery provides the `data()` method.

Still, I'd personally use regular JavaScript objects in most situations. You can add attributes and functions to them, and the likelihood (and magnitude) of memory leaks will be smaller.

Discussion

Pros and cons

As stated by the recipe title, this approach is faster. You will be always triggering events on single objects, instead of the *n* entries on jQuery.cache.

The downside of this approach is that everyone needs to know the event listener object (jQuery.page in the example) in order to bind or trigger one of its known events.

This can be negative if you're aiming to keep your code encapsulated.[*]

The concept of encapsulation is highly enforced in object-oriented programming, where this is one of the things you should be very cautious about.

This is generally not such a great concern with jQuery programming, because it is not object oriented and most users don't get too worried about code encapsulation. Still, it's worth mentioning.

Making the listeners functional

The listener objects mentioned don't have to be simple dummy objects with nothing but bind(), unbind(), and trigger() (as far as we're concerned).

These objects could actually have methods and attributes that would make them much more useful.

The only problem, though, is that if we do something like this:

```
jQuery.page = jQuery({ number:1 });
```

to access the *number* attribute, we would be forced to do this:

```
jQuery.page.number; // undefined
jQuery.page[0].number; // 1
```

This is how jQuery works on HTML nodes and anything else.

But don't give up on me yet! It's easy to work around this. Let's make a small plugin:

```
(function( $ ){

    // These methods will be copied from jQuery.fn to our prototype
    var copiedMethods = 'bind unbind one trigger triggerHandler'.split(' ');

    // Empty constructor
    function Listener(){
    };

    $.each(copiedMethods, function(i,name){
        Listener.prototype[name] = $.fn[name];
    });
```

---

[*] http://en.wikipedia.org/wiki/Encapsulation_(computer_science)

```
// Our "jQuery.fn.each" needs to be replaced
Listener.prototype.each = function(fn) {
    fn.call(this);
    return this;
};

$.listener = function( data ){
    return $.extend(new Listener(), data);
};

})( jQuery );
```

Now we can create objects that will have all the jQuery methods we need that are related to events, but the scope of the functions we pass to bind(), unbind(), etc., will be the object itself (jQuery.page in our example).

Note that our listener objects won't have all jQuery methods but just the ones we copied. While you could add some more methods, most of them won't work. That would require a more complex implementation; we'll stick to this one, which satisfies our needs for events.

Now that we have this mini plugin, we can do this:

```
jQuery.page = jQuery.listener({
    title: 'Start',
    changeTo: function( title ){
        this.title = title;
        this.trigger('change');
    }
});
jQuery.page.changeTo('Inbox');
```

Because you can now access the object from within the handlers, using the this, you don't need to pass certain values like the title as arguments to the handler. Instead, you can simply use this.title to access the value:

```
jQuery.page.bind('change', function(e){
    jQuery('#text1').text( 'Page is ' + this.title );
});
```

9.3 Creating Your Own Events

Problem

You want to provide certain behaviors to an element when it's bound to an event.

Solution

Use jQuery.event.special to do this. This feature requires an object with, at least, a function that will be called each time your event is bound for the time on each element and another function to clean up what you did in the first place.

The syntax looks something like this:

```
jQuery.event.special.myEvent = {
    // Bind the custom event
    setup:function( data, namespaces ){
        this; // The element being bound
        // return false to get the native binding, otherwise,
        // it will be skipped
    },
    // Clean up
    teardown:function( namespaces ){
        this; // The element being bound
        // Ditto about returning false
    }
};
```

After you add your event behavior, you can do something like this:

```
jQuery('#some_element').bind('myEvent', {foo:'bar'}, function(){...});
```

After this, your `setup()` function will be called.

Discussion

Handling every binding to your event

As explained, your `setup()` function will be called only when adding the first handler.

This is enough if the logic you're encapsulating on this event doesn't require some operations to be run each time a new binding is performed.

This option is provided by jQuery, but the approach has changed since jQuery 1.3.3.

If you're using an older version, then you just need to use `jQuery.event.specialAll` instead of `jQuery.event.special`. It will accept the same kind of object, and your callbacks will receive the same arguments. The only difference is that returning false won't bring any change.

As of jQuery 1.3.3, `jQuery.event.specialAll` is gone. To intercept all bindings for an event, you need to include an `add()` (and optionally `remove()`) function in your `jQuery.event.special` namespace. The functions will receive the handler that is about to be bound, and can optionally return a new handler function to be used instead.

A real-world example

Let's make sure this is clear by writing a simple example; I'll use the 1.3.3+ notation.

Let's suppose you want to have an event triggered when an element is selected (clicked) and it isn't disabled. We'll assume that the item is disabled when it has the CSS class `disabled`.

Here's a way of doing that:

```
// Save these to make the code shorter
// Don't do this within the global scope
var event = jQuery.event;
var $selected = event.special.selected = {
    setup:function( data ){
        event.add(this, 'click', $selected.handler);
        return false;
    },
    teardown:function(){
        event.remove(this, 'click', $selected.handler);
        return false;
    },
    handler:function(){
        var $elem = jQuery(this);
        if( !$elem.hasClass('disabled') )
            $elem.triggerHandler('selected');
    }
};
```

As you can see, we provide our own handler for selected. Within the handler, we used triggerHandler() instead of trigger() because we don't need event bubbling, and there's no default action to prevent, so we save some needless processing.

Existing uses for this feature

jQuery.event.special is a great way of adding new behaviors without polluting the jQuery namespace.

It doesn't suit any situation, but it usually comes in handy when you need a custom event that is based on another one (click in our example). It's also useful if you have a plugin that simply binds events or simulates them; then you can "mask" that plugin as a regular event.

jQuery's core uses jQuery.event.special to handle events bound to the document.ready event. Actually, they're stored as regular event handlers, but the first time you bind to this event, you're actually activating the (hacky) detection code.

It is also used to transparently handle mouseenter/mouseleave events (those used by hover()). All the DOM traversal operations needed to achieve this are nicely hidden within the setup() handlers.

There are also plugins that take advantage of jQuery.event.special. Some of these are as follows:

mousewheel
> Provides support for mouse wheel changes.[†]

---

† *http://plugins.jquery.com/project/mousewheel*

drag, drop

Drag and drop support masked as simple events.‡

focusin, focusout

This snippet (not an actual plugin) originally written by Jörn Zaefferer was later added via plugins to achieve event delegation of focus and blur events.

Checking these plugins can be a good start if you're planning on adding new events to jQuery.

9.4 Letting Event Handlers Provide Needed Data

Problem

You need to allow other plugins (or just simple jQuery code) to chime in and modify certain variables before you perform the requested action.

Solution

Use events to notify other scripts about the action that is about to be carried out.

It is possible to get data that is gathered from the actioned event handlers.

If none is provided, you could then use some default option of your choice.

You'll see how to do this according to what jQuery version you are using.

Discussion

How can we do this with jQuery 1.3+?

Since jQuery 1.3, with the addition of jQuery.Event, this can be achieved in a nicer way. The old way still works for triggerHandler() but not for jQuery.trigger().

For the code we'll see now, we will need to create a jQuery.Event:

```
var e = jQuery.Event('updateName');
```

Now, to call the handlers and retrieve the value, we'll pass the event object to trigger() and then fetch the data from the event object:

```
jQuery('#element').trigger(e);
 alert( e.result ); // Charles
```

As I said at the beginning, this doesn't work nicely when many handlers are bound and is, in general terms, a little unreliable and fragile.

So, how can we communicate event handlers and the function triggering the event?

---

‡ *http://plugins.jquery.com/project/drag, http://plugins.jquery.com/project/drop*

The answer is, through the event object that we're passing.

The jQuery.Event object passed to trigger() will be the same that is received by each handler as its first argument.

This means that we can do this:

```
jQuery('#name').bind('updateName', function(e){
    e.name = this.value;
});

var e = jQuery.Event('updateName');
jQuery('#name').trigger(e);
alert( e.name );
```

This example doesn't differ much from simply accessing e.result, but what about multiple event handlers that operate on the same event object?

```
jQuery('#first').bind('update', function(e){
    e.firstName = this.value;
});
jQuery('#last').bind('update', function(e){
    e.lastName = this.value;
});

var e = jQuery.Event('update');
jQuery('#first, #last').trigger(e);
alert( e.firstName );
alert( e.lastName );
```

We now have a way of allowing any number of event handlers to provide needed information for a function to run. Needless to say, you can call trigger() several times, passing the same event object.

As said before, it'd be wise to preset the event object with default values (if applicable). Your code shouldn't rely on the fact that others did subscribe to a certain event.

If no default value can be used, then you can always abort the call or throw an error.

How this was achieved before jQuery 1.3

Older versions of jQuery only allowed the users to get a single value, which would be returned when calling jQuery.trigger() and/or triggerHandler().

It looked something like this:

```
jQuery('#element').bind('updateName', function(){
    return 'Charles';
});

var name = jQuery('#element').triggerHandler('updateName');
alert( name ); // Charles
```

This was OK until you had more than one event handler returning data. At that point, it was a matter of "who comes last" to decide which one's data would be returned.

Allowing event handlers to prevent actions

This is really a specialization of what we just saw. Event objects, by design, have a method called `preventDefault()`. This method is used on native events to abort common actions like clicks on links, but it has no real use on custom events.

We could take advantage of this and use this method to allow other scripts to prevent actions that are about to be performed.

I'll now show you an example of an action. I'll use the mini plugin introduced on Recipe 9.2, but that is certainly not a requirement to use this:

```
var remote = jQuery.listener({
    request:function( url, callback ){
        jQuery.ajax({ url:url, success:callback });
    }
});

// Do a request
remote.request('contact.html', function( html ){
    alert( html );
});
```

Now suppose we want to allow an external script to abort certain requests when needed. We need to modify `remote.request` like this:

```
var remote = jQuery.listener({
    request:function( url, callback ){
        var e = jQuery.Event('beforeRequest');
        e.url = url;
        this.trigger(e);

        if( !e.isDefaultPrevented() )
            jQuery.ajax({ url:url, success:callback });
    }
});
```

`e.isDefaultPrevented()` will return whether `e.preventDefault()` was ever called on this object.

Any external script can now do something like this:

```
remote.bind('beforeRequest', function(e){
    if( e.url == 'contact.html' )
        e.preventDefault();
});
```

Returning false (within the function) would have nearly the same effect as calling `e.preventDefault()`. It will also stop the event propagation, which could be desirable.

Needless to say, in a situation like this, we could use what we learned before to allow the URL (or post data if added) to be modified by handlers.

9.5 Creating Event-Driven Plugins

Problem

You want your plugin to be controllable from the outside. One should be able to "tell" the plugin to do something at any time. There could be many instances (calls) of a plugin, but our action should only be executed in the context we provide.

Solution

One way to do this is indeed using events.

When a plugin is called, it binds functions on each matched element that once triggered, and it will perform the desired actions.

As a possible side solution, each time the plugin is called, instead of respecting the chaining, it could return an object that contains the bindings and allows external manipulation (use the plugin from Recipe 9.2).

This allows you to call the plugin many times on the same element without messing up the events.

Discussion

An example

We'll now create a simple slideshow plugin. I'll base this plugin on an existing plugin of mine called `jQuery.SerialScroll`.§ I first thought of this approach when coding this plugin, and, I must say, it worked pretty well.

We'll name our plugin `slideshow`. It will receive an `<img>` element and an array of URLs, and it will cycle the images. It will allow previous and next movement, jumping to a certain image, and also autocycling.

Let's start with the basics:

```
(function( $ ){
    $.fn.slideshow = function(options){

        return this.each(function(){
            var $img = $(this),
                current = 0;

            // Add slideshow behavior...
        });
    };
})( jQuery );
```

§ *http://flesler.blogspot.com/2008/02/jqueryserialscroll.html*

Now we'll add a few local functions that will allow us to move to different images (URLs) in the collection:

```
function show( index ){
   var total = options.images.length;

   while( index < 0 )
       index += total;

   while( index >= total )
       index -= total;

   current = index;
   $img.attr('src', options.images[index]);
}

function prev(){
   show( current - 1 );
}

function next(){
   show( current + 1 );
}
```

We can now expose this functionality with events:

```
$img.bind('prev', prev).bind('next', next).bind('goto',function(e, index){
   show( index );
});
```

What about autocycling? Let's add a few more functions:

```
var auto = false, id;

function start(){
   stop();
   auto = true;
   id = setTimeout(next, options.interval || 2000);
}

function stop(){
   auto = false;
   clearTimeout(id);
}
```

Here are the events:

```
$img.bind('start', start).bind('stop', stop);
```

We now need to add a few lines to show() to keep autocycling if needed:

```
function show( index ){
   // Same as before...

   if( auto )
       start();
}
```

And that's it! We now have a full slideshow with prev, next, and autocycling.

In order to make the example clear, I made this plugin completely dependent on the outside manipulation.

Here's a model implementation:

```
<ul>
   <li><img id="prev" src="prev.png" /></li>
   <li><img id="slideshow" /></li>
   <li><img id="next" src="next.png" /></li>
 </ul>

 ...

(function( $ ){
   var $image = $('#slideshow');

   $image.slideshow({
       images: ['1.jpg', '2.jpg', '3.jpg', '4.jpg'],
       interval: 3000
   });

   $('#prev').click(function(){
       $image.trigger('prev');
   });

   $('#next').click(function(){
       $image.trigger('next');
   });

   $image.trigger('goto', 0); // Initialize on 0
   $image.trigger('start'); // We want auto cycling

})( jQuery );
```

 I used trigger() because it's nice and short, but the truth is that it would be faster if you used triggerHandler() because trigger() will generate event bubbling (since jQuery 1.3) and you probably don't need it.

What happens if an element already has one of these events?

It could happen (although it's strange) that the #slideshow element could already have a binding on an event by the name of prev, next, goto, start, or stop.

If this is the case, check Recipe 8.4 for a solution.

How can I allow others to clean up the added event handlers?

Because I didn't expose the bound functions, any other external code won't be able to unbind them.

In most cases, you could simply unbind the whole events from the element, something like this:

```
jQuery('#slideshow').unbind('prev next goto start stop'); // Enumerate each event
// or
jQuery('#slideshow').unbind(); // Blindly remove them all
```

If you need a cautious unbinding or if you simply want to unbind all related events, check Recipe 8.3.

What's the difference with other approaches?

There are other existing techniques to allow external manipulation. I'll compare some:

Allowing the plugin to accept commands. This pattern is used by jQuery UI (among others). It consists of executing actions when the plugin is passed a string as the first argument, for example:

```
jQuery('#image').slideshow('goto', 1);
```

This is a little shorter than using events, but the whole approach requires you to save all the needed data (the current index in our case) in a public way, so it can be retrieved afterward. People who use this pattern also tend to use `data()` to store the variables.

If you use events, you can simply use local variables because your event handlers have access to the plugin's local scope.

Returning an object with methods. This pattern is used by the `validate` plugin from Jörn Zaefferer (and others too).

Depending on how it is coded, the object's methods could be able to access local variables. To do so, it must use closures,[‖] which aren't a nice thing to abuse. Also, you need to store this object somewhere (globally). This also requires you to do pseudo-object-oriented code (which you may like or not).

You could create some kind of hybrid between this approach and the one I explained. Instead of binding the events (`prev`, `next`, etc.) to the DOM element, you could create an object (using `jQuery.listener`) and bind the events to it; then it could be returned. As we saw in Recipe 9.2, this listener object wouldn't be restricted to events. It could have methods and even data saved into its attributes.

‖ *http://en.wikipedia.org/wiki/Closure_(computer_science)*

9.6 Getting Notified When jQuery Methods Are Called

Problem

You want to perform a certain action when a DOM element gets modified using jQuery. This could involve changing an attribute such as a CSS property, removing it from the document, etc.

Some browsers already support mutation events,# which would serve this need, but they're not something you can use in a cross-browser fashion yet, and they aren't integrated with jQuery.

Another thing you might ever need is to modify the arguments passed to jQuery methods before they're executed. On the same principle, you could need to alter the data returned by a method after the executing of the function itself.

Solution

This is somehow related to aspect-oriented programming,* but here we won't be nesting functions; instead, we'll overload the desired method once and trigger events every time the method is called.

We'll need one event to be triggered *before* the function is run to allow the arguments to be changed. We'll also need an event *after* the function is run so we can retrieve the returned data and even change it if necessary.

Let's see how to code this as a plugin. I'll show you each step separately.

Discussion

Overloading the desired method

First, let's create a function that replaces jQuery methods with our own function. I'll name it jQuery.broadcast(); you can change its name if you prefer something else:

```
(function($){

    $.broadcast = function(name){
        // Save the original method
        var old = $.fn[name];

        $.fn[name] = function(){
            // Broadcast
        };
    };
```

---

http://www.w3.org/TR/DOM-Level-2-Events/events.html#Events-eventgroupings-mutationevents

* http://en.wikipedia.org/wiki/Aspect_oriented_programming

```
})(jQuery);
```

name needs to be the method name we want to override, for example:

```
jQuery.broadcast('addClass');
```

Triggering an event prior to the execution

Now that we have put our own function as the jQuery method, let's see how to trigger an event that will allow us to change the incoming arguments:

```
// Create an event object
var e = $.Event('before-'+name);
// Save the arguments into the object
e.args = $.makeArray(arguments);
// Trigger the event
this.trigger(e);
```

Assuming you're broadcasting addClass(), we can now do this:

```
jQuery('body').bind('before-addClass',function(e){
  e.args[0]; // The CSS class
});
```

Executing the original method

An event is now triggered, but we still have to call the old addClass(). We'll save the returned data into the event object as well so we can expose it later when we trigger the other event.

```
e.ret = old.apply(this, e.args);
```

As you can see, we don't pass the original arguments array; instead, we use the one we exposed in case it was modified in some way.

Triggering an event after the execution

We now have the returned data saved in our event object. We can now trigger the final event, allowing external modification of the returned data.

We'll reuse the same event object, but we'll change the event's name.

```
e.type = 'after-'+name;
this.trigger(e);
```

Returning the result

All what's left now is to return the resulting data and continue with the normal execution. We'll give out what we saved on e.ret that could have been modified by an event handler:

```
return e.ret;
```

Putting it all together

This is the completed code we've developed:

```
(function($){

    $.broadcast = function(name){
        var old = $.fn[name];

        $.fn[name] = function(){
            var e = $.Event('before-'+name);

            e.args = $.makeArray(arguments);
            this.trigger(e);

            e.ret = old.apply(this, e.args);

            e.type = 'after-'+name;
            this.trigger(e);

            return e.ret;
        };
    };

})(jQuery);
```

Where to go from here?

I tried to keep the example short to illustrate the point. There are a couple of things you can do to improve it; here are a few ideas:

- Use `triggerHandler()` instead of `trigger()`: if you don't need the events to bubble, you could simply use `triggerHandler()`. This will make the whole process faster; note that `triggerHandler()` only triggers the event on the first element of the collection.

- Run the process on each element separately: in the previous example, `trigger()` is called on the whole collection at once. That will be OK for most cases but can yield unexpected results when used on collections with multiple elements.

  You could wrap what we put inside the function with a call to `map()`. That should make the code work once per element.

  The downside is that it will be slightly slower and will also generate an (unexpected) stack entry (`pushStack()`) due to the call to `map()`.

- Allow external code to prevent normal execution: if you're using jQuery 1.3 or higher, you could take advantage of the methods for `jQuery.Event`.

  You can "ask" the event object whether someone called its `preventDefault()` method using `e.isDefaultPrevented()`.

  If this returns `true`, then you don't call the original function.

- Avoid multiple overloads of the same jQuery method: this one is pretty simple; just create an internal object literal where you keep track of which methods were overloaded. Then you just ignore repeated calls.

- Integrate this with `jQuery.event.special`: this one will save you from calling `jQuery.broadcast()` for each method you want to overload.

  Instead, you add an entry to `jQuery.event.special` for each method, and you internally call `jQuery.broadcast()` when someone binds an event. This should be combined with the check for duplicated calls.

9.7 Using Objects' Methods as Event Listeners

Problem

You have objects with methods and attributes, and you want to pass those methods (functions) as event handlers. The problem is that once you do this, the method will "lose the reference" to the object, and you have no way of referencing the object within the event handlers.

Solution

This used to be quite complicated to achieve. It required you to generate closures that would encapsulate the object and then pass them to `bind()`.

Since jQuery 1.3.3, a new parameter has been added to `bind()`. It allows you to specify an object as the scope or `this` of the event handler without using function closures.

This makes the required code both shorter and faster. You can now pass the object's method as the function and the object itself as the scope.

Discussion

Where did the node go?

You will surely wonder this sooner or later. I said before that when you pass a scope object to `bind()`, the `this` of the event handler will be overridden. This means we can't retrieve the node as we always do…but the node is not lost.

When you pass a scope object to the bind() method, events will be delivered with the `this` of the event handler set to the scope object. You can still determine the element being delivered to the event by using the `event.currentTarget` property, which contains a reference to the DOM element.

It's usually not needed because using the `this` is shorter, but in situations like this, it's the only way around.

The example

I'll create a small example that should illustrate how to use the scope parameter and also show you a situation where it is useful.

The objects. For the example, we'll need two objects. Each will have a method that we want to bind as an event handler.

These are the objects:

```
function Person(name){
  this.name = name;
  this.married = false;
}

jQuery.extend( Person.prototype, {
    whatIsYourName: function(){
        alert(this.name);
    },
    updateMarriedState: function(e){
        var checkbox = e.currentTarget;
        this.married = checkbox.checked;
    }
});

var peter = new Person('Peter');
var susan = new Person('Susan');
```

Binding the methods. Let's suppose we have some sort of form and it has two checkboxes (#c1 and #c2). Each will manipulate the *married* state of one of our previous objects.

```
jQuery('#c1').bind('change', peter.updateMarriedState, peter);
jQuery('#c2').bind('change', susan.updateMarriedState, susan);
```

Thanks to the scope attribute, we don't need to create new functions for each binding; we can use the objects' methods instead.

The methods don't even need to be attached to the objects in the first place. You could do something like this:

```
function updatePersonMarriedState(e){
    var checkbox = e.currentTarget;
    this.married = checkbox.checked;
}
jQuery('#c1').bind('change', updatePersonMarriedState, peter);
jQuery('#c2').bind('change', updatePersonMarriedState, susan);
```

As you can see, you're not really forced to put those functions into the objects' prototype, and it could actually make more sense to keep them separated. Why should a method belonging to Person know about checkboxes and the node? It's probably nicer to keep all the specific DOM manipulation apart from the data.

In some cases, the object's method won't need to know about the node or the event object at all. When this happens, we can bind a method directly, and we won't be mixing DOM and data at all.

If we had to have make two buttons (#b1 and #b2) to display the name of one person when clicked, then it'd be as simple as this:

```
jQuery('#b1').bind('click', peter.whatIsYourName, peter);
jQuery('#b2').bind('click', susan.whatIsYourName, susan);
```

It's worth mentioning that both methods are actually the same:

```
peter.whatIsYourName == susan.whatIsYourName; // true
```

The function is created only once and saved into Person.prototype.

CHAPTER 10

HTML Form Enhancements from Scratch

Brian Cherne

10.0 Introduction

Whether you're trying to learn more about JavaScript and jQuery or you just want to code the most direct solution for your immediate problem, sometimes writing code from scratch is the best approach. This chapter aims to provide you with simple, generic solutions that will help you get started writing your own code.

It is important to note that while there are great benefits to starting from scratch, some of the more common problems you'll encounter, such as remaining character count, autoresizing textareas, and form validation (just to name a few), have already been addressed by others. Please see Chapter 11 or visit the jQuery forums and blogs online for more information on how community-critiqued and community-tested plugins can help you. Sometimes it helps to look at someone else's code to find out what you could do better with yours.

When necessary, I provide some sample HTML under the "Problem" heading of each recipe. This isn't a philosophical statement—there isn't anything wrong or problematic with naked HTML. I am, however, trying to reinforce the mind-set that JavaScript should be used for enhancing existing HTML and improving user interaction. Java-Script is, and should be considered, completely separate from your HTML.

In the following recipes I am only showing XHTML code snippets relevant to the problem. Please make sure that your code is a complete XHTML document and that it passes validation.

Also, I am only including `$(document).ready(function(){...})` in the recipes where that is part of the discussion. All other solutions assume you will place the JavaScript in the correct location for your code structure—either in the `.ready()` handler or at the bottom of your file after the XHTML code in question. Please see Chapter 1 for more information.

10.1 Focusing a Text Input on Page Load

Problem

You have a login form on your home page, and you'd like the username text input to be focused on page load.

Solution

Use the jQuery `$(selector).focus()` method:

```
// when the HTML DOM is ready
$(document).ready(function(){
    // focus the <input id="username" type="text" ...>
    $('#username').focus();
});
```

Discussion

Using `$(document).ready()` should be fast enough. However, in situations like retrieving a huge HTML file over a slow connection, the cursor might focus later than desired—the user could have already entered her username and could be in the process of typing her password when `$(document).ready()` executes and puts her cursor back in the username text input. How annoying! In this case you could use inline JavaScript after the `<input>` tag to make focus immediate:

```
<input name="username" id="username" type="text" />

<script type="text/javascript">
    $('#username').focus();
</script>
```

Or, if you prefer to keep your code together in the `$(document).ready()` block, you can check to see whether the text input has any text in it before giving it focus:

```
// when the HTML DOM is ready
$(document).ready(function(){
    var $inputTxt = $('#username');
    if( $inputTxt.val() == '' ) {
        // focus the username input by default
```

```
            $inputTxt.focus();
        }
    });
```

What will happen when JavaScript is disabled? The user will have to manually click into the text input to start typing.

10.2 Disabling and Enabling Form Elements

Problem

Your order form has fields for both shipping and billing contact information. You've decided to be nice and supply the user with a checkbox that indicates the user's shipping information and billing information are the same. When checked, the billing text fields should be disabled:

```
<fieldset id="shippingInfo">
    <legend>Shipping Address</legend>

    <label for="shipName">Name</label>
    <input name="shipName" id="shipName" type="text" />

    <label for="shipAddress">Address</label>
    <input name="shipAddress" id="shipAddress" type="text" />
</fieldset>

<fieldset id="billingInfo">
    <legend>Billing Address</legend>

    <label for="sameAsShipping">Same as Shipping</label>
    <input name="sameAsShipping" id="sameAsShipping" type="checkbox"
value="sameAsShipping" />

    <label for="billName">Name</label>
    <input name="billName" id="billName" type="text" />

    <label for="billAddress">Address</label>
    <input name="billAddress" id="billAddress" type="text" />
</fieldset>
```

Solution 1

If all you want to do is disable the billing fields, it's as simple as using the jQuery .attr() and .removeAttr() methods when the change event is triggered:

```
// find the "sameAsShipping" checkbox and listen for the change event
$('#sameAsShipping').change(function(){

    if( this.checked ){
        // find all text inputs inside billingInfo and disable them
        $('#billingInfo input:text').attr('disabled','disabled');
```

```
        } else {
            // find all text inputs inside billingInfo and enable them
            $('#billingInfo input:text').removeAttr('disabled');
        }

    }).trigger('change'); // close change() then trigger it once
```

Solution 2

While selecting a checkbox and disabling the form fields might be enough to get the point across to the user, you could go the extra mile and prepopulate the billing text fields with data from shipping information.

The first part of this solution is the same in structure as the solution shown previously. However, in addition to disabling the billing fields, we are also prepopulating them with data from the shipping fields. The following code assumes the shipping and billing `<fieldset>` elements contain the same number of text inputs and that they are in the same order:

```
// find the "sameAsShipping" checkbox and listen for the change event
$('#sameAsShipping').change(function(){
    if( this.checked ){
        // find all text inputs inside billingInfo, disable them, then cycle
through each one
        $('#billingInfo input:text').attr('disabled',
'disabled').each(function(i){

            // find the shipping input that corresponds to this billing input
            var valueFromShippingInput =
$('#shippingInfo input:text:eq('+i+')').val();
            // set the billing value with the shipping text value
            $(this).val( valueFromShippingInput );

        }); // close each()

    } else {
        // find all text inputs inside billingInfo and enable them
        $('#billingInfo input:text').removeAttr('disabled');
    }
}).trigger('change'); // close change() then trigger it
```

The second part of this solution updates the billing fields automatically when the user enters information into the shipping fields, but only if the billing fields are otherwise disabled:

```
// find the shippingInfo text inputs and listen for the keyup and change event
$('#shippingInfo input:text').bind('keyup change',function(){

    // if "sameAsShipping" checkbox is checked
    if ( $('#sameAsShipping:checked').length ){

        // find out what text input this is
        var i = $('#shippingInfo input:text').index( this );
        var valueFromShippingInput = $(this).val();
```

```
        $('#billingInfo input:text:eq('+i+')').val( valueFromShippingInput );
    }

}); // close bind()
```

Discussion

In the preceding solution I'm using the `input:text` selector to avoid disabling the checkbox itself.

Using `.trigger('change')` immediately executes the `.change()` event. This will check the state of the checkbox initially, in case it is checked by default. Also, this protects against Firefox and other browsers that hold on to radio button and checkbox states when the page is refreshed.

What will happen when JavaScript is disabled? You should hide the checkbox by default in CSS. Then use JavaScript to add a class name to a parent element that would override the previous CSS rule. In the following example code I've added an extra `<div>` surrounding the checkbox and label so they can be easily hidden:

```
<style type="text/css" title="text/css">
 #sameAsShippingWrapper { display:none; }
 .jsEnabled #sameAsShippingWrapper { display:block }
</style>

...

// when the HTML DOM is ready
$(document).ready(function(){
    $('form').addClass('jsEnabled');
});

...

<form>
 ...
 <div id="sameAsShippingWrapper">
   <label for="sameAsShipping">Same as Shipping</label>
   <input name="sameAsShipping" id="sameAsShipping" type="checkbox" ... />
 </div>
 ....
</form>
```

As an alternative to hiding the checkbox in CSS and showing it using JavaScript, you could add the checkbox to the DOM using JavaScript. I prefer to keep my HTML, CSS, and JavaScript separate, but sometimes this is the better solution:

```
var html_label = '<label for="sameAsShipping">Same as Shipping</label>';
var html_input = '<input name="sameAsShipping" id="sameAsShipping" type="checkbox"
value="sameAsShipping" />';

$( html_label + html_input ).prependTo('#billingInfo").change( ... ).trigger( ... );
```

10.3 Selecting Radio Buttons Automatically

Problem

You have a series of radio buttons. The last radio button is labeled "Other" and has a text input field associated with it. Naturally you'd want that radio button to be selected if the user has entered text in the Other field:

```
<p>How did you hear about us?</p>
<ul id="chooseSource">
    <li>
        <input name="source" id="source1" type="radio" value="www" />
        <label for="source1">Website or Blog</label>
    </li>
    <li>
        <input name="source" id="source2" type="radio" value="mag" />
        <label for="source2">Magazine</label>
    </li>
    <li>
        <input name="source" id="source3" type="radio" value="per" />
        <label for="source3">Friend</label>
    </li>
    <li>
        <input name="source" id="source4" type="radio" value="oth" />
        <label for="source4">Other</label>
        <input name="source4txt" id="source4txt" type="text" />
    </li>
</ul>
```

Solution 1

In the HTML code you'll notice the radio button, label, and associated text input elements are wrapped in an `<li>` tag. You don't necessarily need this structure, but it makes finding the correct radio button much easier—you're guaranteed there's only one radio button sibling:

```
// find any text input in chooseSource list, and listen for blur
$('#chooseSource input:text').blur(function(){

    // if text input has text
    if ( $(this).val() != '' ) {
        // find the radio button sibling and set it be selected
        $(this).siblings('input:radio').attr('checked',true);
    }

});
```

Solution 2

To take the concept one step further, when the radio button is selected, we can `.focus()` the text field. It's important to note that the following code completely replaces the previous solution. Instead of using the `.blur()` method and then chaining a `.each()` method, just use the `.each()` method since that gives us access to all the objects we need:

```
$('#chooseSource input:text').each(function(){

    // these are both used twice, let's store them to be more efficient
    // the text input
    var $inputTxt = $(this);
    // the associated radio button
    var $radioBtn = $inputTxt.siblings('input:radio');

    // listen for the blur event on the text input
    $inputTxt.blur(function(){
        // if text input has text
        if ( $inputTxt.val() != '' ) {
            // select radio button
            $radioBtn.attr('checked',true);
        }
    });

    // listen for the change event on the radio button
    $radioBtn.change(function(){
        // if it is checked, focus on text input
        if ( this.checked ) { $inputTxt.focus(); }
    });

}); // close each()
```

Discussion

The jQuery `.sibling()` method only returns siblings, not the HTML element you're attempting to find siblings of. So, the code `$(this).siblings('input:radio')` could be rewritten `$(this).siblings('input')` because there is only one other input that is a sibling. I prefer including the `:radio` selector because it is more explicit and creates self-commenting code.

It would have been very easy to target the Other text input directly using `$('#source5txt').focus(...)` and have it directly target the radio button using its `id` attribute. While that's a perfectly functional approach, the code as shown previously is more flexible. What if someone decided to change the `id` of the Other radio button? What if each radio button had a text input? The abstract solution handles these cases without additional work.

Why use `.blur()` instead of `.focus()` on the text input? While `.focus()` would be more immediate for selecting the associated radio button, if the user were simply tabbing through the form elements, `.focus()` would accidentally select the radio button. Using `.blur()` and then checking for a value avoids this problem.

What will happen when JavaScript is disabled? The user will have to manually click into the text input to start typing and manually select the radio button. You are left to decide how to validate and process submitted data should the user enter text and select a different radio button.

10.4 (De)selecting All Checkboxes Using Dedicated Links

Problem

You need to select all checkboxes and deselect all checkboxes using dedicated Select All and Deselect All links:

```
<fieldset>

    <legend>Reasons to be happy</legend>

    <a class="selectAll" href="#">Select All</a>
    <a class="deselectAll" href="#">Deselect All</a>

    <input name="reasons" id="iwokeup" type="checkbox" value="iwokeup" />
    <label for="iwokeup">I woke up</label>

    <input name="reasons" id="health" type="checkbox" value="health" />
    <label for="health">My health</label>

    <input name="reasons" id="family" type="checkbox" value="family" />
    <label for="family">My family</label>

    <input name="reasons" id="sunshine" type="checkbox" value="sunshine" />
    <label for="sunshine">The sun is shining</label>

</fieldset>
```

Solution

Target the Select All and Deselect All links directly using their `class` attributes. Then attach the appropriate `.click()` handler:

```
// find the "Select All" link in a fieldset and list for the click event
$('fieldset .selectAll').click(function(event){
    event.preventDefault();
    // find all the checkboxes and select them
    $(this).siblings('input:checkbox').attr('checked','checked');
});

// find the "Deselect All" link in a fieldset and list for the click event
$('fieldset .deselectAll').click(function(event){
    event.preventDefault();
    // find all the checkboxes and deselect them
    $(this).siblings('input:checkbox').removeAttr('checked');
});
```

Discussion

If you are interested in activating and deactivating the dedicated links, you should see Recipe 10.5 in this chapter. In that solution, the individual checkboxes update the toggle state, and you will need this logic to activate and deactivate the dedicated links appropriately.

What will happen when JavaScript is disabled? You should hide the links by default in CSS. Then use JavaScript to add a class name to a parent element that will override the previous CSS rule:

```
<style type="text/css" title="text/css">
.selectAll, .deselectAll { display:none; }
.jsEnabled .selectAll, .jsEnabled .deselectAll { display:inline; }
</style>

...

// when the HTML DOM is ready
$(document).ready(function(){
    $('form').addClass('jsEnabled');
});
```

10.5 (De)selecting All Checkboxes Using a Single Toggle

Problem

You need to select and deselect all checkboxes using a single toggle, in this case another checkbox. Additionally, that toggle should automatically switch states if some (or all) of the checkboxes are selected individually:

```
<fieldset>

    <legend>Reasons to be happy</legend>

    <input name="reasons" id="toggleAllReasons" type="checkbox" class="toggle" />
    <label for="toggleAllReasons" class="toggle">Select All</label>

    <input name="reasons" id="iwokeup" type="checkbox" value="iwokeup" />
    <label for="iwokeup">I woke up</label>

    <input name="reasons" id="health" type="checkbox" value="health" />
    <label for="health">My health</label>

    <input name="reasons" id="family" type="checkbox" value="family" />
    <label for="family">My family</label>

    <input name="reasons" id="sunshine" type="checkbox" value="sunshine" />
    <label for="sunshine">The sun is shining</label>

</fieldset>
```

Solution

Target the toggle directly using its `class` attribute and the `:checkbox` selector. Then cycle through each toggle found, determine the associated checkboxes using `.siblings()`, and attach the `change` event listeners:

```
// find the "Select All" toggle in a fieldset, cycle through each one you find
$('fieldset .toggle:checkbox').each(function(){

    // these are used more than once, let's store them to be more efficient
    // the toggle checkbox
    var $toggle = $(this);
    // the other checkboxes
    var $checkboxes = $toggle.siblings('input:checkbox');

    // listen for the change event on the toggle
    $toggle.change(function(){
        if ( this.checked ) {
            // if checked, select all the checkboxes
            $checkboxes.attr('checked','checked');
        } else {
            // if not checked, deselect all the checkboxes
            $checkboxes.removeAttr('checked');
        }
    });

    // listen for the change event on each individual checkbox (not toggle)
    $checkboxes.change(function(){
        if ( this.checked ) {
            // if this is checked and all others are checked, select the toggle
            if ( $checkboxes.length == $checkboxes.filter(':checked').length ) {
                $toggle.attr('checked','checked');
            }
        } else {
            // if not checked, deselect the toggle
            $toggle.removeAttr('checked');
        }
    }).eq(0).trigger('change'); // close change() then trigger change on first
checkbox only
}); // close each()
```

Discussion

Using `.eq(0).trigger('change')` immediately executes the `.change()` event for the first checkbox. This sets the state of the toggle and protects against Firefox and other browsers that hold on to radio and checkbox states when the page is refreshed. The `.eq(0)` is used to only trigger the first checkbox's change event. Without `.eq(0)`, the `.trigger('change')` would be executed for every checkbox, but since they all share the same toggle, you only need to run it once.

What will happen when JavaScript is disabled? You should hide the toggle checkbox and label by default in CSS. Then use JavaScript to add a class name to a parent element that would override the previous CSS rule:

```
<style type="text/css" title="text/css">
.toggle { visibility:hidden; }
.jsEnabled .toggle { visibility:visible; }
</style>

...

// when the HTML DOM is ready
$(document).ready(function(){
    $('form').addClass('jsEnabled');
});
```

10.6 Adding and Removing Select Options

Problem

You have a drop-down box for colors and want to add new colors to it, as well as remove options from it.

```
<label for="colors">Colors</label>
<select id="colors" multiple="multiple">
    <option>Black</options>
    <option>Blue</options>
    <option>Brown</options>
</select>

<button id="remove">Remove Selected Color(s)</button>


<label for="newColorName">New Color Name</label>
<input id="newColorName" type="text" />

<label for="newColorValue">New Color Value</label>
<input id="newColorValue" type="text" />

<button id="add">Add New Color</button>
```

Solution

To add a new option to the drop-down box, use the .appendTo() method:

```
// find the "Add New Color" button
$('#add').click(function(event){
    event.preventDefault();

    var optionName = $('#newColorName').val();
    var optionValue = $('#newColorValue').val();

    $('<option/>').attr('value',optionValue).text(optionName).appendTo('#colors');
});
```

To remove an option, use the `.remove()` method:

```
// find the "Remove Selected Color(s)" button
$('#remove').click(function(event){
    event.preventDefault();

    var $select = $('#colors');

    $('option:selected',$select).remove();
});
```

Discussion

I use the `.attr()` and `.text()` methods to populate the `<option>` element:

```
$('<option/>').attr("value",optionValue).text(optionName).appendTo('#colors');
```

However, the same line could be rewritten so that the `<option>` element is built in one step, without using the methods:

```
$('<option value="'+optionValue+'">'+optionName+'</option>').appendTo('#colors');
```

Concatenating all the `<option>` data like that would be a fraction of a millisecond faster, but not in any way noticeable by a human. I prefer using the `.attr()` and `.text()` methods to populate the `<option>` element because I think that it is more readable and easier to debug and maintain. With the performance issue being negligible, using one approach or the other is the developer's preference.

What would happen with JavaScript disabled? You would need to provide a server-side alternative that processes the button clicks, and the user would have to wait for the resulting page reloads.

10.7 Autotabbing Based on Character Count

Problem

You have a form for allowing users to register a product online, and you require the user to enter a serial number printed on the installation discs. This number is 16 digits long and separated across four input fields. Ideally, to speed the user along in their data entry, as each input field is filled up, you'd like to automatically focus the next input field until they're finished typing the number:

```
<fieldset class="autotab">
    <legend>Product Serial Number</legend>
    <input type="text" maxlength="4" />
    <input type="text" maxlength="4" />
    <input type="text" maxlength="4" />
    <input type="text" maxlength="4" />
</fieldset>
```

Solution

Inside `<fieldset class="autotab">`, find all the `<input>` elements. Use jQuery's `.bind()` method to listen for the keydown and keyup events. We exit the bound function for a handful of keys that we want to ignore, because they aren't meaningful for automatically tabbing forward or backward. When an `<input>` element is full, based on the `maxlength` attribute, we `.focus()` the next `<input>` element. Conversely, when using the Backspace key, if an `<input>` element is made empty, we `.focus()` the previous `<input>` element:

```
$('fieldset.autotab input').bind('keydown keyup',function(event){

    // the keycode for the key evoking the event
    var keyCode = event.which;

    // we want to ignore the following keys:
    // 9 Tab, 16 Shift, 17 Ctrl, 18 Alt, 19 Pause Break, 20 Caps Lock
    // 27 Esc, 33 Page Up, 34 Page Down, 35 End, 36 Home
    // 37 Left Arrow, 38 Up Arrow, 39 Right Arrow, 40 Down Arrow
    // 45 Insert, 46 Forward Delete, 144 Num Lock, 145 Scroll Lock
    var ignoreKeyCodes =
',9,16,17,18,19,20,27,33,34,35,36,37,38,39,40,45,46,144,145,';
    if ( ignoreKeyCodes.indexOf(',' + keyCode + ',') > -1 ) { return; }

    // we want to ignore the backspace on keydown only
    // let it do its job, but otherwise don't change focus
    if ( keyCode == 8 && event.type == 'keydown' ) { return; }

    var $this = $(this);
    var currentLength = $this.val().length;
    var maximumLength = $this.attr('maxlength');

    // if backspace key and there are no more characters, go back
    if ( keyCode == 8 && currentLength == 0 ) {
        $this.prev().focus();
    }

    // if we've filled up this input, go to the next
    if ( currentLength == maximumLength ) {
        $this.next().focus();
    }
});
```

Discussion

Why do we bind both keydown and keyup events?

You could use just the keydown event. However, when the user is done filling out the first input, there would be no visual indication that their next keystroke would focus the second input. By using the keyup event, after the first input is filled, the second input gains focus, the cursor is placed at the beginning of the input, and most browsers indicate that focus with a border or some other highlight state. Also, the keyup event is required for the Backspace key to focus the previous input after the current input is empty.

You could use just the `keyup` event. However, if your cursor was in the second input and you were using the Backspace key to clear it, once you removed all characters, the focus would be shifted into the first input. Unfortunately, the first is already full, so the next keystroke would be lost, because of the `maxlength` attribute, and then the `keyup` event would focus the second input. Losing a keystroke is a bad thing, so we perform the same check on `keydown`, which moves the cursor to the next input before the character is lost.

Because the logic isn't CPU intensive, we can get away with binding both the `keydown` and `keyup` events. In another situation, you may want to be more selective.

You'll notice that the `ignoreKeyCodes` variable is a string. If we were building it dynamically, it would be faster to create an array and then use `.join(',')` or `.toString()` JavaScript methods. But since the value is always the same, it's easier to simply code it as a string from the very beginning. I also start and end the `ignoreKeyCodes` variable with commas, because I am paranoid about false positives. This way, when searching for a `keyCode` flanked by commas, you are guaranteed to find only the number you're looking for—if you look for 9, it won't find 19, or 39.

Notice there is no code to prevent `$this.next().focus()` from executing when on the last `<input>` element. I'm taking advantage of the jQuery chain here. If `$this.next()` finds nothing, then the chain stops—it can't `.focus()` what it can't find. In a different scenario, it might make sense to precache any known `.prev()` and `.next()` elements.

What will happen when JavaScript is disabled? Nothing. The user will have to manually click from one text input field to the next.

10.8 Displaying Remaining Character Count

Problem

Your company has a contact form on its website. This form has a `<textarea>` element to allow users to express themselves freely. However, you know time is money, and you don't want your staff reading short novels, so you would like to limit the length of the messages they have to read. In the process, you'd also like to show the end user how many characters are remaining:

```
<textarea></textarea>
<div class="remaining">Characters remaining: <span class="count">300</span></div>
```

Solution

Target all `.remaining` messages, and for each find the associated `<textarea>` element and the maximum number of characters as listed in the `.count` child element. Bind an `update` function to the `<textarea>` to capture when the user enters text:

```
// for each "Characters remaining: ###" element found
$('.remaining').each(function(){

    // find and store the count readout and the related textarea/input field
    var $count = $('.count',this);
    var $input = $(this).prev();

    // .text() returns a string, multiply by 1 to make it a number (for math)
    var maximumCount = $count.text()*1;

    // update function is called on keyup, paste and input events
    var update = function(){

        var before = $count.text()*1;
        var now = maximumCount - $input.val().length;

        // check to make sure users haven't exceeded their limit
        if ( now < 0 ){
            var str = $input.val();
            $input.val( str.substr(0,maximumCount) );
            now = 0;
        }

        // only alter the DOM if necessary
        if ( before != now ){
            $count.text( now );
        }
    };

    // listen for change (see discussion below)
    $input.bind('input keyup paste', function(){setTimeout(update,0)} );

    // call update initially, in case input is pre-filled
    update();

}); // close .each()
```

Discussion

The preceding code is generic enough to allow for any number of "Character remaining" messages and `<textarea>` elements on a given page. This could be useful if you were building a content management or data entry system.

To protect against when the user attempts to copy and paste data into the `<textarea>` using a mouse, we need to bind both the `input` and `paste` events. The `mouseup` event cannot be used because it is not triggered when selecting an item from the browser's contextual menu. The `input` event is part of HTML5 (Working Draft) and already implemented by Firefox, Opera, and Safari. It fires on user input, regardless of input device (mouse or keyboard). Safari, at the time of this writing, has a bug and does not fire the input event on `<textarea>` elements. Both Safari and Internet Explorer understand the `paste` event on `<textarea>` elements and understand `keyup` to capture keystrokes. Attaching `keyup`, `input`, and `paste` is redundant but, in this case, benign. The `update` function is simple enough that there aren't any performance issues, and it only manipulates the DOM when needed, so any redundant `update` calls after the first would do nothing.

An alternative to redundant events would be to use `setInterval` when the `<textarea>` element has focus. The same `update` function could be called from the interval, and if it is paired with the `keyup` event, you'd get the immediate updating on key presses and an arbitrary update interval, say 300 milliseconds, for when information is pasted into the `<textarea>` element. If the `update` function were more complex or costly, this might be a better alternative.

When binding events to form elements, it is sometimes important to use a timeout to slightly delay a function call. In the previous example, Internet Explorer triggers the `paste` event before the text from the clipboard is actually added to the `<textarea>` element. Thus, the calculation for characters remaining would be incorrect until the user clicks or presses another key. By using `setTimeout(update,0)`, the update function is placed at the end of the call stack and will fire after that browser has added the text:

```
$input.bind('input keyup paste', function(){setTimeout(update,0)} );
```

What will happen when JavaScript is disabled? You should hide the "Characters remaining" message by default in CSS. Then use JavaScript to add a class name to a parent element that would override the previous CSS rule. Also, it's important to check the length of the message again on the server side:

```
<style type="text/css" title="text/css">
 .remaining { display:none; }
 .jsEnabled .remaining { display:block; }
</style>

...

// when the HTML DOM is ready
$(document).ready(function(){
    $('form').addClass('jsEnabled');
});
```

10.9 Constraining Text Input to Specific Characters

Problem

Your shopping cart page has a quantity field, and you want to make sure users can only enter numbers into that field:

```
<input type="text" class="onlyNumbers" />
```

Solution

Find all elements with the onlyNumbers class, and listen for keydown and blur events. The keydown event handler will prevent users from typing non-numeric characters into the field. The blur event handler is a precautionary measure that cleans any data entered via Paste from the contextual menu or the browser's Edit menu:

```
$('.onlyNumbers').bind('keydown',function(event){

    // the keycode for the key pressed
    var keyCode = event.which;

    // 48-57 Standard Keyboard Numbers
    var isStandard = (keyCode > 47 && keyCode < 58);

    // 96-105 Extended Keyboard Numbers (aka Keypad)
    var isExtended = (keyCode > 95 && keyCode < 106);

    // 8 Backspace, 46 Forward Delete
    // 37 Left Arrow, 38 Up Arrow, 39 Right Arrow, 40 Down Arrow
    var validKeyCodes = ',8,37,38,39,40,46,';
    var isOther = ( validKeyCodes.indexOf(',' + keyCode + ',') > -1 );

    if ( isStandard || isExtended || isOther ){
        return true;
    } else {
        return false;
    }

}).bind('blur',function(){

    // regular expression that matches everything that is not a number
    var pattern = new RegExp('[^0-9]+', 'g');

    var $input = $(this);
    var value = $input.val();

    // clean the value using the regular expression
    value = value.replace(pattern, '');
    $input.val( value )
});
```

Discussion

The keydown event is immediate and prevents users from typing non-numeric characters into the field. This could be replaced with a keyup event that shares the same handler as the blur event. However, users would see a non-numeral appear and then quickly disappear. I prefer just to prevent them from entering the character in the first place and avoid the flickering.

The blur event protects against copying and pasting non-numeric characters into the text field. In the previous scenario, I'm assuming the user is either trying to test the limits of the JavaScript (something that I would do) or trying to copy and paste data from a spreadsheet. Neither situation requires immediate correction in my opinion. However, if your situation requires more immediate correction, please see the "Discussion" section of Recipe 10.8 for more information about capturing changes from the paste event.

If your situation is different and you expect users to be copying and pasting data from a spreadsheet, keep in mind that the regular expression I use does not account for a decimal point. So, a number like "1,000" would be cleaned to "1000" and the number "10.00" would also be cleaned to "1000" as well.

You'll notice that the validKeyCodes variable is a string that starts and ends with commas. As I mentioned in Recipe 10.7, I did this because I am paranoid about false positives—when searching for a keyCode flanked by commas, you are guaranteed to find only the number you're looking for.

What will happen when JavaScript is disabled? The user will be able to enter any characters they please. Always be sure to validate code on the server. Don't rely on JavaScript to provide clean data.

10.10 Submitting a Form Using Ajax

Problem

You have a form that you would like to submit using Ajax:

```
<form action="process.php">

    <!-- value changed via JavaScript -->
    <input type="hidden" name="usingAJAX" value="false" />

    <label for="favoriteFood">What is your favorite food?</label>
    <input type="text" name="favoriteFood" id="favoriteFood" />

    <input type="submit" value="Tell Us" />

</form>
```

Solution

Find the <form> element, and hijack the submit event:

```
$('form').submit(function(event){

    // we want to submit the form using Ajax (prevent page refresh)
    event.preventDefault();

    // this is where your validation code (if any) would go
```

```
// ...

    // this tells the server-side process that Ajax was used
    $('input[name="usingAJAX"]',this).val( 'true' );

    // store reference to the form
    var $this = $(this);

    // grab the url from the form element
    var url = $this.attr('action');

    // prepare the form data to send
    var dataToSend = $this.serialize();

    // the callback function that tells us what the server-side process had to say
    var callback = function(dataReceived){

        // hide the form (thankfully we stored a reference to it)
        $this.hide();

        // in our case the server returned an HTML snippet so just append it to
        // the DOM
        // expecting: <div id="result">Your favorite food is pizza! Thanks for
        // telling us!</div>
        $('body').append(dataReceived)
    };

    // type of data to receive (in our case we're expecting an HTML snippet)
    var typeOfDataToReceive = 'html';

    // now send the form and wait to hear back
    $.get( url, dataToSend, callback, typeOfDataToReceive )

}); // close .submit()
```

Discussion

What will happen when JavaScript is disabled? The form will be submitted, and the entire page will refresh with the results from the server-side script. I use JavaScript to alter the value of the <input type="hidden" name="usingAJAX" /> element from false to true. This allows the server-side script to know what to send back as a response—either a full HTML page or whatever data is expected for the Ajax response.

10.11 Validating Forms

Problem

You have a form that you would like to validate. To get started, you'll want to set up some basic CSS. The only styles that are really important for this enhancement are the display:none declaration of the div.errorMessage selector and the display:block declaration of the `div.showErrorMessage` selector. The rest are just to make things look better:

```
<style type="text/css" title="text/css">
    div.question {
        padding: 1em;
    }
    div.errorMessage {
        display: none;
    }
    div.showErrorMessage {
        display: block;
        color: #f00;
        font-weight: bold;
        font-style: italic;
    }
    label.error {
        color: #f00;
        font-style: italic;
    }
</style>
```

The following HTML snippet is one example of how you might structure this form. The `<div class="question>` element is purely for layout and not important for the validation code. Each `<label>` element's `for` attribute associates it with the form element with that identical `id` attribute. That is standard HTML, but I wanted to call it out because the JavaScript will also be using that (in reverse) to find the correct `<label>` for a given form element. Similarly, you'll notice the error messages have an `id` attribute of `errorMessage_` plus the `name` attribute of the associated form element. This structure may seem redundant, but radio buttons and checkboxes are grouped by the `name` attribute and you'd only want to have one error message per such group:

```
<form action="process.php">

<!-- TEXT -->
<div class="question">
    <label for="t">Username</label>
    <input id="t" name="user" type="text" class="required" />
    <div id="errorMessage_user" class="errorMessage">Please enter your username.</div>
</div>

<!-- PASSWORD -->
<div class="question">
    <label for="p">Password</label>
    <input id="p" name="pass" type="password" class="required" />
    <div id="errorMessage_pass" class="errorMessage">Please enter your password.</div>
</div>

<!-- SELECT ONE -->
<div class="question">
    <label for="so">Favorite Color</label>
    <select id="so" name="color" class="required">
        <option value="">Select a Color</option>
        <option value="ff0000">Red</option>
```

```
            <option value="00ff00">Green</option>
            <option value="0000ff">Blue</option>
        </select>
        <div id="errorMessage_color" class="errorMessage">Please select your favorite
color.</div>
    </div>

    <!-- SELECT MULTIPLE -->
    <div class="question">
        <label for="sm">Favorite Foods</label>
        <select id="sm" size="3" name="foods" multiple="multiple" class="required">
            <option value="pizza">Pizza</option>
            <option value="burger">Burger</option>
            <option value="salad">Salad</option>
        </select>
        <div id="errorMessage_foods" class="errorMessage">Please choose your favorite
foods.</div>
    </div>

    <!-- RADIO BUTTONS -->
    <div class="question">
        <span>Writing Hand:</span>
        <input id="r1" type="radio" name="hand" class="required"/>
        <label for="r1">Left</label>
        <input id="r2" type="radio" name="hand" class="required" />
        <label for="r2">Right</label>
        <div id="errorMessage_hand" class="errorMessage">Please select what hand you
write with.</div>
    </div>

    <!-- TEXTAREA -->
    <div class="question">
        <label for="tt">Comments</label>
        <textarea id="tt" name="comments" class="required"></textarea>
        <div id="errorMessage_comments" class="errorMessage">Please tell us what you
think.</div>
    </div>

    <!-- CHECKBOX -->
    <div class="question">
        <input id="c" type="checkbox" name="legal" class="required" />
        <label for="c">I agree with the terms and conditions</label>
        <div id="errorMessage_legal" class="errorMessage">Please check the box!</div>
    </div>

    <input type="submit" value="Continue" />

</form>
```

Solution

The first part of the solution is fairly straightforward. Find the <form> element, and
hijack the submit event. When the form is submitted, iterate through the required form

elements, and check to see whether the required elements are valid. If the form is error free, then (and only then) trigger the submit event:

```
$('form').submit(function(event){

    var isErrorFree = true;

    // iterate through required form elements and check to see if they are valid
    $('input.required, select.required, textarea.required',this).each(function(){
        if ( validateElement.isValid(this) == false ){
            isErrorFree = false;
        };
    });

    // Ajax alternatives:
    // event.preventDefault();
    // if (isErrorFree){ $.get( url, data, callback, type ) }
    // if (isErrorFree){ $.post( url, data, callback, type ) }
    // if (isErrorFree){ $.ajax( options ) }

    return isErrorFree;

}); // close .submit()
```

The second part of this solution is where all the real validation happens. The isValid() method starts by storing frequently used data from the element we're validating. Then, in the switch() statement, the element is validated. Finally, class names are added to or removed from the <label> and div.errorMessage elements.

```
var validateElement = {

    isValid:function(element){

        var isValid = true;
        var $element = $(element);
        var id = $element.attr('id');
        var name = $element.attr('name');
        var value = $element.val();

        // <input> uses type attribute as written in tag
        // <textarea> has intrinsic type of 'textarea'
        // <select> has intrinsic type of 'select-one' or 'select-multiple'
        var type = $element[0].type.toLowerCase();

        switch(type){
            case 'text':
            case 'textarea':
            case 'password':
                if ( value.length == 0 ||
value.replace(/\s/g,'').length == 0 ){ isValid = false; }
                break;
            case 'select-one':
            case 'select-multiple':
                if( !value ){ isValid = false; }
                break;
```

```
        case 'checkbox':
        case 'radio':
            if( $('input[name="' + name +
'"]:checked').length == 0 ){ isValid = false; };
            break;
    } // close switch()

    // instead of $(selector).method we are going to use $(selector)[method]
    // choose the right method, but choose wisely
    var method = isValid ? 'removeClass' : 'addClass';

    // show error message [addClass]
    // hide error message [removeClass]
    $('#errorMessage_' + name)[method]('showErrorMessage');
    $('label[for="' + id + '"]')[method]('error');

    return isValid;

    } // close validateElement.isValid()
}; // close validateElement object
```

Discussion

The validation in this solution is quite simple. It checks the following:

- `<input type="text">`, `<input type="password">`, and `<textarea>` elements have some data other than whitespace.

- `<select>` elements have something other than the default option selected. Please note that there are two types of `<select>` element: "select-one" and "select-multiple" (see the second code snippet in this section for HTML code and the previous code snippet for JavaScript validation). The first `<option>` element of the "select-one" `<select>` must have a `value=""` in order for validation to work. The "select-multiple" `<select>` is immune from this requirement because its `<option>` elements can be deselected.

- `<input type="radio">` and `<input type="checkbox">` elements have at least one element checked in their respective `name` groups.

The `switch(){}` statement is used because it is more efficient than multiple `if(){}else if(){}` statements. It also allows for elements with shared validation to be grouped together, letting the `break;` statement separate these groups.

The `validateElement` object is in the global scope with the intention that it might be reused on other forms. It also keeps the global scope less cluttered by containing the validation methods—in the future, helper methods could be added to the `validateElement` object without worrying about global naming collisions. For instance, a `stripWhitespace()` method could be implemented like this:

```
var validateElement = {

    stripWhitespace : function(str){
        return str.replace(/\s/g,'');
```

```
        },
        isValid : function(element){

            //... snipped code ...//

                case 'text':
                case 'textarea':
                case 'password':
                    // if text length is zero after stripping whitespace, it's not valid
                    if ( this.stripWhitespace(value).length == 0 ){ isValid = false; }
                    break;

            //... snipped code ...//

        } // close validateElement.isValid()
    }; // close validateElement object
```

When showing and hiding error messages, I used the bracket notation for calling the `.addClass()` and `.removeClass()` jQuery methods:

```
// instead of $(selector).method we are going to use $(selector)[method]
// choose the right method, but choose wisely
var method = isValid ? 'removeClass' : 'addClass';

// show error message [addClass]
// hide error message [removeClass]
$('#errorMessage_' + name)[method]('showErrorMessage');
$('label[for="' + id + '"]')[method]('error');
```

The previous code in bracket notation is functionally identical to the dot notation:

```
if (isValid) {
    $('#errorMessage_' + name).removeClass('showErrorMessage');
    $('label[for="' + id + '"]').removeClass('error');
} else {
    $('#errorMessage_' + name).addClass('showErrorMessage');
    $('label[for="' + id + '"]').addClass('error');
}
```

When we validate on submit, the dot notation is cleaner and more readable. However, let's extend the bracket-notation solution to allow elements to revalidate (after an initial validation) using the change event. This would give the user immediate feedback that their new answers are in fact valid, without requiring them to click the submit button. The following code does not work as expected (see the next paragraph for the real solution), but it illustrates where to `.unbind()` and `.bind()` the change event:

```
// instead of $(selector).method we are going to use $(selector)[method]
// choose the right method, but choose wisely
var method = isValid ? 'removeClass' : 'addClass';

// show error message [addClass]
// hide error message [removeClass]
$('#errorMessage_' + name)[method]('showErrorMessage');
$('label[for="' + id + '"]')[method]('error');
```

```
// after initial validation, allow elements to re-validate on change
$element
    .unbind('change.isValid')
    .bind('change.isValid',function(){ validateElement.isValid(this); });
```

 Because we are unbinding and binding the change event with each validation, I added the .isValid event namespace to target it more directly.
This way, if a form element has other change events bound, they will
remain.

The problem with the previous code isn't syntax but logic. You'll note that the radio
buttons in the HTML have the class="required" attribute. This means that when the
entire form is validated, each radio button is validated, and (more importantly) each
radio button's <label> has a class added or removed to indicate the error. However, if
we allow for a revalidation to occur using the element-specific change event, only that
particular radio button's <label> will be updated—the others would remain in an error
state. To account for this, a single change event would have to look at all radio buttons
and checkboxes in that name group to affect all the <label> classes simultaneously:

```
// instead of $(selector).method we are going to use $(selector)[method]
// choose the right method, but choose wisely
var method = isValid ? 'removeClass' : 'addClass';

// show error message [addClass]
// hide error message [removeClass]
$('#errorMessage_' + name)[method]('showErrorMessage');

if ( type == 'checkbox' || type == 'radio' ) {

    // if radio button or checkbox, find all inputs with the same name
    $('input[name="' + name + '"]').each(function(){
        // update each input elements <label> tag, (this==<input>)
        $('label[for="' + this.id + '"]')[method]('error');
    });

} else {

    // all other elements just update one <label>
    $('label[for="' + id + '"]')[method]('error');

}

// after initial validation, allow elements to re-validate on change
$element
    .unbind('change.isValid')
    .bind('change.isValid',function(){ validateElement.isValid(this); });
```

If the preceding code were to be rewritten using dot-notation syntax, it would have
twice again as many lines. And on a separate note, with this new logic in place, only
one radio button (or checkbox) in a name group would need to have the

`class="required"` in order for all the other elements in that group to be adjusted correctly.

What will happen when JavaScript is disabled? The form will be submitted without client-side validation. Always be sure to validate code on the server. Don't rely on JavaScript to provide clean data. If the server-side code returns the form with errors, it can use the same classes, on the same elements, in the same way. There is no need to use inline style tags or write custom code to handle the server-side errors differently.

HTML Form Enhancements with Plugins

Jörn Zaefferer

11.0 Introduction

Forms are a very common interaction for users of web applications; improving this interaction improves the business of the application.

jQuery and various plugins offer out-of-the-box and customizable solutions for better interactions, with progressive enhancement at heart.

Each problem could be solved with a jQuery solution from scratch, but using a plugin yields a lot of benefits:

- Avoids reinventing the wheel
- Provides functionality that is well tested among different browsers
- Saves a lot of work that hides in the details
- Provides functionality that is tuned to work under extreme conditions

Each recipe will discuss the strengths and weaknesses of the plugin, highlighting where it may make sense to start from scratch instead.

Basic Approach

The basic approach to using jQuery plugins is always the same. First you include jQuery itself, and then you include the plugin file on your page. Some plugins also need a stylesheet. Most plugins require some markup to work with and a line of code that selects this markup element and does something with it. Because of common naming conventions, a plugin "slideshow" would be used like this:

```
<!DOCTYPE html>
<html>
<head>
```

```
<link rel="stylesheet" href="jquery.slideshow.css"/>
<script src="assets/jquery-latest.js"></script>
<script src="assets/jquery.slideshow.js"></script>
<script type="text/javascript">
jQuery(document).ready(function($){
    $("#slideshow").slideshow();
});
</script>
</head>
<body>
    <div id="slideshow">...</div>
</body>
</html>
```

The specific markup necessary for a slideshow is quite different for a slider or form validation, so that's something to look out for in the documentation and examples of each plugin, and that will be covered in the following recipes.

11.1 Validating Forms

Problem

Most registration forms require input of email address, a password (two times), a username, and some other information, like a birth date. This applies to email services, web shops, or forums.

It's easy to imagine John Doe, who wants to buy a new monitor at some web shop where the registration also requires the input of a *captcha* (a barely legible group of random characters to tell the difference between a human and a bot). He fills out the complete form, which takes some time, and then submits the form. After about five seconds, the form is displayed again, with some error message at the top: he forgot to fill out the street field. He fixes that and submits again. Another five seconds pass: now he missed the password and captcha field! Huh? He did fill those in, but he had to fill them in again after the failed first attempt.

Such late feedback can be very frustrating and can ruin an experience that was otherwise good, especially when security concerns limit functionality—here causing the empty password and captcha fields.

Solution

One way to improve the situation is to add client-side validation. The basic idea is to give the user feedback as early as possible, without annoying him. It shouldn't be possible to submit an invalid form, avoiding the issue of filling in passwords or captchas again.

It also makes sense to highlight errors on fields after they are filled in, as in the case of an invalid email address like *john.doe@gmail,com*. Highlighting fields as wrong doesn't help when it happens before the user even has the chance to fill out a field correctly: to

display "too short" on a field that requires at least two characters, after the user t
the first character, isn't helping at all.

A plugin covering these requirements quite well is the validation plugin (*http://jqu
-cookbook.com/go/plugin-validation*).

To get started, download the plugin, extract the files, and copy `jquery.validate.js` to
your project. The following example shows a comment form with fields for name,
email, URL, and actual comment. A call to the plugin method `validate()` sets up the
validation for the form. Validation rules are specified inline using classes and attributes:

```html
<!DOCTYPE html>
<html>
<head>
  <script src="assets/jquery-latest.js"></script>
  <script src="assets/jquery.validate.js"></script>
  <style type="text/css">
    * { font-family: Verdana; font-size: 96%; }
    label { width: 10em; float: left; }
    label.error { float: none; color: red; padding-left: .5em; vertical-align: top; }
    div { clear: both; }
    input, textarea { width: 15em; }
    .submit { margin-left: 10em; }
  </style>
  <script type="text/javascript">
    jQuery(document).ready(function($){
      $("#commentForm").validate();
    });
  </script>
</head>
<body>
  <form id="commentForm" method="get" action="">
    <fieldset>
      <legend>A simple comment form with submit validation and default messages</legend>
      <div>
        <label for="cname">Name</label>
        <input id="cname" name="name" class="required" minlength="2" />
      </div>
      <div>
        <label for="cemail">E-Mail</label>
        <input id="cemail" name="email" class="required email" />
      </div>
      <div>
        <label for="curl">URL (optional)</label>
        <input id="curl" name="url" class="url" value="" />
      </div>
      <div>
        <label for="ccomment">Your comment</label>
        <textarea id="ccomment" name="comment" class="required"></textarea>
      </div>
      <div>
        <input class="submit" type="submit" value="Submit"/>
      </div>
    </fieldset>
  </form>
```

```
    </body>
    </html>
```

Any field with the class `required` is checked to have any content at all. Other methods in this example include the following:

email
> Checks that the field contains a valid email address

url
> Checks that the field contains a valid URL

minlength
> Checks that the field contains at least x characters; here x is specified via an attribute: `minlength="2"`

Discussion

The validation plugin promotes one specific approach to client-side validation: perform as much work as possible in the browser, and ask the server for help only in special cases, which are covered by the remote method (*http://jquery-cookbook.com/go/plugin -validation-remote-method*), for example, to check whether a username is still available.

A different approach would avoid replicating validation rules and methods on both the client and server sides, instead sending the whole form via Ajax to the server, usually on submit of the form. It could then use the same logic on the server side that is in place already. The drawback is that user feedback is slower, because it is impractical to send a request for every keypress. It's also not very likely that the server validation was written with Ajax validation in mind, making it impractical to reuse it. In that case, you'd have to plan up front to use it that way.

The validation plugin can be added to a form later, and apart from remote validation, there is no need to adapt the application in any way. This makes it useful for a simple comment form on a blog, as well as more complex forms on some intranet application and anything in between.

The most important building blocks for the plugin are rules and methods. Methods contain validation logic, like the email method that uses a regular expression to determine whether a value is a valid email address. Rules wire input fields together with methods, where a single rule is a pair of an input field and a method. The email field then has one rule for making it required and one for making it an email address.

Methods

The plugin has about 19 built-in methods. The essential method is `required`—when specified, the field has to be filled out. When left out, most other methods will be ignored on an empty field. The only exception to that is the `equalTo` method, which checks that the content of a field is exactly the same as some other field, which even applies for an empty field. The rule itself is most commonly used for "Confirm password" fields.

The `email`, `url`, `date`, `dateISO`, `dateDE`, `number`, `numberDE`, `digits`, and `creditcard` methods all check for certain data types, with simple variations for different locales. For example, `number` requires a U.S. number format like 1,000.00, and `numberDE` requires the German number format 1.000,00.

The `min` and `max` and `range` methods check the value of a number, while `minlength`, `maxlength`, and `rangelength` check the number of characters.

In case of a select input or checkboxes, `min`, `max`, and `range` validate the number of selected options or checked checkboxes.

In case of file inputs, the `accept` method comes in handy and checks the file extension, by default looking for `.gif`, `.png`, `.jpg`, or `.jpeg`.

The `remote` method is the only method that delegates the actual validation logic elsewhere, to the server side. It gets a URL as the parameter, pointing at some server-side resource. This could be a script that does a database query, for example, for checking if a username is already taken or if a specified email address is already registered. An example of a registration form using the remote method for both username and email fields can be found at *http://jquery-cookbook.com/go/plugin-validation-remote-demo*.

Custom methods. Custom methods are a good way to extend the plugin with application-specific requirements. You may have a form where users enter URLs that have to start with a certain corporate domain. A custom method could encapsulate the necessary validation:

```
jQuery.validator.addMethod("domain", function(value, element) {
    return this.optional(element) || /^http:\/\/mycorporatedomain.com/.test(value);
}, "Please specify the correct domain for your documents");
```

The first argument to `jQuery.validator.addMethod` is the name of the custom method, and it must be a valid JavaScript identifier. The second argument is a function that implements the actual validation. If it returns true, the input is considered valid. It uses `this.optional(element)` to determine whether that input has no value and should therefore be skipped—all default methods use the same call. The third argument specifies the default message for the new method.

Writing methods that accept a parameter works very similarly:

```
jQuery.validator.addMethod("math", function(value, element, params) {
    return this.optional(element) || value == params[0] + params[1];
}, jQuery.format("Please enter the correct value for {0} + {1}"));
```

In this case, the default message is specified with the help of `jQuery.format`, a templating helper the plugin provides. The indexed curly-braced placeholders are replaced with the actual parameters when the validation is run.

Custom methods can also reuse existing methods, which is useful to specify different default messages for a single method. In this example, the `required` method is aliased to `customerRequired` with a different default message:

```
$.validator.addMethod("customerRequired", $.validator.methods.required,
"Customer name required");
```

A collection of ready-to-use custom methods are bundled with the plugin in `additionalMethods.js`.

Rules

There are four distinct ways to specify rules: two in code and two inline as metadata. The previous example uses classes and attributes as metadata, which the plugin supports by default. When the metadata plugin (*http://jquery-cookbook.com/go/plugin-met adata*) is available, rules can be embedded in various ways, for example, inside the `class` attribute:

```
<input type="text" name="email" class="{required:true, email:true}" />
```

Here the class contains JavaScript literals inside curly braces, which is very similar in syntax to specifying rules in code via the `rules` option:

```
$("#myform").validate({
    rules: {
        name: {
            required: true,
            minlength: 2
        },
        email: {
            required: true,
            email: true
        },
        url: "url",
        comment: "required"
    }
});
```

The object keys like `name`, `email`, `url`, and `comment` always refer to the name of the element, not the ID.

Note the shortcuts used for `url` and `comment`, where only a single rule is necessary. This isn't available when specifying rules with parameters, like `minlength`.

Some rules need to be added later, which is possible using the fourth way, the `rules` plugin method:

```
// initialize the validation first
$("#myform").validate();
// some time later, add more rules
$("#username").rules("add", { minlength: 2});
```

Rules can also be removed that way:

```
$("#username").rules("remove", "required");
```

This can come in handy when implementing a "Forgot password" link on a login form:

```
$("#loginform").validate({
    username: "required",
    password: "required"
});
$("a#forgotPassword").click(function(e) {
    $("#password").rules("remove", "required");
    $("#loginform").submit();
    $("#password").rules("add", "required");
    return false;
});
```

That click event code removes the required rule from the password, tries to submit the form (triggering the validation), and adds the rule back. That way, the username field is still being validated, and if the validation fails, the password field will be required again (in case of a normal form submit).

Dependencies. Often the validation behavior of a field depends on some more factors than just a link being clicked. Those can be handled using parameters for the **required** method. The parameter can be a selector or a callback. The selector is useful when the dependency can be written in a simple expression. An email field may be required only when the newsletter checkbox is selected:

```
email: {
    required: "#newsletter:checked"
}
```

A callback can be used for expressions of any complexity, for example, when the field depends on the state of multiple other fields:

```
email: {
    required: function(element) {
        return $("#newsletter:checked").length && $("#telephone:blank");
    }
}
```

Custom expressions. The previous example used the :blank expression to select an element only when it has no value at all or only whitespace. The plugin also provides the :filled expression, the inversion of :blank. jQuery itself provides :checked, and the validation plugin adds the inversion :unchecked. Both are useful when specifying dependencies on radio buttons or checkboxes.

While you could use the :not expression to inverse :filled or :checked, :blank and :unchecked make the selector more readable and therefore easier to understand at a glance.

Error messages

Similar to rules, there are a few ways to specify messages, both in code and inline. Inline messages are read from the title attribute:

```
<input name="email" class="required email" title="A valid email address is
required" />
```

That will produce a single error message for each rule. An alternative inline approach
is to use the metadata plugin (see "Rules" on page 242):

```
<input name="email" class="{required:true, email:true, messages:{required:"Required",
email: "Not a valid email address"}}"/>
```

With this approach, you can specify a message for each rule, which is also possible
when using the `messages` option:

```
$("#myform").validate({
    messages: {
        email: {
            required: "Required",
            email: "Not a valid email address"
        }
    }
});
```

Again, the keys—here, `email`—refer to the name of the input, not the ID, just the same
as specifying rules.

For more dynamic scenarios, the `rules` plugin method can be used:

```
$("#myform").validate();
// sometime later
$("#email").rules("add", {
    messages: {
        email: "A valid email address, please!"
    }
});
```

If you use some of the alternatives to the `title` attribute while using a regular title, you
can suppress the plugin from checking the attribute for messages:

```
$("#myform").validate({
    ignoreTitle: true
});
```

Localization. The default messages are in English (with the exception of `dateDE` and
`numberDE`). In addition, the plugin provides (at the time of this writing) 17 localizations.
Usage is plain and simple: just copy the `messages_xx.js` file you need to your project,
and include it after the validation plugin. For example, here's the code for the Swedish
localization:

```
<script src="assets/jquery-latest.js"></script>
<script src="assets/jquery.validate.js"></script>
<script src="assets/messages_se.js.js"></script>
```

With that in place, instead of "Please enter a valid email address." you'll get "Ange en
korrekt e-postadress."

Error element. By default error messages are inserted into the DOM next to the element
that they are referring to. An error message is inserted as a label element, with the `for`

attribute set to the `id` of the validated element. Using a label with the `for` attribute leverages the browser feature where a click on the label gives focus to the input field. So by default, the user can click the error message to give the invalid field focus.

If you need a different element type, use the `errorElement` option:

```
$("#myform").validate({
    errorElement: "em"
});
```

The plugin will still use the `for` attribute then, but the auto linking the browser provides won't work.

Layout. If you want to customize the position where error messages are inserted, the `errorPlacement` option is useful. We may have a form that uses a table for layout, where the first column contains the regular label, the second the input, and the third the messages:

```
<form id="signupform" method="get" action="">
    <table>
        <tr>
            <td class="label">
                <label id="lfirstname" for="firstname">First Name</label>
            </td>
            <td class="field">
                <input id="firstname" name="firstname" type="text" value=""
maxlength="100" />
            </td>
            <td class="status"></td>
        </tr>
        <!-- more fields -->
    </table>
</form>

$("#signupform").validate({
    errorPlacement: function(error, element) {
        error.appendTo( element.parent("td").next("td") );
    }
});
```

Another common requirement is to display a general message above the form. The `errorContainer` option helps with that:

```
$("#myform").validate({
    errorContainer: "#messageBox1"
});
```

In this example, an element with the ID `messageBox1` would be shown when the form is invalid and would be hidden when valid.

This can also be combined with the `errorLabelContainer` option. When specified, error labels aren't placed next to their input elements but instead added to a single element above or below the form. Combined with the `errorContainer` and `wrapper` options, messages are added to a list of errors above the form:

```
<div class="container">
        <h4>There are a few problems, please see below for details.</h4>
        <ul></ul>
</div>
<form id="myform" action="">
<!-- form content -->
</form>

var container = $('div.container');
// validate the form when it is submitted
$("#myform").validate({
    errorContainer: container,
    errorLabelContainer: $("ul", container),
    wrapper: 'li'
});
```

Handling the submit

Once the form is valid, it has to be submitted. By default that just works as any other
form submit. To submit the form via Ajax, the submitHandler option can be used, together with the form plugin (see Recipe 11.6 for more details):

```
$(".selector").validate({
    submitHandler: function(form) {
        $(form).ajaxSubmit();
    }
});
```

The invalidHandler callback is useful for running code on an invalid submit. The following example displays a summary of the missing fields:

```
$("#myform").validate({
    invalidHandler: function(e, validator) {
        var errors = validator.numberOfInvalids();
        if (errors) {
            var message = errors == 1
                ? 'You missed 1 field. It has been highlighted below'
                : 'You missed ' + errors + ' fields. They have been highlighted below';
            $("div.error span").html(message);
            $("div.error").show();
        } else {
            $("div.error").hide();
        }
    }
});
```

The Marketo demo shows this behavior in action (*http://jquery-cookbook.com/go/plu
gin-validation-marketo-demo*).

Limitations

So, when does it make sense to not use the plugin and write a validation solution from
scratch? There are certain limitations: forms where groups of inputs, like checkboxes,
have different name attributes are hard to validate as a group. Lists of inputs that all have

the same name can't be validated, because each individual input needs its own unique name. If you stick with the naming convention of unique names for individual inputs and one name for groups of checkboxes or radio buttons, the plugin works fine.

If your application has only a login form, the plugin is probably overkill, and it would be difficult to justify the file size; however, if you use the plugin somewhere else on a site, it can be used for the login form as well.

11.2 Creating Masked Input Fields

Problem

There are certain input types that are quite error prone, like a credit card number. A simple typo that goes unnoticed at first can cause weird errors much later. That also applies to dates or phone numbers. These have a few features in common:

- A fixed length
- Mostly numbers
- Delimiting characters at certain positions

Solution

A jQuery plugin that can improve the feedback is the masked input plugin (*http://jquery -cookbook.com/go/plugin-masked-input*). It is applied to one or more inputs to restrict what can be entered while inserting delimiters automatically.

In this example, a phone input is masked:

```
<!DOCTYPE html>
<html>
<head>
    <script src="assets/jquery-latest.js"></script>
    <script src="assets/jquery.maskedinput.js"></script>
    <script>
    jQuery(document).ready(function($) {
        $("#phone").mask("(999) 999-9999");
    });
    </script>
</head>
<body>
    <form>
        <label for="phone">Phone</label>
        <input type="text" name="phone" id="phone" />
    </form>
</body>
</html>
```

The plugin file is included in addition to jQuery itself. In the document-ready callback, the input with ID phone is selected, and the mask method is called. The only argument specifies the mask to use, here describing the format of a U.S. phone number.

Discussion

There are four characters with a special meaning available when specifying the mask:

a
> Any alpha character from a–z and A–Z

9
> Any digit from 0–9

*
> Any alphanumeric character, that is, a–z, A–Z, and 0–9

?
> Anything after this is optional

Any other character, like the parentheses or hyphen in the phone mask, are considered literals, which the plugin automatically inserts into the input and which the user can't remove.

By default, the plugin inserts an underscore (_) for each variable character. For the phone example, the input would display the following value once focused:

(__) __-____

When the user starts typing, the first underscore gets replaced if it is a valid character, here a digit. The other literals are skipped as well.

The underscore placeholder can be customized by passing an additional argument:

```
$("#phone").mask("(999) 999-9999", {placeholder: " "});
```

In this case, whitespace would be displayed instead of the underscore.

It's also possible to define new mask characters:

```
$.mask.definitions['~'] = '[+-]';
$("#eyescript").mask("~9.99 ~9.99 999");
```

Here the new mask character is a tilde, and allowed values for it are + and –, specified as a regular expression character class. The tilde can then be used in a mask.

The quotation mark enables masks with a fixed part and an optional part. A phone number with an optional extension could be defined like this:

```
$("#phone").mask("(999) 999-9999? x99999");
```

When a masked input is combined with the validation plugin (Recipe 11.1), it's important the field proper rules are defined for it. Otherwise, the validation plugin may accept the placeholder characters of the mask plugin as valid input, irritating the user when an invalid field is marked as valid while he just inserted the first character.

Limitations

The significant limitation of the plugin is the fixed-length requirement. It can't be used for anything with a variable length, like currency value. For example, "$ 999,999.99" would require a value between 100,000.00 and 999,999.99 and can't accept anything above or below.

11.3 Autocompleting Text Fields

Problem

There are two HTML input types that allow a user to select one value out of a list of existing values: radio buttons and selects. Radio buttons work well for lists with up to eight items, and selects work well with up to 30 to 150, depending on the type of data. Both fall short when the user can enter a new value as well—in this case they are usually accompanied by an "Other" field. Both become useless when the list is big, maybe 500 or 500,000 items.

Solution

The jQuery UI autocomplete widget (*http://jquery-cookbook.com/go/widget-autocom plete*) can solve the various situations where a select isn't enough. In the simplest case, the data to display is available in a JavaScript array:

```
<label for="month">Select a month:</label>
<input id="month" name="month" />

var months = ['January', 'February', 'March', 'April', 'May', 'June', 'July',
'August', 'September', 'October', 'November', 'December'];
$("#month").autocomplete({
    source: months
});
```

Here we apply the autocomplete plugin to a month input, with the data being a plain JavaScript array.

When the data isn't already available on the client side, the plugin can get it from a server-side resource:

```
$("#month").autocomplete({
    source: "addresses.php"
});
```

The plugin then sends a GET request to that resource, with the user-entered value appended as the q parameter, e.g., addresses.php?q=ma. As a response, the plugin expects a list of newline separated values:

```
Mainstreet
Mallstreet
Marketstreet
```

Discussion

The first decision to make when using the plugin is deciding on local or remote data.

With local data, the complete data set is already present in the browser's memory. It could have been loaded as part of the page or via a separate Ajax request. In any case, it's loaded just once. This mode is practical when the data is small and static—less than 500 rows of data—and doesn't change while selecting a value. The big advantage of local data is that it's extremely fast to find matching values.

Remote data is loaded from the server in small chunks (up to 100 rows per chunk makes sense). This works with both small data sets as well as very big data sets (say, more than half a million rows). As the data is loaded from the server, finding matching values is slower when compared to local data. This is mitigated by loading big enough chunks, which can then be filtered down on the client side without additional requests.

11.4 Selecting a Range of Values

Problem

Imagine a car search interface: the user inputs the price range that's acceptable for him, and while changing the value, the list of available cars in that range is updated. The HTML form elements for that type of input—plain text input, radio buttons, selects— aren't good enough. On the one hand, each requires an exact value. On the other, they fail to visualize the price range. It's also not possible to move the entire range; instead, the user has to update both the start and end values, one by one.

Solution

The jQuery UI slider widget (*http://jquery-cookbook.com/go/widget-slider*) can transform two text inputs into a range slider. The start and end values of the range can be dragged using the mouse or using the cursor keys.

The default slider is applied to a simple `<div>`, with no options necessary:

```
<div id="slider"></div>
```

```
$("#slider").slider();
```

For that to work, jQuery, jQuery UI core, and the slider `.js` files must be included, in addition to a UI theme:

```
<link rel="stylesheet" href="ui.core.css" />
<link rel="stylesheet" href="ui.slider.css" />
<link rel="stylesheet" href="ui.theme.css" />
<script type="text/javascript" src="jquery-1.3.2.js"></script>
<script type="text/javascript" src="ui.core.js"></script>
<script type="text/javascript" src="ui.slider.js"></script>
```

While this adds a nice-looking slider to the page, it doesn't yet really do anything useful.

In the case of the car search, we want to put the selected values into an input field and display them to the user:

```
<p>
    <label for="amount">Price range:</label>
    <input type="text" id="amount" style="border:0; color:#f6931f;
font-weight:bold;" />
</p>

<div id="slider-range"></div>
```

Based on that markup, we can create a range slider:

```
var slider = $("#slider-range").slider({
    range: true,
    min: 0,
    max: 500,
    values: [75, 300],
    slide: function(event, ui) {
        $("#amount").val('$' + ui.values[0] + ' - $' + ui.values[1]);
    }
});
$("#amount").val('$' + slider.slider("values", 0) + ' - $' + slider.slider("values",
1));
```

Setting the range option to true instructs the plugin to create two handles instead of just one. The min and max options specify the total range available; the values option the starting positions.

The slide callback is triggered when a handle is moved. Here it updates the amount input to display the selected price range.

Discussion

Binding a slider to a text input is one option; binding it to a select, and using the options of the select as values, is another.

Let's take the example of a room reservation form where the user enters the minimum number of beds. The maximum number of beds is six; therefore, a slider isn't a bad choice to start with. Using progressive enhancement, we can enhance the select with a slider and feed changes to the slider back to the <select> element:

```
<select name="minbeds" id="minbeds">
    <option>1</option>
    <option>2</option>
    <option>3</option>
    <option>4</option>
    <option>5</option>
    <option>6</option>
</select>

var select = $("#minbeds");
var slider = $('<div id="slider"></div>').insertAfter(select).slider({
    min: 1,
    max: 6,
```

```
        range: "min",
        value: select[0].selectedIndex + 1,
        slide: function(event, ui) {
            select[0].selectedIndex = ui.value - 1;
        }
    });
    $("#minbeds").click(function() {
        slider.slider("value", this.selectedIndex + 1);
    });
```

Instead of using existing markup, which doesn't have any semantic meaning, we generate the `<div>` on the fly and insert it into the DOM, right after the `<select>`.

We have a single value, so we use the `value` option instead of the `values` option. We initialize it with the `selectedIndex` of the select, using the DOM property directly. The property starts at zero, so we add one.

When the slider is updated, on keypresses or while dragging the handle with the mouse, the select is updated by setting its `selectedIndex` to the value read from the `ui` object passed to every `ui` event. The offset of one, which we added during initialization, is now subtracted.

We also set the `range` option, even though we have only one handle. It accepts a string parameter in addition to the Boolean: setting it to `min` displays the range from the start of the slider to the handle; setting it to `max` displays it from the end of the slider to the handle. This helps to visualize the minimum number of beds the hotel room should have.

Finally, we bind a click event to the select to update the slider when the select itself is changed directly by the user. We could also hide the select but would then need to add another form of label to display the selected numerical value.

The plugin also supports two more options, which weren't covered in the example:

- Setting `animate: true` animates the handle to move to the destination when clicking somewhere on the slider.
- Setting `orientation: vertical` displays a vertical slider, instead of the horizontal default.

There are also more events with more fine-grained control:

- `start` is called whenever sliding begins.
- `stop` is called when sliding stops.
- `change` is called when sliding stops and the slider value changes; this is especially useful when a change to the slider triggers an expensive operation, such as sending a request to the server, or updating a graph. Of course, it makes the slider behavior less obvious, because there isn't instant feedback while sliding.

11.5 Entering a Range-Constrained Value

Problem

A slider is good at handling rough inputs and visualizing them but bad for gathering exact values. An example would be a pixel value in a layout component, where the value has to be tuned in very small increments, pixel by pixel. With a standard input, the keyboard has to be used: click the field, remove the current value and enter a new value, repeat for each increment.

Solution

The jQuery UI spinner widget (*http://jquery-cookbook.com/go/widget-spinner*) can solve this problem by adding up and down buttons to the input to enable mouse interaction as well as handle keyboard events like cursor up and down.

All you need is a regular text input:

```
<input id="value" name="value" />
```

to which you then apply the spinner plugin:

```
$("#value").spinner();
```

This will create and position the up/down buttons and add the necessary keyboard handling events.

Use the spinner plugin to add buttons to in- and decrement the value, either by clicking the buttons or giving the input focus and using the cursor keys.

It also restricts the input to numeric values—when entering *abc* into the spinner, it'll get replaced with the default value on blur. Unless specified otherwise, it's a zero.

Discussion

The plugin offers a few options to restrict the input further:

- min sets the lower limit, e.g., –10 or 100.
- max sets the upper limit, e.g., 10 or 200.
- stepping restricts the value to certain increments, e.g., 5; the default is 1.

When the spinner is used to input a currency value, the currency option can be used to display the appropriate symbol inside the input.

The following example puts these all together and creates a form for donating money:

```
<label for="currency">Currency</label>
<select id="currency" name="currency">
    <option value="$">US $</option>
    <option value="€">EUR €</option>
    <option value="¥">YEN ¥</option>
</select>
```

```
<br/>
<label for="amount">Select the amount to donate:</label>
<input id="amount" name="amount" value="5" />
```

We have a select for the currency and a text input for the amount:

```
var currency = $("#currency").change(function() {
    $("#amount").spinner("option", "currency", $(this).val()).blur();
});
$("#amount").spinner({
    currency: currency.val(),
    min: 5,
    max: 1000,
    step: 5
});
```

We bind a change event to the currency select to update the currency option of the spinner whenever the selection changes.

The spinner itself is initialized with the current value, as well as limits for min, max, and step, restricting the value somewhere between 5 and 1,000, with increments of 5, e.g., 10, 15, 20, and so on.

Google Maps integration

The value may also be a decimal number; in that case, the decimal option can be used to specify the number of allowed digits after the decimal point. In the following example, we display a Google map and use spinners to specify the latitude and longitude values.

To start with, we include the Google Maps API scripts:

```
<script type="text/javascript" src="http://maps.google.com/maps/api/js?
sensor=false"></script>
```

With that in place, we can add markup for the spinners and the actual map, along with some minimal styles:

```
<style>
    #map { width:500px; height:500px; }
</style>

<label for="lat">Latitude</label>
<input id="lat" name="lat" value="44.797916" />
<br/>
<label for="lng">Longitude</label>
<input id="lng" name="lng" value="-93.278046" />

<div id="map"></div>
```

Based on that, we can initialize the map and link it with the spinners:

```
function latlong() {
    return new google.maps.LatLng($("#lat").val(),$("#lng").val());
}
function position() {
```

```
    map.set_center(latlong());
}
$("#lat, #lng").spinner({
    precision: 6,
    change: position
});

var map = new google.maps.Map($("#map")[0], {
    zoom: 8,
    center: latlong(),
    mapTypeId: google.maps.MapTypeId.ROADMAP
});
```

The `position` function sets the center of the map to the latitude and longitude values obtained from the spinners. They are initialized with the `decimal` option set to 6, and passing the `position` function for the `change` option. With that, the map is updated whenever one of the spinners changes. Then the map itself is initialized, using the Google Maps API.

The drawback of the spinner in this case is that increments and decrements affect only the digits before the decimal point, so scrolling is rather rough. The `increment` option rounds any value below one up to one, so it can't help here.

11.6 Uploading Files in the Background

Problem

File upload is part of many web applications but badly supported by browsers. The biggest problem is the lack of feedback of the upload status, while any action of the users disrupts the upload. A simple progress bar could improve the feedback but requires quite some work on the server side, while the problem of disruptive actions remains.

Solution

To improve the situation, file uploads should be performed in the background. This allows the application to continue accepting other user input.

The jQuery form plugin (*http://jquery-cookbook.com/go/plugin-form*) makes it trivial to switch from the native browser upload to Ajax background uploading. With this form:

```
<form id="uploadform">
    <input type="file" id="fileupload" name="fileupload" />
    <input type="submit" value="Upload!" />
</form>
```

all you need to add is a call to `ajaxForm`:

```
$("#uploadform").ajaxForm();
```

However, just doing the upload in the background without any feedback of the completed upload isn't enough, so we use the `success` option to display an alert about the successful upload:

```
$("#uploadform").ajaxForm({
    success: function() {
        alert("Upload completed!");
    }
});
```

Discussion

The `ajaxForm` method binds itself to the submit event of the form, which allows it to also include the button used to submit the form in the Ajax request. The latter isn't available when using `ajaxSubmit`. The `ajaxSubmit` method is useful on its own when the form submit is handled elsewhere, for example, by the validation plugin. To integrate validation and Ajax submit, `ajaxSubmit` should be used in the `submitHandler` option:

```
$("#commentform").validate({
    submitHandler: function(form) {
        $(form).ajaxSubmit({
            success: function() {
                $(form).clearForm();
                alert("Thanks for your comment!");
            }
        });
    }
});
```

In addition to the `alert`, the `clearForm` method, also provided by the form plugin, removes all values from the form. This makes it easy for the user to upload another file.

11.7 Limiting the Length of Text Inputs

Problem

It is common to limit the amount of characters in a textarea, like the 140 characters for Twitter or the 500 characters for a YouTube comment. Informing the user that he entered too much, after he submitted a form, is frustrating, so it makes sense to display an indicator of the available characters left.

Solution

The maxlength plugin (*http://jquery-cookbook.com/go/plugin-maxlength*) solves this by adding a "Characters left: x" indicator in front or after the textarea. The plugin, after being applied on a text input or textarea, looks for an element with the class `charsLeft` to update with the count:

```
<form action="/comment">
    <p>Characters left: <span class="charsLeft">10</span></p>
```

```
  <textarea name="commentbody" maxlength="10"></textarea>
</form>

$('textarea').maxlength();
```

To make this less intrusive, we can create the necessary elements with jQuery, resulting in a simpler form markup:

```
<form action="/comment">
  <textarea name="commentbody" maxlength="10"></textarea>
</form>

var textarea = $('textarea');
$('<p>Characters left: <span class="charsLeft">10</span></p>').insertBefore(textarea);
textarea.maxlength();
```

Discussion

In the case of Twitter, the textarea allows you to go over the 140-character limit, but you can't submit. This helps a lot when pasting longer text that wouldn't fit into the 140-character limit and editing it afterward. To get a similar effect with the maxlength plugin, we can set the hardLimit option to false. However, that doesn't affect the actual submit but could be handled elsewhere, e.g., by the validation plugin (see Recipe 11.1).

The plugin also supports counting words instead of characters, by setting the words option to true.

Instead of having the plugin look for the default .charsLeft selector, we can also set the feedback option.

Here is another example using all three of these options:

```
<form action="/comment">
  <textarea name="commentbody" maxlength="10"></textarea>
  <p><span>x</span> characters left</p>
</form>

$('textarea').maxlength({
  feedback: "p>span",
  hardLimit: false,
  words: true
});
```

11.8 Displaying Labels Above Input Fields

Problem

A page layout doesn't have enough space in front of an input element to display a label, the function of the input is obscured, and a title alone isn't visible enough.

Search and login forms are often subject to space constraints. There just isn't enough visual space to display a label in front of the input field. Though without the label, the function of the input is obscured. A `title` attribute isn't enough to fix the problem, because it's rather hard to spot, requiring the user to mouse over the input and rest there.

Solution

The most common example, the search field, can be solved by displaying "search" inside the field with a light gray to emphasize that it's just a label, not the actual text to search for. When focusing the field, the text is removed. When blurring the field, the text is returned, unless something else was entered.

The less common example is a space-constrained login form, consisting of username and password fields. The password field needs to display the watermark as plain text, while the password to be entered (or prefilled by the browser) must still be obfuscated.

In both cases, the watermark shouldn't be submitted as a value.

The watermark plugin (*http://jquery-cookbook.com/go/widget-watermark*) solves this problem by displaying a label element above the actual input, hiding the label when the input gets focus, and displaying it again when the empty field is blurred.

Using a label above the field, instead of modifying the text inside the field, makes this solution also work with password fields and avoids having to clear watermark values on submit.

The default usage calls the watermark plugin method and passes the value to display:

```
$("#search").watermark("Search");
```

Discussion

Instead of passing the value to the plugin, it can also be specified as metadata, using the metadata plugin (*http://jquery-cookbook.com/go/plugin-metadata*), in the markup, which is more practical when several watermarks are used or when those are generated on the server side:

```
<form id="loginform">
    <input type="text" id="email" name="email"
class="{watermark:'E-Mail Address'}" />
    <input type="password" id="password" name="password"
class="{watermark:'Your password'}" />
</form>

$("#loginform input").watermark();
```

Metadata has the drawback that it doesn't build on progressive enhancement. To improve that, label elements should be used as for a normal form, with the plugin positioning the labels at the right position:

```
<form id="loginform">
    <div>
        <label for="email">E-Mail Address</label>
```

```
            <input type="text" id="email" name="email" />
        </div>
        <div>
            <label for="password">Your password</label>
            <input type="password" id="password" name="password" />
        </div>
    </form>
```

In this case, the plugin is applied to the labels instead of the inputs:

```
$("#loginform label").watermark();
```

The plugin then uses the for attribute of each label to find the associated input and position it above the input.

11.9 Growing an Input with Its Content

Problem

A textarea is part of an interface and is often too large or too small, depending on the user's input. Either it's too big and other important elements get out of sight, or it's too small and the user has to scroll too much.

Solution

Use the elastic plugin (*http://jquery-cookbook.com/go/plugin-elastic*) to start with a small default height and have the height autogrow when the user enters a certain amount of text.

Usage is plain and simple. Start with a textarea:

```
<textarea id="commentbody"></textarea>
```

And apply the plugin to it:

```
$("#commentbody").elastic();
```

Discussion

The plugin binds both a timer and a blur event to the textarea to look for changes. When the content changes, it copies the content into a hidden textarea with the same styles applied to it as the original, calculates the new height for that, and if it exceeds the current height of the original, starts an animation to adapt. This allows the textarea to both grow and shrink as content is added or removed.

An alternative is to let the user resize the textarea. Safari offers that by default for any textarea. The jQuery UI resizable plugin (*http://jquery-cookbook.com/go/widget-resizable*) can add that to other browsers as well. Starting with the same textarea, we apply the resizable plugin, customizing the handle option to display only one handle on the bottom right:

```
$("#resizable").resizable({
    handles: "se"
});
```

With that and the jQuery UI base theme included, the handle gets displayed below the textarea. To move it into the bottom-right corner of the textarea, we have to add some CSS:

```
.ui-resizable-handle {
    bottom: 17px;
}
```

11.10 Choosing a Date

Problem

Date inputs are necessary for searching for events, flights, or hotels, or entering a birth date in a registration form. A common solution is to use three selects, for the day, month, and year components. While that works OK for a date of birth, it can get very cumbersome when searching for a flight in a certain time period.

Solution

The jQuery UI datepicker (*http://jquery-cookbook.com/go/widget-datepicker*) can solve the problem by offering a calendar together with a lot of customization options to optimize for various applications.

The default datepicker works by simply applying it to an input:

```
<label for="startAt">Start at:</label>
<input type="text" name="startAt" id="startAt" />

$("#startAt").datepicker();
```

This will bind the events necessary to show the datepicker when the input gets focused, starting with the current date. Next and previous buttons can be used to select the next or previous month, and a calendar can be used to select a day.

To make the datepicker more useful, we need to adapt it to the application where it's used. For the flight-search example, we can assume that the user looks for a flight sometime in the next three months, and therefore it displays three months at once, starting with the next week from the current date:

```
<label for="from">From</label>
<input type="text" id="from" name="from"/>
<label for="to">to</label>
<input type="text" id="to" name="to"/>
```

We start with two inputs, each associated with an appropriate label, and then apply the datepicker to both:

```
var dates = $('#from, #to').datepicker({
    defaultDate: "+1w",
    changeMonth: true,
    numberOfMonths: 3,
    onSelect: function(selectedDate) {
        var option = this.id == "from" ? "minDate" : "maxDate";
        dates.not(this).datepicker("option", option, new Date(selectedDate));
    }
});
```

The default date for the datepicker is the current date plus one week, specified using the `defaultDate` option. A select for changing the months is displayed as well, via `changeMonth: true`. The option `numberOfMonths: 3` indicates that three calendars should be displayed at once.

The `onSelect` option is an event triggered whenever the user selects a date. When the from date is selected, the `minDate` option for the to date is set to the from date, and when the to date is selected, the `maxDate` option for the from date is set.

With that in place, the user can start selecting any of the two dates, and when he continues to select the other, the input is restricted to a positive range already.

Discussion

By default, the datepicker is shown when the input field receives focus. Using the `showOn` option, we can configure the calendar to appear only when clicking a calendar icon next to the input:

```
$("#datepicker").datepicker({
    showOn: 'button',
    buttonImage: 'images/calendar.gif',
    buttonImageOnly: true
});
```

The `buttonImage` option specifies the path to an image to use as the button, where `buttonImageOnly` specifies to use only that image, instead of a button element with an embedded image.

The `showOn` option also supports `both` as a value, displaying the datepicker on focus of the input and on clicks on the button.

Localization

The jQuery UI datepicker supports 41 locales, provided as `ui.datepicker-xx.js` files, where *xx* is the locale. Each file adds a property to `$.datepicker.regional`. The `ui.datepicker-ar.js` file adds these:

```
$.datepicker.regional['ar'] = {
    closeText: 'إغلاق',
    prevText: '&#x3c;السابق',
    nextText: 'التالي&#x3e;',
    currentText: 'اليوم',
    dayNames: ['الخم','الأربعاء','الثلاثاء','الاثنين','الأحد','السبت',
```

```
جمعة' ,'يس'],
    dayNamesShort: ['خم' ,'أربعاء' ,'ثلاثاء' ,'اثنين' ,'أحد' ,'سبت'
جمعة' ,'يس'],
    dayNamesMin: ['خم' ,'أربعاء' ,'ثلاثاء' ,'اثنين' ,'أحد' ,'سبت'
جمعة' ,'يس'],
    dateFormat: 'dd/mm/yy',
    firstDay: 0,
    isRTL: true
};
```

To initialize a datepicker with the Arabic locale, we refer to that property:

```
$("#datepicker").datepicker($.datepicker.regional.ar);
```

To mix in other options as well, we use $.extend:

```
$("#datepicker").datepicker($.extend({}, $.datepicker.regional.ar, {
    changeMonth: true,
    changeYear: true
});
```

We create an empty object literal via {} and then use $.extend to copy the regional options as well as values for changeMonth and changeYear into the empty object, which is then used to initialize the datepicker.

jQuery Plugins

Mike Hostetler

12.0 Introduction

A primary goal of the jQuery JavaScript library is to remain a fast and concise alternative to other JavaScript libraries that are available in the open source world. A key principle toward this goal is ensuring that the jQuery core addresses the needs of most developers, while remaining fast and concise. Developers may have needs that aren't completely satisfied by the jQuery core. Or, a developer may write an extension to core jQuery functionality that may be useful to a significant segment of jQuery users but shouldn't be included in the jQuery core.

jQuery was designed to be extensible in a variety of ways. The recipes in this chapter are intended to introduce the reader to the world of jQuery plugins.

12.1 Where Do You Find jQuery Plugins?

Problem

You're trying to build something with jQuery that requires functionality that doesn't exist in the jQuery core. The problem is one that other developers have likely run into before, and you think a plugin may exist. Where should you start looking to find plugins, and how should you evaluate the plugins that you find?

Solution

Search through the following repositories for jQuery plugins:

jQuery Plugin Repository
    http://plugins.jquery.com
Google Code
    http://code.google.com

GitHub
    http://github.com

Google with special queries
    http://google.com

SourceForge
    http://sourceforge.net

Discussion

There are a few places around the Web that jQuery plugins may be found. Because of the nature of jQuery plugins, there are certain open source hosting sites that tend to attract jQuery plugins more than others. Additionally, the jQuery project hosts a central repository for jQuery plugins at *http://plugins.jquery.com*.

It's best to look through all of the available resources and collect several potential plugins, if they are available, for your review. Plugins that are built to solve the same problem often take very different approaches or were built for alternate versions of the jQuery core library.

When looking for a jQuery plugin, the following are the best steps to find the most updated and recent versions of plugins.

Search through the jQuery Plugin Repository

The jQuery Project hosts a plugin repository (*http://plugins.jquery.com*) that currently boasts more than 1,200 plugins at the time of this writing. Most authors who host their own plugins will post their plugins here.

Plugins hosted in the jQuery Plugin Repository are organized into a number of categories, which can assist with narrowing your search. Plugins may be organized into multiple categories. Plugins are also required to be listed by API compatibility, ensuring that any plugins you find are likely to work with a particular version of the jQuery core library. Lastly, you may also browse plugins by release date, allowing you to keep up with your favorite plugins as new versions are released.

Search through Google Code

Google Code (*http://code.google.com/*) hosting offers a very rich repository of jQuery plugins. More often than not, if you can't find a plugin hosted on the main Plugin Repository, there's a good chance it could be on Google Code.

Search through GitHub

GitHub (*http://github.com*) is a rising star in the code hosting world that many jQuery plugin authors are turning toward. More and more plugins end up here, and it is certainly a site that warrants a search when looking for a specific plugin. One of the most compelling features of GitHub is the ability to "fork" a repository in a friendly way by utilizing the features of the Git source code management system. In the event that you need to modify an existing plugin, utilizing the features of GitHub are a compelling way to keep track with upstream updates.

The best way to find a plugin on GitHub is to utilize GitHub's excellent search. GitHub supports a number of advanced operators when searching. All of these options may be viewed in greater detail at *http://github.com/search*. When looking specifically for a jQuery plugin, searching for repositories using JavaScript will return the best results.

Perform a Google search

While the previous suggestions are known sources of plugins, searching throughout the entire Web via Google is useful as well. Because the body of search material tends to be larger, so does the number of potential results to sift through. Using a few of the suggested searches can result in finding plugins quicker:

```
{searchterm} "jquery*.js" - Best practice plugin naming is jquery-{myplugin}.js or
jquery.{myplugin}.js

{searchterm} "*jquery.js" - Alternate best practice plugin naming
```

Search through SourceForge

There tends to be very few actual jQuery plugins hosted on SourceForge (*http://source forge.net*). However, a number of projects on this site offer jQuery support tools, such as IDE code completion extensions. If you're out of options, or are looking for something unique, SourceForge is a good place to do a quick search.

12.2 When Should You Write a jQuery Plugin?

Problem

After searching for an existing jQuery plugin to fit your needs, the plugins that were found either don't meet your needs or are not constructed in a way that you can take advantage of them properly. Is it worth writing a new jQuery plugin that can be shared with others who have the same need?

Solution

There's no cut and dried solution to this problem. The number of available jQuery plugins is large, but there are valid cases where plugins don't exist to meet a particular need.

In my opinion, the decision to write and publish your own jQuery plugin comes down to three things:

• Is it likely there are others who have the same problem?

- What level of support are you willing to provide?
- What level of community participation do you desire?

Discussion

Build a plugin if there is a potential audience

If you're facing a problem that remains unsolved, there are likely other developers who have encountered the same issue. How others before you have solved the issue is the key question. It's assumed that you've done some homework at this point, searching for a solution. During that search, clues that may surface that point toward a need for a plugin can be found in forum posts or mailing list questions that have gone unanswered. There's no easy way to decide whether a plugin is worth building, and the decision ultimately comes down to the person who is planning to build the plugin. However, a general feel of whether there is a potential audience is worth exploring.

The other potential reason to build and publish your own plugin is if a plugin exists to meet your needs but does not fully do what you want. If this is the case, it is worth considering the potential for writing a patch and submitting that patch back to the original author for inclusion in the plugin. Participating in the open source process by submitting a patch to an existing project tends to be a much more efficient application of a developer's most precious resource: time.

Know and communicate the level of support you are willing to provide

If writing your own plugin is the best option, a bit of forethought and planning will help make sure the process of hanging out your own open source shingle goes well.

Whenever you decide to publish your code, the first and biggest consideration is licensing. The jQuery core project is dual-licensed as MIT and GPL, but many other open source licenses are worthy of consideration. A more thorough discussion on the intricacies of open source licensing can be found at Wikipedia (*http://en.wikipedia.org/ wiki/Open_source_license*).

Second, it is important to consider and communicate the level of support that you, the plugin author, are willing to provide to others who may download and use your code. Choosing to simply publish your code and provide no support is a completely valid option and is much better than keeping your code to yourself for fear of the potential support issues. The key is communication; writing a quick note about your support plan into the comments of your plugin will go a long way.

If you are willing to provide deeper support for a plugin that you want to publish, there are several great source code hosting sites that offer several features to assist in supporting your plugin. See Recipe 12.1 for a list of the best places to host and support your plugin.

Plan for participation from others

Lastly, think through and gauge your willingness to accept participation from others. Participation is a key component of the open source ecosystem, and it is wise to communicate your intention from the moment you publish your plugin. The attraction of allowing participation is that you can benefit from the work of others. Plugins that accept participation from others tend to attract additional users, partly because of the appearance of activity and partly because active code tends to be more trustworthy code.

Communicating the path to participation is key. Whether you intend to or not, any piece of code that is published tends to attract some sort of participation once users find it. Having a plan to engage that participation in an open and public way is essential.

One last word of advice: engaging participation simply by publishing your email address and allowing people to email you with comments and questions is generally a bad idea for a couple reasons. First, email isn't a public forum that displays activity to potential users, and second, it introduces you, the plugin author, as a bottleneck to integrating that activity back into the plugin.

12.3 Writing Your First jQuery Plugin

Problem

You've decided that you want to write a jQuery plugin. How do you write a plugin in jQuery? What best practices should you follow?

Solution

jQuery is designed to make writing a plugin very simple and straightforward. You can extend the existing jQuery object by writing either methods or functions. Simply declaring the following JavaScript after inclusion of the jQuery core library will allow your code to use your new custom method or function.

Writing a custom jQuery method

jQuery methods are available to be chained and thus can take advantage of jQuery selectors. jQuery methods are defined by extending the `jQuery.fn` object with your method name. Because the jQuery object must be able to handle multiple results, you must wrap your custom functionality inside a call to the `each()` function to apply your code to all of the results:

```
jQuery.fn.goShop = function() {
  return this.each(function() {
    jQuery('body').append('<div>Purchase: ' + this.innerHTML + '</div>');
  });
};
```

Accessing this new plugin is as simple as calling jQuery like you normally would and utilizing your new method name:

```
jQuery('p').goShop();
```

Writing a custom jQuery function

Functions are attached to the main jQuery object. Functions are designed to be called outside of a jQuery selection:

```
jQuery.checkout = function() {
  jQuery('body').append('<h1>Checkout Successful</h1>');
};
```

This new function can be manipulated and called normally:

```
jQuery.checkout();
```

Discussion

Attaching new methods and functions to the main jQuery object are a powerful feature of jQuery. Many of the core methods are built into the library using this same technique. By leveraging this existing foundation in jQuery, users of jQuery and users of your plugin have a fast and concise way to add new functionality, extend existing functionality, and mold the jQuery code into whatever form suits them best. This flexibility is a key feature and enables jQuery and its plugins to be used by a wider audience.

The choice to extend jQuery via a new method or a function mainly depends on the needs of the developer. In general, focusing on extending jQuery via adding a new method is best because this allows that new method to be chained along with other methods, and it allows the code in the method to take advantage of jQuery's selector engine.

12.4 Passing Options into Your Plugin

Problem

Your first plugin adds a method to jQuery. However, there are a few options that would be helpful to others if they were exposed properly. What is the best method of passing options into a custom method?

Solution

Options are best passed into your custom plugin method via an options object. Using a single options object to pass in parameters promotes cleaner code, is easier to work with, and provides flexibility down the road.

When allowing options to be utilized in your plugin, it's wise to provide sensible defaults. After providing sensible default options, it's also important that your plugin provide a method for the user of the plugin to override the defaults. Both of these goals are easily accomplished by declaring a default options object, overriding the default options with user-supplied options and the jQuery extend() method, and then utilizing the options in your code:

```
jQuery.fn.pulse = function(options) {
  // Merge passed options with defaults
  var opts = jQuery.extend({}, jQuery.fn.pulse.defaults, options);

  return this.each(function() {
    // Pulse!
    for(var i = 0;i<opts.pulses;i++) {
      jQuery(this).fadeTo(opts.speed,opts.fadeLow).fadeTo(opts.speed,opts.fadeHigh);
    }

    // Reset to normal
    jQuery(this).fadeTo(opts.speed,1);
  });
};

// Pulse plugin default options
jQuery.fn.pulse.defaults = {
  speed: "slow",
  pulses: 2,
  fadeLow: 0.2,
  fadeHigh: 1
};
```

By specifying option defaults, developers using your plugin have the ability to provide as many or as few options when they call your function. It is important to place your options' defaults after you've defined your plugin entry method; otherwise, you will encounter an error.

```
// Override only one option
jQuery('p').pulse({pulses: 6});

// Override all options
jQuery('p').pulse({speed: "fast", pulses: 10, fadeLow: 0.3, fadeHigh: 0.8});
```

Lastly, by specifying your options as an object attached as a child to your plugin function, the default options may be overridden only once in a project. A developer then has the ability to specify their own set of default options, minimizing the amount of code required to produce the desired behavior:

```
// Plugin code included above

// Reset pulse default options
jQuery.fn.pulse.defaults = {
  speed: "fast",
  pulses: 4,
  fadeLow: 0.2,
  fadeHigh: 1
};
```

```
// This call will use the new defaults
jQuery('p').pulse();
```

Discussion

Supporting options in your plugin is a powerful way to add tremendous flexibility to the plugin. Plugins that support a rich set of options are more likely to fit the needs of a wider audience, perform a wider variety of tasks, and generally gain more popularity than plugins that don't support options.

Including a set of default options with your plugin is another way to give developers who use your plugin flexibility and choice in how the plugin is implemented. A handy side benefit is that the plugin can always rely on certain options being defined, reducing the amount of code required to check whether an option has been passed. This leaves plugin users with the ability to override a single option, multiple options, or even all of the options every time they call your plugin. Lastly, by attaching the default options to the jQuery object, the options can be overridden globally, giving your users another tool to leverage in new and creative ways.

12.5 Using the $ Shortcut in Your Plugin

Problem

Other JavaScript libraries make use of the $ shortcut. jQuery itself uses $ only as a shortcut, with the main object being named jQuery. How can you ensure that your plugin maintains compatibility with other plugins and libraries?

Solution

jQuery itself uses the $ function as a custom alias for the jQuery object. When jQuery is set into compatibility mode, it passes back control of the $ alias to the original library that defined it. Plugins can be crafted to use the same technique.

By wrapping your plugin in an anonymous function and immediately executing that function, the $ shortcut is kept inside the plugin. Code outside of the plugin can use $ normally. Inside the plugin, $ will reference the jQuery object as normal:

```
;(function($) {
  $.fn.pulse = function(options) {
    // Merge passed options with defaults
    var opts = $.extend({}, $.fn.pulse.defaults, options);

    return this.each(function() {
      // Pulse!
      for(var i = 0;i<opts.pulses;i++) {
        $(this).fadeTo(opts.speed,opts.fadeLow).fadeTo(opts.speed,opts.fadeHigh);
      }

      // Reset to normal
```

```
        $(this).fadeTo(opts.speed,1);
    });
};

// Pulse plugin default options
$.fn.pulse.defaults = {
    speed: "slow",
    pulses: 2,
    fadeLow: 0.2,
    fadeHigh: 1
};
})(jQuery);
```

Discussion

Wrapping your distributed code in an anonymous function is a very straightforward and simple step that adds several features and ensures that your plugin code can play nicer in the wider world that your users may live within.

Adding a semicolon at the beginning of your function definition helps protect against another developer who may have forgotten to include an ending semicolon in their library. The JavaScript language breaks statements on newline by default, but many users take advantage of minimization tools that compress the entire set of JavaScript in their projects into a single file. This process removes the line endings and can cause errors if your code follows immediately after. Adding the initial semicolon is a quick and easy trick to protect against that possibility.

The open parenthesis immediately begins the anonymous function definition. Within our anonymous function, we define a function that passes the variable that we want to use in place of the fully named jQuery object. In this case, we want to take advantage of using $ as the variable. Defining an additional function is required because of the way the JavaScript language handles scoping. In more traditional languages such as Java and C++, scope is limited to the block statement. In JavaScript, scope is wrapped in functions. Therefore, the reason for using a function here is really to set up a scope boundary that we can define our plugin within.

What follows is a new version of our plugin, with the sole change of swapping out the way we utilize the jQuery object. Because we've wrapped this plugin anonymously and limited the scope of the $ variable, we can now use $ freely without conflict from any other code.

The last line wraps up the scoping function and anonymous function with a close bracket and close parenthesis, respectively. The last bit is what actually calls our anonymous function immediately after it has been defined. This is where we tell our function to pass in the jQuery object, which is what gets renamed to $ within our function. Lastly, we close off our new statement with a semicolon to protect against JavaScript minimization and compression errors.

The $ shortcut can be incredibly useful in writing JavaScript code. It cuts down on code size, promotes good code design, and has become extremely popular and well known. Thus, many libraries take advantage of the $ shortcut, tying it into their own context. With each library supporting their own version of the $ shortcut, conflicts can easily arise. By wrapping your plugin code within an anonymous function, you can ensure that your plugin maintains a level of scope around usage of the $ shortcut that will reduce the potential for conflicts with other JavaScript libraries.

One additional side effect of wrapping your plugin in an anonymous function, as described earlier, is that a closure is created. Utilizing a closure in JavaScript aids in properly namespacing any methods or variables that you may need to define, further reducing the chance for variable names or function names to conflict with other code.

12.6 Including Private Functions in Your Plugin

Problem

Your plugin code is growing and needs to be organized. How can you implement a private method that's unavailable to code outside your plugin?

Solution

By utilizing the plugin design pattern started in Recipe 12.4, private functions may be defined normally within the anonymous function that we've wrapped our plugin in. Because the function is enclosed in an anonymous function, outside code won't see our private method. Code outside will only be able to see functions or methods that are attached to the jQuery object.

```
;(function($) {

    $.fn.pulse = function(options) {

        // Merge passed options with defaults
        var opts = $.extend({}, $.fn.pulse.defaults, options);

        return this.each(function() {
            doPulse($(this),opts);
        });
    };

    function doPulse($obj,opts) {
        for(var i = 0;i<opts.pulses;i++) {
            $obj.fadeTo(opts.speed,opts.fadeLow).fadeTo(opts.speed,opts.fadeHigh);
        }

        // Reset to normal
        $obj.fadeTo(opts.speed,1);
    }
```

```
    // Pulse plugin default options
    $.fn.pulse.defaults = {
        speed: "slow",
        pulses: 2,
        fadeLow: 0.2,
        fadeHigh: 1
    };

})(jQuery);
```

Discussion

Because we now have our plugin wrapped in an anonymous function, defining private functions within our plugin is as simple as adding a new function as you normally would.

Grouping and organizing your plugin with public and private methods offers many advantages to your users and to the plugin author. As your plugin matures and you receive feedback from the community, you can leverage the use of public and private methods to provide a consistent API between plugin versions. The consistency of your API can be a major factor in your plugin's success.

The ability to break code down into private and public messages also has significant advantages in code organization as your plugin grows. Well-organized code is easier to read, to maintain, and to test. Well-tested, clean code can lead to less error-prone code.

12.7 Supporting the Metadata Plugin

Problem

Several plugins utilize the metadata plugin to pass custom options into their methods. How can integration with the metadata plugin be constructed?

Solution

Leveraging the metadata plugin is as simple as checking whether the plugin is available and then extending your plugin options with the metadata parameters. Using this technique, you can supply default options when making the call to your plugin and override those default options for each object to be operated on through the metadata written into the markup:

```
<!-- Include the metadata plugin -->
<script type="text/javascript" src="metadata/jquery.metadata.js"></script>

<!-- Example of markup containing metadata -->
<p class="{pulses: 8, speed: 'slow'}">Starship Enterprise</p>
<p>Battlestar Galactica</p>
<p class="{speed: 100}">Serenity</p>

;(function($) {
```

```
$.fn.pulse = function(options) {
  // Merge passed options with defaults
  var opts = $.extend({}, $.fn.pulse.defaults, options);

  return this.each(function() {

    // Merge in the metadata elements for this specific node
    var o = $.metadata ? $.extend({}, opts, $.metadata.get(this)) : opts;

    doPulse($(this),o);
  });
};

function doPulse($obj,opts) {
  for(var i = 0;i<opts.pulses;i++) {
    $obj.fadeTo(opts.speed,opts.fadeLow).fadeTo(opts.speed,opts.fadeHigh);
  }

  // Reset to normal
  $obj.fadeTo(opts.speed,1);
}

// Pulse plugin default options
$.fn.pulse.defaults = {
  speed: "slow",
  pulses: 2,
  fadeLow: 0.2,
  fadeHigh: 1
};
})(jQuery);
```

Discussion

Including the metadata plugin is a great example of how jQuery plugins can build off of one another. The jQuery plugin ecosystem is vast, and chances are there are other plugins that you can utilize.

To include and use the metadata plugin, you first must actually include it into your script. The metadata plugin is hosted along with jQuery at Google Code. The metadata plugin works by allowing you to embed additional data into your HTML, while still producing valid HTML. We take advantage of this by allowing users to embed element-specific options into the class element of the items we can operate on.

The options are embedded into the HTML using standard JSON. All of the options may be embedded, or none may be embedded; it's up to your users. There are several other methods and options for using the metadata plugin that are described on its documentation page (*http://docs.jquery.com/Plugins/Metadata*).

Within our plugin, we first check to see whether a user has included the metadata plugin. This is done to ensure that we keep this additional feature optional and to provide backward compatibility, if necessary. Because the metadata plugin operates on a single element, we split up how we handle options. The first step is to use the options provided when the plugin was called. These options are extended with our default options, creating our starting point for this first instantiation of our plugin. The second step is to extend those locally default options with the metadata that may be defined for each element. All that is required is for us to extend our locally default options with the metadata options, if the metadata plugin exists.

The metadata plugin provides another option for users of your plugin to pass in options. Providing options to potential users is a great way to show that you are committed to your plugin, being a good citizen of the jQuery ecosystem. The metadata plugin is also a great way to offer your users the ability to write less code by embedding custom options into the HTML elements.

12.8 Adding a Static Function to Your Plugin

Problem

In addition to making your plugin available through the jQuery function, you want to expose a static function. How can you add a static function to your jQuery plugin?

Solution

Adding a static method to your plugin requires extending the jQuery object in much the same way you would add a method. The difference is simply that functions are called without using jQuery selectors:

```
;(function($) {
  $.fn.pulse = function(options) {
    // Merge passed options with defaults
    var opts = $.extend({}, $.fn.pulse.defaults, options);

    return this.each(function() {

      // Merge in the metadata elements for this specific node
      var o = $.metadata ? $.extend({}, opts, $.metadata.get(this)) : opts;

      doPulse($(this),o);
    });
  };

  function doPulse($obj,opts) {
    for(var i = 0;i<opts.pulses;i++) {
      $obj.fadeTo(opts.speed,opts.fadeLow).fadeTo(opts.speed,opts.fadeHigh);
    }

    // Reset to normal
    $obj.fadeTo(opts.speed,1);
  }

  // Define our base to add to
  $.pulse = {};
```

```
    // Static Function
    $.pulse.impulse = function($obj) {
      var opts = {
        speed: 2500,
        pulses: 10,
        fadeLow: 0.2,
        fadeHigh: 0.8
      };
      doPulse($obj,opts);
    }

    // Static Function
    $.pulse.warpspeed = function($obj) {
      var opts = {
        speed: 25,
        pulses: 100,
        fadeLow: 0.2,
        fadeHigh: 0.8
      };
      doPulse($obj,opts);
    }

    // Pulse plugin default options
    $.fn.pulse.defaults = {
      speed: "slow",
      pulses: 2,
      fadeLow: 0.2,
      fadeHigh: 1
    };
})(jQuery);
```

Calling the static methods available in your plugin is very straightforward, requiring only that you explicitly pass a valid object to operate on:

```
// Call the impulse method on the first element returned
jQuery.pulse.impulse(jQuery('p:first'));

// Call the warpspeed method on the first element returned
jQuery.pulse.impulse(jQuery('p:first'));
```

Discussion

Adding a static function within the scope of your plugin only requires adding a way for code outside of your plugin to call it. This is accomplished by attaching the functions to the jQuery object.

In the previous example, we've added a namespace object to aid in organizing our code better. If all that your plugin required was a single static function, it would be completely appropriate to expose your static function without adding a namespacing object. After adding our namespace object, we simply define our functions like normal and attach them to the namespace object we created. Doing this exposes our function to the global namespace, while allowing the contents of the functions to access private functions and variables.

Taking advantage of the static function is as simple as calling it using the jQuery object we attached it to. This function is called without utilizing jQuery selectors, so in order to operate on a DOM element, that element must be explicitly passed to the function.

A static function attached to the jQuery object is another example of the flexibility of the jQuery library. Your entire plugin could be made up of adding static functions that simply extend the jQuery core in interesting new ways. A static function could be the entry point you provide to your plugin, or it could be a simple shortcut method you've found useful that's packaged in your plugin in a way that makes it easier to share with other developers. Whatever the need, static functions can be a useful and powerful tool when building your own jQuery plugin.

12.9 Unit Testing Your Plugin with QUnit

Problem

You want to raise the quality and reliability of your jQuery plugin by creating unit tests for it. How do you write and ship tests with your jQuery plugin?

Solution

The easiest method to write unit tests for a jQuery plugin is to utilize QUnit, the same unit testing framework that the jQuery project uses. With QUnit, you can write your tests right in JavaScript and ship them with your plugin for your users to run in their own browsers:

```
<!DOCTYPE html PUBLIC "-//W3C//DTD XHTML 1.0 Transitional//EN"
    "http://www.w3.org/TR/xhtml1/DTD/xhtml1-transitional.dtd">
<html xmlns="http://www.w3.org/1999/xhtml" xml:lang="en" lang="en">
<head>
  <script type="text/javascript" src="../jquery-1.3.2.min.js"></script>
  <script type="text/javascript" src="metadata/jquery.metadata.js"></script>
  <script type="text/javascript" src="jquery.pulse.js"></script>

  <link rel="stylesheet"
href="http://jqueryjs.googlecode.com/svn/trunk/qunit/testsuite.css" type="text/css"
media="screen" />
  <script type="text/javascript"
src="http://jqueryjs.googlecode.com/svn/trunk/qunit/testrunner.js"></script>
</head>
<body>

  <script type="text/javascript">
    module("Testing the jQuery Pulse Plugin");
    test("Test Pulse with basic options", function() {
      $("div.starship").pulse();
```

```
      equals($("#enterprise").css("opacity"),1,"The element should be visible");
      equals($("#galactica").css("opacity"),1,"The element should be visible");
    });

    test("Test Impulse", function() {
      $.pulse.impulse($("#galactica"));

      equals($("#galactica").css("opacity"),1,"The element should be visible");
    });

    test("Test Warp Speed", function() {
      $.pulse.warpspeed($("#enterprise"));

      equals($("#enterprise").css("opacity"),1,"The element should be visible");
    });
  </script>

  <div id="main">
    <div class="starship" id="enterprise">USS Enterprise - NC-1701-A</div>
    <div class="starship" id="galactica">Battlestar Galactica</div>
  </div>

</body>
</html>
```

Discussion

Learning how to effectively test code is beyond the scope of this chapter. The tests written in the previous example are intended to simply show an example of what can be done with unit testing. Chapter 18 goes into great detail about unit testing and specifically the QUnit framework. For a discussion on how to use QUnit, what types of things you can test, and how to effectively test your code, please refer to that chapter.

Shipping unit tests with your plugin is another great way to show developers you are committed to the success and stability of the code that you publish. This builds trust with your user base and shows that your plugin is a good member of the jQuery plugin ecosystem. Tests also make it easy for users of your plugins to find bugs that can creep up in another runtime environment, such as a different browser. This allows you, the plugin author, to better address the bug that was found by having a working test bed, allowing you, the plugin developer, to directly address the bug that was found.

Interface Components from Scratch

Nathan Smith

13.0 Introduction

While the official jQuery UI widget collection offers a wealth of ready-made functionality, from time to time you might choose to create a customized element that meets a specific need. Perhaps you desire greater control over the HTML markup or simply want to keep your JavaScript code base lighter. Maybe you are looking to build something not already covered by existing solutions. Whatever the reason, this chapter will show you how to tersely write customized components for your projects. These recipes have been written with ease of use in mind, favoring simplicity over configuration.

Recipe 13.1 will show you how to create custom tool tips, for occasions where you need to direct the user's attention via providing additional content or instruction. Recipe 13.2 will explain how to build a file tree–style menu, allowing the user to drill down and explore the depth of a site hierarchy. In Recipe 13.3 you will learn how to create a vertically folding accordion. Recipe 13.4 will explain how to use interpage links and their respective targets to create document tabs. Recipe 13.5 shows how to create a basic modal window via appropriate action. Recipe 13.6 explains how to build a simple drop-down menu. Recipe 13.7 delves into the creation of an image rotator that can be controlled via buttons, reusing the interpage link technique from Recipe 13.4. Recipe 13.8 takes lessons learned from Recipe 13.3, creating horizontal panels instead of a vertical accordion.

The following paradigms are used throughout this chapter and will not be called out specifically for each example.

Each recipe begins by checking whether the necessary element actually exists in the document. If not, then we exit the function. There is no need to go any further if that criterion is not met, and this keeps code from executing unnecessarily:

```
// Does element exist?
if (!$('#foobar').length) {

 // If not, exit.
 return;
}
```

A snippet of generic code is used throughout to cancel the following links that only serve to trigger JavaScript events. The `blur()` method is applied to get rid of dotted borders that would otherwise be permanent (until the user clicked something new), and `return false` tells the browser not to follow the link's `href`:

```
// Nofollow.
this.blur();
return false;
```

To actually kick off the dynamic functionality, each recipe ends with a call to jQuery's `document.ready()` function, ensuring that the DOM has finished loading (but not necessarily all image assets) before attempting to apply event listeners and so forth:

```
// Kick things off.
$(document).ready(function() {
 init_foobar();
});
```

Some of the recipes have the following bit of code in the `<head>` of the HTML document. For the most part, `document.write()` is considered an antiquated practice in JavaScript, because it forces the browser to pause, rendering the page when it encounters such a command. However, when prehiding content with CSS that will later be shown via JavaScript, this is *exactly* the outcome we want:

```
<script type="text/javascript">
/* <![CDATA[ */
document.write('<link rel="stylesheet" type="text/css" href="preload.css" />');
/* ]]> */
</script>
```

Essentially, before the page even begins to render, a CSS file is written to the `<head>` that prehides all the content that will later be shown as the user interacts with the page. The reason we write the CSS reference with JavaScript is that with JavaScript off, all the content is visible and fully accessible. For more on that technique, read Peter-Paul Koch's "Three JavaScript articles and one best practice" (*http://www.quirksmode.org/ blog/archives/2005/06/three_javascrip_1.html#link4*).

13.1 Creating Custom Tool Tips

Problem

From time to time, a graphical element or interface aspect may need further clarification, but because of restraints on space (or for the sake of aesthetics), a designer might not want to take up precious screen real estate by adding explanatory text. In such a case, there is a need to provide a bit of guidance to the user, who would need it initially but whose need would diminish as familiarity with the interface grew. In such cases, a tool tip makes for an ideal solution. However, HTML leaves us with scarce resources to create a tool tip, and often the `title="..."` attribute does not cut it.

Tool tips can be a good solution for user interface clarification, especially if tied to some sort of dismissible user preference (i.e., "Don't show me this again"). However, dynamic tool tips have often been abused, most notably on blogs, where every single element on a page with a `title="..."` attribute causes a tool tip to appear when the mouse passes over it. Such cases should be avoided, because if everything is treated as a special case via a tool tip, then the importance is diminished, and in reality nothing on the page is emphasized. It is the equivalent of shouting every single word in a sentence. Just as with any web project, the context of the content should dictate the approach, not vice versa.

Solution

To solve this problem, we can use jQuery to get the mouse position within our area of interest on the page and then dynamically place a `<div>` element offset from the point of origin, which could contain instructions, additional information (in the case of e-commerce), or just about anything the developer needs to appear. This would be done by creating a dynamically generated `<div>` before the close of the `</body>` tag, allowing it to have a higher z-index than the rest of the page, which would look like Figure 13-1. Additionally, just to be sure the tool tip takes precedence, it is explicitly given an extremely high z-index of `9999`.

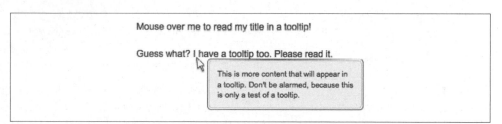

Figure 13-1. A tool tip generated with jQuery

Tool tip—HTML code

```
<!DOCTYPE html PUBLIC "-//W3C//DTD XHTML 1.0 Transitional//EN"
"http://www.w3.org/TR/xhtml1/DTD/xhtml1-transitional.dtd">
<html xmlns="http://www.w3.org/1999/xhtml" xml:lang="en" lang="en">
<head>
<meta http-equiv="content-type" content="text/html; charset=utf-8" />
<meta http-equiv="imagetoolbar" content="false" />
<title>jQuery Cookbook - Ch.13 - Creating Custom Tooltips</title>
<link rel="stylesheet" type="text/css" href="../_common/basic.css" />
<link rel="stylesheet" type="text/css" href="tooltip.css" />
<script type="text/javascript" src="../_common/jquery.js"></script>
```

```
<script type="text/javascript" src="tooltip.js"></script>
</head>
<body>
<div id="container">
  <p>
    <span class="tooltip" title="This is my title. There are many like it, but
        this one is mine. You will see it as you hover your mouse over me.">
      Mouse over me to read my title in a tooltip!
    </span>
  </p>
  <p>
    <span class="tooltip" title="This is more content that will appear in a
        tooltip. Don't be alarmed, because this is only a test of a tooltip.">
      Guess what? I have a tooltip too. Please read it.
    </span>
  </p>
</div>
</body>
</html>
```

Tool tip—jQuery code

```
// Initialize.
function init_tooltip() {

  // Does element exist?
  if (!$('.tooltip').length) {

    // If not, exit.
    return;
  }

  // Insert tool tip (hidden).
  $('body').append('<div id="tooltip_outer"><div id="tooltip_inner"></div></div>');

  // Empty variables.
  var $tt_title, $tt_alt;

  var $tt = $('#tooltip_outer');
  var $tt_i = $('#tooltip_inner');

  // Watch for hover.
  $('.tooltip').hover(function() {

    // Store title, empty it.
    if ($(this).attr('title')) {
      $tt_title = $(this).attr('title');
      $(this).attr('title', '');
    }

    // Store alt, empty it.
    if ($(this).attr('alt')) {
      $tt_alt = $(this).attr('alt');
      $(this).attr('alt', '');
    }
```

```
      // Insert text.
      $tt_i.html($tt_title);

      // Show tool tip.
      $tt.show();
    },
  function() {

      // Hide tool tip.
      $tt.hide();

      // Empty text.
      $tt_i.html('');

      // Fix title.
      if ($tt_title) {
        $(this).attr('title', $tt_title);
      }

      // Fix alt.
      if ($tt_alt) {
        $(this).attr('alt', $tt_alt);
      }

    // Watch for movement.
    }).mousemove(function(ev) {

      // Event coordinates.
      var $ev_x = ev.pageX;
      var $ev_y = ev.pageY;

      // Tool tip coordinates.
      var $tt_x = $tt.outerWidth();
      var $tt_y = $tt.outerHeight();

      // Body coordinates.
      var $bd_x = $('body').outerWidth();
      var $bd_y = $('body').outerHeight();

      // Move tool tip.
      $tt.css({
        'top': $ev_y + $tt_y > $bd_y ? $ev_y - $tt_y : $ev_y,
        'left': $ev_x + $tt_x + 20 > $bd_x ? $ev_x - $tt_x - 10 : $ev_x + 15
      });
    });
}

// Kick things off.
$(document).ready(function() {
  init_tooltip();
});
```

Discussion

It is worth mentioning that `$('.tooltip')` is not the most performant way to retrieve elements. For the sake of this demo, all tags on the page are being parsed, which is the equivalent of `document.getElementsByTagName('*')`. Depending on the size of the document, and depending on the browser, this can be quite slow. So, when actually employing this code, be sure to specify which tags you are looking for. For example, you would use `$('a.tooltip, span.tooltip')` instead of just `$('.tooltip')`. While more modern browsers will map such class selectors to `getElementsByClassName` or `querySelectorAll` (if available), older browsers have to first iterate through tag names and then determine whether the relevant class is present.

Assuming that one or more elements exist that match `class="tooltip"`, we append the dynamic markup at the end of the page, right before the close of the body. It does not yet appear anywhere visibly, because in the CSS file we have applied `display: none` to the `#tooltip_outer` ID.

Next, we create empty variables called `$tt_title` and `$tt_alt`. These will be used to temporarily store the `title` and `alt` (if it exists) attributes of our matched `class="tooltip"` elements. The astute reader might wonder, "Aren't we just interested in the `title` attribute? Why worry about `alt`?" Good question. We store the `alt` attribute in addition to the `title`, just in case `class="tooltip"` is used on an image. Internet Explorer causes its own tool tip to appear showing the `alt` contents, and we don't want that.

The rest of the code deals with `class="tooltip"` elements. When one such element is hovered over with the mouse, we store the contents of the `title` and (possibly) `alt` attributes and then zero them out by setting each one equal to an empty text string. This way, there is no browser default tool tip interfering with our custom one. The contents of the `title` attribute are copied to `#tooltip_inner`, and then the `#tooltip_outer` is shown.

Likewise, when the mouse leaves the target element, we want to undo what happened when it was it first entered. The `#tooltip` is hidden, the `#tooltip_inner` content is set to an empty string, and the `title` and `alt` attributes are restored to their original values.

Lastly, the `.mousemove()` method monitors mouse movement once it has entered the boundaries of a `class="tooltip"` element. The tool tip is offset relative to the mouse position, appearing to the right side of the cursor; that is, unless the tool tip is dangerously close to extending beyond the width of the browser. In such a case, a horizontal scroll bar would appear, and we do not want that. To solve this snafu, we have a bit of logic that flips the tool tip to the left side of the cursor. The same is true vertically. If the tool tip is too far at the bottom of a page, it will flip itself to be above the mouse cursor.

13.2 Navigating with a File-Tree Expander

Problem

On content-heavy sites with multiple tiers of information architecture, occasionally a need arises to present several levels of nested data. If all of the info was presented in its entirety, it would be too unwieldy to be useful and would take up too much vertical space on a page. Enter the file-tree paradigm. This functionality, seen most notably in the desktop UI of Windows Explorer (not to be confused with Internet Explorer), allows a user to expand and compact layers of directories.

Solution

By using jQuery's descendant selectors on nested unordered lists, we can hide/show additional portions of a tree structure, as needed. This is done by adding `class="tree"` to the top-level unordered list and using a combination of CSS and Java-Script to unveil its sublevels, producing a tree like that in Figure 13-2. Additionally, we make use of event delegation to support numerous tiers without the overhead of attaching event listeners to multiple elements. Instead, the event is captured at the top level of the `<ul class="tree">` via jQuery's `.live()` method.

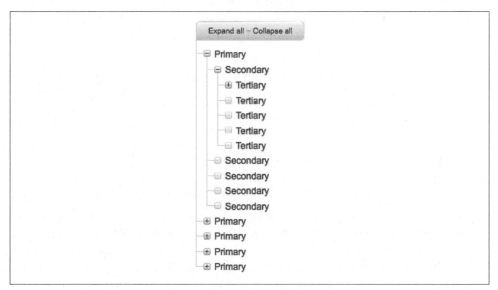

Figure 13-2. Presenting multiple levels of data through a file tree

File tree—HTML code

```
<!DOCTYPE html PUBLIC "-//W3C//DTD XHTML 1.0 Transitional//EN"
"http://www.w3.org/TR/xhtml1/DTD/xhtml1-transitional.dtd">
<html xmlns="http://www.w3.org/1999/xhtml" xml:lang="en-us" lang="en-us">
```

```html
<head>
<meta http-equiv="content-type" content="text/html; charset=utf-8" />
<meta http-equiv="imagetoolbar" content="false" />
<title>jQuery Cookbook - Ch.13 - Navigating a File Tree Expander</title>
<link rel="stylesheet" type="text/css" href="../_common/basic.css" />
<link rel="stylesheet" type="text/css" href="tree.css" />
<script type="text/javascript">
/* <![CDATA[ */
document.write('<link rel="stylesheet" type="text/css" href="preload.css" />');
/* ]]> */
</script>
<script type="text/javascript" src="../_common/jquery.js"></script>
<script type="text/javascript" src="tree.js"></script>
</head>
<body>
<div id="container">
  <p class="tree_controls">
    <a href="#" class="expand_all">Expand all</a> ~
    <a href="#" class="collapse_all">Collapse all</a>
  </p>
  <ul class="tree">
    <li>
      <a href="#" class="tree_trigger"> </a> Primary
      <ul class="tree_expanded">
        <li>
          <a href="#" class="tree_trigger"> </a> Secondary
          <ul class="tree_expanded">
            <li>
              <a href="#" class="tree_trigger"> </a> Tertiary
              <ul>
                <li>
                  <span class="tree_slug"> </span> Quaternary
                </li>
                <li>
                  <span class="tree_slug"> </span> Quaternary
                </li>
                <li>
                  <span class="tree_slug"> </span> Quaternary
                </li>
                <li>
                  <span class="tree_slug"> </span> Quaternary
                </li>
                <li>
                  <span class="tree_slug"> </span> Quaternary
                </li>
              </ul>
              ...
            </li>
            ...
          </ul>
          ...
        </li>
        ...
      </ul>
      ...
```

```
        </li>
        ...
    </ul>
</div>
...
</body>
</html>
```

File tree—jQuery code

```
// Initialize.
function init_tree() {

  // Does element exist?
  if (!$('ul.tree').length) {

    // If not, exit.
    return;
  }

  // Expand and collapse.
  $('p.tree_controls a.expand_all, p.tree_controls a.collapse_all').click(function() {

    // Look at the class.
    if ($(this).hasClass('expand_all')) {
        $(this).parent('p').next('ul').find('a.tree_trigger')
              .addClass('trigger_expanded')
              .end().find('ul').addClass('tree_expanded');
        return false;
    } else {
        $(this).parent('p').next('ul').find('a.tree_trigger')
              .removeClass('trigger_expanded')
              .end().find('ul').removeClass('tree_expanded');
    }

    // Nofollow.
    this.blur();
    return false;
  });

  // Listen for tree clicks.
  $('ul.tree a.tree_trigger').live('click', function() {

    // Is the next <ul> hidden?
    if ($(this).next('ul').is(':hidden')) {
      $(this).addClass('trigger_expanded').next('ul')
            .addClass('tree_expanded');
    } else {
      $(this).removeClass('trigger_expanded').next('ul')
            .removeClass('tree_expanded');
    }

    // Nofollow.
    this.blur();
    return false;
```

```
  });

  // Add class for last <li>.
  $('ul.tree li:last-child').addClass('last');

  // Change state of trigger.
  $('ul.tree_expanded').prev('a').addClass('trigger_expanded');
}

// Kick things off.
$(document).ready(function() {
  init_tree();
});
```

Discussion

The tree code begins by attaching event handlers to links with class names of expand_all and collapse_all. If either link is clicked, then we traverse the DOM upward to the parent <p>, over to the next <ul>, and then down into its children. Each child link with class="tree_trigger" receives the class of trigger_expanded, and each subsequent <ul> receives the class tree_expanded. These class names correspond to the CSS rules that change their visual appearance. In the case of the trigger links, they have an expanded icon. As for the lists, they are now display: block instead of display: none.

The "live" event listener listens for clicks anywhere within the tree. Basically, this listens for clicks anywhere within the <ul class="tree"> and then determines whether the click happened on a link with class="trigger". If so, it executes the associated code. The benefit of using .live(), as opposed to adding a click handler directly to each link, is that the code is associated with all existing and future elements that match the criteria. The benefit of this is twofold: you don't waste time attaching event listeners to numerous elements, and if dynamic content is inserted via Ajax, it is affected by the "live" event listener as well.

Next, we add a style hook of class="last" via JavaScript to each <li> that is the :last-child of its parent. This allows us to position a background image that simulates connectivity throughout the tree, via a light gray line. Finally, if any child <ul> has been hard-coded to be visible when the page loads via class="tree_expanded", we traverse the DOM and add class="tree_trigger_expanded" to the nearest trigger link.

13.3 Expanding an Accordion

Problem

The situation in which one might use an accordion could be somewhat akin to when a file tree might be useful. The paradigms are similar in that each one allows for additional information to be initially obscured from view and then revealed as the user interacts further. They differ, however, in that an accordion is not meant to contain an entire taxonomy of data but rather is used more as a novelty to draw attention to several facets of a site or product. One such accordion example can be seen at *http://www.apple .com/iphone*. This allows for panels of info to be expanded at the user's leisure, without completely dominating the vertical space allotted to the sidebar. It conserves space not unlike high-density shelving or movable bookcases in a library, allowing one aisle to serve several racks of storage versus having an ever-present aisle between each one.

It is worth noting that there is a jQuery UI accordion widget that is highly customizable and can be given a theme/skin to match the rest of the UI widgets. You can see it in action at *http://jqueryui.com/demos/accordion*. The benefit of using the official widget is that it is officially supported by the jQuery UI community and will continue to evolve and become more robust. The potential drawback is the amount of extra code required, if all you need is a simple accordion. On the flip side, the reason one might choose to build a custom accordion component is for a smaller code footprint. This comes at the disadvantages of having the animation not be pixel-perfect and having to set the height in pixels of each accordion panel. It is advised that you consider both options and do what best fits the project at hand.

Solution

Using jQuery's excellent DOM traversal capabilities, namely, adjacent sibling selectors, it is possible to write a script generically enough to handle multiple accordion elements. Additionally, this script is able to handle more elements being added to the accordion, if need be. Figure 13-3 shows an accordion that hasn't yet expanded, while Figure 13-4 shows its contents, revealed by expanding it.

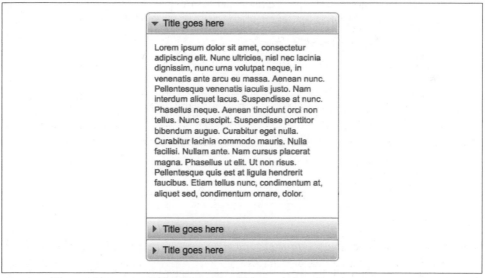

Figure 13-3. Accordion, waiting for the user to expand

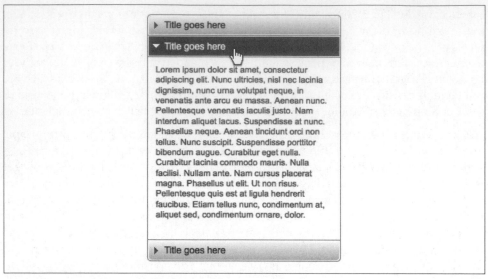

Figure 13-4. The expanded accordion

Accordion—HTML code

```
<!DOCTYPE html PUBLIC "-//W3C//DTD XHTML 1.0 Transitional//EN"
"http://www.w3.org/TR/xhtml1/DTD/xhtml1-transitional.dtd">
<html xmlns="http://www.w3.org/1999/xhtml" xml:lang="en-us" lang="en-us">
<head>
<meta http-equiv="content-type" content="text/html; charset=utf-8" />
<meta http-equiv="imagetoolbar" content="false" />
<title>jQuery Cookbook - Ch.13 - Expanding an Accordion</title>
<link rel="stylesheet" type="text/css" href="../_common/basic.css" />
<link rel="stylesheet" type="text/css" href="accordion.css" />
<script type="text/javascript">
/* <![CDATA[ */
document.write('<link rel="stylesheet" type="text/css" href="preload.css" />');
/* ]]> */
</script>
<script type="text/javascript" src="../_common/jquery.js"></script>
<script type="text/javascript" src="accordion.js"></script>
</head>
<body>
<div id="container">
  <dl class="accordion">
    <dt>
      <a href="#"><span></span> Title goes here</a>
    </dt>
    <dd>
      <p>
        Lorem ipsum...
      </p>
    </dd>
    <dt>
```

```
          <a href="#"><span></span> Title goes here</a>
        </dt>
        <dd>
          <p>
            Lorem ipsum...
          </p>
        </dd>
        <dt>
          <a href="#"><span></span> Title goes here</a>
        </dt>
        <dd>
          <p>
            Lorem ipsum...
          </p>
        </dd>
      </dl>
      ...
    </div>
  </body>
</html>
```

Accordion—jQuery code

```
// Initialize.
function init_accordion() {

  // Does element exist?
  if (!$('dl.accordion').length) {

    // If not, exit.
    return;
  }

  // Gather all accordions.
  $('dl.accordion').each(function() {

    // Reveal first accordion item.
    $(this).find('dt:first a').addClass('accordion_expanded')
          .end().find('dd:first').show();

    // Added to round corners via CSS.
    $(this).find('dt:last').addClass('last');
  });

  // Event listener for click.
  $('dl.accordion dt a').click(function() {

    // Get parent <dl>.
    var $dl = $(this).parents('dl:first');

    // Get the next <dd>.
    var $dd = $(this).parent('dt').next('dd');

    // Class final <dt>.
    function findLast() {
```

```
    if ($dl.find('dd:last').is(':hidden')) {
      $dl.find('dt:last').addClass('last');
    }
  }

  // Is it visible?
  if ($dd.is(':hidden')) {

    // Expand the <dd>, hide others.
    $dd.slideDown('fast').siblings('dd:visible').slideUp('fast', findLast);

    // Change arrow state, remove class="last" from <dt>.
    $(this).addClass('accordion_expanded').parent('dt')
          .removeClass('last').siblings('dt').find('a')
          .removeClass('accordion_expanded');
  }

  // Nofollow.
  this.blur();
  return false;
  });
}

// Kick things off.
$(document).ready(function() {
  init_accordion();
});
```

Discussion

This function begins by finding all definition lists with the class of `accordion` and applying jQuery's `.each()` method to them. Inside each one, the first `<dt>` link is given the class `accordion_expanded`, and the first `<dd>` is shown (the rest remain hidden because of CSS `display: none`). Additionally, the last `<dt>` is given `class="last"`, allowing us to style it uniquely with rounded corners for those browsers that support it. This differs from the file-tree example, in which we patched browsers that lacked `:last-child`. In the case of the accordion, `class="last"` will be removed and reapplied based on user interaction.

The second part of the code handles the crux of the accordion. All links that reside inside the accordion's `<dt>` are given a click event listener. When any of these links is clicked, we traverse the DOM upward to the parent `<dt>` and then over to the next `<dd>`. If that `<dd>` is hidden, then we animate it into place via jQuery's `.slideDown()` method, while simultaneously calling `.slideUp()` on all the other sibling `<dd>`. When this is completed, the callback function `findLast` is executed, which determines whether to assign `class="last"` to the last visible `<dt>`, depending on whether its accompanying `<dd>` is hidden.

If that last `<dd>` is visible, then no action is taken, because the `<dd>` itself is being rounded via CSS, targeted via `:last-child`. Again, the astute reader may wonder, "Why are we not patching Internet Explorer 6 and 7, since they don't understand `:last-child`?" The reason is, while IE 6 and 7 don't support `:last-child`, neither do they support rounded corners via CSS, so in this case there is nothing to be gained.

Finally, the class of `accordion_expanded` is added to the `<dt>` link that was clicked, and that class is removed from all other `<dt>` links. This causes the arrows in each `<dt>` to all point to the right, indicating that they are collapsed, with the exception of the most recently clicked `<dt>` link.

13.4 Tabbing Through a Document

Problem

You might have a page that has quite a bit of data that all belongs together because of site architecture, as opposed to separating it into distinct pages. In such a case, instead of simply having a lengthy document with headings and paragraphs, a tabbed interface often makes better sense. In this case, the tabs work as one might expect a desktop application to function. Instead of leaving the page that you are on, the relevant information associated with each tab is brought to the forefront, as shown in Figure 13-5. One such example of this type of functionality is the Yahoo! home page.

Solution

By grabbing the `href="..."` of an interpage anchor link, we can use jQuery to then find the ID of the target, hide its siblings, and bring the target element into the foreground. This is by far one of the simpler applications of jQuery yet can be used to great effect.

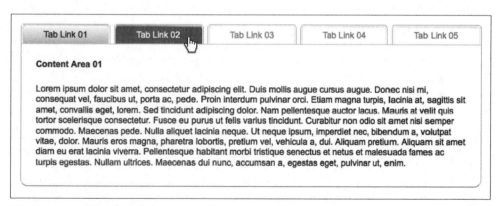

Figure 13-5. Using tabs to help users navigate information

Tabs—HTML code

```
<!DOCTYPE html PUBLIC "-//W3C//DTD XHTML 1.0 Transitional//EN"
"http://www.w3.org/TR/xhtml1/DTD/xhtml1-transitional.dtd">
<html xmlns="http://www.w3.org/1999/xhtml" xml:lang="en-us" lang="en-us">
<head>
```

```
<meta http-equiv="content-type" content="text/html; charset=utf-8" />
<meta http-equiv="imagetoolbar" content="false" />
<title>jQuery Cookbook - Ch.13 - Tabbing Through a Document</title>
<link rel="stylesheet" type="text/css" href="../_common/basic.css" />
<link rel="stylesheet" type="text/css" href="tabs.css" />
<script type="text/javascript">
/* <![CDATA[ */
document.write('<link rel="stylesheet" type="text/css" href="preload.css" />');
/* ]]> */
</script>
<script type="text/javascript" src="../_common/jquery.js"></script>
<script type="text/javascript" src="tabs.js"></script>
</head>
<body>
<div id="container">
  <ul class="tabs">
    <li>
      <a href="#tab_content_primary_01" class="current">Tab Link 01</a>
    </li>
    <li>
      <a href="#tab_content_primary_02">Tab Link 02</a>
    </li>
    <li>
      <a href="#tab_content_primary_03">Tab Link 03</a>
    </li>
    <li>
      <a href="#tab_content_primary_04">Tab Link 04</a>
    </li>
    <li>
      <a href="#tab_content_primary_05">Tab Link 05</a>
    </li>
  </ul>
  <div class="tab_content_wrap">
    <div id="tab_content_primary_01" class="tab_content">
      <p>
        <strong>Content Area 01</strong>
      </p>
      <p>
        Lorem ipsum...
      </p>
    </div>
    <div id="tab_content_primary_02" class="tab_content">
      <p>
        <strong>Content Area 02</strong>
      </p>
      <p>
        Duis ultricies ante...
      </p>
    </div>
    <div id="tab_content_primary_03" class="tab_content">
      <p>
        <strong>Content Area 03</strong>
      </p>
      <p>
        Morbi fringilla...
```

```
      </p>
    </div>
    <div id="tab_content_primary_04" class="tab_content">
      <p>
        <strong>Content Area 04</strong>
      </p>
      <p>
        Sed tempor...
      </p>
    </div>
    <div id="tab_content_primary_05" class="tab_content">
      <p>
        <strong>Content Area 05</strong>
      </p>
      <p>
        Nulla facilisi...
      </p>
    </div>
  </div>
  ...
  </div>
  </body>
  </html>
```

Tabs—jQuery code

```javascript
// Initialize.
function init_tabs() {

  // Does element exist?
  if (!$('ul.tabs').length) {

    // If not, exit.
    return;
  }

  // Reveal initial content area(s).
  $('div.tab_content_wrap').each(function() {
    $(this).find('div.tab_content:first').show();
  });

  // Listen for click on tabs.
  $('ul.tabs a').click(function() {

    // If not current tab.
    if (!$(this).hasClass('current')) {

      // Change the current indicator.
      $(this).addClass('current').parent('li').siblings('li')
             .find('a.current').removeClass('current');

      // Show target, hide others.
      $($(this).attr('href')).show().siblings('div.tab_content').hide();
    }
```

```
    // Nofollow.
    this.blur();
    return false;
  });
}

// Kick things off.
$(document).ready(function() {
  init_tabs();
});
```

Discussion

When the function runs initially, the first tabbed content area is revealed, while the rest remain hidden because of the `display: none` style rule in our `preload.css` file.

Beyond that, all we have to do is listen for any link within `<ul class="tabs">` to be clicked. If it doesn't already have `class="current"`, then we know its content is obscured, so we add `class="current"` to the clicked link and remove it from any sibling tabs that might have it. Next, we grab the `href="..."` or the clicked link, which points to an ID in the same page, and we reveal that element via jQuery's `.show()` method, while simultaneously hiding any sibling tabbed content areas that might be visible.

Note that if you want enhanced functionality, such as firing custom events when tab states change or loading remote content via Ajax, be sure to check out the official jQuery UI Tab widget.

13.5 Displaying a Simple Modal Window

Problem

With the prevalence of pop-up blocking features being included in most browsers, gone are the days of being able to reliably use `window.open()` to create a dialog box. Instead, a much more popular and usable solution is to create a modal overlay within the current page, which will take visual precedence until the user interacts with or dismisses it.

It is worth noting that there is a jQuery UI dialog widget that is highly customizable and can be given a theme/skin to match the rest of the UI widgets. You can see it in action at *http://jqueryui.com/demos/dialog*. The benefit of using the official widget is that it is officially supported by the jQuery UI community and will continue to evolve and become more robust. The potential drawback is the amount of extra code required, if all you need is a simple modal. On the flip side, the reason one might choose to build a custom modal component is for a smaller code footprint. It is advised that you consider both options and do what best fits the project at hand.

If you want an even more robust solution, one particularly geared toward showing a wide variety of content and particularly well suited to image galleries, look no further than ThickBox. It is a popular jQuery add-on written by Cody Lindley (one of the coauthors of this book). You can see it in action at *http://jquery.com/demo/thickbox/*.

Solution

Using jQuery, we can easily find the width and height of the browser viewport and create a dimmed layer to sit atop the entire site design. Using CSS positioning, we can then place our modal "window" (which in fact is simply a `<div>` layer) front and center to draw the user's attention to it, as shown in Figure 13-6. Various types of content can be displayed, including images, Ajax-loaded HTML fragments, and in-page markup.

Figure 13-6. A modal window, created with jQuery

Modal—HTML code

```
<!DOCTYPE html PUBLIC "-//W3C//DTD XHTML 1.0 Transitional//EN"
"http://www.w3.org/TR/xhtml1/DTD/xhtml1-transitional.dtd">
<html xmlns="http://www.w3.org/1999/xhtml" xml:lang="en-us" lang="en-us">
<head>
```

```
<meta http-equiv="content-type" content="text/html; charset=utf-8" />
<meta http-equiv="imagetoolbar" content="false" />
<title>jQuery Cookbook - Ch.13 - Displaying a Simple Modal Window</title>
<link rel="stylesheet" type="text/css" href="../_common/basic.css" />
<link rel="stylesheet" type="text/css" href="modal.css" />
<script type="text/javascript" src="../_common/jquery.js"></script>
<script type="text/javascript" src="modal.js"></script>
</head>
<body>
<div id="container">
  <a href="#modal_anchor" class="modal">In-page</a>
  | <a href="modal_markup.html#load_me" class="modal">Remote markup</a>
  | <a href="modal_text.txt" class="modal">Remote text</a>
  | <a href="../_common/photo_1.jpg" class="modal" title="Baltic Sea - Estonia">Image
file</a>.
  <br />
  <br />
  <select><option>-- SHOULD BE OVERLAPPED IN IE6 --</option></select>
  <br />
  <br />
  <div id="modal_anchor">
    <p>
      This content will be copied into the modal window, if its #anchor is targeted.
    </p>
  </div>
  Lots of line breaks, to simulate scrolling content...
  <br />
  It's the end of the world, as we know it, and I feel fine.
</div>
</body>
</html>
```

Modal—jQuery code

```
// Initialize.
function init_modal() {

  // Does element exist?
  if (!$('a.modal').length) {

    // If not, exit.
    return;
  }

  // Detect IE6 (boolean).
  var $IE6 = typeof document.addEventListener !== 'function' && !window.XMLHttpRequest;

  // Do some math.
  function sizeModal() {

    // Modal dimensions.
    var $modal = $('#modal_window');
    var $modal_width = $modal.outerWidth();
    var $modal_height = $modal.outerHeight();
    var $modal_top = '-' + Math.floor($modal_height / 2) + 'px';
```

```
      var $modal_left = '-' + Math.floor($modal_width / 2) + 'px';

      // Set modal.
      $('#modal_window').css('margin-top', $modal_top)
                        .css('margin-left', $modal_left);
    }

    /* For IE6. */
    function positionModal() {
      // Force modal into place.
      $('#modal_wrapper').css('top', $(document).scrollTop() + 'px');
    }

    // Reveal the modal.
    function showModal() {
      if ($IE6) {
        positionModal();
      }

      // Unveil the wrapper.
      $('#modal_wrapper').show();

      // Size it.
      sizeModal();

      // Reveal modal window.
      $('#modal_window').css('visibility', 'visible').show();

      // Resize as images load.
      $('#modal_content img').each(function() {
        $(this).load(function() {
          $(this).removeClass('modal_placeholder').show();
          sizeModal();
        });
      });
    }

    // Insert modal at end of </body>.
    $('body').append('
                    <div id="modal_wrapper">
                      <!--[if IE 6]>
                        <iframe id="modal_iframe"></iframe>
                      <![endif]-->
                      <div id="modal_overlay"></div>
                      <div id="modal_window">
                        <div id="modal_bar">
                          <strong>Modal window</strong>
                          <a href="#" id="modal_close">Close</a>
                        </div>
                        <div id="modal_content"></div>
                      </div>
                    </div>
    ');

    // Look for modal links.
    $('a.modal').click(function() {
```

```
    // Check the href="..."
    var $the_link = $(this).attr('href');

    // Determine link target.
    if ($the_link.match(/^#./)) {

      // Assume #anchor content.
      $('#modal_content').html($($(this).attr('href')).html());
      showModal();

    } else if ($the_link.match(/.jpg$/) ||
               $the_link.match(/.png$/) ||
               $the_link.match(/.gif$/)) {

      // Assume image content.
      $('#modal_content').html('
        <p id="modal_image_wrapper">
          <img src="' + $the_link + '" class="modal_placeholder" />
        </p>
        ');
      showModal();

    } else {

      // Assume external Ajax content.
      $('#modal_content').load($(this).attr('href')
                         .replace('#', ' #'), '', showModal);
    }

    // Determine modal title.
    if ($(this).attr('title')) {

      // Insert title.
      $('#modal_bar strong').html($(this).attr('title'));

    } else if ($(this).html() !== '') {

      // Insert link text.
      $('#modal_bar strong').html($(this).html());
    }

    // Nofollow.
    this.blur();
    return false;
  });

  // Hide modal elements.
  $('#modal_overlay, #modal_close').click(function() {

    // Hide the modal.
    $('#modal_wrapper').hide();

    // Hide, because images might load later.
    $('#modal_window').css('visibility', 'hidden');
```

```
    // Unbind image listeners.
    $('#modal_content img').each(function() {
      $(this).unbind();
    });

    // Destroy modal content.
    $('#modal_content').html('');

    // Reset modal title.
    $('#modal_bar strong').html('Modal window');

    // Nofollow.
    this.blur();
    return false;
  });

  // Listen for browser scroll, if IE6.
  if ($IE6) {
    $(window).scroll(function() {
      if ($('#modal_wrapper').is(':visible')) {
        positionModal();
      }
    });
  }
}

// Kick things off.
$(document).ready(function() {
  init_modal();
});
```

Discussion

Our modal solution begins by defining a variable that acts as a Boolean value, representing whether the browser is Internet Explorer 6. To determine this, we perform two quick evaluations. Once we know if we are faced with IE 6, we can use that knowledge to patch functionality. You will also notice that there is a conditional comment included in the markup fragment that we dynamically create:

```
<!--[if IE 6]><iframe id="modal_iframe"></iframe><![endif]-->
```

At first glance, this might be confusing because if the browser is Internet Explorer 6, an empty `iframe` is inserted that does not reference any included page content. The reason we do this is to trick IE 6 into allowing our modal to overlap any `<select>` form elements that might be in the page. If we do not use this workaround, then all `<select>` elements on the page will essentially "poke through" the modal overlay, making for a quite disorienting user experience.

Next, we create a function to house all the calculations that need to be performed in order to center the modal window inside the viewport. While we could have done this all in CSS and simply hard-coded the width and height, this allows for greater flexibility.

The developer implementing this JavaScript need only set the width of the modal in CSS, and our function takes care of the rest, even allowing for content of varying height.

The next function exists for, and is only ever called by, Internet Explorer 6. This patches IE 6's lack of CSS support for `position: fixed`. For all other browsers, our modal will remain centered vertically and horizontally as the user scrolls a long document. In IE 6, however, we need to specifically tell the modal to adjust its position as the user scrolls. We will do so by calling this function later in the file.

Actually revealing the modal window is simple enough. We have bundled all the necessary code for that into `showModal()`. It contains a call to `positionModal()` if the browser is IE 6. It shows the modal wrapper `<div>` and calls `sizeModal()` to center the modal and size it according to its content's height. Once sized correctly, the modal window itself is shown. An `onload` function is also attached to any dynamically inserted images. This is to account for browsers not knowing the dimensions of an image until it is fully cached. Note that `showModal()` isn't actually called until later in the file.

When the document loads, we attach the modal markup right before the close of the `</body>`.

Click listeners are attached to all links with `class="modal"`. When a modal link is clicked, there is a series of evaluations done in order to determine what type of content is to be loaded. First if the link begins with a hash (#) and is followed by one or more characters, we know that there is in-page content being linked to. In such cases, the HTML content is copied from that ID into the modal. The second case involves images. If the `href` ends in `.jpg`, `.png`, or `.gif`, then an `<img>` tag is created, and the `href` is copied into the `src`. Thirdly, if none of the previous criteria is met, we are most likely dealing with an external page. In this case, jQuery's `.load()` method is called, retrieving the HTML from that page (and from a specific ID if a hash exists) and inserting it into the modal.

The next chunk of code adds click event listeners to the modal overlay (the gray background) and the close button. If either of these is clicked, the modal will be hidden, all modal images will be stripped of their event listeners, the modal content will be set to an empty string, and the text in the modal window's title bar will be reset.

Last is an event listener specifically for IE 6 that watches for the window to scroll. If the modal window wrapper is visible (and implicitly everything else associated with the modal window), then `positionModal()` is called continuously as the user scrolls the page. This ensures that the modal window stays in place via mimicking `position: fixed`.

13.6 Building Drop-Down Menus

Problem

Inevitably, there will be a client or boss who wants everything "one click away" in a site navigation structure. While this is not an altogether ignoble aspiration, placing links to every single section of a site on a single page could add significant clutter to a page. Enter the drop-down menu.

Solution

In desktop programs and operating systems, these menus are often activated by clicking a term, after which you see a variety of subterms and categories. On the Web, however, the paradigm seems to be that drop-down menus appear when the user hovers over a top-level link, as shown in Figures 13-7 and 13-8. By using a combination of CSS `:hover` rules and positioning techniques, most of the heavy lifting can be done without much JavaScript at all. jQuery can simply offer minor enhancements for IE 6.

A mild warning for developers: take into account the accessibility implications of users who do not have the manual dexterity to use a mouse. It's like the old adage: "If all you have is a hammer, everything looks like a nail." Before resorting to drop-downs as an easy off-the-shelf solution, check that the information architecture of the project has been well thought through. Be sure that a drop-down paradigm is the best choice. For example, Microsoft Word, long known for its ridiculous levels of drop-downs and toggleable options (most of which the average user never touched), was redesigned in Office 2007 with a tabbed UI dubbed the "ribbon." Suddenly, once obscure options are being used regularly, because of a better executed interface.

Figure 13-7. Drop-down menu ready for use

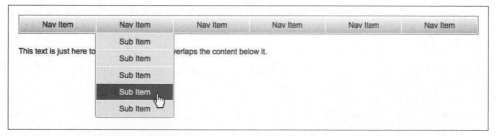

Figure 13-8. Drop-down menu in action

Drop-down—HTML code

```
<!DOCTYPE html PUBLIC "-//W3C//DTD XHTML 1.0 Transitional//EN"
"http://www.w3.org/TR/xhtml1/DTD/xhtml1-transitional.dtd">
<html xmlns="http://www.w3.org/1999/xhtml" xml:lang="en-us" lang="en-us">
<head>
<meta http-equiv="content-type" content="text/html; charset=utf-8" />
<meta http-equiv="imagetoolbar" content="false" />
<title>jQuery Cookbook - Ch.13 - Building Drop-Down Menus</title>
<link rel="stylesheet" type="text/css" href="../_common/basic.css" />
<link rel="stylesheet" type="text/css" href="dropdown.css" />
<!--[if IE 6]>
<script type="text/javascript" src="../_common/jquery.js"></script>
<script type="text/javascript" src="dropdown.js"></script>
<![endif]-->
</head>
<body>
<div id="container">
  <ul class="dropdown">
    <li class="dropdown_trigger">
      <a href="#">Nav Item</a>
      <ul>
        <li>
          <a href="#">Subitem</a>
        </li>
        <li>
          <a href="#">Subitem</a>
        </li>
        <li>
          <a href="#">Subitem</a>
        </li>
        <li>
          <a href="#">Subitem</a>
        </li>
        <li>
          <a href="#">Subitem</a>
        </li>
      </ul>
    </li>
    ...
  </ul>
  <p>
    This text is just here to show that the menu overlaps the content below it.
  </p>
  ...
</div>
</body>
</html>
```

Drop-down—jQuery code

```
// Initialize.
function init_dropdown() {

    // Does element exist?
```

```
if (!$('ul.dropdown').length) {

    // If not, exit.
    return;
}

// Add listener for hover.
$('ul.dropdown li.dropdown_trigger').hover(function() {

    // Show subsequent <ul>.
    $(this).find('ul').fadeIn(1);
},
function() {

    // Hide subsequent <ul>.
    $(this).find('ul').hide();
});
}

// Kick things off.
$(document).ready(function() {
  init_dropdown();
});
```

Discussion

In this example, jQuery is only employed if the browser is IE 6. You might be wondering, "Why is fadeIn being called with only a one-millisecond animation?" This fixes a bug in IE 6, which has trouble rendering vertical CSS borders. Visually, it is the same as .show() but without any border issues. Aside from that, everything else is pretty simple. When a list item with class="dropdown_trigger" is hovered over, the subsequent <ul> is shown. When the mouse leaves that area, the <ul> is hidden. That's all there is to it! Note that we are conditionally including the jQuery library only for IE 6. Chances are, if you are reading this book, you will want to use jQuery for more than just this one particular demo. In that case, move your inclusion of jQuery *outside* of the conditional comments.

13.7 Cross-Fading Rotating Images

Problem

On pages that contain a large masthead or "hero" image, often seen on e-commerce sites, many different products and/or departments are vying for that top spot. Often, the compromise is to simply have a series of images fade in and out, repeating on a loop. This is all well and good but can often be frustrating to use, because far too many sites overlook the need to pause the rotation in order to glean the very information that is attempting to be conveyed.

The implications of a constant animation should be considered. Most users have learned to ignore annoying ads that contain a lot of motion. The designer/developer must take into account those users who might not want to see the animation, while also trying to read the rest of the page. Worse yet is when a user attempts to read one of the rotating slides, only to have it continue to animate. Therefore, play/pause functionality is be included in this recipe, lest our users be caught in an endless, animated loop.

Solution

Using jQuery's `.fadeIn()` and `.fadeOut()` methods, we can create a nice cross-fade animation that will iterate through an array, changing each image's opacity based on a set timer. By implementing what we learned from the tabbed document portion of this chapter, we can create links to each image, which not only will cause the target image to come to the forefront but also sets a flagged variable of **pause** to either true or false, which will start or stop the animation. This makes for a truly usable image rotator versus pure eye candy.

Rotator—HTML code

```
<!DOCTYPE html PUBLIC "-//W3C//DTD XHTML 1.0 Transitional//EN"
"http://www.w3.org/TR/xhtml1/DTD/xhtml1-transitional.dtd">
<html xmlns="http://www.w3.org/1999/xhtml" xml:lang="en" lang="en">
<head>
<meta http-equiv="content-type" content="text/html; charset=utf-8" />
<meta http-equiv="imagetoolbar" content="false" />
<title>jQuery Cookbook - Ch.13 - Cross-fading Rotating Images</title>
<link rel="stylesheet" type="text/css" href="../_common/basic.css" />
<link rel="stylesheet" type="text/css" href="rotator.css" />
<script type="text/javascript">
/* <![CDATA[ */
document.write('<link rel="stylesheet" type="text/css" href="preload.css" />');
/* ]]> */
</script>
<script type="text/javascript" src="../_common/jquery.js"></script>
<script type="text/javascript" src="rotator.js"></script>
</head>
<body>
<div id="container">
  <div id="rotator_wrapper">
    <ul id="rotator">
      <li id="photo_1">
        <img src="../_common/photo_1.jpg" alt="Photo" />
      </li>
      <li id="photo_2">
        <img src="../_common/photo_2.jpg" alt="Photo" />
      </li>
      <li id="photo_3">
        <img src="../_common/photo_3.jpg" alt="Photo" />
      </li>
      <li id="photo_4">
```

```
            <img src="../_common/photo_4.jpg" alt="Photo" />
         </li>
         <li id="photo_5">
            <img src="../_common/photo_5.jpg" alt="Photo" />
         </li>
      </ul>
      <ul id="rotator_controls">
         <li>
            <a href="#photo_1" class="current">1</a>
         </li>
         <li>
            <a href="#photo_2">2</a>
         </li>
         <li>
            <a href="#photo_3">3</a>
         </li>
         <li>
            <a href="#photo_4">4</a>
         </li>
         <li>
            <a href="#photo_5">5</a>
         </li>
      </ul>
      <a href="#" id="rotator_play_pause">PAUSE</a>
   </div>
</div>
</body>
</html>
```

Rotator—jQuery code

```
// Initialize.
function init_rotator() {

   // Does element exist?
   if (!$('#rotator').length) {

      // If not, exit.
      return;
   }

   // Rotate speed.
   var speed = 2000;

   // Pause setting.
   var pause = false;

   // Rotator function.
   function rotate(element) {

      // Stop, if user has interacted.
      if (pause) {
         return;
      }
```

```
  // Either the next /first <li>.
  var $next_li = $(element).next('li').length ?
                  $(element).next('li') :
                  $('#rotator li:first');

  // Either next / first control link.
  var $next_a = $('#rotator_controls a.current').parent('li').next('li').length ?
                  $('#rotator_controls a.current').parent('li').next('li').find('a') :
                  $('#rotator_controls a:first');

  // Animate.
  $('#rotator_controls a.current').removeClass('current');
  $next_a.addClass('current');

  // Continue.
  function doIt() {
    rotate($next_li);
  }

  // Fade out <li>.
  $(element).fadeOut(speed);

  // Show next <li>.
  $($next_li).fadeIn(speed, function() {

    // Slight delay.
    setTimeout(doIt, speed);
  });
}

// Add click listeners for controls.
$('#rotator_controls a').click(function() {

  // Change button text.
  $('#rotator_play_pause').html('PLAY');

  // Show target, hide other <li>.
  $($(this).attr('href')).show().siblings('li').hide();

  // Add class="current" and remove from all others.
  $(this).addClass('current').parent('li').siblings('li')
        .find('a').removeClass('current');;

  // Pause animation.
  pause = true;

  // Nofollow.
  this.blur();
  return false;
});
```

```
// Pause / Play the animation.
$('#rotator_play_pause').click(function() {

    // What does the button say?
    if ($(this).html() === 'PAUSE') {

        // Stop rotation.
        pause = true;

        // Change the text.
        $(this).html('PLAY');

    } else {

        // Remove class="pause".
        pause = false;

        // Start the rotation.
        rotate('#rotator li:visible:first');

        // Change the text.
        $(this).html('PAUSE');
    }

    // Nofollow.
    this.blur();
    return false;
});

// Hide all but first <li>.
$('#rotator li:first').siblings('li').hide();

// Wait for page load.
$(window).load(function() {

    // Begin rotation.
    rotate($('#rotator li:visible:first'));
});
}

// Kick things off.
$(document).ready(function() {
    init_rotator();
});
```

Discussion

This recipe starts off by defining two key variables: speed (a numeric value in milliseconds) and pause (a Boolean to tell the rotator whether to play). Initially, speed has been set to two seconds, and pause is set to false, allowing the rotator to autoplay when the page loads.

Inside the `rotate()` function, a variable has been set called `$next_li`, which will correspond either to the next `<li>` after the one currently being animated or to the first `<li>` in the array (in the case of reaching the end of the array and needing to begin anew). Likewise, the same premise is being applied to links within `<ul id="rotator_con trols">` in order to add a visual indicator of which image's button is currently active. After a slight delay of two seconds, the whole sequence is kicked off again.

If that were where this demo ended, it could get pretty tiresome seeing images rotate uncontrollably. Luckily, we can reuse the in-page anchor link technique from the tabbed document recipe. We simply assign click listeners to each of the links in `<ul id="rotator_controls">` and then reveal the target image while hiding the rest. We also add a play/pause button that will start and/or stop the rotator from animating.

Last is the code that sets everything into motion. All but the first `<li>` within `<ul id="rotator">` are hidden, and then when the window has finished loading, the animation begins. Note that `$(window).load()` differs from `$(document).ready()` because the former waits for all assets to load completely, including images, which is especially important for the case of an image rotator. The latter simply waits for the HTML structure to be intact, which is important for applying functionality even as the rest of the images on a page are loading. Both are important, and each one has its place.

13.8 Sliding Panels

Problem

Occasionally, you might need to display a variety of choices horizontally, and do so with a bit of panache, but might have more choices than the width of a layout will allow. Or, perhaps the approach simply dictates that there be some fancy user interaction. Either way, the sliding panels approach (sometimes called a *horizontal accordion*) is one possible way to present such information. Figure 13-9 shows a closed panel, while Figure 13-10 shows a panel that has slid out to become visible.

Solution

In this recipe, we will revisit some of the concepts applied in the accordion demo, but instead of expanding and collapsing content panels vertically, we will be animating them horizontally. We will also use a CSS positioning trick to work around the slight miscalculation of simultaneously animating panels. Rather than worry about synchronization between each panel, animating with pixel-perfect precision at exact fractions of a second, we simply take the last `<li>` in the `<ul class="panels">` and position it absolutely to the top right of the `<ul>`. That way, when the sum width of all the panels occasionally adds up to greater than 100 percent of the `<ul>` as they animate, the last `<li>` never breaks to the next line.

Figure 13-9. Horizontal panel, still closed

Figure 13-10. Horizontal panel, opened

Panels—HTML code

```
<!DOCTYPE html PUBLIC "-//W3C//DTD XHTML 1.0 Transitional//EN"
"http://www.w3.org/TR/xhtml1/DTD/xhtml1-transitional.dtd">
<html xmlns="http://www.w3.org/1999/xhtml" xml:lang="en" lang="en">
<head>
<meta http-equiv="content-type" content="text/html; charset=utf-8" />
<meta http-equiv="imagetoolbar" content="false" />
<title>jQuery Cookbook - Ch.13 - Sliding Panels</title>
<link rel="stylesheet" type="text/css" href="../_common/basic.css" />
<link rel="stylesheet" type="text/css" href="panels.css" />
<script type="text/javascript" src="../_common/jquery.js"></script>
<script type="text/javascript" src="panels.js"></script>
</head>
<body>
<div id="container">
  <ul class="panels">
    <li>
      <a href="#">1</a>
    </li>
    <li>
      <a href="#">2</a>
    </li>
    <li>
      <a href="#">3</a>
    </li>
    <li>
      <a href="#">4</a>
    </li>
    <li>
```

```
      <a href="#">5</a>
    </li>
  </ul>
  <ul class="panels">
    <li>
      <a href="#">A</a>
    </li>
    <li>
      <a href="#">B</a>
    </li>
    <li>
      <a href="#">C</a>
    </li>
    <li>
      <a href="#">D</a>
    </li>
    <li>
      <a href="#">E</a>
    </li>
  </ul>
</div>
</body>
</html>
```

Panels—jQuery code

```
// Initialize.
function init_panels() {

  // Does element exist?
  if (!$('ul.panels').length) {

    // If not, exit.
    return;
  }

  // Animation speed.
  var speed = 200;

  // Add class for last <li>.
  $('ul.panels li:last-child').addClass('last');

  // Begin with mouseover.
  $('ul.panels li').hover(function() {

    // Alter target <li>.
    $(this).stop().animate({
      width: '360px',
      fontSize: '150px'

    // Speed.
    }, speed)

    // Alter sibling <li>.
    .siblings('li').stop().animate({
```

```
      width: '135px',
      fontSize: '50px'

    // Speed.
    }, speed);
  },

  // End with mouseout.
  function() {

    // Restore target <li>.
    $(this).stop().animate({
      width: '180px',
      fontSize: '100px'

    // Speed.
    }, speed)

    // Restore sibling <li>.
    .siblings('li').stop().animate({
      width: '180px',
      fontSize: '100px'

    // Speed.
    }, speed);
  });
}

// Kick things off.
$(document).ready(function() {
  init_panels();
});
```

Discussion

The recipe begins by defining a variable for **speed**. In this case, it is set to 200 milliseconds. We then add **class="last"** to each ending **<li>**. We then attach a hover event listener (in reality, this maps to both a mouseover and mouseout, but let's not get technical). When an **<li>** is hovered over with the mouse, its width is animated to **40%** and font size to **150px**, while the other **<li>** are each animated to **15%** wide with a font size of **50px**. Likewise, when the mouse exits the **<li>**, the widths of all **<li>** elements are set to **20%**, and their font sizes are set to **100px**.

User Interfaces with jQuery UI

Richard D. Worth

14.0 Introduction

A couple years back, there was a set of quite popular jQuery plugins bundled in a package called Interface, written by Stefan Petre. These offered really great interactions, such as dragging-and-dropping, selecting, sorting, and resizing, and great widgets such as a tool tip, an autocomplete, and an accordion. The 1.2 release of jQuery had some API changes that would've required changes to Interface for it to be compatible, but Interface was never updated.

jQuery UI (*http://jqueryui.com/*), started by Paul Bakaus, picked up where Interface left off. jQuery UI is a suite of plugins with a consistent API and complete documentation that has been tested in all major browsers. With it, you can create rich web interfaces and rich Internet applications (RIAs). Oh yeah, and the plugins work well together and are easy to use, accessible, extensible, and "themeable."

jQuery UI is a sister project of jQuery. Version 1.0 of jQuery UI was released in September 2007. Version 1.5 was released in June 2008. About halfway through the development of 1.6, the team changed directions and ended up releasing 1.7 with some major changes, most specifically the introduction of the jQuery UI CSS Framework (*http://jqueryui.com/docs/Theming/API*). jQuery UI 1.6 was released later for legacy compatibility. The latest stable release is 1.7.2 and includes the following interactions, widgets, and effects.

Interactions

- Draggable (drag)
- Droppable (and drop)
- Resizable
- Selectable
- Sortable

Widgets

- Accordion
- Datepicker
- Dialog
- Progressbar
- Slider
- Tabs

Effects

- Blind, bounce, clip, drop down/up/left/right, explode, fold, highlight, pulsate, puff, scale, shake, slide down/up/left/right, transfer
- Color animations
- Class animations (`addClass`/`removeClass`/`toggleClass` with interval)

Basic Usage

This chapter will forgo covering some of the more common ways to use these interactions, widgets, and effects, because they are well covered in demos on the jQuery UI website (*http://jqueryui.com/demos*). These same demos, with full source code and descriptions, are included in every download of jQuery UI, along with full documentation.

How This Chapter Is Organized

The first two recipes get you started by helping you to download jQuery UI, or reference it on a content delivery network (CDN), and include it on your page for use.

The next seven recipes of this chapter cover the jQuery UI API. This API first built on top of the jQuery plugin pattern but has grown to include what is needed by jQuery UI widgets, which are a unique style of jQuery plugin. Namely, they're state and method calls. So, in addition to specifying options on `init`, you can modify options after `init`. You can also call methods on jQuery UI plugins to change the state and programmatically trigger custom events.

The remainder of the chapter focuses on a project where multiple jQuery UI widgets are combined to create a single user interface that includes flexible and themeable controls for a music player.

14.1 Including the Entire jQuery UI Suite

Problem

You want to include the entire jQuery UI suite. This might be because you don't know yet what parts you'll use and what parts you won't. Or it might be because you'll use enough of the suite that it's easier or more efficient to include the whole suite, rather than each individual piece you'll use.

Solution

Link to a jQuery UI theme, then a compatible version of the jQuery script, and then the jQuery UI script:

```
<link rel="stylesheet" type="text/css" href="themename/jquery-ui.css" />
<script type="text/javascript" src="jquery.js"></script>
<script type="text/javascript" src="jquery-ui.js"></script>
```

Discussion

This chapter covers the latest stable version of jQuery UI: 1.7.2. It requires at a minimum jQuery 1.3. When you download jQuery UI, included in the ZIP package is the latest stable version of jQuery that is compatible.

Rather than host your own version of jQuery and jQuery UI, you can use Google's AJAX Libraries API. Simply change your script URLs like so:

```
<script type="text/javascript"
  src="http://ajax.googleapis.com/ajax/libs/jquery/1.3.2/jquery.min.js"></script>
<script type="text/javascript"
  src="http://ajax.googleapis.com/ajax/libs/jqueryui/1.7.2/jquery-ui.min.js"></script>
```

Google also hosts the 20 or so themes that are in the jQuery UI ThemeRoller gallery.

```
<link rel="stylesheet" type="text/css" href="http://ajax.googleapis.com/ajax/libs/
jqueryui/1.7.2/themes/{themename}/jquery-ui.css" />
```

This includes the 13 images per theme that are referenced by relative URLs in the theme CSS.

You can replace {themename} with base, black-tie, blitzer, cupertino, dark-hive, dot-luv, eggplant, excite-bike, flick, hot-sneaks, humanity, le-frog, mint-choc, overcast, pepper-grinder, redmond, smoothness, south-street, start, sunny, swanky-purse, trontastic, ui-darkness, ui-lightness, or vader. For a preview of each of these, see the jQuery UI ThemeRoller gallery (*http://jqueryui.com/themeroller/#themeGallery*).

Theming with jQuery UI is well covered in the next chapter. For our purposes, we'll just be sure to include one of these themes, because a theme is required.

14.2 Including an Individual jQuery UI Plugin or Two

Problem

You only want to use one or two jQuery UI widgets. You don't want to import the whole library and an entire theme's CSS. You just want the minimum required to use the plugins you need.

Solution

So, you only want Sortable and Tabs. You have two options for including individual jQuery UI components rather than the entire suite:

- Use the jQuery UI Download Builder (*http://jqueryui.com/download*) to create a custom build of jQuery UI containing only those plugins you are interested in. For this example, select Sortable and Tabs. The Download Builder will automatically select any dependencies, in this case, UI Core. The ZIP you download includes a single *.js* file with UI Core, Sortable, and Tabs:

  ```
  js/jquery-ui-1.7.2.custom.min.js
  ```

  Include this file on your page after the jQuery script, which is provided in the same folder:

  ```
  <script type="text/javascript" src="js/jquery-1.3.2.min.js"></script>
  <script type="text/javascript" src="js/jquery-ui-1.7.2.custom.min.js"></script>
  ```

- Download the jQuery UI development bundle, reference the *development-bundle* folder in a custom Download Builder ZIP, or use SVN (*http://jqueryui.com/docs/Subversion*). Each individual plugin file is in the *ui* subfolder. Reference each file individually:

  ```
  <script type="text/javascript" src="jquery-1.3.2.js"></script>
  <script type="text/javascript" src="ui/ui.core.js"></script>
  <script type="text/javascript" src="ui/ui.sortable.js"></script>
  <script type="text/javascript" src="ui/ui.tabs.js"></script>
  ```

The CSS for each individual plugin is also available in separate files, if you go with the second option (*development-bundle*). You'll need to include the core CSS, each plugin-specific CSS, and the theme CSS:

```
<link rel="stylesheet" type="text/css" href="themes/base/ui.core.css" />
<link rel="stylesheet" type="text/css" href="themes/base/ui.tabs.css" />
<link rel="stylesheet" type="text/css" href="themes/base/ui.theme.css" />
```

In this case, one of the plugins we've selected, Sortable, doesn't have any plugin-specific CSS.

Discussion

Whether using JavaScript or CSS, there are trade-offs between using a single large include and multiple smaller (overall) includes. It's not always clear-cut, like "Use individual plugin files in development. Use one large file in production." For example, it may be simpler in development to point to the whole suite, where performance testing isn't a big consideration. But then in production you might need to include only the files for the plugins used on each page to minimize load.

On the other hand, for debugging purposes, it may be beneficial to have a script and CSS reference to each plugin file during development, and in production you may use the Google AJAX Libraries API and the visitor's cache to make up for the file size, even if the file includes functions that are not ever used. The ideal setup will depend on your architecture, how many and which of the plugins you use, and the specific needs of your development and production environments.

14.3 Initializing a jQuery UI Plugin with Default Options

Problem

You want to start using a jQuery UI plugin as quickly and easily as possible, accepting the built-in default options.

Solution

All jQuery UI plugins are called like traditional jQuery plugins, so after you get a matched set of elements, simply call the plugin name as a function on the jQuery object:

```
<script type="text/javascript">
$(function() {
    $('#topnav').tabs();
});
</script>
```

Discussion

Because JavaScript is case sensitive, care is taken in the naming of jQuery UI plugins. All jQuery UI plugins start lowercase, and, like the jQuery API, most are only one word. If more than one word is needed, any after the first will start uppercase. There aren't currently any jQuery UI plugins with more than one word, so here's a made-up example:

```
$('p.long').succinct();
```

```
$('.short').longerPluginName();
```

The initialized element gets a class of `ui-pluginname`. For example, here's the before and after HTML if you call `$('div').draggable();`:

```
<div>A simple DIV</div>

<div class="ui-draggable">A simple DIV</div>
```

There are some exceptions to this. The element on which you call `.dialog()` gets the class of `ui-dialog-content` and is wrapped in a generated element with a class of `ui-dialog`. Another exception is if you call `.datepicker()` on a text input. The input will not get the `ui-datepicker`, but the `<div>` that appears when the input is focused has the `ui-datepicker` class.

Here are a few points to keep in mind when initializing a jQuery UI plugin:

- If you call a jQuery UI plugin `init` method on a set containing more than one element, it will be called as a separate `init` on each element individually. So, the following:

```
$('img').draggable();
```

is equivalent to this:

```
$('img').each(function() {
    $(this).draggable();
});
```

- Each `DOMElement` can be initialized by each jQuery UI plugin only once. Any future `init` calls, whether with options specified or not, will be ignored. See later in this chapter for recipes on changing options after `init` as well as destroying a plugin, which undoes an `init`. If you really want to, you can call `init` again after that.

- All options are optional. You can always safely initialize a jQuery UI plugin by simply calling the plugin name method. Not only is it safe, but it should be supremely useful. Each has been designed to have the most common options as defaults. If they don't make you happy, see the next two recipes.

14.4 Initializing a jQuery UI Plugin with Custom Options

Problem

You want to use a jQuery UI plugin but with options other than those selected by the plugin author to be the built-in defaults.

Solution

Specify default option overrides in an options hash as the first argument to the plugin `init` method call:

```
$('#myDiv').dialog({
    height: 100,          // overrides default: 'auto'
    width: 350            // overrides default: 300
});
```

Discussion

Any option values you specify on `init` will override the default value. All unspecified options values will maintain the default.

The options hash, whether all defaults or some defaults plus some custom options, is the basis for the initial state of the plugin. That state is specific to the combination of that `DOMElement` with that jQuery UI plugin. For example, you might initialize a single element with two different jQuery UI plugins that each has a color option:

```
$('#myDiv').foo({ color: 'black' });
$('#myDiv').bar({ color: 'green' });
```

Now, `#myDiv`, what's your `foo` color? Black. What's your `bar` color? Green. Both are separate from the CSS color. In some later recipes, we'll get into how to ask elements what their plugin values are, as well as how to give them new values.

Also important to note is now that `#myDiv` is initialized as a `foo` and a `bar`, it is no longer affected by those plugin defaults. The defaults are only used on `init` as a template for the plugin's initial state.

14.5 Creating Your Very Own jQuery UI Plugin Defaults

Problem

Every time you create a jQuery UI dialog, you find yourself specifying the same few options, among others:

```
$('#msg').dialog({
    height: 300,
    width: 400,
    draggable: false,
    modal: true,
    buttons: {
        'OK': function(event, ui) {
            $(this).dialog('close');
        }
    }
    ...
});
```

You long for your code to be as succinct as it once was. What happened to the simple beauty of `$('#msg').dialog();`?

Solution

Override the plugin defaults before `init` by extending `$.ui.pluginname.defaults`:

```
$.extend($.ui.dialog.defaults, {
    height: 300,
    width: 400,
    draggable: false,
    modal: true,
    buttons: {
        'OK': function(event, ui) {
            $(this).dialog('close');
        }
    }
});
...
$('#msg').dialog();
...
$('#note').dialog();
```

Discussion

If you were only looking to improve the readability a bit, you could simply put the options in a variable and pass them to the plugin `init`:

```
var options = {
    height: 300,
    width: 400,
    draggable: false,
    modal: true,
    buttons: {
        'OK': function(event, ui) {
            $(this).dialog('close');
        }
    }
};

$('#msg').dialog(options);
```

But this recipe is about more than just readability and code beauty. It's about changing the default behavior of a plugin you didn't write. Plus, it makes it so you can get back to the simple no-options `init`:

```
$('#msg').dialog();
```

As Dave Methvin famously said, "It couldn't get any shorter unless it read your mind."

Of course, you still have the option of overriding even these custom defaults by passing custom options to the plugin `init`, as in the previous recipe.

Don't forget that plugin options are cloned and extended from the defaults at the time of `init`. So, extending `$.ui.dialog.defaults` after a `<div>` has already been initialized as a dialog will have no effect on that dialog, even if that `init` was done with no custom options. The effect will be on any dialogs initialized after the defaults were overridden.

14.6 Getting and Setting jQuery UI Plugin Options

Problem

You need to check or change the value of a jQuery UI plugin option after it has been initialized.

Solution 1: Getting the Value

Call the plugin's `option` method, passing the name of the option:

```
var active = $('#myDiv').accordion('option', 'active');
```

When called with only an option name, the `option` method gets and returns the value, so it's not chainable.

Solution 2: Setting the Value

Call the plugin's `option` method, passing the name of the option and the new value:

```
$('#myDiv').accordion('option', 'active', 3);
```

When called with an option name and value, the `option` method sets the value and returns the jQuery object, so it's chainable.

Discussion

The `option` method get/set follows the same pattern as jQuery getters and setters such as `.css()` and `.attr()`. If you provide a value, it's a setter; if you omit the value, it's a getter.

As with other jQuery setters, you can set multiple options at once by passing a hash to the `option` method:

```
$('#myDiv').accordion('option', {
    active: 2,
    collapsible: true
});
```

14.7 Calling jQuery UI Plugin Methods

Problem

You need to make a jQuery UI plugin do something programmatically.

Solution

Call the jQuery UI plugin name method, and pass the name of the plugin method you want to call as the first argument. For example, to close a dialog, use this:

```
$('#msg').dialog('close');
```

If the method takes arguments, pass them after the name of the method. For example, to select the third tab, use this:

```
$('#nav').tabs('select', 2); // tabs method select accepts a 0-based index
```

Discussion

Every jQuery UI plugin provides at least four common base methods:

- option
- enable
- disable
- destroy

The option method was covered in the previous recipe. The destroy method is covered in a later recipe. The enable and disable methods are pretty self-explanatory. These work by setting the disabled option for that plugin, which defaults to false:

```
$('img').draggable('disable');

$('#mySlider').slider('enable');
```

Calling these methods also toggles the ui-pluginname-disabled class on the element, which can be used for styling or selecting.

To see whether a plugin is currently disabled, use the option method to get the value of the disabled option:

```
var isDisabled = $('#tempature').slider('option', 'disabled');
```

14.8 Handling jQuery UI Plugin Events

Problem

You need to react to, or be notified of, an event that occurs on a jQuery UI plugin. This could be a dialog opening, an accordion panel closing, or a tab being selected.

In this recipe, we're going to handle a draggable being dropped onto a droppable, which triggers the drop event on the droppable element.

Solution 1: Pass a Callback Function to the Event Name Option

On init, or later using the option method, you can declare a callback function to be called when that event occurs:

```
// Declaring an event callback option on init
$('#shopping-cart').droppable({
    drop: function(event, ui) {
        addProduct(ui.draggable);
```

```
        }
});

// Declaring an event callback after init using the option method
$('#shopping-cart').droppable();
...
$('#shopping-cart').droppable('option', 'drop', function(event, ui) {
    addProduct(ui.draggable);
});
```

Note that this solution allows for only one function to be called at each event trigger. You can call multiple handling functions by using a proxy method or by using the bind solution, shown next.

Solution 2: Bind to the Custom Event Using the Event Type

Use the jQuery `.bind()` method, and bind to the type of the event:

```
// Declaring an event callback option on init
$('#shopping-cart').bind('drop', function(event, ui) {
    addProduct(ui.draggable);
});
```

This binding can be done on the plugin element itself, or some container, taking advantage of custom event bubbling and delegation.

Discussion

Every jQuery UI event receives two arguments, `event` and `ui`. The event argument is similar to the event argument passed to all browser events, such as `click` and `keypress`. The difference is that this is a custom event object. As with browser events, the type can be found in `event.type`.

Many jQuery UI plugin events have corresponding browser events that will typically trigger them. For example, the draggable sequence, `dragstart`, `drag`, `dragstop`, is most likely triggered by the browser events `mousedown`, `mousemove`, and `mouseup`. If the custom event was triggered by a browser event, that browser event will be in the `event.originalEvent` property. This can be really useful if you need to determine whether something was done via the keyboard, the mouse, or programmatically. Or it can be helpful if you need to find out whether a modifier key was held while the mouse was clicked or moved.

The `ui` argument is a hash that contains any values that are particularly applicable to that event at that time, as well as ones that couldn't be had by calling the `option` or some other method on the plugin. For example, when a droppable gets a draggable dropped on it, that draggable element is passed to the drop event in `ui.draggable`. The contents of this `ui` hash are unique to each plugin event.

Note that the event name is most often different from the event type. For example, both Draggable and Slider have a `start` event. This is the event name. The types of the same are dragstart and slidestart. Since each plugin has its own option namespace, each can have the same option name, simply, start:

```
$('img').draggable({
    start: function(event, ui) {
        //event.type == 'dragstart'
    }
});
$('#mySlider').slider({
    start: function(event, ui) {
        //event.type == 'slidestart'
    }
});
```

But since events are bound and triggered in the same namespace, a prefix is required to make the event types unique:

```
$('img').bind('dragstart', function(event, ui) {
        //event.type == 'dragstart'
    }
});
$('#mySlider').bind('slidestart', function(event, ui) {
        //event.type == 'slidestart'
    }
});
```

This prefix is most commonly the name of the plugin, yielding event types such as dialogfocus, tabsadd, and progressbarchange. In some cases, a custom verb prefix is used instead, if it's a better fit. So, you use dragstart instead of draggablestart, and you use slidestart instead of sliderstart.

If the event type prefix happens to match the event name exactly, it is dropped to avoid a doubling up like dragdrag or slideslide. In these cases, the event type will match the event name, like drag and slide.

14.9 Destroying a jQuery UI Plugin

Problem

You're done with a particular plugin, and you want your element back the way it was. This is bigger than disable; this is un-init.

Solution

Call the destroy method:

```
$('#queue').sortable('destroy');
```

Discussion

Calling the `destroy` method will completely uninitialize that element as that plugin. It will remove any classes added by the `init` or any later method call or event. If the `init` caused the element to be wrapped, it will unwrap. It's like a big undo.

Destroying a jQuery UI plugin doesn't remove the element from the DOM. It simply removes that plugin state saved on that element, putting the element back as close as possible to its pre-`init` state. After a jQuery UI plugin is destroyed, it can be initialized as the same again.

If you want to both destroy and remove a plugin element, you can simply call `.remove()`. The `destroy` method will be called automatically by jQuery UI as it's removed. This is true even if the element has been initialized as more than one jQuery UI plugin.

14.10 Creating a jQuery UI Music Player

Problem

You need a music player that supports a common set of interface controls whether the music is being played by Flash Player or HTML5 audio or some other browser audio capability. You need the controls to be accessible, flexible, and themeable. A few basic features will do:

- Play
- Pause
- A track bar to show and control the current point in the playback
- A progress meter to show how much of the song is buffered
- Volume

In addition to these basic features, you want one more feature. This music player needs to be scalable. The same interface should work at any size, whether resized by the browser, the user, or the application—all the way up to full screen.

Solution

Let's build a music player using jQuery UI. We're going to create the play and pause buttons using jQuery UI CSS Framework icons, and we're going to create the track bar using the jQuery UI Slider plugin. The progress meter will be a jQuery UI Progressbar. Finally, the volume control will be one more jQuery UI Slider. We'll wrap these elements in a common container to provide for some nice widget theming so that not only will each of our controls be themed but also our music player as a whole will be themed.

We will not be building this music player as a reusable plugin. We're simply going to wire together some jQuery UI widgets to work as something that will appear to the user as one component. But the music player itself won't be a jQuery plugin or a jQuery UI plugin. For this recipe, it's just a collection of HTML, JavaScript, and CSS. That way, we can focus on how to use the jQuery UI plugins underneath, without the additional complexity of building a new plugin out of existing plugins.

HTML5 audio

To keep things simple, we're going to use a minimal subset of the HTML5 Media Element API (*http://dev.w3.org/html5/spec/Overview.html#htmlmediaelement*). This is available in a number of recent browsers, such as Firefox 3.5. We'll implement it as a compatibility layer so that another playback mechanism, such as Flash Player, could be substituted easily. For this recipe, we need the following from our audio API:

- Start or resume playback (`play`)
- Pause the playback (`pause`)
- Get the length of the song (`duration`)
- Get the current point that the playback is at (`timeupdate`)
- Change to a certain point in the song (`currentTime`)
- Get the volume the song is being played at (`volumechange`)
- Change to a certain volume (`volume`)

Assuming an HTML5 `audio` element (*http://dev.w3.org/html5/spec/Overview.html#audio*) exists in the document, here's the compatibility layer code:

```
var $audio = $('audio'), audioEl = $audio[0];
var audio = {
        currentTime: 0,
        duration: secondsTotal,
        volume: 0.5,
        set: function(key, value) {
                this[key] = value;
                try { audioEl[key] = value; } catch(e) {}
                if (key == 'currentTime') {
                        $audio.trigger('timeupdate');
                }
                if (key == 'volume') {
                        $audio.trigger('volumechange');
                }
        },
        play: function() {
                audioEl.play && audioEl.play();
        },
        pause: function() {
                audioEl.pause && audioEl.pause();
        }
};
```

```
$audio.bind('timeupdate', function() {
        audio.currentTime = audioEl.currentTime;
});
audio.set('currentTime', 0);
audio.set('volume', 0.5);
```

The music player

Let's use the CSS class `mplayer` for our music player. This will be the class for our main `<div>`, and will be used as a prefix in all our CSS rules and jQuery selectors. Here's the CSS and HTML for our bare player:

```
.mplayer { position: relative; width: 40%; height: 2.5em; margin: 50px 0 100px 0; }
```

```
<div class="mplayer ui-widget"></div>
```

I've set the width to 40 percent so that we can see we have a flexible player from the ground up. Just resize your browser and watch the player resize. This will be even easier to see when the player isn't empty.

In addition to the `mplayer` class, our main `<div>` gets a `ui-widget` class. This is to ensure elements within it get styled appropriately. See the next chapter for more on theming with jQuery UI CSS Framework classes.

An empty `<div>` and no JavaScript make for an invisible and quiet music player. Let's add a play button and get our music on.

Play and pause button

There's not yet a button plugin in jQuery UI. We can make do in the meantime with an **a** element and some semantically named jQuery UI CSS Framework icon classes:

Here's the CSS:

```
.mplayer .buttons-container { position: absolute; top: 10px; left: 10px; }
.mplayer .buttons-container .playpause { height: 1.2em; width: 1.2em; display: block;
        position: relative; top: -2px; left: -2px; }
.mplayer .buttons-container .playpause .ui-icon { margin: -1px 0 0 -1px; }
.mplayer .playpause .ui-icon-play, .paused .playpause .ui-icon-pause { display: none; }
.paused .playpause .ui-icon-play { display: block; }
```

Here's the HTML:

```
<div class="mplayer ui-widget">
        <div class="buttons-container">
                <a class="playpause ui-state-default ui-corner-all" href="#">
                        <span class="ui-icon ui-icon-play"></span>
                        <span class="ui-icon ui-icon-pause"></span>
                </a>
        </div>
</div>
```

With a couple CSS rules, we're able to have one button serve as both the pause and the play button. With the previous CSS, only one icon, play or pause, will be visible at once, depending on whether our `div.mplayer` has the `paused` class. But the same HTML allows for a different designer to decide that both icons will be visible at once, but perhaps with different colors and opacity, depending on whether the song is playing.

Here's the JavaScript:

```
$('.mplayer .playpause').click(function() {
        var player = $(this).parents('.mplayer');
        if (player.is('.paused')) {
                $('.mplayer').removeClass('paused');
                audio.play();
        } else {
                $('.mplayer').addClass('paused');
                audio.pause();
        }
        return false;
})
.hover(function() { $(this).addClass('ui-state-hover'); },
        function() { $(this).removeClass('ui-state-hover'); })
.focus(function() { $(this).addClass('ui-state-focus'); })
.blur(function() { $(this).removeClass('ui-state-focus'); });
$('.mplayer').addClass('paused');
```

Our button needs JavaScript to do the following:

- Call the `audio.play()` or `audio.pause()` function, depending on whether the `paused` class is on `div.mplayer` when clicked.
- Toggle the `paused` class on the `.mplayer`.
- React to mouse and keyboard `focus`, `hover`, and `blur`. This is where a button plugin might come in handy (there's one being built), but for a simple icon button like this, it's not too much code.

Don't forget the `return false;` since our button is an `<a>` with an href of `#`.

With jQuery, jQuery UI, and the UI Lightness theme loaded, Figure 14-1 shows what our music player looks like with just the play/pause button.

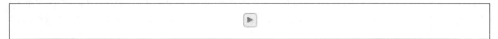

Figure 14-1. Play and pause button

If you click the play button, it should change to a pause button. If you click again, it should change back. Also notice that you get a hover effect, as well as a visual cue, when tabbing in and out of the button with the keyboard. If you're in a browser that supports the `audio` element and it has a `src` attribute that points to a supported music file, you should even hear something when you click play.

Current and total time labels

The next step is to add two labels, one that shows the current point we're at in the song and another that shows the total time in the song. These are pretty straightforward.

Here's the CSS:

```css
.mplayer .currenttime { position: absolute; top: 0.6em; left: 2.2em;
        width: 3em; text-align: center; background: none; border: none; }
.mplayer .duration { position: absolute; top: 0.6em; right: 2.2em;
        width: 3em; text-align: center; background: none; border: none; }
```

Here's the HTML:

```html
<div class="mplayer ui-widget">
        <div class="buttons-container">
                <a class="playpause ui-state-default ui-corner-all" href="#">
                        <span class="ui-icon ui-icon-play"></span>
                        <span class="ui-icon ui-icon-pause"></span>
                </a>
        </div>
        <span class="currenttime ui-state-default"></span>
        <span class="duration ui-state-default"></span>
</div>
```

Here's the JavaScript:

```javascript
function minAndSec(sec) {
        sec = parseInt(sec);
        return Math.floor(sec / 60) + ":" + (sec % 60 < 10 ? '0' : '') +
Math.floor(sec % 60);
}
$('.mplayer .currenttime').text(minAndSec(audio.currentTime));
$('.mplayer .duration').text(minAndSec(secondsTotal));

$audio
        .bind('timeupdate', function(event) {
                $('.mplayer .currenttime').text(minAndSec(audio.currentTime));
        });
```

We've put the current time on the left and total time on the right, leaving room in the middle for the track bar (see Figure 14-2). We want the current time to always reflect where we are in the song, so we bind to audio's **timeupdate** notification event. The event itself doesn't give us the **currentTime**. For that, we go to the **audio.currentTime** property. We need a small function to format it as minutes:seconds, since times in the audio layer are in seconds.

Figure 14-2. Current and total time labels

Slider track for song position

Now we're getting somewhere. Next is our track bar. It consists of a simple `<div>`, but we're going to give it a track and handle by calling `.slider()` on it. We'll use Slider's `range: 'min'` option so that the region between 0:00 and the current time will be shaded. Oh yeah, and we have to set `max` to the duration of the song, in seconds. So if it's a 3.5-minute song, we'll set `max` to 210. No calculations are needed, because `audio.duration` already gives us the total number of seconds in the song. The other defaults for Slider work for us here: `max: 0`, `step: 1`.

Here's the CSS:

```
.mplayer .track { top: 11px; margin: 0 5.2em; margin-top: -2px;
        border-style: none; }
.mplayer .track .ui-slider-handle { border-left-width: 0; height: 1.1em;
        top: -0.24em; width: 2px; margin-left: -3px; }
```

Here's the HTML:

```
<div class="mplayer ui-widget">
        <div class="buttons-container">
                <a class="playpause ui-state-default ui-corner-all" href="#">
                        <span class="ui-icon ui-icon-play"></span>
                        <span class="ui-icon ui-icon-pause"></span>
                </a>
        </div>
        <span class="currenttime ui-state-default"></span>
        <div class="track"></div>
        <span class="duration ui-state-default"></span>
</div>
```

Here's the JavaScript:

```
$('.mplayer .track')
        .slider({
                range: 'min',
                max: audio.duration,
                slide: function(event, ui) {
                        $('.ui-slider-handle', this).css('margin-left',
                                (ui.value < 3) ? (1 - ui.value) + 'px' : '');
                        if (ui.value >= 0 && ui.value <= audio.duration) {
                                audio.set('currentTime', ui.value);
                        }
                },
                change: function(event, ui) {
                        $('.ui-slider-handle', this).css('margin-left',
                                (ui.value < 3) ? (1 - ui.value) + 'px' : '');
                }
        })
        .find('.ui-slider-handle').css('margin-left', '0').end()
        .find('.ui-slider-range').addClass('ui-corner-left').end();

$audio
        .bind('timeupdate', function(event) {
                $('.mplayer .track').each(function() {
```

```
                    if ($(this).slider('value') != audio.currentTime) {
                            $(this).slider('value', audio.currentTime);
                    }
            });
            $('.mplayer .currenttime').text(minAndSec(audio.currentTime));
    });
```

Slider handles are center aligned, meaning at the min value, the left half of the handle goes beyond the left of the slider, and when at the max point, the right half of the handle goes beyond the right of the slider. We already made the handle skinnier than normal and got rid of the left border so it sticks to the range a little better. But we still need a little bit of adjustment when near the min. That's what these lines are for:

```
slide: function(event, ui) {
        $('.ui-slider-handle', this).css('margin-left',
                (ui.value < 3) ? (1 - ui.value) + 'px' : '');
        if (ui.value >= 0 && ui.value <= audio.duration) {
                audio.set('currentTime', ui.value);
        }
},
change: function(event, ui) {
        $('.ui-slider-handle', this).css('margin-left',
                (ui.value < 3) ? (1 - ui.value) + 'px' : '');
}
```

Also, in the slide callback, we're checking whether the value is valid before telling the audio to go to that point. This is a case where the user is dragging the slider around, and we need to move around the playback point in the song. This allows for "scrubbing." If we only handled this in the change callback, the audio wouldn't change until the user let go of the mouse, after clicking or dragging the slider handle to a new point. Figure 14-3 shows the slider we've created.

Figure 14-3. Slider track for song position

Progress bar in track to show buffering

Get ready for some fun. What if I told you we can call two different jQuery UI plugins on the same element? It works really well in this case. We already have a track bar, which we created as a <div>, calling .slider() on it. In addition to adding a ui-slider class to our .track element, the jQuery UI Slider plugin created and appended a couple elements to our track, a slider handle (.ui-slider-handle) and a slider range (.ui-slider-range), since we specified range: 'min'. Fortunately, that's as much as it did to our <div>. It's still a <div>, and it's still our <div>. So, let's dual-purpose it and call .progressbar() on it. This will make it so our buffer display runs behind the range display that shows our current time. Check this out.

Here's the CSS:

```
.mplayer .ui-progressbar .ui-progressbar-value { border-style: none; }
```

Here's the JavaScript:

```
var secondsCached = 0, cacheInterval;
$('.mplayer .track')
        .progressbar({
                value: secondsCached / secondsTotal * 100
        })
        .find('.ui-progressbar-value').css('opacity', 0.2).end();

cacheInterval = setInterval(function() {
        secondsCached += 2;
        if (secondsCached > secondsTotal) clearInterval(cacheInterval);
        $('.mplayer .track.ui-progressbar')
                .progressbar('value', secondsCached / secondsTotal * 100);
}, 30);
```

There's no HTML, since we're reusing the .track element from the previous section. Oh, and in case you hadn't noticed, that buffering code is totally bogus. Well, it works; it just isn't representing a song being buffered, only simulating it. But it works great! If you really had a music resource that was coming in and buffering and your audio API supported notifying you of that, you'd bind to the event and set the progress bar value as shown earlier, between 0 and 100. Unlike Slider, you can't specify a custom max for progress. But that makes sense, right? Progress goes from 0 percent to 100 percent.

OK, so we have got some proof-of-concept code here. When the page loads, the buffer progress will race away as if the file is flying in, but not quite as if it's local. It's fun to watch. Figure 14-4 shows the progress bar we've created. The other thing that's bogus about our buffer progress indicator? Since it isn't a real buffer progress, you can jump beyond it. What will happen? That depends on your audio API and backend. So, if you don't have a buffer progress or don't want or need one, skip this. Or leave it in for looks.

Figure 14-4. Progress bar in track to show buffering

Volume slider

So, we need to add a volume control. Slider is a good fit. Drag from volume: 0 to volume: 1 and set step to 0.01:

```
$('.mplayer .volume').slider({
        max: 1,
        step: 0.01,
        value: audio.volume,
        slide: fnSlide,
        change: fnChange
});
```

Bam. Why not? Well, that would certainly work. But it would take up a bit of space. And orientation may be an issue. If we lay it out horizontally, which is the default for Slider, we're competing with the track for horizontal space. Not to mention we're "lopsiding" our player. OK, so should we add `orientation: 'vertical'` to the slider options? Well, that too would work, but it would mean our player is now 100 pixels tall and only in order to fit the volume control. The rest of the controls need just over 30 pixels. There has to be a better way.

There is. Keep the volume slider's bar hidden when not in use. We'll keep the slider handle visible and add a little speaker icon to it. Then we'll hide the rest by setting the height of the control to 0. When the user hovers over the handle, we'll set the height to 100 pixels. On mouseout, we'll remove that, and it will go back to 0 height. Also, with its container positioned absolutely in a relative wrapper, it won't affect the overall height of the player when it is fully visible.

There's one problem. When the bar appears, let's say the volume is at 0.10, or 10 percent. That would mean the handle is near the bottom. Should the handle jump down? Or the bar up? And what about while the user slides it? What if they drag from 10 percent up to 90 percent and then let go? It would jump back down when the bar hides again. Yuck.

So, here's what we're going to do. We're going to keep the handle fixed the whole time. The user will drag up for increase and down for decrease. The bar, including the `range: "min"` shaded portion below the handle, will move down and up accordingly.

Here's the CSS:

```
.mplayer .volume-container { position: absolute; top: 12px; right: 12px; }
.mplayer .volume { height: 0; margin-top: 5px; }
```

Here's the HTML:

```
<div class="mplayer ui-widget">
        <div class="buttons-container">
                <a class="playpause ui-state-default ui-corner-all" href="#">
                        <span class="ui-icon ui-icon-play"></span>
                        <span class="ui-icon ui-icon-pause"></span>
                </a>
        </div>
        <span class="currenttime ui-state-default"></span>
        <div class="track"></div>
        <span class="duration ui-state-default"></span>
        <div class="volume-container">
                <div class="volume">
                        <a href="#" class="ui-state-default ui-corner-all
ui-slider-handle">
                                <span class="ui-icon ui-icon-volume-on"></span>
                        </a>
                </div>
        </div>
</div>
```

Here's the JavaScript:

```javascript
$('.mplayer .volume')
    .slider({
        max: 1,
        orientation: 'vertical',
        range: 'min',
        step: 0.01,
        value: audio.volume,
        start: function(event, ui) {
            $(this).addClass('ui-slider-sliding');
            $(this).parents('.ui-slider').css({
                'margin-top': (((1 - audio.volume) * -100) + 5) + 'px',
                'height': '100px'
            }).find('.ui-slider-range').show();
        },
        slide: function(event, ui) {
            if (ui.value >= 0 && ui.value <= 1) {
                audio.set('volume', ui.value);
            }
            $(this).css({
                'margin-top': (((1 - audio.volume) * -100) + 5) + 'px',
                'height': '100px'
            }).find('.ui-slider-range').show();
        },
        stop: function(event, ui) {
            $(this).removeClass('ui-slider-sliding');
            var overHandle = $(event.originalEvent.target)
                .closest('.ui-slider-handle').length > 0;
            if (!overHandle) {
                $(this).css({
                    'margin-top': '',
                    'height': ''
                }).find('.ui-slider-range').hide();
            }
        },
        change: function(event, ui) {
            if (ui.value >= 0 && ui.value <= 1) {
                if (ui.value != audio.volume) {
                    audio.set('volume', ui.value);
                }
            }
        }
    })
    .mouseenter(function(event) {
        if ($('.ui-slider-handle.ui-state-active').length) {
            return;
        }
        $(this).css({
            'margin-top': (((1 - audio.volume) * -100) + 5) + 'px',
            'height': '100px'
        }).find('.ui-slider-range').show();
    })
```

```
        .mouseleave(function() {
                $(this).not('.ui-slider-sliding').css({
                        'margin-top': '',
                        'height': ''
                }).find('.ui-slider-range').hide();
        })
        .find('.ui-slider-range').addClass('ui-corner-bottom').hide().end();
```

While it's being dragged, we're adjusting the negative `margin-top` of the bar in inverse proportion to the current value, keeping the handle static. This happens here:

```
$(this).parents('.ui-slider').css({
        'margin-top': (((1 - audio.volume) * -100) + 5) + 'px',
        'height': '100px'
})
```

Figure 14-5 shows the volume slider in our player.

Figure 14-5. Volume slider

This interaction requires recognizing that you're not dragging the bar, which is what's moving, in the opposite direction of your mouse. But meanwhile, your mouse, the size of the shaded range, and your volume do move in logical concert: down for down, up for up. Also, if you prefer, you can hover so that the bar appears, move your mouse to the position on the bar where you want to set the volume, and click.

Widget background and top styling

OK, let's add a couple elements with jQuery UI CSS Framework classes to style the player in a way that matches the controls within it:

Here's the CSS:

```
.mplayer .bg { position: absolute; width: 100%; height: 100%; top: 0;
        bottom: 0; left: 0; right: 0; border: none; }
.mplayer .rod { position: absolute; top: -2px; left: -0.4%; right: -0.4%;
        width: 100.8%; height: 3px; overflow: hidden; border: none; }
.mplayer .hl { position: absolute; top: 2px; left: 1%; right: 1%; width: 98%;
        height: 1px; overflow: hidden; border: none; }
.mplayer .hl2 { position: absolute; top: 2px; left: 2%; right: 2%; width: 96%;
        height: 3px; overflow: hidden; border: none; }
```

Here's the JavaScript:

```
$('.mplayer').each(function() {
        $('.bg:first', this).css('opacity', 0.7);
        $('.bg:last', this).css('opacity', 0.3);
})
$('.mplayer .rod').css('opacity', 0.4);
$('.mplayer .hl').css('opacity', 0.25);
$('.mplayer .hl2').css('opacity', 0.15);
```

Here's the HTML:

```
<div class="mplayer ui-widget">
        <div class="bg ui-widget-header ui-corner-bottom"></div>
        <div class="bg ui-widget-content ui-corner-bottom"></div>
        <div class="rod ui-widget-header"></div>
        <div class="hl ui-widget-content"></div>
        <div class="hl2 ui-widget-content"></div>
        <div class="buttons-container">
                <a class="playpause ui-state-default ui-corner-all" href="#">
                        <span class="ui-icon ui-icon-play"></span>
                        <span class="ui-icon ui-icon-pause"></span>
                </a>
        </div>
        <span class="currenttime ui-state-default"></span>
        <div class="track"></div>
        <span class="duration ui-state-default"></span>
        <div class="volume-container">
                <div class="volume">
                        <a href="#" class="ui-state-default ui-corner-all
ui-slider-handle">
                                <span class="ui-icon ui-icon-volume-on"></span>
                        </a>
                </div>
        </div>
</div>
```

Here we're using opacity and layering to squeeze a couple more shades out of any jQuery UI theme. Figure 14-6 shows the finished product:

Figure 14-6. Widget background and top styling

Finally, Figure 14-7 shows a sampling of the jQuery UI music player in a few prebuilt jQuery UI themes.

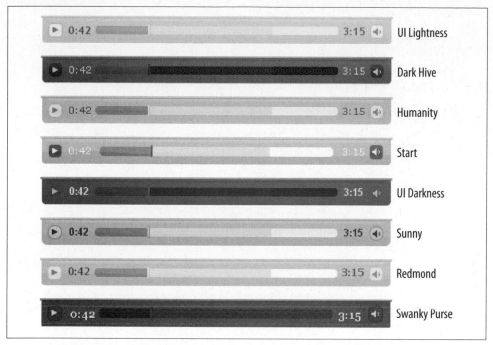

Figure 14-7. jQuery UI media player in a few different ThemeRoller themes

jQuery UI Theming

Maggie Wachs, Scott Jehl, Todd Parker, and Patty Toland
(Filament Group, Inc.)

15.0 Introduction

One of the advantages of jQuery UI is its ease of integration into such a wide range of websites and applications. And a major factor for successful integration is the ability to apply a look and feel to jQuery UI widgets that's consistent with a larger site or system design.

jQuery UI is expressly designed to make custom theming easy. You can create highly customized visual styles for your widgets—that automatically include not only colors and textures but a full complement of interaction states—using the following:

- The jQuery UI CSS Framework, a comprehensive set of CSS classes for applying consistent styles and behaviors across widgets
- ThemeRoller, jQuery UI's tool for theme creation

Together, they provide ways to easily and consistently change the look and feel of both official jQuery UI widgets and your own custom components so they blend seamlessly with your site or application.

This chapter focuses how to get the most out of these tools, whether you're using them to customize an official jQuery UI widget or incorporating them into your own custom development workflow. We'll start with a summary of the jQuery UI CSS and how it works with ThemeRoller, and then we'll present four theming recipes in this order:

1. Styling jQuery UI widgets with ThemeRoller
2. Overriding jQuery UI layout and theme styles
3. Applying a ThemeRoller theme to non-jQuery UI components
4. Referencing multiple themes on a single page

Each recipe starts with a basic sample design challenge and progressively applies techniques to customize the theme. For that reason, you'll frequently see references from one recipe to another in this chapter.

Before we dive into styling the widgets, it's important to understand how all of the jQuery UI classes are structured and how they work with ThemeRoller.

Understanding the Components of jQuery UI CSS

Our primary goal when creating the jQuery UI CSS was to simplify the setup process so that developers could deploy widgets quickly and seamlessly in their code without having to sift through complex markup or CSS.

In our early experience integrating third-party JavaScript widgets into our own projects, customizing the appearance of library widgets was significantly harder than setting up the scripts to run properly. Unlike the scripts, which were designed to be customized—core and widget plugin scripts handle complex tasks behind the scenes and configurable options are made easily accessible for customization—widget styles were generally keyed off of a single class or baked into the markup. We had to identify classes in the markup and deconstruct their style rules before we could modify them, which usually involved several hours of sifting through the code and CSS, using Firebug to figure out where classes are assigned or find inline styles, retrofitting background images, and then replacing style rules or editing classes in the markup to make the appearance approximate our project's design. (And that was only when the code and CSS were reasonably organized and consistent.)

To us, this felt backward; it would be much easier to add a custom look and feel to a mostly unstyled widget than to pick apart the CSS of an already-styled widget and try to figure out which rules can safely be replaced. We resolved to develop a better way to apply styles consistently so they would work coherently across a group of widgets and within a larger site or application design system.

To solve this problem for jQuery UI, we divided the jQuery UI CSS into logical components, similarly to how the scripts are structured, and separated core structural styles required for a widget to function properly (positioning, floats, and padding) from the customizable theme styles (colors and background images). So, the classes that developers can modify to make the widgets match their project are now grouped into two basic categories:

- Widget-specific classes include all styles required to format a particular widget's structure and layout, including positioning, spacing and dimensions, and other layout-related styles to help it function correctly. For instance, Widget classes for the tabs include styles that float tabs so they appear in a horizontal row and selectively hide the associated tab content panels.

  Widget-specific classes are included in the accompanying CSS when you download one or more jQuery UI widgets (see Recipe 15.1 to learn how to download and reference jQuery UI CSS). Classes are named for the specific widget they control, and the class name always begins with the prefix ui-[widgetname], e.g., ui-tabs.

- Framework classes apply a customized theme look and feel—including a base font, background colors and textures, font and icon colors, shape (corner radius), and interaction state feedback—across all widgets. Framework classes are named according to their basic purpose—for example, some provide state feedback (ui-state-default, ui-state-hover) or apply rounded corners (ui-corner-all, ui-corner-top)—and are intended for reuse throughout a website or application. In fact, they can be applied to any widget, including those created by jQuery UI or another JavaScript library or your custom widgets.

In practice, we style jQuery UI widgets by assigning a combination of these classes—one or more descriptive Widget-specific classes along with a series of generic Framework classes—that work together to create the final appearance. For example, look at the markup for the accordion header:

```
<h3 class="ui-accordion-header ui-state-active ui-corner-top">code</h3>
```

Three classes are applied that assign very specific styles:

- ui-accordion-header is a Widget-specific class unique to this component; it sets structural style rules (positioning, dimensions, margin, padding) but does not apply any colors or images.
- ui-state-active is a Framework class that adds the theme colors and background images to show its active state.
- ui-corner-top, another Framework class, specifies that the header should have rounded top corners.

Although this approach means that multiple classes are assigned to some elements, it's a powerful system that makes it easy to apply a very lightweight theme to an unlimited number of widgets, even your own custom components. The careful separation of the structural styles from the theme also means that you can drop in a new theme at any time without worrying about it breaking your existing widgets.

We also wanted to make it easy to create a new look and feel, or accurately match an existing design, without deep expertise in CSS or photo-editing tools like Adobe Photoshop. ThemeRoller lets developers edit style rules set by the Framework classes without having to touch the CSS or do any manual image production.

ThemeRoller is a web application that offers a fun and intuitive interface for designing and downloading custom themes for jQuery UI. ThemeRoller provides levers to change the following theme styles:

- *Base font for all widgets*: The base font sets a standard typeface, size, and weight (normal or bold) that will be used throughout all the widgets in the theme. By default, font size is specified in "em" units. We recommend using ems over pixels so text will scale with the widget containers when the user manipulates browser text size, but you can specify pixels if you like. As with standard CSS, it's good practice to provide a range of fonts in case your first font of choice is not installed on a user's computer and to end the font string with the generic font style like "serif" or "sans-serif."

- *Corner radius*: A corner radius can be applied consistently across all widgets in the theme to give them a rounded appearance. Each radius value must be followed by a unit: pixels for a fixed radius, ems for a radius that responds to text size changes, or a value of zero for perfectly square corners. Smaller pixel values make the corners of widgets more square, while larger values make the corners more round.

 As of this writing, corners set in CSS3 as we do in the Framework are not supported in some modern browsers, including Internet Explorer. Please see the sidebar in Recipe 15.1 to learn how to bring rounded corner support to these browsers.

- *Headers, toolbars, and content areas*: Each of these levers sets a background color with a semitransparent texture and colors for border, text, and icons. For example, the header style is used for the title bar of a dialog or datepicker and the selected range of a slider or progress bar, while the content style is used for the content area of a selected accordion or tab.

- *Default, active, and hover states for clickable elements*: There are three states that represent different points in the user interaction: `default` is the standard clickable state, `hover` is used to provide visual feedback when the mouse is placed over the item, and `active` is used when the item is currently selected. Each clickable state is defined by a background color with a semitransparent texture and by colors for border, text, and icons. Keep in mind that each state should be different enough to provide adequate feedback to the user.

- *Highlight and error states*: These are special styles for communicating states in a system. The highlight state is used on text messages to draw a user's attention, as well as to indicate today's date in the calendar widget, and is also useful for highlighting when an Ajax screen update has occurred. The error state can be used to indicate that there is a problem that requires the user's attention such as displaying a form validation issue or alerting the user to a system failure. Both are defined by a background color with a semitransparent texture and by colors for border, text, and icons. These states should contrast with the standard content text and background colors in your theme and should also be different enough from each other so that it's clear which one is meant to draw attention versus communicate an alert or warning message.

- *Modal screen for overlays*: The modal screen is a layer that sits between a modal dialog and the page content beneath it and is commonly used to make page content appear temporarily disabled while the modal is showing. This lever styles the modal screen's background color and opacity. If you don't want a modal overlay at all for a particular widget, that can be toggled through the widget's `modal` option.

- *Drop shadow styles*: As with the highlight and error states, a dropshadow style can be optionally applied to overlays. Drop shadows have background color, texture, and opacity (like headers and clickable elements), and also have a shadow thickness specifying how far the shadow should be offset from the top-left corner of its component and a corner radius. To make the shadow appear evenly around the component, the top and left offset values should be negative and equal to the shadow thickness. As with standard corner radius, you can set a shadow corner radius in pixels or ems or enter zero to make corners square.

The ThemeRoller interface lets you directly edit all of the previous Framework class styles and preview your design changes in functioning jQuery UI widgets. Once you've created a theme, ThemeRoller automatically generates and packages all required CSS and background images—you simply download the resulting theme stylesheet and reference it in your project. (You'll find ThemeRoller in the Themes section of the jQuery UI site or at *http://themeroller.com*.)

Now that we've reviewed the jQuery UI CSS and ThemeRoller, we'll look at four recipes that use them to customize themes. First, we'll start with the simple step of creating a theme and styling widgets with ThemeRoller (Recipe 15.1); then we'll move through slightly more complex steps of overriding Framework classes for more customized themes (Recipe 15.2), using Framework classes throughout your project (Recipe 15.3), and finally looking at multiple themes on a single page for complex interfaces (Recipe 15.4).

 For designers and developers who are interested in editing and previewing themes for jQuery UI and custom ThemeRoller-ready components in place in your website or application, we developed a downloadable ThemeRoller bookmarklet tool. To learn more about and download the bookmarklet, go to ui.jquery.com/themeroller (*http://ui.jquery.com/themeroller*).

15.1 Styling jQuery UI Widgets with ThemeRoller

Problem

jQuery UI widgets used in your website or application must match an established design.

Solution

Use ThemeRoller, a simple web application for editing the jQuery UI CSS Framework classes to customize the look and feel of the jQuery UI widgets.

This recipe makes the following assumptions:

- You have a basic knowledge of how CSS works and, specifically, how styles cascade, take precedence, and can be scoped using selector classes, ids, or elements. (For our recommended resources, please refer to the Appendix at the end of this chapter.)

- You're already familiar with jQuery UI CSS classes. (If not, just review "Understanding the Components of jQuery UI CSS" on page 342.)

Let's walk through an example.

We're working on a new website for booking travel reservations, and specifically, we're building out the part of the interface for booking a flight. The design consists of a set of tabs for selecting the type of reservation (flight, car rental, or package deal), and the Book a Flight tab includes a form for entering the number of passengers, selects for the departure and arrival cities, calendars to set departure and return travel dates, and a submit button (see Figure 15-1).

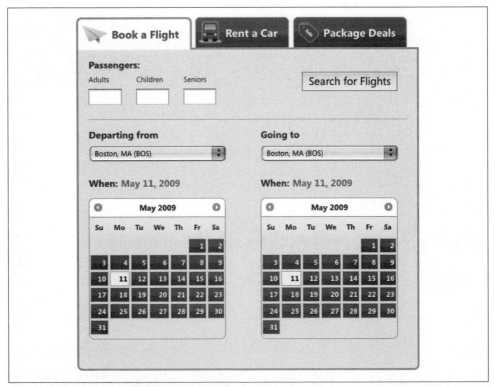

Figure 15-1. Final target design for travel application

For this recipe, we'll use the jQuery UI widgets for the tabs and datepickers, and style them with a custom theme created in ThemeRoller. (You can also modify the theme stylesheet beyond the standard ThemeRoller output to more closely match your design—you'll see how in Recipes 15.2–15.4).

Step 1. Open ThemeRoller

Open the jQuery UI website at *http://jqueryui.com* and choose Themes from the top navigation bar, or go directly to *http://themeroller.com*.

The interface for ThemeRoller is grouped into two main sections, as shown in Figure 15-2:

- *ThemeRoller toolbar pane in the left column*, which provides tools to set and change all style settings in a theme
- *Sample widgets preview pane on the right* for previewing your style selections—each widget is interactive to show the full range of styles (use your mouse to see hover and active styles, for example) and updates in real time when you edit styles using the toolbar

Figure 15-2. The default view of ThemeRoller, with the toolbar pane on the left and widgets preview pane on the right

The ThemeRoller toolbar provides two distinct ways to customize themes, accessible with the tabs at the top of the toolbar column:

- *The Roll Your Own tab* (Figure 15-3) is the workspace where you create custom styles for your theme. Customizable settings are grouped into sections with inputs and tools for quick style selection, including setting the base font and corner radius across all widgets and setting background colors and textures, text color, and icon color.

  Each section is closed by default and displays current styles in the form of a small icon to the right of the label. Open/close sections as needed while you edit, and preview sample widgets to the right, which update to reflect your changes in real time.

> JavaScript is not required to use ThemeRoller. If JavaScript is disabled, a Preview button appears that may be clicked to view changes.

- *The Gallery tab* (Figure 15-3) offers a range of preconfigured themes that can be downloaded as is or used as a starting point for a more customized theme.

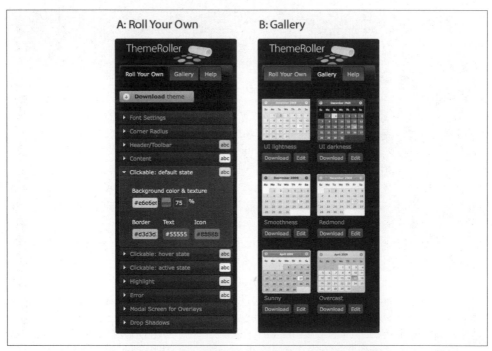

Figure 15-3. ThemeRoller's Roll Your Own tab (A) provides controls to change the font, corner radius, and colors for a range of interaction states; the Gallery tab (B) provides one-click access to a variety of prebuilt themes

Step 2. Create and preview a theme

For our travel reservations app, we'll select a gallery theme called Sunny that's close to our final design (as shown in Figure 15-4).

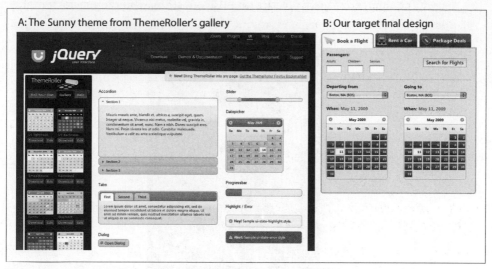

Figure 15-4. ThemeRoller's gallery themes offer a wide range of starting points for customizing designs; Sunny (A) shares many styles with our target design (B)

Sunny specifies similar overall background, font face, and font colors to our final design, but a couple of styles will need to be edited to more closely match our design—for instance, Sunny's tabs are yellow with a gray background, while our tabs are dark gray with a white background.

We can easily change those settings by either clicking the Edit button below the Sunny image in the gallery (which will move you over to the Roll Your Own view) or clicking the Sunny image in the gallery to activate it and then clicking over to the Roll Your Own tab at the top of the toolbar.

Once you have the Sunny settings in the Roll Your Own tab, the toolbar prefills with all the theme's settings, and you can start editing. Let's tweak the following settings to make the Sunny theme match our design:

- *Set the base font for all widgets*: The default font in the Sunny theme and our target design seem very similar, but we can simply open the Font Settings section (as shown in Figure 15-5) and either confirm that they are correct or fill in alternate values for font family, weight, and size. The font family accepts multiple comma-separated font names (as in standard CSS notation). Here are some design notes and tips:

—By default, the font size is specified in "em" units. We recommend using ems in favor of pixel text sizes so widget text will scale with the widget containers when the user manipulates browser text size.

—Provide a range of fonts in case your first font of choice is not installed on a user's computer. It's good practice to end a font string with the generic font style like "serif" or "sans-serif."

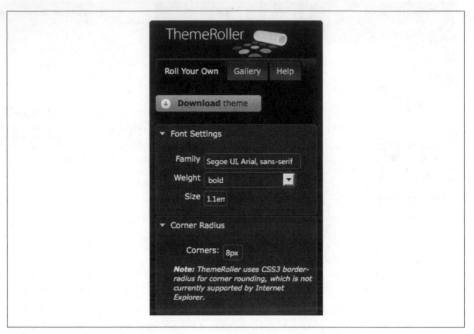

Figure 15-5. The Font Settings and Corner Radius sections

- *Apply a corner radius*: Our design includes rounded corners on the datepicker and tabs. You can set a corner radius on jQuery UI widgets in ThemeRoller by opening the Corner Radius section (as shown in Figure 15-5) and entering a value followed by a unit: pixels for a fixed radius, or ems for a radius that responds to text size. Smaller pixel values make the corners of widgets more square, while larger values make the corners more round. For perfectly square corners, set the value to zero.

At the time of writing of this edition, some modern browsers, most notably Internet Explorer, do not support the CSS3 `border-radius` property and as a result do not render the rounded corner styles applied by Framework classes. Corners appear square instead. If your design includes rounded corners and must render consistently across all browsers, you may want to use a corner-rounding JavaScript library like ddRoundies.

We've written a basic tutorial on our Filament Group lab explaining how to incorporate ddRoundies into your project: "Achieving Rounded Corners in Internet Explorer for jQuery UI with DD_roundies" (*http://www.filamentgroup.com/lab/achieving_roun ded_corners_in_internet_explorer_for_jquery_ui_with_dd _roundi*).

- *Make the default tabs and buttons gray.* Unselected tabs, like accordion section headers or datepicker buttons, are clickable elements, and each is assigned a class that represents its current clickable state: default, hover, or active. In this case we'll change the default state background color from gray to yellow and update text and border color to match our design (Figure 15-6):

  1. Open the "Clickable: default state" section.

  2. Focus your cursor on the background color field (it contains a hexadecimal value preceded by #), and pick a new dark gray color or enter a hexadecimal value; in this case we'll enter the value #333333

  3. The text color is dark gray and now blends with our background, so we'll also update the default state text color to contrast with the background. We'll change the text color value to #FFFFFF.

  4. As with the text, the icons that appear in the header are gray and need to be updated so they don't disappear against the gray background. Let's give them a value of #EEEEEE, a color that will complement but won't appear higher contrast than the text.

  5. Finally, let's change the border color from yellow to light gray; enter value #D2D2D2.

  6. Hit the Tab or Enter key, or click elsewhere on the page, to preview the changes in the widgets on the right.

Figure 15-6. ThemeRoller's section for the Clickable: default state

- *Update the hover state to match the new tab color*: The clickable hover state style is intended to be shown whenever you mouse over a clickable component like a tab, accordion section, or datepicker button. Now that the default state is gray, we'll adjust the hover state's background and text colors to coordinate and use a complementary darker shade of gray for the background with white text and icons:

    1. Open the "Clickable: hover state" section.

    2. In the background color field enter the value #111111.

    3. Update the text and icon colors to #FFFFFF.

    4. Let's also make the border color better match our design by setting it to a slightly darker gray than the default border, #888888.

- *Change the tabs and datepicker header backgrounds to white*: The header style appears in several jQuery UI widgets: behind the tabs, at the top of datepicker's month/year feedback and navigation buttons, as the slider range, and as the progress bar completion indicator. In our design the header is a flat white color with gray text and dark yellow icons:

    1. Open the Header/Toolbar section.

    2. In the background color field enter a hexadecimal value of #FFFFFF.

    3. Click the texture icon next to the background input, and choose the first option, "flat." (Hover over any texture image to see the name.) Doing this removes the background image so that the style only sets a flat background color.

    4. Set the background opacity to 100 percent to ensure that the header is fully opaque.

5. The text color is white and doesn't show up on our new background, so let's change it to dark gray to match our default clickable state, #333333.

6. Finally, change the border and icon colors to #EDAA12, and the text color to white, #FFFFFF.

- *Change the content container border color to yellow*: Content borders appear around accordion sections, and define the tabs, dialog, slider, datepicker, and progress bar containers. In the design the border is the same light yellow we used for the header border:

    1. Open the Content section.

    2. Focus on the border color field, and enter the value #EDAA12.

- *Update the "active" state border color to blend with the container*: After updating the container border color, you'll see that the selected accordion section and selected tab still have dark gray borders. This color is set with the clickable active state class:

    1. Open the "Clickable: active state" section.

    2. Focus on the border color field, and enter the value #EDAA12.

You can "save" a theme at any point simply by bookmarking the page; ThemeRoller updates the URL with all relevant styles each time the preview pane refreshes. Bookmark your custom theme—even bookmark multiple themes to compare them side by side—and reload any theme from its bookmark to modify and refine it for download.

Also, for any theme downloaded from ThemeRoller, a complete theme URL is included in the stylesheet. Open the stylesheet (e.g., jquery-ui-1.7.1.custom.css), and search for the comment that starts with this: "To view and modify this theme, visit http://jqueryui.com/themeroller/..."

At this point, we have made our ThemeRoller theme match the design of our travel reservations app as closely as we can (see Figure 15-7). It's now ready for download.

Figure 15-7. Our final customized ThemeRoller theme that closely matches our design

Step 3. Download the jQuery UI widgets and theme

Click the "Download theme" button at the top of the ThemeRoller toolbar's Roll Your Own tab, which navigates you to the jQuery UI download builder (see Figure 15-8).

In the right column under Theme, you'll see Custom Theme pre-selected in the drop-down.

 If you chose a default theme from the gallery and made no changes to it, you'll see the name of that theme, e.g., Smoothness.

Next, we'll select which jQuery UI components to download with our theme. All are selected by default; simply uncheck those you don't want to download, or click "Deselect all components" at the top of the Components section to download only the theme stylesheet. For our travel reservations app, we need the jQuery UI core scripts and those for tabs and the datepicker.

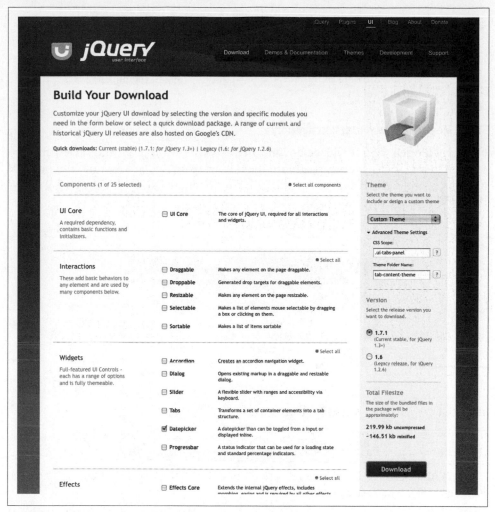

Figure 15-8. The jQuery downloader combines UI core, any interactions and widgets you select, and your theme into a single zipped file

Finally, select which version of jQuery UI you'd like to use; the latest stable version is selected by default. Click Download, and save the ZIP file locally. The downloaded ZIP file will be named like *jquery-ui-1.7.1.custom.zip*.

(The Advanced Theme Settings section in the download builder's Theme section allows you to download a scoped theme—we'll get to that in detail in Recipe 15.4.)

The jQuery UI CSS is updated with each new version of jQuery UI—e.g., new releases will include not only updated scripts but may also include modifications and updates to the CSS as well.

At the time of this writing, the version of jQuery UI is 1.7, and recipes and techniques in this chapter are applicable only to theming features in that version.

Step 4. Merge files into your project directory

Next, we'll open the ZIP file we downloaded in the previous step and review its contents. jQuery UI files are arranged into the following directory structure; the order of the folders and files may vary depending on your operating system (Figure 15-9 shows the folder opened on Mac OS X).

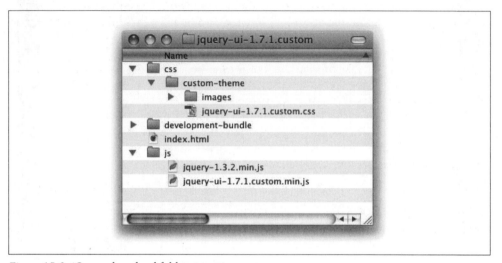

Figure 15-9. jQuery download folder structure

index.html

> Sample markup for the UI components you selected.

 If you chose not to download any components, this file will not be included in the download.

/css

> Contains a theme folder (e.g., *custom-theme*) with the following files:
>
> • An images directory with framework icons and background textures.

- Your theme stylesheet, e.g., `jquery-ui-1.7.1.custom.css`, which includes the styles you just edited and, if downloaded, the widget-specific styles necessary for the widgets to function properly.

/js

Compiled jQuery UI JavaScript files.

/development-bundle

Individual component scripts and CSS used to create the compiled versions found in the *css* and *js* folders, open source license text, and related resources necessary for advanced development with jQuery UI.

When working on your own project, be sure to review the markup in *index.html* and use it as a guide along with the Demos & Documentation at *http://jqueryui.com* to integrate the component markup and scripts into your project.

For our travel application, we'll copy the theme folder in the *css* directory and paste it to the styles directory in our project; to keep it simple, we named the styles folder *css* to match.

 It's important to maintain the established directory structure within the theme folder so that the icon images are referenced properly by the theme classes. If you do change the theme directory structure, you will likely have to replicate those changes if later you decide to upgrade to a newer version of the jQuery UI scripts and CSS.

Step 5. Reference the theme stylesheet in your project

Finally, we'll include a reference to the theme stylesheet in the `<head>` of our page.

Keep in mind that *the stylesheet reference should always appear before any references to jQuery UI scripts* so that the CSS loads first; this is necessary because some widgets depend on the CSS to function properly.

We'll reference the theme stylesheet (in bold) before all scripts in our travel reservations app:

```
<!doctype html>
<html>
<head>
    <meta charset="UTF-8">
    <title>travel application | Book a Flight, Rent a Car, or Find Package
Deals</title>
    <!-- jQuery UI styles -->
    <link rel="stylesheet" type="text/css" href="css/custom-theme/jquery-ui-
1.7.1.custom.css" />

    <!-- jQuery core & UI scripts -->
    <script type="text/javascript" src="js/jquery-1.3.2.min.js"></script>
    <script type="text/javascript" src="js/jquery-ui-1.7.1.custom.min.js"></script>

    <script type="text/javascript">
```

```
$(function(){
    $('#travel').tabs();
    $("#departure-date-picker").datepicker({altField: '#departure-date',
altFormat: 'MM d, yy'});
    $("#arrival-date-picker").datepicker({altField: '#arrival-date',
altFormat: 'MM d, yy'});
});
</script>
</head>
```

When the jQuery UI widget markup and styles are in place for your project, preview your page in a browser to confirm that the styles are being applied correctly. Previewing our travel application reveals that the theme is applied correctly—as you can see in Figure 15-10, our default tabs are gray, the headers are white, and the text and icon colors match our selections.

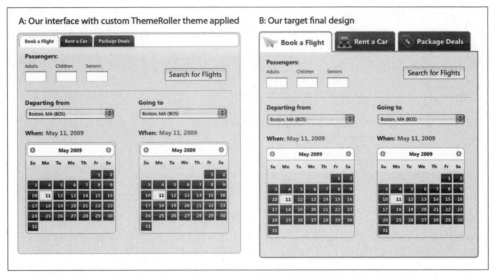

Figure 15-10. Our design interface with customized ThemeRoller theme applied (A) and our target final design (B)

But our interface clearly needs more work to match our target design (Figure 15-10): the tabs are too small and are missing their custom icons, and the datepicker header is enclosed within the datepicker widget when it should appear on top. In Recipe 15.2 we'll review how to make small adjustments to theme styles so that these elements better match our design.

If the jQuery UI widgets in your page are not picking up the theme stylesheet, double-check the directory path to the theme stylesheet against the reference in your page, and correct any typos. If that doesn't solve the issue, temporarily disable any non-jQuery styles or scripts to test whether they're interfering with how the theme stylesheet is loaded or rendered, and fix any related bugs.

Discussion

Since ThemeRoller themes are structured to deliver a holistic experience and apply across multiple widgets, it helps to think about how the various Framework classes interact with one another. If you choose to create your own theme from scratch, or substantially modify an existing theme, here are some points you might want to consider:

To create uniform backgrounds for headers and toolbars and content areas to make the "on" state tab appear seamlessly connected to the visible content panel, and match the content area background and borders to your clickable active state background and borders.

For clickable elements, states should be clearly different enough to provide adequate feedback to the user. Here are a couple of ways to make sure the states work together to deliver distinctive visual differentiation:

- Use mirror image textures for the default and active clickable states to achieve a three-dimensional look and feel. For instance, a "highlight" texture for the default button state pairs well with an "inset" texture for the active button state. The button will look like it physically depresses on click.
- If you do use the same texture for clickable and hover, make sure the background color and image opacity are different enough (generally at least a 10 percent shift) to provide a clear visual change.

Optimize your theme for speed by using the same image for multiple styles. For example:

- When you use the same icon color for multiple states, the stylesheet will make fewer HTTP requests, improving page performance.
- You can also use the same background image (color plus texture opacity) for multiple states as well. If you do this, it's important to make sure that the other style elements—border, text, and icon colors—are distinct enough to make a clear differentiation.

To make changes to your custom theme without having to start from scratch, open the original theme stylesheet, search for the comment that starts with "To view and modify this theme, visit http://jqueryui.com/themeroller/...," and copy and paste the theme URL into a browser's address bar to open ThemeRoller with that theme's settings preloaded.

15.2 Overriding jQuery UI Layout and Theme Styles

Problem

The customized (or standard gallery) theme you created in ThemeRoller, downloaded, and referenced in your project is a partial match to your target design but doesn't match exactly. You need to modify the styles, but at the same time you want to ensure that edits to these styles don't make it difficult for you to upgrade to newer versions of jQuery UI scripts and CSS.

Solution

Create custom override styles, scoped to the components that need additional non-ThemeRoller styling, and structure them so that they don't conflict with or overwrite any standard jQuery UI CSS files.

The following recipe makes the following assumptions:

- You have a basic knowledge of how CSS works and, specifically, how styles cascade, take precedence, and can be scoped using selector classes, IDs, or elements. (For our recommended resources, please refer to the Appendix at the end of this chapter.)

- You're already familiar with how to create and edit a theme using ThemeRoller. (If not, review Recipe 15.1, which describes in detail how to create a theme and apply it to your pages.)

Each jQuery UI widget is styled to work out of the box when you download the jQuery UI scripts and a theme stylesheet; no changes to the CSS are necessary to incorporate the widget or styles into your site. But it's possible that the styling may not exactly match the design conventions established in your project. For example, you may want to reduce the padding or use a custom background image for a header.

Let's pick up where we left off in the previous recipe and continue working on our travel reservations application. We created, downloaded, and applied the theme stylesheet correctly; however, the default jQuery UI styles for the tabs and datepickers don't quite match the design for our project, as shown in Figure 15-11.

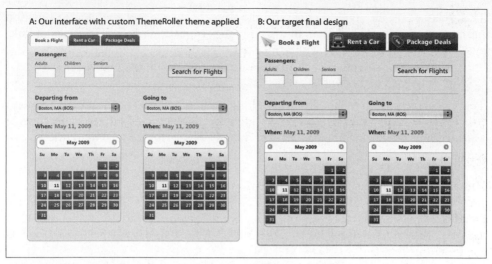

Figure 15-11. Our design interface with customized ThemeRoller theme applied (A) and the target design provided by the designer (B)

Step 1. Review the widget markup and styles for jQuery UI plugins

First, we'll review how classes are assigned in the jQuery UI widget markup to better understand how they're applied (and can therefore be overridden).

Let's start with the tabs markup. When the jQuery UI tabs widget is initialized on the page, the plugin script assigns several classes to the widget markup, as shown next. (Please note that this is the markup that is transformed or inserted by the plugin script; it's the finished product, not the markup served to the page before JavaScript is run.)

Pay particular attention to the classes that begin with the prefix ui-tabs—the Widget-specific classes for the tabs—highlighted in bold:

```
<div class="ui-tabs ui-widget ui-widget-content ui-corner-all" id="travel">
    <ul class="ui-tabs-nav ui-helper-reset ui-helper-clearfix ui-widget-header
ui-corner-all">
        <li class="ui-state-default ui-corner-top ui-tabs-selected ui-state-active">
<a href="#travel-flight" id="tab-flight">Book a Flight</a></li>
        <li class="ui-state-default ui-corner-top"><a href="#travel-car"
id="tab-car">Rent a Car</a></li>
        <li class="ui-state-default ui-corner-top"><a href="#travel-package"
id="tab-package">Package Deals</a></li>
    </ul>
    <div id="travel-flight" class="ui-helper-clearfix ui-tabs-panel
ui-widget-content ui-corner-bottom"></div><!-- /flight -->
    <div id="travel-car" class="ui-tabs-panel ui-widget-content ui-corner-bottom
ui-tabs-hide"></div><!-- /car -->
    <div id="travel-package" class="ui-tabs-panel ui-widget-content ui-corner-bottom
ui-tabs-hide"></div><!-- /package -->
</div><!-- /travel -->
```

These classes set the styles that control the widget's layout and enable it to function properly according to its design. In this case, they transform an unordered list of links and `<div>` elements into tabs with associated content panels. (Widget-specific classes are discussed in detail in "Understanding the Components of jQuery UI CSS" on page 342 earlier in this chapter.)

They also identify a widget's individual components—like the header or content panels—and as such they're ideal for writing override rules to adjust layout features or add customizations like drawn icons. The Widget classes for the tabs mark the following components:

ui-tabs
> Outer container that wraps around the tab navigation and content.

ui-tabs-nav
> Container for the navigation options. The tab list items and links are styled using descendant selectors, i.e., `ui-tabs-nav li`.

ui-tabs-selected
> Selected tab "on" state, which is dynamically by the script. This class is assigned to only one tab at a time.

ui-tabs-panel
> Content areas that map to tabs.

ui-tabs-hide
> Default state for the content panels. They're hidden until selectively shown by the user.

To see the style rules associated with these classes, open the theme stylesheet and find (Ctrl/Command-F) or scroll to the block that begins with `ui-tabs`. Notice that the rules only apply to layout characteristics, like positioning, padding, or border width, and are absent any theme styles, like background or border colors:

```css
.ui-tabs { padding: .2em; zoom: 1; }
.ui-tabs .ui-tabs-nav { list-style: none; position: relative;
padding: .2em .2em 0; }
.ui-tabs .ui-tabs-nav li { position: relative; float: left;
border-bottom-width: 0 !important; margin: 0 .2em -1px 0; padding: 0; }
.ui-tabs .ui-tabs-nav li a { float: left; text-decoration: none;
padding: .5em 1em; }
.ui-tabs .ui-tabs-nav li.ui-tabs-selected { padding-bottom: 1px;
border-bottom-width: 0; }
.ui-tabs .ui-tabs-nav li.ui-tabs-selected a, .ui-tabs .ui-tabs-nav
li.ui-state-disabled a, .ui-tabs .ui-tabs-nav li.ui-state-processing
a { cursor: text; }
.ui-tabs .ui-tabs-nav li a, .ui-tabs.ui-tabs-collapsible .ui-tabs-nav
li.ui-tabs-selected a { cursor: pointer; } /* first selector in group seems
obsolete, but required to overcome bug in Opera applying cursor: text overall
if defined elsewhere... */
.ui-tabs .ui-tabs-panel { padding: 1em 1.4em; display: block; border-width: 0;
background: none; }
.ui-tabs .ui-tabs-hide { display: none !important; }
```

Your theme stylesheet will contain the `ui-tabs` style rules only if you've also downloaded the tabs plugin.

Step 2. Create an override stylesheet

We've found the best way to safely fine-tune a widget's appearance is to write new style rules that override the jQuery UI theme styles and append these "override rules" in a separate stylesheet. Override rules are written against jQuery UI CSS class names and as such *must appear in the source order after your theme stylesheet*; since styles are read in order, the last style rule always takes precedence.

The jQuery UI library is constantly evolving to include more features with better-streamlined code. By maintaining override styles in a separate file, you can customize the widget styles as much or as little as you'd like and still preserve the ability to easily upgrade the jQuery UI files as needed and simply overwrite your existing theme stylesheet knowing that your override rules remain intact. Override rules can be listed in a dedicated stylesheet for overriding default theme styles, or if you prefer to limit the number of files linked to your pages (and therefore limit the number of requests to the server), append override rules to the master stylesheet for your entire project.

As we work through this recipe, we'll append override styles to the master stylesheet for our project, `travel.css`, just below the block of custom styles we developed for our application:

```
/* ----- CUSTOM STYLES for the travel application */
body { font-size: 62.5%; }
fieldset { padding: 0 0 1.5em; margin: 0 0 1.5em; border: 0; }
p, label { padding: 0 0 .5em; margin: 0; line-height: 1.3; }
p label { display: block; }
...
/* ----- OVERRIDE RULES for jQuery UI widgets */
/* tabs background styles go here */
...
```

And we'll reference `travel.css` after the theme stylesheet in our page:

```
<!doctype html>
<html>
<head>
    <meta charset="UTF-8">
    <title>travel application | Book a Flight, Rent a Car, or Find Package
Deals</title>

    <!-- jQuery UI styles -->
    <link rel="stylesheet" type="text/css" href="css/custom-theme/jquery-ui-
1.7.1.custom.css" />

    <!-- overrides & custom styles for the travel application -->
    <link rel="stylesheet" type="text/css" href="css/travel.css" />
....
```

Step 3. Edit the style rules in your override stylesheet

Now that we've reviewed how the Widget classes are named and applied, and also how to reference override styles in our project, let's update our travel reservations application with our customized tabs navigation bar and datepicker header style. We'll tackle the tabs first.

Scope overrides. The design we created for the tabs is specific to the travel reservations application, and we don't necessarily want the same customizations, like the icons or font size, to apply to every tab widget in our entire application. To ensure that these styles only apply to the travel application, we'll scope the override rules to our travel application's unique ID.

Each new rule will start with the Widget-specific class assigned to the component we want to change; for example, when changing styles for the tab's navigation bar, we'll write a rule against the `.ui-tabs-nav` class:

```
.ui-tabs-nav { /* our override style rule */ }
```

And scope it to our travel application by prepending its ID, `travel`:

```
#travel .ui-tabs-nav { /* our override style rule */ }
```

Write override rules. After applying the theme stylesheet, our tab's navigation panel looks like Figure 15-12: the individual tabs are small and surrounded by a border that's separated from the outermost container by a few pixels of padding.

Figure 15-12. Our tabs with ThemeRoller theme applied before overrides

However, our design (Figure 15-13) calls for large tabs with icons and without a background—they appear to sit above the tab content.

Figure 15-13. Our target tab design

To override the default tab styles, we'll make a handful of style changes:

1. First we'll remove the outermost border. The entire tabs widget is surrounded by a 1-pixel border and has a few pixels of padding. For the tabs to appear above the content panels, we'll remove both:

   ```
   #travel.ui-tabs { padding: 0; border-width: 0; }
   ```

There's intentionally no space between our scoping ID, `#travel`, and the `.ui-tabs` class because both are applied to the same element in the markup:

```
<div id="travel" class="ui-tabs ui-widget ui-widget-content ui-corner-all">
```

2. Next, we'll flatten the bottom of the tab navigation bar (set the bottom-corner radius to zero) and remove its top and side borders. We'll also remove any extra padding so that the tabs appear flush with the left side of the widget, and we'll thicken the border width to 3 pixels to match our design:

```
#travel .ui-tabs-nav {
    border-width: 3px;
    border-top-width: 0;
    border-left-width: 0;
    border-right-width: 0;
    -moz-border-radius-bottomleft: 0;
    -webkit-border-bottom-left-radius: 0;
    -moz-border-radius-bottomright: 0;
    -webkit-border-bottom-right-radius: 0;
    padding: 0;
}
```

3. The tabs are a little too close together, so let's add some right margin:

```
#travel .ui-tabs-nav li {
margin-right: .5em;
}
```

4. And update the selected tab, `.ui-tabs-selected`, so that it appears connected to the tab content area. We'll increase the border width to 3 pixels so that it matches the design, and we'll then fix the gap between the tab and content. The amount of space between the tab and its content panel is directly related to the tab navigation bar's border thickness, so we can close the gap by applying a negative 3-pixel bottom margin:

```
#travel .ui-tabs-nav li.ui-tabs-selected {
    border-width: 3px;
    margin-bottom: -3px;
}
```

5. Next, we'll apply our custom icons. Because each icon is unique to its tab, we can apply each icon as a background image using the unique ID of each tab. (Technically these aren't override styles, but we'll need to reference these rules when we style the selected tab's icon next.)

```
#tab-flight {
    background: url(../images/icon-tab-flight.png) no-repeat .3em center;
    padding-left: 50px;
}

#tab-car {
    background: url(../images/icon-tab-car.png) no-repeat .1em center;
    padding-left: 45px;
}
```

```
#tab-package {
        background: url(../images/icon-tab-package.png) no-repeat .1em center;
        padding-left: 45px;
}
```

6. The selected tab uses a slightly different icon that sits on a white, not gray, background. For each tab, we'll add a rule that keys off the Widget-specific class for the selected state, `.ui-tabs-selected`:

```
#travel .ui-tabs-nav li.ui-tabs-selected #tab-flight {
        background-image: url(../images/icon-tab-flight-on.png);
}

#travel .ui-tabs-nav li.ui-tabs-selected #tab-car {
        background-image: url(../images/icon-tab-car-on.png);
}

#travel .ui-tabs-nav li.ui-tabs-selected #tab-package {
        background-image: url(../images/icon-tab-package-on.png);
}
```

7. Our tabs should also have more padding and a larger font size:

```
#travel .ui-tabs-nav a {
    font-size: 1.5em;
    padding-top: .7em;
    padding-bottom: .7em;
}
```

8. To finish up the tabs, we'll adjust the border around the content panel so that it matches the 3-pixel border width we set on the selected tab:

```
#travel .ui-tabs-panel {
    border-width: 3px;
    border-top-width: 0;
    padding-top: 1.5em;
}
```

Now that our tabs match the design, let's update the datepicker's header. As illustrated in Figure 15-14, with a few adjustments we can make the datepicker's header component—the bar above the calendar that contains navigation arrows and month/year feedback—appear above, not contained within, the datepicker.

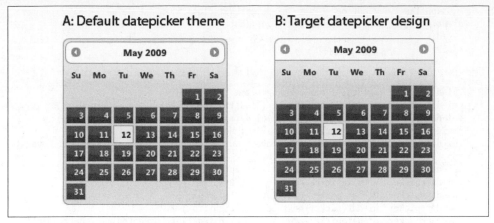

Figure 15-14. *Our datepicker with ThemeRoller theme applied (A) and our target design (B)*

Like the tabs, when the datepicker plugin is initialized on the page, the script writes widget markup to the page that contains jQuery UI Widget-specific and Framework classes to set its structural and themed appearance. In an abridged version of the datepicker markup, you can see that Widget-specific classes conform to the naming convention and begin with `ui-datepicker`, and identify each component:

```
<div id="ui-datepicker-div" class="ui-datepicker ui-widget ui-widget-content
ui-helper-clearfix ui-corner-all ui-helper-hidden-accessible">
    <div class="ui-datepicker-header ui-widget-header ui-helper-clearfix
ui-corner-all">
        <a class="ui-datepicker-prev ui-corner-all">title="Prev"><span class="ui-icon
ui-icon-circle-triangle-w">Prev</span></a>
        <a class="ui-datepicker-next ui-corner-all" title="Next"><span class="ui-icon
ui-icon-circle-triangle-e">Next</span></a>
        <div class="ui-datepicker-title">
            <span class="ui-datepicker-month">January</span><span class="ui-datepicker-
year">2009</span>
        </div>
    </div>
    <table class="ui-datepicker-calendar">
        <thead>
        <tr>
            <th class="ui-datepicker-week-end"><span title="Sunday">Su</span></th>
            ...
        </tr>
        </thead>
        <tbody><tr>
            <td class="ui-datepicker-week-end ui-datepicker-other-month"> 1 </td>
            ...
        </tr>
        </tbody>
    </table>
    <div class="ui-datepicker-buttonpane ui-widget-content">
        <button type="button" class="ui-datepicker-current ui-state-default
ui-priority-secondary ui-corner-all">Today</button>
```

```
    <button type="button" class="ui-datepicker-close ui-state-default
ui-priority-primary ui-corner-all">Done</button>
  </div>
</div>
```

The datepicker Widget classes are assigned the following default style rules:

```
.ui-datepicker { width: 17em; padding: .2em .2em 0; }
.ui-datepicker .ui-datepicker-header { position:relative; padding:.2em 0; }
.ui-datepicker .ui-datepicker-prev, .ui-datepicker .ui-datepicker-next {
position:absolute; top: 2px; width: 1.8em; height: 1.8em; }
.ui-datepicker .ui-datepicker-prev-hover, .ui-datepicker .ui-datepicker-next-hover {
top: 1px; }
.ui-datepicker .ui-datepicker-prev { left:2px; }
.ui-datepicker .ui-datepicker-next { right:2px; }
.ui-datepicker .ui-datepicker-prev-hover { left:1px; }
.ui-datepicker .ui-datepicker-next-hover { right:1px; }
.ui-datepicker .ui-datepicker-prev span, .ui-datepicker .ui-datepicker-next span {
display: block; position: absolute; left: 50%; margin-left: -8px; top: 50%;
margin-top: -8px;  }
.ui-datepicker .ui-datepicker-title { margin: 0 2.3em; line-height: 1.8em;
text-align: center; }
.ui-datepicker .ui-datepicker-title select { float:left; font-size:1em;
margin:1px 0; }
.ui-datepicker select.ui-datepicker-month-year {width: 100%;}
.ui-datepicker select.ui-datepicker-month,
.ui-datepicker select.ui-datepicker-year { width: 49%;}
.ui-datepicker .ui-datepicker-title select.ui-datepicker-year { float: right; }
.ui-datepicker table {width: 100%; font-size: .9em; border-collapse: collapse;
margin:0 0 .4em; }
.ui-datepicker th { padding: .7em .3em; text-align: center; font-weight: bold;
border: 0;   }
.ui-datepicker td { border: 0; padding: 1px; }
.ui-datepicker td span, .ui-datepicker td a { display: block; padding: .2em;
text-align: right; text-decoration: none; }
.ui-datepicker .ui-datepicker-buttonpane { background-image: none; margin: .7em
0 0 0; padding:0 .2em; border-left: 0; border-right: 0; border-bottom: 0; }
.ui-datepicker .ui-datepicker-buttonpane button { float: right; margin: .5em .2em
.4em; cursor: pointer; padding: .2em .6em .3em .6em; width:auto; overflow:visible; }
.ui-datepicker .ui-datepicker-buttonpane button.ui-datepicker-current { float:left; }
...
```

This is just a subset of the datepicker's style rules; to view all, in the theme stylesheet find the style block that starts with ui-datepicker.

Returning to our travel application, let's write a few override rules to make the datepicker's header appear like our design:

1. First we'll remove the padding that separates the header from the datepicker's outer container:

    ```
    #travel .ui-datepicker { padding: 0; }
    ```

2. Like the tab navigation bar, we want to flatten the bottom and remove its top and side borders:

```
#travel .ui-datepicker-header {
    border-top-width: 0;
    border-left-width: 0;
    border-right-width: 0;
    -moz-border-radius-bottomleft: 0;
    -webkit-border-bottom-left-radius: 0;
    -moz-border-radius-bottomright: 0;
    -webkit-border-bottom-right-radius: 0;
}
```

3. Finally, we'll remove the border and background image from the next and previous navigation arrows on hover:

```
#travel .ui-datepicker-prev-hover,
#travel .ui-datepicker-next-hover {
    border-width: 0;
    background-image: none;
}
```

With the override styles applied, our working travel application now accurately matches the final design (Figure 15-15).

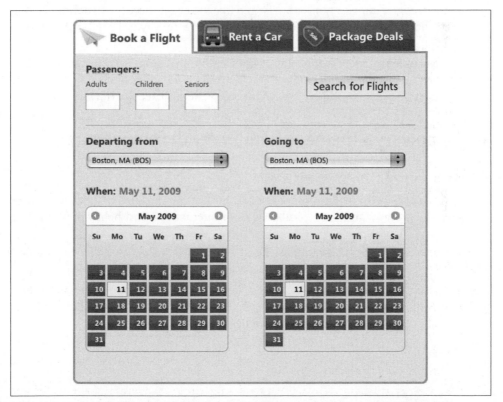

Figure 15-15. Our final design, with both standard ThemeRoller and override styles applied

Discussion

Consider whether you'd like to apply override rules to all widgets in your project or whether you only want to override theme styles for a subset of widgets. If there's even a small chance that you may want to present the widget in different ways, apply override styles by scoping them to a container element's class or ID so that you don't alter the default formatting of the widget.

Here are some editing tips/reminders:

- If you want to remove the bottom border on a widget header, use `border-bottom-width: 0;` instead of `border-bottom:0;`. The former will retain the border style and color in the event you want it back.

- For variation in stacked elements that have the same class, you might disable just the background image in one, letting the difference in background color show through.

- If you need to change the color of a particular portion of a widget, design the theme to accommodate that change instead of hard-coding a color into your stylesheet.

- If you need to remove a border but would like to keep it there for structural layout, you can set it to transparent. To do this in an IE-safe way, set the border style to `dashed`.

- Use em units whenever possible for structural dimensions such as padding and margins, and more importantly for font sizes. Write styles assuming 1em is the standard widget size, and try not to dip below .8em to keep text legible.

15.3 Applying a Theme to Non-jQuery UI Components

Problem

Other page components—like content boxes, buttons, and toolbars—are sitting next to jQuery UI widgets and have similar types of interactions and behaviors, but their designs don't match.

Solution

You can assign Framework classes to non-jQuery UI elements to apply the same theme as ThemeRoller-styled elements. (As a bonus, those elements will automatically update when you apply an updated ThemeRoller theme.)

The following recipe makes the following assumptions:

- You have a basic knowledge of how CSS works and, specifically, how styles cascade, take precedence, and can be scoped using selector classes, IDs, or elements. (For our recommended resources, please refer to the Appendix at the end of this chapter.)
- You're already familiar with how to create and edit a theme using ThemeRoller. (If not, review Recipe 15.1, which describes in detail how to create a theme and apply it to your pages.)

In the previous two recipes we used ThemeRoller to create and download a theme and then wrote a few CSS rules to override default theme styles and make it more closely match our finished design. Now we'll take it another step further and apply Framework classes to elements in our project so that they coordinate with the jQuery UI widgets and the theme we created.

Step 1: Review available Framework classes to identify those you can apply to your components

Framework classes are part of the jQuery UI theme stylesheet you download when you create a theme in ThemeRoller. They're named according to their purpose and apply theme styles like background colors and textures, border and font colors, rounded corners, and icons. Framework classes are built into jQuery UI widgets, but they may also be applied to any other elements—like custom widgets you've developed or extended from a third party—to achieve a consistent look and feel across your site or application.

The following is an overview of the classes that make up the framework, the styles applied by each, and general rules for referencing them in your own code.

Unless noted otherwise, all styles set by Framework classes are inherited by child elements, including any text, link, and icon styles.

Layout helper classes hide content or fix common structural issues, like completely wrapping a container around floated child elements:

`.ui-helper-hidden`
Applies `display: none`. Content hidden this way may not be accessible to screen readers.

`.ui-helper-hidden-accessible`
Positions an element off the page so that it's not visible but is still accessible to screen readers.

`.ui-helper-reset`
> Removes inherited padding, margin, border, outline, text decoration, and `list-style`; sets `line-height` to 1.3 and `font-size` to 100 percent.

`.ui-helper-clearfix`
> Forces nonfloated container elements to completely wrap around floated child elements.

Widget container classes should only be applied to the elements for which they're named because their child links will inherit styles from them:

`.ui-widget`
> Applies the theme's font family and size on the entire widget and explicitly sets the same family and 1em font size to child form elements to force inheritance.

`.ui-widget-header`
> Applies bold font.

`.ui-widget-content`
> Applies border color, background color and image, and text color.

Interaction states style clickable elements—like buttons, accordion headers, and tabs—to provide the appropriate state feedback as the user interacts with them; each class applies border color, background color and image, and text color. The `-hover`, `-focus`, and `-active` classes are intended to replace their CSS pseudoclass counterparts (`:hover`, `:active`, `:focus`) and must be assigned to an element with client-side scripting. State classes were designed this way to avoid style conflicts and added selector complexity that occurs when pseudoclasses are built into the CSS. (If pseudoclasses are necessary for your project, you can add them to your override stylesheet as described in Recipe 15.2.)

- `.ui-state-default`
- `.ui-state-hover`
- `.ui-state-focus`
- `.ui-state-active`

Interaction cues style content to convey feedback in the form of highlight or error messaging, disabled form elements, or visual hierarchy. All apply border color, background color and image, and text color:

`.ui-state-highlight`
> Assign this class to temporarily highlight a component.

`.ui-state-error`
> Assign this class to any components that contain error messaging.

`.ui-state-error-text`
> Applies only the "error" text and icon colors without the background.

`.ui-state-disabled`

Styles a form element to appear disabled using low opacity and therefore works alongside other classes used to style the element. The element is still usable when this class is applied; to disable functionality, use the `disabled` form element attribute.

`.ui-priority-primary`

Assign this class to a button when its action takes priority over another (i.e., Save over Cancel). Applies bold text.

`.ui-priority-secondary`

Assign this class to a button when its action is secondary to another (i.e., Cancel). Applies normal font weight and reduced opacity.

Icon classes provide additional feedback in the form of directional arrows and informational symbols, like an *x* or a trash can to mark a button that deletes. An icon is applied to an element with two classes:

`.ui-icon`

Base class that sets the element's dimensions to a 16-pixel square, hides any text, and sets the ThemeRoller-generated icon sprite image as a background.

`.ui-icon-[type]`

Where "type" is a descriptor for the icon graphic that will be displayed. Type can be a single word (`ui-icon-document`, `ui-icon-print`) or a combination of words, numbers, and shorthand; for example, `.ui-icon-caral-1-n` will display a single caret symbol that points north, and `.ui-icon-arrow-2-e-w` will display a double arrow icon that points east-west.

Because the `ui-icon` base class affects an element's dimension and hides all inner text, it's good practice to assign icons to their own elements, like `<span>` tags, so that the styles don't adversely affect any child content or elements. For accessibility purposes, include a brief description in the icon's `<span>` tag; it's hidden from the user's view but will be available to screen readers.

Also, each element with the `.ui-icon` class is assigned a sprite background image depending on the state of its parent container. For example, an icon element within a `.ui-state-default` container will display icons in the `ui-state-default` icon color you set in ThemeRoller.

jQuery UI provides a full suite of Framework icons (Figure 15-16). In ThemeRoller you can preview their default and hover interaction states by hovering over an icon in the widget example column, and you can mouse over an icon to see its class name.

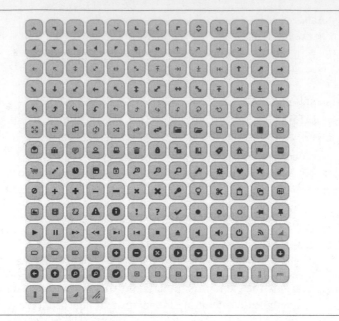

Figure 15-16. jQuery UI includes a full set of themed icons in a single sprite image; their interaction states are previewable in ThemeRoller

Corner radius helper classes apply rounded corners to a subset or all corners of a container. The last segment of the corner class name indicates where the corner will appear, as noted here:

.ui-corner-tl
  Top left

.ui-corner-tr
  Top right

.ui-corner-bl
  Bottom left

.ui-corner-br
  Bottom right

.ui-corner-top
  Both top

.ui-corner-bottom
  Both bottom

.ui-corner-right
  Both right

.ui-corner-left
  Both left

`.ui-corner-all`
>All four corners

Overlay and shadow classes can be used to add depth and dimension to a site or application:

`.ui-widget-overlay`
>Applies 100 percent width and height dimensions, background, and opacity to the modal screen, a layer that sits between a modal dialog and the page content that is commonly used to make page content appear temporarily disabled while the modal is showing.

`.ui-widget-shadow`
>Applies background, corner radius, opacity, top/left offsets to position the shadow behind a widget, and shadow thickness (similar to border width).

Because these Framework classes apply theme styles to jQuery UI widgets and can be used to style any component on your page, we can use them throughout an interface to create a uniform appearance. In this recipe, we'll review how to assign three types of Framework classes:

- Clickable state classes, including `.ui-state-default`, `.ui-state-hover`, and `.ui-state-active`
- A corner class, `.ui-corner-all`
- An interaction cue class for disabling a form element, `.ui-state-disabled`

Step 2: Apply clickable-state Framework classes

Let's continue refining the look of our travel reservations application.

After applying a theme we created in ThemeRoller and modifying default styles with override rules, the interface of our travel application's flight selector is almost done: the clickable elements in our jQuery UI widgets have a consistent appearance—by default, the tabs and datepicker buttons are all dark gray with a glassy texture.

But our Search for Flights submit button doesn't conform to this design and instead looks like a standard, unstyled browser button (Figure 15-17). We want it to look more like our polished theme style.

To make the search button look like other clickable elements in our travel application, we'll assign the Framework classes that set clickable state styles—`.ui-state-default`, `.ui-state-hover`, and `.ui-state-active`—to the button markup and then write a short jQuery script to apply the styles when the user interacts with the button. We'll also apply rounded corners with the same radius value set for the tabs and datepicker widget.

First, let's assign the default state class to the button so that it matches the other clickable elements. We'll simply write (or copy from the theme stylesheet) `ui-default-state` into the button's `class` attribute:

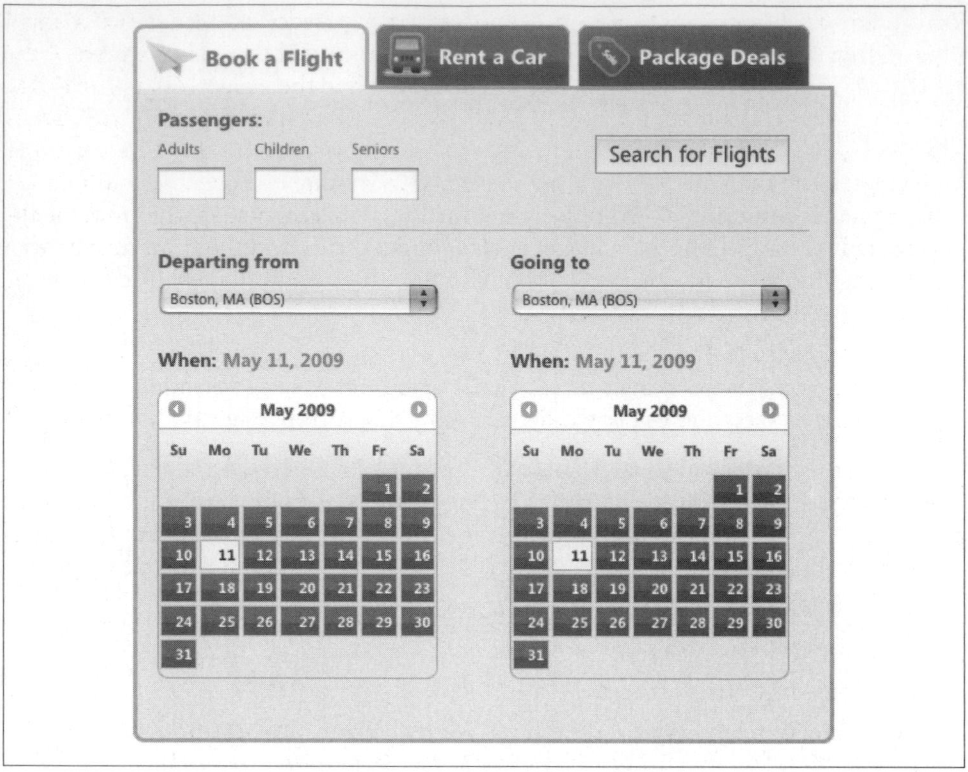

Figure 15-17. *Our interface is nearly complete, except for the unstyled Search for Flights button*

```
<button id="search-flights" class="ui-state-default">Search for Flights</button>
```

Other clickable elements like our tabs have rounded corners, so we'll add rounded corners to all sides of the button and append ui-corner-all to the class attribute:

```
<button id="search-flights" class="ui-state-default ui-corner-all">Search for
Flights</button>
```

With these quick additions to the markup, we've applied our default theme style for clickable elements to the search button and also made it "themeable"—later if we decide to create and apply a new theme to our travel application widget, the search button will pick up the default clickable and corner styles from the new stylesheet.

Finally, let's apply the hover and mousedown (active) states to provide visual feedback to users when they're interacting with the button (Figure 15-18).

Figure 15-18. *Three Framework classes are used to assign clickable states*

To update the button's appearance on hover and mousedown, we'll write a small jQuery script. Since we've already downloaded and included the latest version of the jQuery core library in our page and have already initialized the widget plugins on DOM ready, we'll append a function to the DOM ready block that toggles the state classes assigned to our search button. As noted in the following script block, the hover event contains two functions—the first removes the default state class and adds the hover state on mouseover, and the second reverses these class assignments on mouseout—and the mousedown event replaces the default and hover state classes with the active class:

```
$(function(){
    // initialize tabs and datepickers
        $('#travel').tabs();
        $('#departure-date-picker').datepicker({altField: '#departure-date', altFormat:
'MM d, yy'});
        $('#arrival-date-picker').datepicker({altField: '#arrival-date', altFormat: 'MM
d, yy'});

    // search button hover & active states
        $('#search-flights')
            .hover(
                function(){ $(this).removeClass('ui-state-default').addClass('ui-state-
hover'); },
                function(){ $(this).removeClass('ui-state-hover').addClass('ui-state-
default'); }
            )
            .mousedown(
                function(){ $(this).removeClass('ui-state-default, ui-state-
hover').addClass('ui-state-active'); }
            );
});
```

 Why write a script to update button states when CSS pseudoclasses (:hover, :active, :focus) do the same thing? We weighed this question when designing the jQuery UI CSS and decided against using pseudoclasses for a few key reasons:

- They introduce a degree of complexity to the stylesheet that made it nearly impossible to keep it lean, and including them required that we account for every possible scenario where these states may clash.

- They also add CSS bloat and would have significantly increased the size of the stylesheet.

- Some browsers, like older but still popular versions of Internet Explorer, only support pseudoclasses on link elements (anchor tags), so we had to create classes for all clickable states anyway.

Ultimately, our button will look like the one in Figure 15-19.

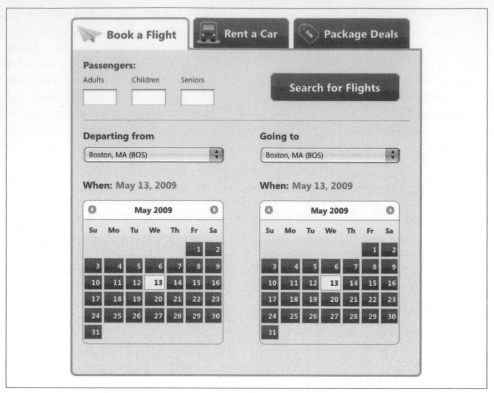

Figure 15-19. Our final design with theme classes applied to the Search button

Now that the button is styled to match our application, we can conditionally add an interaction cue class, `ui-state-disabled`, to provide visual feedback when the button is disabled (see Figure 15-20). For example, let's assume all fields in our flight reservation form are required for submission. In this case, the search button should appear disabled until the user enters a valid entry for every field; when the form is complete, we'll enable the button for submission.

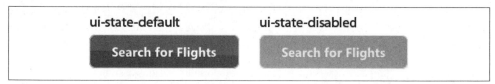

Figure 15-20. Add the ui-state-disabled state to make a form element appear disabled

To apply a disabled appearance to our search button, we'll append the Framework class `ui-state-disabled` to our default button. (Both classes are necessary to create the final appearance because the disabled state styles simply reduce the default button's opacity.)

```
<button id="search-flights" class="ui-state-default ui-state-disabled ui-corner-
all">Search for Flights</button>
```

Applying the disabled state class only changes the appearance of the button and does not affect its functionality; it's still capable of accepting user input to submit the form. To ensure that the button is actually disabled, be sure to add the `disabled` attribute and value to the button markup:

```
<button id="search-flights" class="ui-state-default ui-state-disabled ui-corner-all"
disabled="disabled">Search for Flights</button>
```

Discussion

Framework classes are designed to be reused throughout an application, and as such they provide developers with a ready set of classes for styling related components in an application, like our travel application's Search for Flights button, or even your own widgets. Because Framework classes are named according to their purpose, applying them to component parts of a custom widget is fairly intuitive:

- Clickable state classes can be added to buttons, links, or other elements that require a hover or active state.
- Corner classes can be applied to any element with block properties.
- Layout helpers can be used throughout the layout structure for fixing float containers or toggling content visibility.
- Interaction cue classes can be assigned to elements that must convey visual priority or error messaging.

Adding Framework classes to non-jQuery UI elements also makes them themeable; if you decide to edit and download an updated theme using ThemeRoller, the new theme will automatically also apply your styles to those elements.

15.4 Referencing Multiple Themes on a Single Page

Problem

More than one theme must be applied to your application and appear on a single page. For example, your jQuery UI tabs must be styled according to a primary theme, and widgets within the tab panels must conform to a different theme.

Solution

Create a second theme using ThemeRoller, and apply it selectively to widgets or components in your application by associating the new theme with a class, an ID, or other scoping selector during the download process.

The following recipe makes the following assumptions:

- You have a basic knowledge of how CSS works and, specifically, how styles cascade, take precedence, and can be scoped using selector classes, IDs, or elements. (For our recommended resources, please refer to the Appendix at the end of this chapter.)
- You're already familiar with how to create and edit a theme using ThemeRoller. (If not, review Recipe 15.1, which describes in detail how to create a theme and apply it to your pages.)

jQuery UI themes are intended to create a consistent look and feel in jQuery UI widgets and other interface components across an entire application, but sometimes the design is more complex, and a different look and feel must be applied to certain widgets depending on where they appear in the application.

In the case of our travel application, let's say the designer reviews our final design and feels that using dark gray on all clickable elements makes it difficult to distinguish the reservation type tabs from the form fields within the set. He decides the top tabs should retain their current style, but all interactive components inside the tabs—including the datepickers and search button—should be styled differently and have a yellow default state. Figure 15-21 shows our current and our new design.

Figure 15-21. Our original theme (A) sets the clickable default state to gray for all interactive elements; the new design (B) keeps the top tabs gray but shifts all interactive components inside the tabs to yellow

There are a couple of ways to create style exceptions for the tab contents. As described in Recipe 15.2, we could write and reference override rules to modify the default theme styles for the datepicker and button. To do that, we'd have to use a design editing tool like Adobe Photoshop to figure out all of the new color hexadecimal values and then produce new yellow background images.

Or, we could just create a new theme in ThemeRoller that matches our secondary theme (in this case, yellow clickable elements), scope it to our tab content area specifically, and then reference it after our original theme stylesheet. The jQuery UI download builder provides a simple interface for scoping a theme in this way: the Advanced Theme Settings area on the Download page can be set to specify a scoping selector—a class, an ID, or other hierarchical CSS selector—that allows you to pinpoint exactly which components will be styled with the additional theme.

Returning to our travel reservations application, at this point we've completed the steps described in Recipes 15.1 through 15.3:

- Created and downloaded a theme and referenced it in our project (Recipe 15.1)
- Wrote and appended override rules to modify a few of the theme's default styles (Recipe 15.2)
- Added a few Framework classes to our search button to apply our theme styles (Recipe 15.3)

Now we'll review how to scope a second theme and apply it to our project.

Step 1. Create another theme using ThemeRoller

Open the jQuery UI website at *http://jqueryui.com* and choose Themes from the top navigation bar, or go directly to *http://themeroller.com*.

We created the original theme to style all of the widgets used in our design. However, in this case we only want to style the widgets within the tab content panel; we can disregard the top navigation tabs for now.

As we did in Recipe 15.1, we'll start with the Sunny theme, since it closely matches the yellow clickable states and header styles in our new design by default (Figure 15-22).

 You can use an existing custom theme as a starting point without having to start from scratch. To do so, open the theme stylesheet, search for the comment that starts with "To view and modify this theme, visit http://jqueryui.com/themeroller/..." and copy and paste the theme URL into a browser's address bar to open ThemeRoller with that theme's settings preloaded.

The Sunny theme is very close to our new target design, with a couple of exceptions: the header that sits above the datepicker is gray when ours is yellow, and the content area and active state border color is a darker brown than is specified in our design. We'll return to the Roll Your Own tab to tweak a few settings:

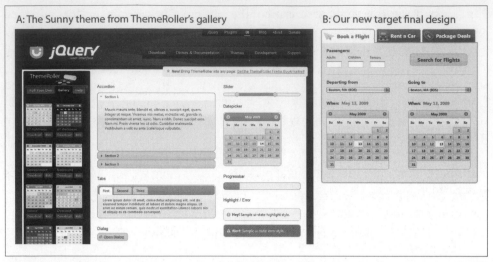

A: The Sunny theme from ThemeRoller's gallery   B: Our new target final design

Figure 15-22. The new target design with yellow clickable states and headers for tab contents closely matches the Sunny gallery theme

- *Change the header background from gray to yellow*: The background color and border of our additional theme needs to match that of our "Clickable: default state."

    1. Open the Header/Toolbar section.

    2. In the background color field enter #FECE2F; we don't need to make any changes to the texture or opacity settings.

    3. The white text is now barely visible against the yellow background, so we'll darken it to match the gray text elsewhere in our application; enter the value #333333.

    4. Likewise, the icons in the datepicker header need to contrast more with the background, so we'll make them medium brown; enter #A27406.

    5. Finally, change the border color to #D19405.

- *Change the content and active state borders to light brown*: Content borders appear around accordion sections and define the tabs, dialog, slider, datepicker, and progress bar outer containers.

    1. Open the Content section.

    2. Update the border color to match that of the header border, #D19405.

    3. Hit the Tab or Enter key, or click elsewhere on the page, to preview the changes in the widgets on the right.

Step 2. Scope the new theme and download it

When you're finished editing the Sunny theme, click the "Download theme" button in the toolbar's Roll Your Own tab, which navigates you to the jQuery UI download builder.

Before we edit the download builder settings, we need to determine which scoping selector we'll use to apply our new theme to the travel application's content panels. We want to ensure that we only affect the tab contents and don't alter the original theme we applied to our top navigation tabs.

A scoping selector is a class, an ID, or an HTML tag that specifically identifies the parent container of the elements we want to style. It's best to choose a scoping selector with the most limited range so that you don't inadvertently scope styles to elements that should assume the base theme styles. In our travel reservations application, the scoping selector should identify the container that encloses the tabs' content and does not also enclose the tabs' navigation panel.

When we look at the generated markup in our application, we see that each content panel is assigned the class `ui-tabs-panel`:

```
<div class="ui-tabs ui-widget ui-widget-content ui-corner-all" id="travel">
    <ul class="ui-tabs-nav ui-helper-reset ui-helper-clearfix ui-widget-header ui-
corner-all">
        <li class="ui-state-default ui-corner-top ui-tabs-selected ui-state-active">
<a href="#travel-flight" id="tab-flight">Book a Flight</a></li>
        <li class="ui-state-default ui-corner-top"><a href="#travel-car" id="tab-
car">Rent a Car</a></li>
        <li class="ui-state-default ui-corner-top"><a href="#travel-package"
id="tab-package">Package Deals</a></li>
    </ul>
    <div id="travel-flight" class="ui-helper-clearfix ui-tabs-panel
ui-widget-content ui-corner-bottom"></div><!-- /flight -->
    <div id="travel-car" class="ui-tabs-panel ui-widget-content ui-corner-bottom
ui-tabs-hide"></div><!-- /car -->
    <div id="travel-package" class="ui-tabs-panel ui-widget-content
ui-corner-bottom ui-tabs-hide"></div><!-- /package -->
</div><!-- /travel -->
```

Because the content panel markup appears after and is separate from that of the tabs' navigation, we can safely scope our new styles to the `ui-tabs-panel` class without affecting the styles applied to the top tabs.

With our scoping selector identified, we can return to the jQuery UI download builder. In the right column under Theme, we'll specify how this new theme should be scoped within our application. Click Advanced Theme Settings to expand this section; you'll see two input fields (Figure 15-23):

- CSS Scope accepts the scoping selector (class, ID, or HTML tag). When compiling the theme stylesheet, the download builder prefixes every style rule with this value, which applies all style rules only to elements within the specified container.

Figure 15-23. The jQuery UI download builder's Advanced Theme Settings expands to provide fields for CSS scope and the new theme folder name

For our travel reservations application, we'll enter the class we chose to scope our styles, `.ui-tabs-panel`. Be sure to include the preceding period (.) or, if specifying an ID, the hash (#)—these marks are necessary for the stylesheet to render properly.

 When this field is left blank, the theme is applied globally across all widgets in your application and is not scoped to any particular container.

- Theme Folder Name accepts a folder name for the new theme that's included in the downloaded ZIP; this folder contains the theme stylesheet and image files. This value defaults to the name of the selected theme, which in our case should be "custom-theme" since we've arrived at the download builder after designing a custom theme in ThemeRoller.

  When you type a CSS scope in the first field, the download builder suggests a folder name based on that scope. This is meant to be helpful, but you may want to override the suggestion with something more meaningful to your project's directory structure.

  For the travel reservations application, we'll write our own folder name and use "tab-content-theme" to better describe the folder contents.

Now that we've set up the CSS scope and folder name, we'll select all jQuery UI widgets that will use the new scoped theme (Figure 15-24).

Figure 15-24. Download a scoped theme by filling in Advanced Theme Settings and selecting any widgets that will use the scoped theme on the jQuery UI Download page

Getting New Widgets

You'll need to download any widgets that will use the scoped theme so that the appropriate styles are included in the scoped CSS. JavaScript for these widgets will automatically be included in the download as well. However, if you need only the scoped theme, you can discard the JavaScript, since it will likely be a duplicate of what you already have.

If you reach this step and realize that you need to download additional widgets for your project that you had not included in your original download (for example, you need to add a progress bar), we strongly advise that you not download new widgets with a scoped theme. Merging JS files is just too complicated.

Instead, to add new widgets to the project, we recommend that you redo the download process wholesale: reopen the original theme in ThemeRoller, and then download all jQuery UI components used in the project. That way, you can simply overwrite the original theme stylesheet and your jQuery UI JavaScript file with files that cover all widgets in your application. To do this, simply open the original theme stylesheet, search for the comment that starts with "To view and modify this theme, visit http://jqueryui.com/themeroller/...," copy and paste the theme URL into a browser's address bar to open ThemeRoller with that theme's settings preloaded, and then click "Download theme" to select additional widgets.

Select which version of jQuery UI you'd like to use (the latest stable version is selected by default), click Download, and save the ZIP file locally (the file will be named like *jquery-ui-1.7.1.custom.zip*).

Step 3. Merge files into your project directory

The download folder contains the CSS directory (*css*) with your scoped theme folder; the widget JavaScript (*js*), which may be a duplicate of what you're already using (to stay safe, double check before overwriting any files); and the development bundle (*development-bundle*), which contains individual CSS files used to create the compiled version found in the *css* folder, open source license text, and related resources necessary for advanced development. The order of the folders and files may vary depending on your operating system (Figure 15-25 shows the folder opened on Mac OS X).

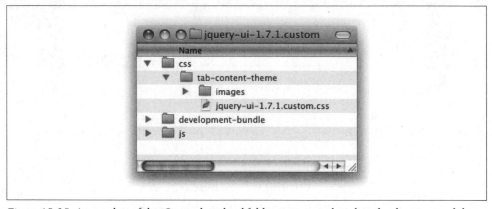

Figure 15-25. A snapshot of the jQuery download folder structure when downloading a scoped theme

Now we'll copy and paste the *tab-content-theme* folder into the styles directory for our travel reservations project.

 It's important to maintain the established directory structure within the theme folder so that the icon images are referenced properly by the theme classes. If you do change the theme directory structure, you will likely have to replicate those changes if later you decide to upgrade to a newer version of the jQuery UI scripts and CSS.

The new theme folder will sit alongside the original theme folder in the styles directory, as shown in Figure 15-26.

Figure 15-26. Scoped theme folders are appended to the styles directory

Step 4. Reference the scoped theme stylesheet in your project

We'll reference our scoped stylesheet after the original theme stylesheet and before all jQuery UI scripts. The order in which theme stylesheets are referenced on the page is not important:

```html
<!doctype html>
<html>
<head>
    <meta charset="UTF-8">
    <title>Travel widget | Book a Flight, Rent a Car, or Find Package Deals</title>

    <!-- jQuery UI styles -->
    <link rel="stylesheet" type="text/css" href="css/custom-theme/jquery-ui-
1.7.1.custom.css" />
    <link rel="stylesheet" type="text/css" href="css/tab-content-theme/jquery-ui-
1.7.1.custom.css" />

    <!-- jQuery core & UI scripts -->
    <script type="text/javascript" src="js/jquery-1.3.2.min.js"></script>
    <script type="text/javascript" src="js/jquery-ui-1.7.1.custom.min.js"></script>

    <script type="text/javascript">
    $(function(){
        $('#travel').tabs();
        $("#departure-date-picker").datepicker({altField: '#departure-date',
altFormat: 'MM d, yy'});
        $("#arrival-date-picker").datepicker({altField: '#arrival-date', altFormat:
'MM d, yy'});
    });
    </script>
</head>
...
```

When the theme stylesheet links are in place, we'll preview the page in a browser to confirm that the styles are being applied correctly. Because we scoped the new theme to the tab content panel, the styles are only applied to the content's widgets and not to the tabs above, as illustrated in Figure 15-27.

 For another example of this technique, visit this article: *http://www.fil amentgroup.com/lab/using_multiple_jquery_ui_themes_on_a_single _page/*.

Figure 15-27. Final application with scoped theme applied

15.5 Appendix: Additional CSS Resources

To get the most out of the jQuery UI CSS Framework and ThemeRoller, it helps to have a basic knowledge of how CSS works and, specifically, how styles cascade, take precedence, and can be scoped using selector classes, IDs, or elements.

We recommend the following books and online resources for a primer on these concepts:

CSS Basics Tutorial
   http://www.cssbasics.com/

CSS Cheat Sheet
   http://lesliefranke.com/files/reference/csscheatsheet.html

Designing with Web Standards
   http://www.zeldman.com/dwws/

Web Standards Solutions
   http://www.friendsofed.com/book.html?isbn=1590593812

Eric Meyer on CSS
   http://www.ericmeyeroncss.com/

jQuery, Ajax, Data Formats: HTML, XML, JSON, JSONP

Jonathan Sharp

16.0 Introduction

Web developers work with a number of data formats and protocols in transferring information between browsers and servers. This chapter provides a number of recipes for handling and working with some of the most common data formats, Ajax techniques, and jQuery.

16.1 jQuery and Ajax

Problem

You want to make a request to the server for some additional data without leaving the page the visitor is currently on.

Solution

Here's a simple Ajax request:

```
(function($) {
    $(document).ready(function() {
        $('#update').click(function() {
            $.ajax({
                type: 'GET',
                url: 'hello-ajax.html',
                dataType: 'html',
                success: function(html, textStatus) {
                    $('body').append(html);
                },
                error: function(xhr, textStatus, errorThrown) {
                    alert('An error occurred! ' + ( errorThrown ? errorThrown :
```

```
        xhr.status );
                    }
                });
            });
        });
    })(jQuery);
```

Discussion

At the core of jQuery's Ajax architecture is the `jQuery.ajax()` method. This provides the basis of all browsers to server requests and responses. So, let's look at this in a little more detail. To initiate a request to the server, a settings object that contains parameters for the request is passed to the `$.ajax` method. A vast number of options are available, with the most common options of a request being `type`, `url`, `complete`, `dataType`, `error`, and `success`:

```
var options = {
    type: 'GET'
};
```

The first option that needs to be addressed when starting an Ajax request is the type of HTTP request you're going to make to the server, which in the majority of cases will be either a GET or POST type:

```
var options = {
    type: 'GET',
    url: 'hello-ajax.html',
    dataType: 'html'
};
```

Next we'll look at the `URL` and `dataType` options. `URL` is fairly self-explanatory with the following interactions worth noting. When setting the `cache` option to `false`, jQuery will append a get variable of `_=<random number>` (for example `/server-ajax-gateway?_=6273551235126`), which is used to prevent the browser, proxies, and servers from sending a cached response. Finally, the `dataType` option specifies the data format that is the expected response from the server. For example, if you're expecting the server to return XML, then a value of `xml` would be appropriate:

```
var options = {
    type: 'GET',
    url: 'hello-ajax.html',
    dataType: 'html',
    error: function(xhr, textStatus, errorThrown) {
        alert('An error occurred! ' + errorThrown);
    },
    success: function(data, textStatus) {
        $('body').append( data );
    }
};
```

The next two options that we define are two callback methods, one called **error** and the other called **success**. They function as they are appropriately titled, with **error** being called when there is an error with the request and **success** being called with a successful response (determined if a server response type of 200 is returned). The other common option mentioned is the `complete` option, which defines a callback to execute upon after either success or error of the response:

```
var options = {
    type: 'GET',
    url: 'hello-ajax.html',
    dataType: 'html',
    complete: function(xhr, textStatus) {
        // Code to process response
    }
};
```

Once the settings have been defined, we can go ahead and execute our request:

```
var options = {
    type: 'GET',
    url: 'hello-ajax.html',
    dataType: 'html',
    complete: function(xhr, textStatus) {
        // Code to process response
    }
};
$.ajax( options );
```

We can also set our options inline:

```
$.ajax({
    type: 'GET',
    url: 'hello-ajax.html',
    dataType: 'html',
    complete: function(xhr, textStatus) {
        // Code to process response
    }
});
```

Our final solution requests the file `hello-ajax.html` and appends the contents (`html`) to the `<body>` element upon the return of a successful request. If the request fails, the `error` method is triggered instead, alerting the user with a message:

```
(function($) {
    $(document).ready(function() {
        $('#update').click(function() {
            $.ajax({
                type: 'GET',
                url: 'hello-ajax.html',
                dataType: 'html',
                success: function(html, textStatus) {
                    $('body').append(html);
                },
                error: function(xhr, textStatus, errorThrown) {
                    alert('An error occurred! ' + errorThrown);
                }
            });
        });
```

```
        });
    })(jQuery);
```

16.2 Using Ajax on Your Whole Site

Problem

You have a large web application with Ajax calls occurring throughout the code base and need to define default settings for all requests throughout the application.

Solution

```
(function($) {
    $(document).ready(function() {
        $('#loadingIndicator')
            .bind('ajaxStart', function() {
                $(this).show();
            })
            .bind('ajaxComplete', function() {
                $(this).hide();
            });
        $.ajaxSetup({
            cache: true,
            dataType: 'json',
            error: function(xhr, status, error) {
                alert('An error occurred: ' + error);
            },
            timeout: 60000, // Timeout of 60 seconds
            type: 'POST',
            url: 'ajax-gateway.php'
        }); // Close $.ajaxSetup()
    }); // Close .read()
})(jQuery);
```

Discussion

When working with larger applications, often there is a common Ajax gateway through which all requests are passed. Using the $.ajaxSetup() method, we can set Ajax request default settings. This would result in an ease of Ajax requests throughout the application such as follows:

```
$.ajax({
    data: {
        // My request data for the server
    },
     success: function(data) {
         // Now update the user interface
    }
});
```

A brief side point is that the timeout option takes its value in milliseconds (seconds × 1,000), so a timeout of 6,000 would be six seconds. One thing to consider when setting this value is the extent to which the Internet has grown globally. Some of your visitors or users may be in locations that have a higher latency than you would expect for users within your region. So, don't set this value too low (for example five seconds). Specifying a higher timeout value such as 30 or 60 seconds will allow users with higher-latency connections (such as those using satellite) to still enjoy the benefits of your application.

In the previous example, the request will be a POST to `ajax-gateway.php`. If an error occurs, it will be handled by the error function as defined in `$.ajaxSetup()`. It is possible to still override settings for a specific request as follows:

```
$.ajax({
    url: 'another-url.php',
        data: {
            // My request data for the server
        },
        success: function(data) {
            // Now update the user interface
        }
});
```

The previous request would be sent to `another-url.php` instead of `ajax-gateway.php`. One beneficial feature of jQuery's Ajax architecture is the global events available such as `ajaxComplete`, `ajaxError`, `ajaxSend`, `ajaxStart`, `ajaxStop`, and `ajaxSuccess`. These events may be set up using the `.bind('event', callback)` method or the short-cut `.event(callback)`. The following example shows the two methods for binding the callback for the `ajaxError` event:

```
(function($) {
    $(document).ready(function() {
        $('#loadingIndicator')
            .ajaxError(function() {
                // Your code
            });
        // Or using bind()
        $('#loadingIndicator')
            .bind('ajaxError', function() {
                // Your code
            });
    });
})(jQuery);
```

Here is a rundown and description of the events that are available as well as the order in which they're triggered:

ajaxStart

> Triggered at the start of an Ajax request if no other requests are in progress

ajaxSend

> Triggered before each individual request is sent

ajaxSuccess *or* ajaxError

> Triggered upon a successful or an unsuccessful request

ajaxComplete

> Triggered every time a request is complete (regardless of whether it was a success or had an error)

ajaxStop

> Triggered if there are no additional Ajax requests in progress

In the next recipe we will build upon these events in more detail.

16.3 Using Simple Ajax with User Feedback

Problem

You need to show a status indicator to the user when Ajax requests are in progress and hide it upon completion.

Solution

```
(function($) {
    $(document).ready(function() {
        $('#ajaxStatus')
            .ajaxStart(function() {
                $(this).show();
            })
            .ajaxStop(function() {
                $(this).hide();
            });

        // Start our ajax request when doAjaxButton is clicked
        $('#doAjaxButton').click(function() {
            $.ajax({
                url: 'ajax-gateway.php',
                    data: { val: "Hello world" },
                    dataType: 'json',
                success: function(json) {
                    // Data processing code
                    $('body').append( 'Response Value: ' + json.val );
                }
            });
        });
    });
})(jQuery);
```

Discussion

One of the huge benefits of jQuery's Ajax implementation is the exposure of global Ajax events that are triggered on all elements with each Ajax request. In the following solution, we bind two of the events, ajaxStart and ajaxStop using the shortcut methods to the XHTML element with the ID ajaxStatus. When the Ajax request is triggered upon clicking #doAjaxButton, the ajaxStart event is also dispatched and calls show()

on the #ajaxStatus element. Notice that these events are triggered automatically and are a by-product of using the $.ajax() (or other shortcut methods such as $.get()). This provides an elegant decoupled solution for having an application-wide request status as Ajax requests are submitted:

```
(function($) {
    $(document).ready(function() {
        $('#ajaxStatus')
            .ajaxStart(function() {
                $(this).show();
            })
            .ajaxStop(function() {
                $(this).hide();
            });

        // Start our ajax request when doAjaxButton is clicked
        $('#doAjaxButton').click(function() {
            $.ajax({
                url: 'ajax-gateway.php',
                data: { val : 'Hello world' },
                dataType: 'json',
                success: function(json) {
                    // Data processing code
                    $('body').append( 'Response value: ' + json.val );
                }
            });
        });
    });
})(jQuery);
```

Let's look at some of the additional events and the difference between local and global Ajax events. Local Ajax events (set up using $.ajaxSetup() or defined at the time of $.ajax()) consist of beforeSend, success, error, and complete. These events are defined inline and tightly coupled to each Ajax request. Global Ajax events are interleaved with the local events but are triggered for any element that binds to them and also make use of jQuery's native event-handling architecture. Here's a quick review on how to handle local Ajax events (such as the complete event):

```
$.ajax({
    type: 'GET',
    url: 'ajax-gateway.php',
    dataType: 'html',
    complete: function(xhr, textStatus) {
        // Code to process response
    }
});
```

Now let's examine the breakdown, order, and scope in which events are triggered on a successful Ajax request:

- ajaxStart (global)
- beforeSend (local)

- ajaxSend (global)
- success (local)
- ajaxSuccess (global)
- complete (local)
- ajaxComplete (global)
- ajaxStop (global)

For an unsuccessful Ajax request, the order of triggered events would be as follows with success and ajaxSuccess being replaced by error and ajaxError, respectively:

- ajaxStart (global)
- beforeSend (local)
- ajaxSend (global)
- error (local)
- ajaxError (local)
- complete (local)
- ajaxComplete (global)
- ajaxStop (global)

ajaxStart and ajaxStop are two special events in the global scope. They are different in that their behavior operates across multiple simultaneous requests. ajaxStart is triggered when a request is made if no other requests are in progress. ajaxStop is triggered upon completion of a request if there are no additional requests in progress. These two events are only triggered once when multiple simultaneous requests are dispatched:

```
(function($) {
    $(document).ready(function() {
        $('#ajaxStatus')
            .ajaxStart(function() {
                $(this).show();
            })
            .ajaxStop(function() {
                $(this).hide();
            });

        // Start our Ajax request when doAjaxButton is clicked
        $('#doAjaxButton').click(function() {
            $.ajax({
                url: 'ajax-gateway.php',
                complete: function() {
                    // Data processing code
                }
            });
            $.ajax({
                url: 'ajax-data.php',
                complete: function() {
                    // Data-processing code
```

```
            }
        });
    });
  });
})(jQuery);
```

One setting that can be passed into the `$.ajax()` method is `global`, which can be set to either `true` or `false`. By setting `global` to `false`, it's possible to suppress the global events from being triggered.

 If you experience performance issues in your application, it may be because of the cost of event propagation if there is a significantly large number of elements. In this case, setting `global` to `false` may give you a performance improvement.

The `beforeSend` callback is a local event that allows for modifying the `XMLHttpRequest` object (which is passed in as an argument) prior to the request being sent. In the following example, we specify a custom HTTP header for the request. It is possible to cancel the request by returning `false` from the callback:

```
(function($) {
    $(document).ready(function() {
        // Start our ajax request when doAjaxButton is clicked
        $('#doAjaxButton').click(function() {
            $.ajax({
                url: 'ajax-gateway.php',
                beforeSend: function(xmlHttpRequest) {
                    xmlHttpRequest.setRequestHeader('X-SampleHeader',
'Hello world');
                },
                complete: function() {
                    // Data processing code
                }
            });
        });
    });
})(jQuery);
```

Now taking all of the events if we revise our solution, we come up with the following:

```
(function($) {
    $(document).ready(function() {
        $('#ajaxError')
            .ajaxError(function(evt, xhr, ajaxOptions, error) {
                $(this)
                    .html( 'Error: ' + ( xhr ? xhr.status : '' )
                            + ' ' + ( error ? error :'Unknown' ) )
                    .show();
            })
            .ajaxSuccess(function() {
                $(this).hide();
            });
```

```
      $('#ajaxStatus')
          .ajaxStart(function() {
              $(this).show();
          })
          .ajaxSend(function() {
              $(this).html('Sending request...');
          })
          .ajaxStop(function() {
              $(this).html('Request completed...');
              var t = this;
              setTimeout(function() {
                  $(t).hide();
              }, 1500);
          });

      // Start our ajax request when doAjaxButton is clicked
      $('#doAjaxButton').click(function() {
          $.ajax({
              url: 'ajax-gateway.php',
              complete: function() {
                  // Data processing code
              }
          });
      });
    });
  })(jQuery);
```

16.4 Using Ajax Shortcuts and Data Types

Problem

You need to make a GET Ajax request to the server and place the contents of the
resulting HTML in a <div> with an ID of contents.

Solution

```
(function($) {
 $(document).ready(function() {
      $('#contents').load('hello-world.html');
});
})(jQuery);
```

Discussion

This recipe differs slightly from others in that we'll survey a variety of the functions and
shortcuts provided by jQuery in an effort to clearly present their differences.

jQuery provides a number of shortcuts for making Ajax requests. Based upon
the previous recipes covering Ajax, the following shortcuts exist: .load(), $.get(),
$.getJSON(), $.getScript(), and $.post(). But first, let's review our solution:

```
$('#contents').load('hello-world.html');
```

The `.load(url)` method is making a GET Ajax request to `hello-world.html` and placing the contents of that result into the element `#contents`. Two optional parameters to the `.load()` method are `data` and `callback`. The `data` parameter can be either a map (or JavaScript object) or as of jQuery 1.3 a string. The following example is passing in the variable `hello` with the value `world`. (This is the same as the following URL: `hello-world.html?hello=world`.)

```
$('#contents').load('hello-world.html', { hello: 'world' });
```

The third optional parameter is a callback function that is called when the request completes (either on `success` or `error`). In the following example, an alert message is being triggered upon the completion of the request:

```
$('#contents').load('hello-world.html', { hello: 'world' }, function() {
    alert('Request completed!');
});
```

The next two methods we will look at are `$.get()` and `$.post()`. Both methods accept the same arguments, with the `$.get()` method sending a GET HTTP request and the `$.post()` method sending a POST HTTP request. We'll look at a sample using the `$.get()` request. The `$.get()` method accepts `url`, `data`, `callback`, and `type` parameters. The first three parameters function the same as with the previous `load()` method, so we'll only cover the final `type` parameter:

```
$.get(
    'hello-world.html',
    { hello: 'world' },
    function(data) {
        alert('Request completed!');
    },
    'html'
);
```

The `type` parameter can accept one of the following: `xml`, `html`, `script`, `json`, `jsonp`, or `text`. These `type` values determine how the response text from the Ajax request is processed prior to being passed to the callback function. In the previous example, since we specified a `type` of `html`, the data argument of our callback will be in DOM object form. Specifying `xml` as the `type` will result in an `xml` DOM object being passed in. If you specify `script` as the `type`, the resulting data returned by the server will be executed prior to the `callback` method being triggered. Both `json` and `jsonp` formats result in a JavaScript object being passed to your `callback` method, with the difference of `jsonp` being that jQuery will pass in a method name in the request and map that callback method to the anonymous function defined with the request. This allows for cross-domain requests. Finally, the `text` format is just as the name suggests: plain text that is passed in as a string to your `callback` method.

We'll now look at the final two shortcuts: `$.getJSON()` and `$.getScript()`. The `$.getJSON()` method accepts `url`, `data`, and `callback` as arguments. `$.getJSON()` is essentially a combination of the `$.get()` method with appropriate parameters being set for JSON or JSONP. The following example would make a JSONP request to Flickr and request photos from the public timeline:

```
$.getJSON(
    'http://www.flickr.com/services/feeds/photos_public.gne?
format=json&jsoncallback=?',
    function(json) {
    }
);
```

Since this request is cross-domain, jQuery will automatically treat the request as a JSONP and fill in the appropriate `callback` function name. This also means that jQuery will initiate the request by inserting a `<script>` tag into the document instead of using the `XMLHttpRequest` object. Flickr's API allows for the `callback` function name to be specified by setting the `jsoncallback` get variable. You'll notice the `jsoncallback=?` portion of the URL. jQuery will intelligently replace the ? with the appropriate function name automatically. By default jQuery will append a `callback=` variable but allows for easily modifying this, as demonstrated. The `callback` replacement works on both GET and POST request URLs but will not work with parameters passed in the data object. See Recipes 16.7 and 16.8 for working with JSON and Recipe 16.9 for a full JSONP implementation of our Flickr example.

`$.getScript()` executes a request either via an Ajax request or via dynamically inserting a `<script>` tag for cross-domain support and then evaluating the returned data and finally triggering the callback provided. In the following example, we're adding a script to the document and then calling one of the functions it provides in the callback:

```
// hello-world.js
function helloWorld(msg) {
    alert('Hello world! I have a message for you: ' + msg);
}

// hello-world.html
(function($) {
    $(function() {
        $.getScript('hello-world.js', function() {
            helloWorld('It is a beautiful day!');
        });
    });
})(jQuery);
```

16.5 Using HTML Fragments and jQuery

Problem

You want to take a string of HTML and convert it into a series of DOM nodes and then insert it into the document.

Solution

```
(function($) {
    $(document).ready(function() {
        $('<div>Hello World</div>')
            .append('<a href="http://jquery.com">A Link</a>')
            .appendTo('body');
    });
})(jQuery);
```

Discussion

Manipulating strings of HTML is one of the more common tasks when using jQuery. At the heart of jQuery is an elegant interface for translating a string of markup into its DOM representation. Instead of passing in a selector, we can simply pass in a string of HTML. (The following does not work for XML; see Recipe 16.6 for converting a string of XML to a DOM.)

```
$('<div>Hello World</div>');
```

At this point our HTML has been converted into a DOM representation and is ready for manipulation with jQuery. We can operate on this fragment using any of the jQuery methods:

```
$('<div>Hello World</div>')
    .append('<a href="http://jquery.com">A Link</a>')
    .appendTo('body');
```

One caveat worth noting is that prior to the HTML fragment being appended to the document, some visual attributes such as `width` and `height` may not be available. So in the following example, calling `.width()` will return a value of `0`.

```
$('<div>Hello World</div>').width();
// Returns '0'
```

16.6 Converting XML to DOM

Problem

You need to convert a string of XML to a DOM object for use with jQuery.

Solution

```
<h1 id="title"></h1>

(function($) {
    $(document).ready(function() {
        var xml = '<myxml><title>Hello world!</title></myxml>';
        var title = $.xmlDOM( xml ).find('myxml > title').text();
        $('#title').html( title );
    });
})(jQuery);
```

Discussion

A frequent question appearing on the jQuery mailing list is how to convert a string of XML to its DOM representation that jQuery is able to operate on. When making an Ajax request with a response type of xml, the browser will automatically parse the returned XML text into a DOM object.

So, what would you do if you had a string of XML that you needed to process with jQuery? The xmlDOM plugin provides native cross-browser parsing of a string of XML and returns a jQuery-wrapped DOM object. This allows you to convert and access the XML in one step:

```
(function($) {
    $(document).ready(function() {
        var xml = '<myxml><title>Hello world!</title></myxml>';
        var title = $.xmlDOM( xml ).find('myxml > title').text();
        $('#title').html( title );
    });
})(jQuery);
```

Another common practice is passing in the DOM object as the second argument to jQuery (the context) as follows:

```
(function($) {
    $(document).ready(function() {
        var $xml = $.xmlDOM( '<myxml><title>Hello world!</title></myxml>' );
        var title = $('myxml > title', $xml).text();
        $('#title').html( title );
    });
})(jQuery);
```

This allows you to run your jQuery selection against the context object passed in; otherwise, jQuery runs the query against the document object.

The xmlDOM plugin by the author may be downloaded from *http://jquery-cookbook
.com/go/plugin-xmldom*.

16.7 Creating JSON

Problem

You have a JavaScript object that contains data that needs to be serialized for easier
storage and retrieval.

Solution

```
(function($) {
    $(document).ready(function() {
        var messageObject = { title: 'Hello World!', body: 'It\'s great to be
alive!' };
        var serializedJSON = JSON.stringify( messageObject );
    });
})(jQuery);
```

Discussion

JavaScript Object Notation (JSON) is a common data format used to exchange data
between the browser and the server. It is lightweight in nature and is easy to use and
parse in JavaScript. Let's first look at a simple object:

```
var messageObject = { title: 'Hello World!', body: 'It\'s great to be alive!' };
```

In this example, we have a simple object with two attributes, `title` and `body`. Being able
to store a serialized version of the object is quite simple. The serialized version is as
follows:

```
var serializedJSON = '{"title":"Hello World!","body":"It\'s great to be alive!"}';
```

The two common tasks when working with JSON are serialization (encoding an object
into a string representation) and deserialization (decoding a string representation into
an object literal). Currently, only a handful of browsers have native built-in JSON handling (such as Firefox 3.1+ and Internet Explorer 8). Other browsers have plans to add
support because JSON is now part of the ECMA 3.1 specification. In the meantime,
there are two main approaches to take when working with JSON data. Douglas
Crockford has written a JavaScript implementation for encoding and decoding JSON,
which you can get from *http://jquery-cookbook.com/go/json*. Let's serialize the previous
object utilizing the `JSON` library:

```
var serializedJSON = JSON.stringify( messageObject );
```

We now have a string representation that we can send to our server such as in an Ajax
request or submit in a form.

16.8 Parsing JSON

Problem

You're passed a string of JSON data and need to convert it to object format.

Solution

```
(function($) {
    $(document).ready(function() {
        var serializedJSON = '{"title":"Hello World!","body":"It\'s great to be
alive!"}';
        var message = JSON.parse( serializedJSON );
    });
})(jQuery);
```

Discussion

As discussed in the previous recipe, we'll now look at parsing or decoding a JSON string.

 It is important to note that some of the approaches outlined here are unsafe and may cause potential security issues. Make sure that you trust the source of your data.

The easiest approach in consuming JSON data is to `eval()` the message. There are some inherent security issues though with this approach because `eval()` encompasses the entire JavaScript specification instead of simply the JSON subset. What this means is that a malicious person could execute code embedded in the JSON string. So, we don't recommend this approach. Instead, let's use Douglas Crockford's `JSON` library mentioned in the previous recipe. (Note that his library does utilize `eval()` except that it pre-processes the data to make sure the data is safe.)

```
var serializedJSON = '{"title":"Hello World!","body":"It\'s great to be alive!"}';
var message = JSON.parse( serializedJSON );
```

So, now we can work with our message object as we would any other JavaScript object:

```
alert( "New Message!\nTitle: " + message.title + "\nBody: " + message.body);
```

The `JSON` library as well as additional JSON resources may be downloaded from *http://jquery-cookbook.com/go/json*.

16.9 Using jQuery and JSONP

Problem

You want to consume a list of photos from Flickr's public photo stream and display the first three images.

Solution

```
(function($) {
    $(document).ready(function() {
        var url     = 'http://www.flickr.com/services/feeds/photos_public.gne?
jsoncallback=?';
        var params  = { format: 'json' };
        $.getJSON(url, params, function(json) {
            if ( json.items ) {
                $.each( json.items, function(i, n) {
                    var item = json.items[i];
                    $('<a href="' + item.link + '"></a>')
                        .append('<img src="' + item.media.m + '" />')
                        .appendTo('#photos');
                    // Display the first 3 photos (returning false will
                    // Exit the loop
                    return i < 2;
                });
            }
        });
    });
})(jQuery);
```

Discussion

Security is a critical issue when building a website or application and especially so with the advent of Ajax. Web browsers have enforced a same origin policy on requests, which means that you're restricted to making requests to the same domain as the page's URL or a subdomain of the current domain. So, for example, a page served from *http://www.example.com* is allowed to make Ajax requests to *http://www.example.com* and *http://x.www.example.com* but not *http://example.com* or *http://y.example.com*. As the semantic Web emerged and websites such as Flickr started exposing an API for other users and services to consume, the security policy enforced by web browsers became a hindrance. One area that has never had same origin policies was the use of the script element with a src attribute. It's possible for *http://www.example.com* to include a script from *http://static.example2.com*, but the issue of dynamically including that script and managing program flow became an issue. Thus, JSONP emerged as a standard to overcome the same origin limitation.

It is important to note that some of the approaches outlined here are unsafe and may cause potential security issues. Make sure that you trust the source of your data. Also, when including a script element in a page, that entire script will have access to the entire HTML DOM and any private or sensitive data that it may contain. It could be possible for a malicious script to send this data to an untrusted party. Take extra precaution such as placing the script in a sandbox. Extended security is outside the scope of this recipe, but we wanted to make sure you were aware of it.

JSONP makes use of requesting data through a `<script>` tag with a `src` attribute as well as manages the program flow for the developer by wrapping the data in a callback function that the developer can implement. Let's first look at a sample JSON message.

```
{"title":"Hello World!","body":"It's great to be alive!"}
```

Here is the same message wrapped in a callback:

```
myCallback({"title":"Hello World!","body":"It's great to be alive!"})
```

What this allows for is when the resource is requested upon being loaded in the browser the `myCallback` function will be called and have the JSON object passed in as the first argument. The developer can then implement the `myCallback` function as follows to process the data:

```
function myCallback(json) {
    alert( json.title );
}
```

Now let's review our Flickr solution. First we define the URL of the Flickr web service followed by declaring a `params` object for the get variables. The `jsoncallback` param is a special param defined by the Flickr service that allows for us to pass in a function name. Since we've set this parameter to a ?, jQuery will automatically generate a function name and bind it with our callback method.

jQuery detects that this is a JSONP (cross-domain request) by the =? in the URL. It is not possible to pass this in the `params` array.

```
var url     = 'http://www.flickr.com/services/feeds/photos_public.gne?
jsoncallback=?';
var params  = { format: 'json' };
```

Next, we call jQuery's `$.getJSON()` method, passing in our `url`, `params`, and our callback function, which will accept a JSON object. In our callback method, we check and make sure that an item's array exists and then use jQuery's `$.each()` to iterate over the first three items, create a link, append an image to it, and then append the link to an element with an ID of `photos`. Finally, our callback function will return `false` on the third iteration (when `i = 2`), breaking the loop.

```
$.getJSON(url, params, function(json) {
    if ( json.items ) {
        $.each( json.items, function(i, n) {
            var item = json.items[i];
            $('<a href="' + item.link + '"></a>')
                .append('<img src="' + item.media.m + '" />')
                .appendTo('#photos');
            return i < 2;
        });
    }
});
```

With the combination of the JSON data format and the cross-domain capabilities of JSONP, web developers are able to create new applications aggregating and transforming data in new and innovative ways and growing the semantic Web.

Using jQuery in Large Projects

Rob Burns

17.0 Introduction

jQuery is often used to add small user interface enhancements to a website. However, for larger, more complex web applications, jQuery is also quite useful. The sample recipes throughout this chapter show how jQuery can be used to address the needs of more substantial and interactive web content. The first three recipes explore different methods of persisting data in a web browser. These are followed by a look at easing the use of Ajax and JavaScript as the quantity of code and data in your application grows.

17.1 Using Client-Side Storage

Problem

You are writing a rich Internet application that processes nontrivial amounts of user data in the web browser. Motivated by the desire to cache this data for performance reasons or to enable offline use of your application, you need to store data on the client.

Solution

A simple to-do list will be used to illustrate storing data on the client. As with many of the recipes in this chapter, a jQuery plugin will be used to handle browser inconsistencies:

```
<!DOCTYPE html>
<html><head>
    <title>17.1 - Using Client-Side Storage</title>
    <script type="text/javascript" src="../../jquery-1.3.2.min.js"></script>
    <script type="text/javascript" src="jquery.jstore-all.js"></script>
</head>
```

```
<body>
    <h1>17.1 - Using Client-Side Storage</h1>
    <p>Storage engine: <span id="storage-engine"></span></p>
    <input id="task-input"></input>
    <input id="task-add" type="submit" value="Add task"></input>
    <input id="list-clear" type="submit" value="Remove all tasks"></input>
    <ul  id="task-list"></ul>
</body></html>
```

The HTML consists of form elements for manipulating the to-do list: a text field to
input a task, and buttons for adding a task and deleting all tasks. The current tasks will
be listed using an unordered list:

```
(function($) {
    $.jStore.ready(function(ev,engine) {
        engine.ready(function(ev,engine) {
            $('#storage-engine').html($.jStore.CurrentEngine.type);
            $('#task-list').append($.store('task-list'));
        });
    });
```

The jStore plugin provides two callbacks: `jStore.ready()` and `engine.ready()`. Much
like jQuery's `ready()` function, these allow us to do some initial setup once jStore and
the current storage engine have completed their internal initialization. This opportunity
is used to display the currently used storage engine and any saved to-do items on
the page:

```
$('document').ready(function() {
    $('#task-add').click(function() {
        var task = $('#task-input').val();
        var taskHtml = '<li><a href="#">done</a> ' + task + '</li>';
        $.store('task-list',$('#task-list').append(taskHtml).html());
        return false;
    });
```

Once the document is ready, click events are bound to the appropriate controls. When
the "Add task" button is clicked, a list-item element is constructed with the contents
of the task text field and a link to mark this task as done. The list item is then appended
to the contents of the task list, and the task list is saved in local storage using the `task-
list` key. At a later time, the list can be retrieved using this key, as is being done in the
`engine.ready()` callback:

```
$('#list-clear').click(function() {
    $('#task-list').empty();
    $.remove('task-list');
    return false;
});
```

When the "Remove all tasks" button is clicked, the element containing the to-do list
is emptied of its contents. The `task-list` key and its associated value are then removed
from local storage:

```
        $('#task-list a').live('click',function() {
            $(this).parent().remove();
            var taskList = $('#task-list').html();
            if( taskList ) { $.store('task-list',taskList); }
            else { $.remove('task-list'); }
            return false;
        });
    });
})(jQuery);
```

Lastly, a live event is bound to the done links for each item in the to-do list. By using the live() function, instead of the bind() function or a shortcut such as click(), all elements that match #task-list a will have the given function bound to the click event, even elements that do not yet exist at the time live() is called. This allows us to insert "done" links for each new item, without rebinding the click event each time the insertion occurs.

When an item is marked as done, it is removed from the list, and the updated list saved in local storage using the task-list key. Some care needs to be taken when saving the updated list:

```
        if( taskList ) { $.store('task-list',taskList); }
        else { $.remove('task-list'); }
```

In the case that the last item in the list is being removed, the taskList variable will be empty. This causes the store() function to be evaluated as if it were called with a single parameter, not two. When store() is passed a single parameter, the value held at that key is retrieved, and the saved list is unmodified. The goal is to save an empty list. The remove() function in the else clause removes the task-list key and its associated value. This meets the goal of setting the saved state to an empty list.

Discussion

Traditionally, the only option available to store data on the client was cookies. The amount of data that can be stored in a cookie is very limited. Better alternatives now exist. The following table contains currently available storage mechanisms and their browser compatibility.

	Firefox	Safari	Internet Explorer
DOM Storage	2.0+	no	8.0+
Gears	yes	yes	yes
Flash	yes	yes	yes
SQL Storage API	no	3.1+	no
userData behavior	no	no	5.0+

DOM Storage and the SQL Storage API are part of emerging HTML standards. As such, they don't yet enjoy thorough cross-browser support. Google Gears and Flash are browser plugins that can be used for client-side storage. Internet Explorer has, for some time, included the userData behavior for client-side storage. If a single mechanism to support all major browsers is needed, a Flash or Google Gears–based approach offers support for the widest variety. However, it requires users to have a browser plugin installed.

 The 1.0.3 release of the jStore plugin contains a bug. A typo needs to be corrected. Line 403 of `jquery.jstore-all.js` should read as follows:

```
return !!(jQuery.hasFlash('8.0.0'));
```

Fortunately, jStore (available at *http://plugins.jquery.com/project/jStore*) affords a layer of abstraction, which enables cross-browser and client-side storage and, in most cases, doesn't rely on browser plugins. jStore provides a unified interface to the storage mechanisms listed previously. While manual selection is supported, this example illustrates jStore's ability to automatically select the appropriate storage mechanism for the browser currently in use. When viewed in different browsers, this recipe displays the currently selected storage mechanism.

17.2 Saving Application State for a Single Session

Problem

You want to persist data on the client only until the current session is ended, i.e., the window or tab is closed.

Solution

In this example there are two HTML pages. Each page contains a set of selectable elements. When elements are selected and deselected, the state of the page is persisted. By navigating to and from the two pages, you can see how the state of any given page can be maintained as a user navigates through a website. The `sessionStorage` object is used for data that doesn't require persisting between a user's subsequent visits:

```html
<!DOCTYPE html>
<html><head>
    <title>17.2 Saving Application State for a Single Session</title>
    <style>
        .square {
            width: 100px; height: 100px; margin: 15px;
            background-color: gray; border: 3px solid white; }
        .selected {
            border: 3px solid orange; }
    </style>
    <script src="../../jquery-1.3.2.min.js"></script>
</head>
```

```
<body>
    <h1>17.2 Saving Application State for a Single Session</h1>
    <a href="one.html">page one</a>
    <a href="two.html">page two</a>
    <div id="one" class="square"></div>
    <div id="two" class="square"></div>
    <div id="three" class="square"></div>
</body></html>
```

Each of the two HTML pages (one.html and two.html) have the same content. The
following JavaScript code takes care of managing the state of each page, such that each
page reflects past user manipulation:

```
jQuery(document).ready(function() {
    $('.square').each(function(){
        if( sessionStorage[window.location + this.id] == 'true' ) {
            $(this).addClass('selected');
        }
    });

    $('.square').click(function() {
        $(this).toggleClass('selected');
        sessionStorage[window.location + this.id] = $(this).hasClass('selected');
        return false;
    });
});
```

When the document is loaded, the sessionStorage object is queried for keys comprising
the current URL and the id of each of the selectable squares. Each square has a CSS
class applied if appropriate. When a square is clicked, its display is affected by toggling
a CSS class, and its state is persisted accordingly. Each square's state is persisted using
a key generated from the current URL and current element id pair.

Discussion

Similar session-delimited client-side storage is available when using the jStore plugin
from the previous recipe. By using jStore, you gain the benefits of cross-browser compatibility. This recipe will only work in Internet Explorer 8.0 and Firefox 2.0 or higher.
Safari 3.1 doesn't have this feature, though future versions are slated to include it.

The DOM storage API is attractive in cases where broad browser compatibility isn't a
concern. Applications developed for internal company intranets may fall into this category. It is also part of the upcoming HTML5 specification. In the future its availability
is likely to spread. Using a built-in storage API has the benefit of incurring no overhead
from additional JavaScript code. The minified jStore plugin and jStore.swf flash component are 20 KB in size.

17.3 Saving Application State Between Sessions

Problem

You want to persist data on the client between sessions. Recipe 17.1 saves the state of the to-do list in between sessions. This recipe illustrates how to enable similar functionality without using the jStore plugin.

Solution

For the HTML part of this solution, please refer to Recipe 17.1 (as it is identical). The JavaScript is listed here:

```
(function($) {
    $('document').ready(function() {
        if( window.localStorage ) { appStorage = window.localStorage; }
        else { appStorage = globalStorage[location.hostname]; }

        var listHtml = appStorage['task-list'];
        $('#task-list').append(listHtml.value ? listHtml.value : listHtml);
```

The initial setup is somewhat more verbose than the jStore-based solution. Firefox has a nonstandard implementation of the long-term storage portion of the DOM storage API. It uses the `globalStorage` array, as opposed to the `localStorage` object to persist data between sessions. Each storage object in the `globalStorage` array is keyed on the domain that the current document is being served from. This code will use `localStorage` if it is available. Otherwise, it will fall back to `globalStorage`.

In the next section of code, the unordered list is populated with any existing tasks. In the jStore-based example this was a single line of code. The additional complexity here is because of Firefox's particular behavior. A string is returned from `localStorage`. But, an object with two attributes, `value` and `secure`, is returned when accessing `globalStorage`. The `value` attribute is used if present. Otherwise, a string returned from `localStorage` is assumed:

```
$('#task-add').click(function() {
    var task = $('#task-input').val();
    var taskHtml = '<li><a href="#">done</a> ' + task + '</li>';
    appStorage['task-list'] = $('#task-list').append(taskHtml).html();
    return false;
});

$('#list-clear').click(function() {
    $('#task-list').empty();
    appStorage['task-list'] = '';
    return false;
});

$('#task-list a').live('click',function() {
    $(this).parent().remove();
    appStorage['task-list'] = $('#task-list').html();
```

```
            return false;
        });
    });
})(jQuery);
```

The remainder of the code adds new tasks, removes tasks when marked "done," and clears the task list by attaching events to DOM elements like the previous jStore-based recipe. However, instead of using the jStore function-based interface for manipulating persisted data, values in the `appStorage` object created earlier can be assigned directly. This allows the code to remove a task to be simplified.

Discussion

The DOM Storage API consists of two interfaces: `sessionStorage` and `localStorage`. Firefox has included this feature since version 2.0, when the standard was still in development. Since then, the standard has undergone revision. Internet Explorer 8.0 has an implementation of the current API. Forthcoming versions of Safari and Firefox will conform to the current specification as well. That said, Firefox 2.0–3.0 browsers will persist for some time. Coding an application to support `globalStorage` will additionally serve these legacy browsers.

17.4 Using a JavaScript Template Engine

Problem

You want to use a JavaScript template engine to display JSON data.

Solution

This recipe is a book listing. It grabs information about a book from a server-side script and adds it to a list of books displayed in the browser. The book details are returned from the server as a JSON string. The Pure templating engine (available at *http://plugins .jquery.com/project/pure*) is used to format the data and insert it into the web page:

```
<!DOCTYPE html>
<html><head>
    <title>jQuery Cookbook - 17.4 Using a Javascript Template Engine</title>
    <style>.hidden { display: none }</style>
    <script type="text/javascript" src="../../jquery-1.3.2.min.js"></script>
    <script type="text/javascript" src="pure.js"></script>
</head>

<body>
    <h1>17.4 - Using a Javascript Template Engine</h1>
    <input type="button" id="add-book" value="Add book"></input>
    <input type="button" id="clear-list" value="Clear booklist"></input>
    <div id="book-list"></div>
```

There are two buttons. One will fetch book details from the server when clicked. The other will clear the locally displayed book list. The book list will be displayed inside a `<div>` element with an `id` of `book-list`. These elements are visible when the page is loaded:

```
<div id="book-template" class="hidden book">
    <ul class="author-list"><li class="author"><span class="name"></span>
</li></ul>
    <p class="title"></p>
    <p class="year"></p>
    <div class='book-footer'>
        <div class="rating-div">Rating: <span class="rating"></span></div>
        <div>Location: <span class="location"></span></div>
    </div>
</div>
</body></html>
```

The `<div>` with an `id` of `book-template` has a class `hidden` assigned to it. This `<div>` is not displayed. It will be used as a template for the data received from the server. The Pure templating engine associates attributes in a data structure with HTML elements that have the same class. Therefore, the contents of the paragraph element with class `year` will reflect the value of the `year` attribute in our data structure:

```
{
    "title": "Democracy and the Post-Totalitarian Experience",
    "author": [
        {
            "name": "Leszek Koczanowicz"
        },
        {
            "name": "Beth J. Singer"
        }
    ],
    "year": "2005",
    "rating": "3",
    "location": "Mandalay"
}
```

The preceding code is an example of the JSON data that is returned from the server. The `title`, `year`, `rating`, and `location` attributes have a single value and map directly to a single element in the HTML template. In order to repeat any of these values more than once, one only has to assign the appropriate class to additional elements in the template.

The `author` attribute contains an array of objects. Each object has a single attribute: `name`. Multiple authors are represented this way in order to illustrate the iteration capabilities of the templating engine. The template contains a single list item element with class `author`. The list item contains a `<span>` element with class `<name>`. For attributes within the data structure that have an array value, an instance of the associated HTML element will be created for each element of the array. In this way, an arbitrary number of list items can be created:

```
(function($) {
    $('document').ready(function() {
        $('#add-book').data('id',1);
```

Once the document is ready, the JavaScript code starts by using the jQuery `data()` function to store the current `id` of the book we will be requesting. This `id` will be incremented each time a book is requested. The `data()` function allows arbitrary data to be stored in DOM elements:

```
        $('#add-book').click(function() {
            var curId = $(this).data('id');
            $.getJSON('server.php', {id: +curId}, function(data) {
                if( data.none ) { return false; }
                var divId = 'book-' + curId;
                $('#book-list').append($('#book-template').clone().attr('id',divId));
                $('#'+divId).autoRender(data).removeClass('hidden');
                $('#add-book').data('id', curId + 1);
            });
            return false;
        });
```

When the "Add book" button is clicked, a request is made to the server using the jQuery `getJSON()` function. The templating process starts by making a clone of the hidden `<div>` in our HTML. The `id` of this clone must be changed before it is appended to the book list. If the `id` isn't changed, then a DOM element with a non-unique `id` will have been introduced. The `autoRender()` function from the Pure plugin is then called with the JSON data as an argument. This renders the template using the provided data. Lastly, the `hidden` class is removed, making the book details visible:

```
        $('#clear-list').click(function() {
            $('#add-book').data('id',1);
            $('#book-list').empty();
            return false;
        });
    });
})(jQuery);
```

The function to clear the book list is fairly straightforward. The appropriate `<div>` element is emptied, and the book `id` counter is reset to 1.

Discussion

There are two benefits to using JavaScript-based templating engines. One is that they allow the transformation of a JSON data structure into styled and structured HTML without manually manipulating each element of the data structure. This benefit can be realized by applying a templating engine to the variety of small chunks of data that are commonly retrieved by Ajax calls, as this example illustrated.

The second benefit of using a JavaScript templating engine is that it produces pure HTML templates. These templates contain no traces of the scripting languages, which are usually used to denote the data to be templated, and implement functionality such as iteration. It's difficult to take advantage of this when using the templating engine in the browser, as done in this recipe. The negative impact this has on a site's appeal to search engines dissuades most people from going this route. However, jQuery and the Pure templating engine can be run in server-side JavaScript environments, as well. Jaxer (*http://www.aptana.com/jaxer*), Rhino (*http://www.mozilla.org/rhino/*), and SpiderMonkey (*http://www.mozilla.org/js/spidermonkey/*) have all been known to work.

17.5 Queuing Ajax Requests

Problem

You want to have greater control over the order of many separate Ajax requests.

Solution

This recipe illustrates two different ways to queue Ajax requests. The first fills a queue with requests, sending subsequent requests once the previous request has returned a response. The second sends groups of requests in parallel. But, it doesn't execute the callback functions for each request until all responses have returned. An example of normal unqueued requests is included for comparison:

```
<!DOCTYPE html>
<html><head>
    <title>jQuery Cookbook - 17.5 - Queuing Ajax Requests</title>
    <script type="text/javascript" src="../../jquery-1.3.2.min.js"></script>
    <script type="text/javascript" src="jquery-ajax-queue_1.0.js"></script>
</head>

<body>
    <h1>17.5 - Queuing Ajax Requests</h1>
    <input type="button" id="unqueued-requests" value="Unqueued requests"></input>
    <input type="button" id="queued-requests" value="Queued requests"></input>
    <input type="button" id="synced-requests" value="Synced requests"></input>
    <p id="response"></p>
</body></html>
```

The ajaxqueue jQuery plugin (available at *http://plugins.jquery.com/project/ajax queue/*) is used for queuing behaviors. Three buttons trigger each set of Ajax requests. A log of the responses is displayed in a paragraph element:

```
(function($) {
    $('document').ready(function() {
        $('#unqueued-requests').click(function() {
            $('#response').empty();
            $.each([1,2,3,4,5,6,7,8,9,10], function() {
                $.get('server.php',{ data: this }, function(data) {
                    $('#response').append(data);
                });
            });
            return false;
        });
```

The first button triggers normal Ajax requests. Ten requests are sent, each with a number for their position in the sequence. The `server.php` script simulates a server under load by sleeping random amounts of time before returning a response. When it arrives, the response is appended to the contents of the `#response` paragraph:

```
$('#queued-requests').click(function() {
    $('#response').empty();
    $.each([1,2,3,4,5,6,7,8,9,10], function() {
        $.ajaxQueue({url: 'server.php',
            data: { data: this },
            success: function(data) { $('#response').append(data); }
        });
    });
    $.dequeue( $.ajaxQueue, "ajax" );
    return false;
});
```

The "Queued requests" button adds each request to a queue by calling the `ajaxQueue()` function. Internally, the `ajax()` function is called with the provided options, each time a request is dequeued. After each of the requests has added to the queue, a call to `dequeue()` with the `ajaxQueue` function as a parameter triggers the first request. Each subsequent request will be sent in turn:

```
$('#synced-requests').click(function() {
    $('#response').empty();
    $.each([1,2,3,4,5,6,7,8,9,10], function() {
        $.ajaxSync({url: 'server.php',
            data: { data: this },
            success: function(data) { $('#response').append(data); }
        });
    });
    return false;
    });
  });
})(jQuery);
```

The final set of requests use the `ajaxSync()` function to send the requests in parallel but synchronize the execution of the provided callbacks when the responses return.

Discussion

Responses from the unqueued requests come back out of order. This behavior is not necessarily undesirable and in many cases may be preferred. However, there are scenarios where one would like more control over Ajax requests and their responses. The functionality provided in `ajaxQueue()` suits the case where each subsequent request is dependent upon the response to the previous request, whereas `ajaxSync()` supports the use case of manipulating data, which is gathered from a variety of servers. In this scenario, processing is unable to commence until all servers have returned a response and the complete set of data is present.

17.6 Dealing with Ajax and the Back Button

Problem

Populating web pages using Ajax creates a convenient, interactive user experience, which can't be replicated with traditional HTTP requests. Unfortunately, each time you update the contents of the browser window with Ajax, that content becomes inaccessible to the back and forward buttons of your browser. The bookmarking functionality found in most browsers is also rendered nonfunctional.

Solution

The solution to this problem is to relate each Ajax request to a unique URL. This URL can then be bookmarked and accessed by the back and forward browser buttons. One method for doing this is to use hash values. Hash values are generally used to link into a specific position within a document. *http://en.wikipedia.org/wiki/Apple#History* links to the history section of the Wikipedia page for Apple. For the purposes of this recipe, the hash value will refer to content loaded by an Ajax request.

In this example, the sample project is a small glossary. It has three entries. When you click each entry, the definition for the word is retrieved and displayed via Ajax. Granted, the content could easily be displayed all at once on a single page. However, this same approach is appropriate for larger, more varied data, such as the contents of each tab in a tabbed interface:

```
<!DOCTYPE html>
<html><head>
    <title>17.6 Dealing with Ajax and the Back Button</title>
    <script src="../../jquery-1.3.2.min.js"></script>
    <script src="jquery.history.js"></script>
</head>

<body>
    <h1>17.6 Ajax and the Back Button</h1>
    <a href="#apples" class='word'>apples</a>
    <a href="#oranges" class='word'>oranges</a>
    <a href="#bananas" class='word'>bananas</a>
    <p id='definition'></p>
</body></html>
```

Necessary JavaScript files are included in the head of the document. The jquery.history.js file contains the jQuery history plugin (available at *http://plugins.jquery.com/project/history*). There is an anchor element for each of the three entries in the glossary. The definition for each entry will be displayed in the paragraph with an id of definition:

```
(function($) {
    function historyLoad(hash) {
        if(hash) { $('#definition').load('server.php',{word: hash}); }
        else { $('#definition').empty(); }
```

```
        }
        $(document).ready(function() {
            $.history.init(historyLoad);
            $('a.word').click(function() {
                $.history.load($(this).html());
                return false;
            });
        });
    })(jQuery);
```

The history plugin has two functions that are of concern: `init()` and `load()`. The `init()` function is called inside the **ready** function. A callback to handle Ajax requests is passed in as an argument. `load()` is bound to the word links. The content of each anchor tag is passed in as an argument. The callback `historyLoad()` takes care of requesting the content for the passed-in hash value. It also needs to be able to handle instances where there is no hash value.

Discussion

There are two instances when the `historyLoad()` callback is called. First, it is called inside the `$.history.init()` function, when the page is loaded. The hash value is stripped from the end of the URL and passed as the argument. If there is not a hash value present, the argument is empty. The `load()` function also calls `historyLoad()`. The argument we pass to `$.history.load()`, the word we clicked, in this case, is passed on as the hash argument to our callback.

In this solution, a jQuery plugin was used. It is relatively easy to implement similar functionality without a plugin, by using JavaScript's `window.location.hash` object. The jQuery history plugin comprises only 156 lines of code. The reason it was chosen over writing a solution from scratch is that a large part of the plugin code handles cross-browser inconsistencies. When handling browser differences, it's often more effective to draw from the communal pool of experience that accumulates in a plugin than try and to account for every implementation discrepancy oneself.

17.7 Putting JavaScript at the End of a Page

Problem

As a project grows in size, often the amount of JavaScript it contains grows as well. This results in slower page load times. Combining several disparate JavaScript files into one monolithic file, using minification, and using compression can help reduce the JavaScript size and reduce the number of HTTP requests made. But, one will always be left with some amount of code to load. It would be nice if the impact of this code on perceived load times could be reduced.

Solution

A user perceives load times based on what they see on the screen. A browser has a limited number of HTTP connections at its disposal to load external content, such as JavaScript, CSS stylesheets, and images. When JavaScript is placed at the top of the document, it can delay the loading of other visible resources. The solution is to place your JavaScript files at the end of your page:

```
<!DOCTYPE html>
<html><head>
    <title>17.7 Putting JavaScript at the End of a Page</title>
</head>

<body>
    <h1>17.7 Putting JavaScript at the End of a Page</h1>
    <p>Lorem ipsum dolor...</p>
    <script src="../../jquery-1.3.2.min.js"></script>
    <script type="text/javascript">
        jQuery(document).ready(function() {
            jQuery('p').after('<p>Ut ac dui ipsum...</p>').show();
        });
    </script>
</body></html>
```

Discussion

By placing the JavaScript just before the closing <body> tags, any images or CSS stylesheets that are referenced previously in the document are loaded first. This won't cause the page to load any faster. However, it will decrease the perceived load time. Visible elements will be given priority over the JavaScript code. Loading the JavaScript files late in the page doesn't incur any drawbacks because it generally shouldn't be executed until the entire page is loaded.

No benefit is gained from putting the inline JavaScript at the end of the document. It is placed there in this example because the jQuery function can't be called until jquery-1.3.2.min.js is loaded. If we placed the inline JavaScript in the <head> element, an error would be generated because of jQuery not being defined.

Unit Testing

Scott González and Jörn Zaefferer

18.0 Introduction

Automated testing of software is an essential tool in development. Unit tests are the basic building blocks for automated tests: each component, the unit, of software is accompanied by a test that can be run by a test runner over and over again without any human interaction. In other words, you can write a test once and run it as often as necessary without any additional cost.

In addition to the benefits of good test coverage, testing can also drive the design of software, known as *test-driven design*, where a test is written before an implementation. You start writing a very simple test, verify that it fails (because the code to be tested doesn't exist yet), and then write the necessary implementation until the test passes. Once that happens, you extend the test to cover more of the desired functionality and implement again. By repeating those steps, the resulting code looks usually much different from what you'd get by starting with the implementation.

Unit testing in JavaScript isn't much different from in other programming languages. You need a small framework that provides a test runner, as well as some utilities to write the actual tests.

18.1 Automating Unit Testing

Problem

You want to automate testing your applications and frameworks, maybe even benefit from test-driven design. Writing your own testing framework may be tempting, but it involves a lot of work to cover all the details and special requirements of testing Java-Script code in various browsers.

Solution

While there are other unit testing frameworks for JavaScript, we will take a look at QUnit (*http://jquery-cookbook.com/go/qunit*). QUnit is jQuery's unit test framework and is used by a wide variety of projects.

To use QUnit, you need to include jQuery and two QUnit files on your HTML page. QUnit consists of `testrunner.js`, the test runner and testing framework, and `testsuite.css`, which styles the test suite page to display test results:

```
<!DOCTYPE html>
<html>
<head>
 <title>QUnit basic example</title>
 <script src="http://code.jquery.com/jquery-latest.js"></script>
 <link rel="stylesheet"
href="http://jqueryjs.googlecode.com/svn/trunk/qunit/testsuite.css" type="text/css"
media="screen" />
 <script type="text/javascript"
src="http://jqueryjs.googlecode.com/svn/trunk/qunit/testrunner.js"></script>

<script type="text/javascript">
   test("a basic test example", function() {
    ok( true, "this test is fine" );
    var value = "hello";
    equals( value, "hello", "We expect value to be hello" );
    });
</script>

</head>
<body>
 <div id="main"></div>
</body>
</html>
```

Opening this file in a browser gives the result shown in Figure 18-1.

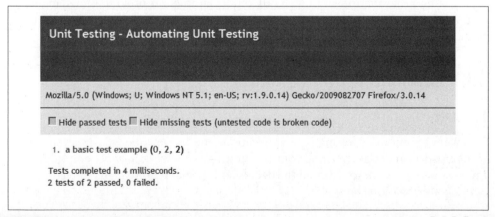

Figure 18-1. Test result in a browser

The only markup necessary in the `<body>` element is a `<div>` with `id="main"`. This is required for all QUnit tests, even when the element itself is empty. This provides the fixture for tests, which will be explained in Recipe 18.6.

The interesting part is the `<script>` element following the `testrunner.js` include. It consists of a call to the `test` function, with two arguments: the name of the test as a string, which is later used to display the test results, and a function. The function contains the actual testing code, which involves one or more assertions. The example uses two assertions, `ok()` and `equals()`, which are explained in detail in Recipe 18.2.

Note that there is no `document-ready` block. The test runner handles that: calling `test()` just adds the test to a queue, and its execution is deferred and controlled by the test runner.

Discussion

The header of the test suite displays the page title, a green bar when all tests passed (a red bar when at least one test failed), a gray bar with the `navigator.userAgent` string (handy for screenshots of test results in different browsers), and a bar with a few checkboxes to filter test results.

"Hide passed tests" is useful when a lot of tests ran and only a few failed. Checking the checkbox will hide everything that passed, making it easier to focus on the tests that failed.

"Hide missing tests" is useful when you have a lot of tests that are just placeholders, indicated by the test name "missing test—untested code is broken code." This can be useful when you have a large untested code base and added placeholders for every test that still needs to be written. In order to focus on tests that are already implemented, you can use the checkbox to temporarily hide the placeholder tests.

The actual contents of the page are the test results. Each entry in the numbered list starts with the name of the test followed by, in parentheses, the number of failed, passed, and total assertions. Clicking the entry will show the results of each assertion, usually with details about expected and actual results. Double-clicking will run just that test (see Recipe 18.8 for details).

Below the test results is a summary, showing the total time it took to run all tests as well as the overall number of total and failed assertions.

18.2 Asserting Results

Problem

Essential elements of any unit test are assertions. The author of the test needs to express the results expected and have the unit testing framework compare them to the actual values that an implementation produces.

Solution

QUnit provides three assertions.

ok(boolean[, message])

The most basic one is ok(), which requires just one Boolean argument. When the argument is true, the assertion passes; otherwise, it fails. In addition, it accepts a string to display as a message in the test results:

```
test("ok test", function() {
    ok(true, "ok succeeds");
    ok(false, "ok fails");
});
```

equals(actual, expected[, message])

The equals assertion uses the simple comparison operator (==) to compare the actual and expected arguments. When they are equal, the assertion passes; otherwise, it fails. When it fails, both actual and expected values are displayed in the test result, in addition to a given message:

```
test("equals test", function() {
    equals("", 0, "equals succeeds");
    equals("three", 3, "equals fails");
});
```

Compared to ok(), equals() makes it much easier to debug tests that failed, because it's obvious which value caused the test to fail.

same(actual, expected[, message])

The same() assertion can be used just like equals() and is a better choice in most cases. Instead of the simple comparison operator (==), it uses the more accurate comparison operator (===). That way, undefined doesn't equal null, 0, or the empty string (""). It also compares the content of objects so that {key: value} is equal to {key: value}, even when comparing two objects with distinct identities.

same() also handles NaN, dates, regular expressions, arrays, and functions, while equals() would just check the object identity:

```
test("same test", function() {
    same(undefined, undefined, "same succeeds");
    same("", 0, "same fails");
});
```

In case you want to explicitly not compare the content of two values, equals() can still be used. In general, same() is the better choice.

18.3 Testing Synchronous Callbacks

Problem

When testing code with a lot of callbacks, it happens every once in a while that a test that actually should fail just passes, with the assertions in question never showing up in the test results. When the assertions are in a callback that is never called, the assertions aren't called either, causing the test to silently pass.

Solution

QUnit provides a special assertion to define the number of assertions a test contains. When the test completes without the correct number of assertions, it will fail, no matter what result the other assertions, if any, produced.

Usage is plain and simple; just call `expect()` at the start of a test, with the number of expected assertions as the only argument:

```
test("a test", function() {
    expect(1);
    $("input").myPlugin({
        initialized: function() {
            ok(true, "plugin initialized");
        }
    });
});
```

Discussion

`expect()` provides the most value when actually testing callbacks. When all code is running in the scope of the test function, `expect()` provides no additional value—any error preventing assertions to run would cause the test to fail anyway, because the test runner catches the error and considers the test as failed.

18.4 Testing Asynchronous Callbacks

Problem

While `expect()` is useful to test synchronous callbacks (see Recipe 18.3), it falls short when testing asynchronous callbacks. Asynchronous callbacks conflict with the way the test runner queues and executes tests. When code under test starts a timeout or interval or an Ajax request, the test runner will just continue running the rest of the test, as well as other tests following it, instead of waiting for the result of the asynchronous operation.

Solution

There are two functions to manually synchronize the test runner with the asynchronous operation. Call `stop()` before any asynchronous operation, and call `start()` after all assertions are done, and the test runner can continue with other tests:

```
test("a test", function() {
    stop();
    $.getJSON("/someurl", function(result) {
        equals(result.value, "someExpectedValue");
        start();
    });
});
```

Discussion

A shortcoming of this approach to manual synchronization is the risk that `start()` is never called when the code under test fails elsewhere. In that case, the test runner never continues and therefore never finishes to display the end result. It can't even display the result for the current test, so all that is displayed is the result of the previous test.

When that happens, you first need to identify the test that doesn't finish by looking for the previous test that finished and then finding that test in code and skipping to the next test. Once that is done, you can ease debugging by adding a timeout argument to the call to `stop()`:

```
test("a test", function() {
    stop(500);
    $.getJSON("/someurl", function(result) {
        equals(result.value, "someExpectedValue");
        start();
    });
});
```

In this example, the test runner would wait 500 ms for the test to finish (using `setTimeout`); otherwise, it would declare the test as failed and continue running. By seeing the result of other tests, it can be much easier to identify the actual problem and fix it.

Nonetheless, the timeout argument shouldn't be used for regular tests. If you added it for debugging, remove it once the test works again.

Why is that? The drawback of the timeout is that it makes tests undeterministic. When running the test on a slow machine or under heavy load, the timeout may be too short, causing an otherwise perfectly fine test to fail. Hunting a bug that doesn't exist at all is a very time-consuming and frustrating experience—avoid it.

18.5 Testing User Actions

Problem

Code that relies on actions initiated by the user can't be tested by just calling a function. Usually an anonymous function is bound to an element's event, e.g., a click, which has to be simulated.

Solution

You can trigger the event using jQuery's `trigger()` method and test that the expected behavior occurred. If you don't want the native browser events to be triggered, you can use `triggerHandler()` to just execute the bound event handlers. This is useful when testing a click event on a link, where `trigger()` would cause the browser to change the location, which is hardly desired behavior in a test.

Let's assume we have a simple key logger that we want to test:

```
var keylogger = {
    log: null,
    init: function() {
        keylogger.log = [];
        $(document).unbind("keydown").keydown(function(event) {
            keylogger.log.push(event.keyCode);
        });
    }
};
```

We can manually trigger a keypress event to see whether the logger is working:

```
test("basic keylogger behavior", function() {
    // initialize
    keylogger.init();

    // trigger event
    var event = $.Event("keydown");
    event.keyCode = 9;
    $(document).trigger(event);

    // verify expected behavior
    same(keylogger.log.length, 1, "a key was logged");
    same(keylogger.log[0], 9, "correct key was logged");
});
```

Discussion

If your event handler doesn't rely on any specific properties of the event, you can just call `.trigger(eventType)`. However, if your event handler does rely on specific properties of the event, you will need to create an event object using `$.Event` and set the necessary properties, as shown previously.

It's also important to trigger all relevant events for complex behaviors such as dragging, which is comprised of mousedown, at least one mousemove, and a mouseup. Keep in mind that even some events that seem simple are actually compound; e.g., a click is really a mousedown, mouseup, and then click. Whether you actually need to trigger all three of these depends on the code under test. Triggering a click works for most cases.

18.6 Keeping Tests Atomic

Problem

When tests are lumped together, it's possible to have tests that should pass but fail or tests that should fail but pass. This is a result of a test having invalid results because of side effects of a previous test:

```
test("2 asserts", function() {
    $("#main").append("<div>Click here for <span class='bold'>messages</span>.</div>");
    same($("#main div").length, 1, "added message link successfully");
    $("#main").append("<span>You have a message!</span>");
    same($("#main span").length, 1, "added notification successfully");
});
```

Notice the first append() adds a <span> that the second assert doesn't take into account.

Solution

Use the test() method to keep tests atomic, being careful to keep each assertion clean of any possible side effects. You should only rely on the fixture markup, inside the #main element. Modifying and relying on anything else can have side effects:

```
test("test 1", function() {
    $("#main").append("<div>Click here for <span class='bold'>messages
</span>.</div>");
    same($("#main div").length, 1, "added message link successfully");
});
test("test 2", function() {
    $("#main").append("<span>You have a message!</span>");
    same($("#main span").length, 1, "added notification successfully");
});
```

QUnit will reset the elements inside the #main element after each test, removing any events that may have existed. As long as you use elements only within this fixture, you don't have to manually clean up after your tests to keep them atomic.

Discussion

In addition to the #main fixture element, QUnit will also clean up properties of jQuery itself: $.event.global and $.ajaxSettings. Any global events like $().ajaxStart() are managed by jQuery in $.event.global—if your test had bound lots of them, it could slow down the test runner significantly when running a lot of tests. By cleaning the property, QUnit ensures that your tests aren't affected by global events.

The same applies to `$.ajaxSettings`, which is usually used via `$.ajaxSetup()` to configure common properties for `$.ajax()` calls.

In addition to the filters explained in Recipe 18.8, QUnit also offers a `?noglobals` flag. Consider the following test:

```
test("global pollution", function(){
    window.pollute = true;
    same(pollute, true);
});
```

In a normal test run, this passes as a valid result. Running the same test with the noglobals flag (*http://jquery-cookbook.com/examples/18/06-keeping-tests-atomic/glob als.html?noglobals*) will cause the test to fail, because QUnit detected that it polluted the window object.

There is no need to use this flag all the time, but it can be handy to detect global namespace pollution that may be problematic in combination with third-party libraries. And it helps to detect bugs in tests caused by side effects.

18.7 Grouping Tests

Problem

You've split up all of your tests to keep them atomic and free of side effects, but you want to keep them logically organized and be able to run a specific group of tests on their own.

Solution

You can use the `module()` function to group tests together:

```
module("group a");
test("a basic test example", function() {
    ok( true, "this test is fine" );
});
test("a basic test example 2", function() {
    ok( true, "this test is fine" );
});

module("group b");
test("a basic test example 3", function() {
    ok( true, "this test is fine" );
});
test("a basic test example 4", function() {
    ok( true, "this test is fine" );
});
```

All tests that occur after a call to `module()` will be grouped into that module. The test names will all be preceded by the module name in the test results. You can then use that module name to select tests to run (see Recipe 18.8).

Discussion

In addition to grouping tests, `module()` can be used to extract common code from tests within that module. The `module()` function takes an optional second parameter to define functions to run before and after each test within the module:

```
module("module", {
    setup: function() {
        ok(true, "one extra assert per test");
    }, teardown: function() {
        ok(true, "and one extra assert after each test");
    }
});
test("test with setup and teardown", function() {
    expect(2);
});
```

You can specify both setup and teardown properties together, or just one of them.

Calling `module()` again without the additional argument will simply reset any setup/teardown functions defined by another module previously.

18.8 Selecting Tests to Run

Problem

When debugging a failing test, it can be a huge waste of time to rerun the entire test suite after every little change to your code just to see whether a single test now passes.

Solution

QUnit offers URL filtering to select the tests to run. This works best when combined with modules. You can run just the tests from a given module by appending a query string with the module name to the test suite URL. For example, `test.html?validation` will run all tests in the module named `validation`:

```
// test.html?validation - just the validation module
// test.html?validation&tooltip - validation and tooltip module
// test.html?!validation - exclude the validation module
// test.html?test 3 - just "test 3", the url will be displayed as test.html?test%203
module("validation");
test("test 1", function () {
    ok(true, "bool succeeds");
});
test("test 2", function () {
    equals(5, 5.0, "equals succeeds");
});
```

```
module("tooltip");
test("test 3", function () {
    same(true, 3 == 3, "same succeeds");
});

test("test 4", function () {
    ok(false, "bool fails");
});
module("other");
test("test 5", function () {
    equals(3, 5, "equals fails");
});
```

Discussion

You can combine tests from various modules by specifying multiple modules at once, delimited with the ampersand; e.g., `test.html?validation&tooltip` would run tests that contain `validation` or `tooltip`.

You can exclude tests using the exclamation mark; e.g., `test.html?!validation` would run all tests except those from the `validation` module.

Instead of manually modifying the URL, you can also double-click any of the test results to rerun just that test. QUnit will use the same filtering mechanism by appending the name of the test to the current location.

Index

We'd like to hear your suggestions for improving our indexes. Send email to *index@oreilly.com*.

F

fadeIn() method, 166, 306
fadeOut() method, 166
fadeTo() method, 155, 166
fading elements, 153–155, 161
fields
    autocompleting text fields, 249
    creating masked input fields, 247
    displaying labels above input fields, 257
:file filter, 46
file-tree expander, 285–288
files
    uploading in background, 255
filter selectors
    creating, 50
filter() method, 16, 19, 44, 45, 47
filtering
    arrays with grep(), 80
    wrapper sets of DOM elements, 16
filters
    :animated filter, 41
    :button filter, 46
    :checkbox filter, 46
    :contains filter, 42
    :data filter, 51
    :eq filter, 40
    :even filter, 40
    :file filter, 46
    :has filter, 42
    :hidden filter, 44, 46
    :image filter, 46
    list of form filters, 46
    :lt filter, 40
    :not filter, 43
    :odd filter, 40
    :password filter, 46
    :radio filter, 46
    :reset filter, 46
    :submit filter, 46
    :text filter, 46
    :visible filter, 44
find() method, 16, 18, 24, 76
finding
    bottlenecks, 101–105
    descendant elements in wrapper sets, 18
    jQuery plugins, 263
Firebug
    timing problem, 103
fn object, 96

defining plugins, 267
focus() method, 216, 223
focusin plugin, 198
focusout plugin, 198
font size, 157
for..in loop, 114
form elements
    enabling and disabling, 213–215
    selecting by type, 46
    selecting input elements, 15
form plugin, 255
formatting
    jQuery chains, 92
forms (see HTML forms)
fraction parameter, 167
Framework classes
    about, 343
    list of, 371
Function(), 103
functions, 82
    (see also callbacks)
    attaching to main jQuery object, 268
    private functions in jQuery plugins, 272
    reusing handler functions, 173
    static functions in jQuery plugins, 275

G

general sibling combinator (~), 38
get() method, 59, 401
getJSON() method, 409
getTime() method, 102
getting
    DOM element attributes, 29
    HTML content, 31
    jQuery UI plugin options, 323
    text content, 32
GitHub, 264
global conflicts
    using $ alias, 33
global events
    Ajax architecture, 395
    triggering, 192–195
Google
    minified version of jQuery, 10
    themes in the jQuery UI ThemeRoller
        gallery, 317
Google Code, 264
Google maps, 254
greater than (>)

namespace
    jQuery and other libraries, 71
    plugins, 175
    triggering event handlers, 176
nested data
    presenting, 285
next() method, 39
nextAll() method, 38
noCloneEvent attribute, 78
noConflict() method, 70
:not filter, 43
not() method, 43
notifications
    jQuery methods, 205–208

O

objects
    attaching to DOM using data(), 84
    DOM objects, 59–61
    extending with extend(), 85
    iterating over with, 79
    jQuery objects, 59–61, 105
    objects' methods as event listeners, 208
:odd filter, 40
offset method, 139, 141
offsetParent method, 139
offsets
    elements, 139–141
ok(), 428
one(), 173
opacity attribute, 78
operating on DOM elements, 23
optimization
    selectors, 35
option method, 324
options
    metadata plugin, 274
    passing to plugins, 268
outerHeight method, 137
outerWidth method, 137
overloads
    jQuery events, 208

P

packing
    JavaScript, 125
padding
    animation methods, 151

pages
    accessibility, 130–133
    loading, 12
    putting JavaScript at the end of a page, 423
    referencing multiple themes on a single
        page, 379–388
    text input on page load, 212
panels
    sliding panels in jQuery UI, 310–313
parsing JSON, 406
participation
    in plugin development, 267
passing options to jQuery plugins, 268
:password filter, 46
performance, 87–133
    animation speeds, 152
    attributes, 99
    bare-metal loops, 112
    bottlenecks, 101–105
    code from other libraries, 94
    custom iterators, 96–99
    debugging chains, 118
    debugging jQuery code, 120
    event propagation, 399
    global event triggering, 192–195
    jQuery chains, 92
    jQuery objects, 105
    making your pages accessible, 130–133
    name lookups, 115
    progressive enhancement, 128
    redundant repetition, 91
    selectors, 107
    server requests, 123
    tables, 109–112
    tracing into jQuery, 121
    updating DOM, 117
    writing unobtrusive JavaScript, 126
period (.)
    operators, 93
persisting data
    web browsers, 411
philosophy of jQuery, 4
players
    creating a jQuery UI music player, 327–
        339
plugins, 237–262, 263–278, 315–339
    (see also jQuery plugins)
    $ shortcut, 270
    adding functionality with, 72–74

stop(), 165, 186, 430
stopImmediatePropagation() method, 182
stopping
    animations, 165
    handler execution loops, 182
storage
    browsers, 413
    client-side, 411–414
strings
    removing whitespace from using trim(), 83
style attribute, 78
stylesheets
    switching, 148–150
styling
    overriding jQuery UI layout and theme
        styles, 360–370
    styling jQuery widgets with ThemeRoller,
        345–360
:submit filter, 46
submitHandler, 246
submitting
    forms using Ajax, 228
subsets
    performing actions on, 67–68
success callback method, 392
support
    for plugins, 266
support object, 78
swing function, 166
switch(){} statement, 233
switching
    stylesheets, 148–150
synchronous callbacks
    unit testing, 429

T

tabbing
    through documents, 293–296
<table> element, 111
tables
    loading, 109–112
tbody attribute, 78
template
    effects, 152
testing, 425
    (see also unit testing)
    callback functions with isFunction(), 82
    jQuery plugins with QUnit, 277
    selector speed test pages, 108

using debuggers, 123
text
    constraining text input to specific
        characters, 226
    limiting length of text inputs, 256
    text input on page load, 212
text content
    getting and setting, 32
text fields
    autocompleting, 249
:text filter, 46
text() method, 32, 222
textarea
    size of, 256, 259
<textarea> element, 224
ThemeRoller
    about, 343
    referencing multiple themes on a single
        page, 379
    styling jQuery widgets, 345–360
theming, 341–389
    applying themes to non-jQuery UI
        components, 370–379
    overriding jQuery UI layout and theme
        styles, 360–370
    referencing multiple themes on a single
        page, 379–388
    styling jQuery widgets with ThemeRoller,
        345–360
ThickBox, 297
this(), 88
tilde (~)
    general sibling combinator, 38
time() function, 102, 114
toggleAttr() method, 99
toggleCheck() method, 99
.toggleCheck() plugin, 99
toggleClass, 170
toggling
    attributes, 99
tool tips
    creating, 280–284
<tr> element, 111
tracing
    into jQuery, 121
traversing DOM, 22
trigger() method, 92, 177, 192, 207, 431
triggerHandler(), 199, 431
triggerHandler() method, 207

triggering
global events, 192–195
trim() method, 84
removing whitespace from strings or form values, 83
Twitter
character limit, 256
type
selecting form elements by, 46
type parameter, 401
typeof operator, 83

U

UI (see jQuery UI)
ui argument, 325
unbind(), 173, 234
unique() function, 82
filtering out duplicate array entries, 82
unit testing, 425–435
asserting results, 427
asynchronous callbacks, 429
atomic, 432
automatic unit testing, 425–427
grouping tests, 433
selecting test to run, 434
synchronous callbacks, 429
user actions, 431
updating
DOM, 117
uploading
files in background, 255
URL, 392
user actions
unit testing, 431
user events
defined, 171
user feedback
Ajax, 396–399
user interface (see jQuery UI)
utilities, 77–86
data(), 84
each(), 79
extend(), 85
grep(), 80
isFunction(), 82
map(), 81
merge(), 81
support(), 77
trim(), 83

unique(), 82

V

validating forms, 229–236, 238–247
valueOf() method, 102
values
entering range-constrained values, 253
removing whitespace from using trim(), 83
selecting ranges of, 250–252
viewports
elements, 143, 146
height and width in browser, 297
views
scrolling elements into, 141
visibility
selecting elements based on, 43
visibility property, 44
:visible filter, 44

W

watermark plugin, 258
web pages (see pages)
whitespace
removing from strings or form values, 83
Widget-specific classes, 342
widgets
ARIA, 130
bottom borders on widget headers, 370
jQuery UI, 316
library widgets compared to setting up scripts, 342
styling jQuery widgets with ThemeRoller, 345–360
width method, 135
window.onload event, 11
windows
dimensions, 135
displaying modal windows, 296–302
wrapper sets
about, 6
DOM elements, 16
finding descendant elements, 18
writing
custom iterators, 96–99
jQuery plugins, 265–268
selectors, 107

X

XML
 converting to DOM, 404

Colophon

The animal on the cover of the *jQuery Cookbook* is an ermine (*Mustela erminea*), also known as a stoat. "Ermine" sometimes refers to the animal's white winter fur, and "stoat" to the brown fur it has during the rest of the year. It belongs to the weasel family, which includes martens, ferrets, minks, otters, and polecats, though it is distinguished from these other members by its black-tipped tail.

The ermine lives in northern woodland regions of Europe, Asia, and North America. It is mainly nocturnal and makes dens in tree roots, under stones, and in tunnels. A solitary animal, the ermine can travel up to 10 miles in one night searching for food. Its predators include foxes, badgers, cats, and birds of prey.

The ermine's slender body helps it run swiftly, even across snow, as well as climb and swim. Although this shape has advantages, it also causes the ermine to quickly lose heat from its body. Thick fur and a fast metabolism help compensate, and the ermine must eat daily to meet its energy demands. Its diet includes small mammals, birds, fish, and insects. When the ermine spots its prey, it sneaks up on it in a series of leaps, grasps the victim's neck, and kills it with repeated bites.

White ermine fur is highly prized and is used in trimming coats, although demand has dropped in recent years. Typically, several furs are sewn together to form a pattern of black dots on a white field. This pattern was imitated in heraldry—the design of coats of arms— as early as the 12th century, most famously in the arms of Brittany. Ermine fur is also a symbol of royalty or purity, which is perhaps why Elizabeth I of England, "the Virgin Queen," was painted with an ermine by her side.

The cover image is from Riverside Natural History. The cover font is Adobe ITC Garamond. The text font is Linotype Birka, the heading font is Adobe Myriad Condensed; and the code font is LucasFont's TheSansMonoCondensed.